Publisher: Katherine Schowalter
Senior Editor: Diane Cerra
Managing Editor: Jacqueline A. Martin
Composition: Kevin Shafer & Associates

This text is printed on acid-free paper.

This publication is designed to provide accurate and authoritative information in regard to the subject matter covered. It is sold with the understanding that the publisher is not engaged in rendering professional services. If legal, accounting, medical, psychological, or any other expert assistance is required, the services of a competent professional person should be sought.

Library of Congress Cataloging-in-Publication Data

Selic, Bran
    Real-Time Object-Oriented Modeling/Bran Selic, Garth Gullekson, Paul T. Ward
    p.   ca.
    Includes index
    ISBN 0-471-59917-4 (cloth)
    1. Real-time programming. 2. Object-oriented programming
(Computer science)   I. Gullekson, Garth   II. Ward, Paul T.   III. Title.
QA76.54.S295   1994
005.1 -- dc20   93-20757
                                                     CIP

Printed in the United States of America

10 9 8 7 6 5 4 3 2

Real-Time Object-Oriented Modeling

Bran Selic
Garth Gullekson
Paul T. Ward

John Wiley & Sons, Inc.

New York ■ Chichester ■ Brisbane ■ Toronto ■ Singapore

To:
Lillian, Andrew, Matthew, and Sandy
Joanne, Ray, and Corinne
Pamela

Contents

Foreword

I find it exciting to live in a time when systems thinking is making major inroads into Western thought. As I write this, the passing of one of the great system thinkers of our time, W. Edwards Deming, is only a few weeks past. And earlier this very day, I read the vision of United States Vice President Al Gore for a telecommunications system that would integrate video, telephony, and computing for every school, library, hospital, and clinic by the year 2000. Nobody could have foreseen a single system for all these services just a decade ago. But advances in technology and in systems thinking, propelled by each other, have brought such grand schemes within reach.

Software is a young discipline, and systems thinking in software is even younger. Software systems evolved from the primordial soup of computer programs just decades ago. As these systems grew, they became too large for a single person to understand. Software engineering responded with decomposition techniques that let each programmer (or programming team) work in its own corner of the world. The system view became ever more elusive, the internal interfaces of software systems became increasingly complex, and software became more difficult to reshape and extend. This complexity precipitated a "software crisis" that has been with us for 20 or 30 years.

The challenge worsens daily. Powerful new hardware and sophisticated customer expectations impose increasing demands on the software that serves them. Today, we are building fewer programs and more systems. A software system used to be a one-of-a-kind effort bankrolled by a dollar figure having six or more trailing zeroes. But systems thinking isn't just for computer system or telecommunications giants any more. Today, the spreadsheet "program" I can buy for about $100 at my local software supermarket is a million-line system. We will find systems thinking to be a crucial survival skill for the software concern of the 1990s and beyond.

The object paradigm is a decomposition technique that came of age in the 1980s, and it is one of the darlings of large system development today. It raised expectations for software quality and productivity among credible advocates and curious onlookers alike. Objects emphasize independence. Each object is a locus of expertise, an island of administration and maintenance, a participant in a loosely coupled community of parts. A "popular culture" emerged from the object community that brought disproportionate focus to autonomy and decoupling as measures of good software architecture. This culture often oversimplified things in two stages: make everything an object and let every object manage its own responsibilities. The "me" generation had come of age in software. A few system-level concepts from the object paradigm found their way into popular programming culture (for example, type hierarchies and programming languages to express them). But systems thinking and the big picture took a back seat in the popular object movement.

The problem wasn't that objects and systems thinking were incompatible. On the contrary, the Smalltalk vision is one of the best examples of systems thinking we have. Smalltalk isn't just a language, but a finely tuned library, a development environment, and little short of a way of life. The C++ language shows systems thinking as well, supporting many styles of programming and facilitating compatibility with existing systems. The Eiffel vision drove home the importance of the broad view of life-cycle system maintenance. Many of the credible advocates and some of the curious onlookers were able to reach into the core of these visions and maintain a system view. But the system view never really found a home in a language, and it is scarcely present in most development methods. Why?

Among programers (or practitioners of any craft) we find few individuals who can grasp the big picture, who can abstract the myriad details of a complex digital system into patterns of regularity and rich structure. In the 1960s, we called such individuals "designers." In light of the complexity these individuals face in today's intricate, rich systems, they deserve the title of "architect." Architects are not only masters of scale, but employ a delightful assortment of tools and techniques that simultaneously attack system complexity from multiple angles. Their vision goes beyond the familiar term "object-oriented analysis," to the disturbingly foreign term "object-oriented synthesis"; beyond any given paradigm, to multiple paradigms; beyond rote, to a sense of aesthetics in the literature we call software. Architecture is a way of thinking—a way of systems thinking—and it is this way of thinking that distinguishes architects from implementors. An architect sees interwoven patterns of structure and interaction in complex systems, a far cry from the idyllic isolationism of the object model. The role of such patterns in architecture has emerged over the past two years as an important theme at object-oriented happenings.

You will find many of these ideas behind the approaches described in the following pages. You will find this book to be a useful framework for thinking about programs as systems, and for looking at systems in new and useful ways. ROOM gives voice to the unspoken language in the architect's mind, a multidimensional panorama of system structure. It is this kind of "thinking-systems thinking" that is key to the ROOM approach. It is a style of thinking beyond "what are the right objects?" to the question of "what is the right way to put objects together?" It is a style of thinking that goes beyond the static architecture to the structure and behavior of the running, living system.

The ROOM method and the ObjecTime environment are thinking aids, not thinking substitutes. The ROOM method encourages architects to collect and organize their thoughts online, where they are available to support the thought processes of downstream developers. The graphical ROOM language is friendly and expressive, with abstractions that remove the clutter that would otherwise distract the architect and implementor from systems thinking. It is this primary focus on supporting reason and creativity (that is, on the human element) that distinguishes the ROOM method from many CASE-based methods.

One important advantage of the ObjecTime environment is that architects and implementors can explore run-time structure and behavior at many levels of abstraction. Using executable modeling as a tool to explore requirements and architecture (rather than as a "final filter" to remove bugs) is a surprisingly underappreciated strategy among contemporary software architects. A run-time view lets the architect nurture insights that would never germinate or grow in a field of just bubbles and arrows. This view is particularly important to developers of real-time and fault-tolerant systems. As Bertrand Meyer notes, "bubbles don't crash." A running system offers unique architectural insights, and a systems-thinking perspective takes that into account.

While tools and methods have their places in quality and productivity, I view the future of software to lie in the hands of mature experts and in their ability development. Design tools aren't an end. They should be a means to architectural insight. If we leverage the architect, everyone benefits. That is the message of the ROOM approach. The architect can use the ROOM language to capture design decisions that object-oriented modeling alone may lose. ROOM models can document the architect's patterns, and guide the implementor through the architect's vision. But more importantly, ROOM lacks the fixed restrictions and dogmatic limitations of programming approaches for the masses. Controversial design rules are left to the discretion of the designer. The good news is that a knowledgable designer can violate design dogma (such as "inheritance-should-reflect-subtyping") where it makes good architectural sense. The bad news is that nothing protects the system from a sorcerer's apprentice who lacks design insight (such as a sense of goodness in an inheritance hierarchy). This is perhaps the best measure of a true power tool: Its results reflect the skill of the designer more than any characteristic of the tool itself.

Design and architecture can be learned from no book alone. No method or tool can instill the taste and vision that inspire a gifted architect. But accomplished architects and system thinkers will find tools in this book that leverage their insights through the programming teams they work with. And programming teams will be able to work with renewed architectural awareness. Garth Gullekson, Bran Selic, and Paul Ward dare to give us tools to capture the deep, rich, intricate architectures of systems all the way up to large, distributed, real-time, fault-tolerant systems—systems that few methods approach with confidence. They let us look at such a system from many perspectives, and to reconcile those perspectives in an architecture that can long serve customer needs. I have long been looking forward to this book, and I know anyone who does serious work on large systems will find it a treasure.

James O. Coplien
Wheaton, IL
January 14, 1994

Preface

For most of us, true understanding of complex subjects comes primarily through direct experience. Like learning to ride a bicycle or parenting, no amount of "book knowledge" or systematic planning can quite prepare us for the reality of it. The development of a large software system belongs in this category of activities. Its myriad aspects often are too difficult to absorb by a purely rational process. Instead, we learn best about its essential nature by participating in its construction. As we proceed, we uncover new facts and relationships about the system. Much of this information is absorbed intuitively, a side effect of experience. Over time, from a seemingly arbitrary collection of disjointed facts, there emerges a single and consistent mental model that constitutes our understanding of the system. In its totality, this mental structure is typically far beyond what the rational mind can focus on. Reason enters the picture only after the fact. It selectively views portions of this framework and derives abstract conclusions from it. The value of these abstractions comes from the underlying structure. Without that, these abstractions are just knowledge devoid of understanding.

Experience plays a key role in the methodology described in this book. First, the methodology itself is the result of extensive experience of the authors and their colleagues in analyzing, designing, and implementing distributed real-time systems for a variety of applications. In addition, the methodology is based on the provision of continuous empirical feedback throughout the development process. This is a consequence of the view that complex systems are not only difficult to construct properly on the first try, but, perhaps more significantly, that they are often difficult to *specify* correctly the first time. This emphasis on constructive experience sets this approach apart from many traditional software development methodologies in which system construction either is intentionally avoided until the final phases of development, or is viewed as a supplementary technique at best (for example, small-scale prototyping).

The Construction of Real-Time Systems

The subject of this book is an approach to the specification, design, and construction of software for distributed real-time systems. Real-time and distributed systems design has proven to be one of the most difficult and intricate engineering problems ever faced. This is primarily because of the complexity of the real world in which these systems operate. This environment can be bewilderingly diverse, dynamic, and unpredictable—components fail at random, communications are corrupted, interruptions occur when they are most inappropriate, and so on.

This complexity is mirrored in the size and structure of real-time software. In some cases, it has reached a point where it is comparable in organizational complexity to large biological systems. For example, the software that controls standard telephone-switching equipment typically comprises many millions of lines of high-level language code, and is designed and implemented by programming teams consisting of hundreds and even thousands of individuals. Anyone who has experienced the petty annoyances of trying to make even a simple program of several hundred lines run properly can certainly appreciate the magnitude of this task. In spite of this, there is a steadily growing demand for even more complex systems. For instance, telephone switches today are being amalgamated into so-called "intelligent" networks that span entire continents. This means that the stakes are getting higher. The cost of a telephone network outage, for example, easily can exceed tens of millions of dollars. In one well-documented case, such an outage was triggered by a simple and relatively common programming error [Meyers90].

Experiences such as this are making it increasingly obvious that current approaches to real-time software development will be inadequate to satisfy the heightened expectations for the coming generation of systems. The challenge then is to devise new organizational and technological means for dealing with this problem. A relatively recent and promising technological development is the *object paradigm*. A primary thesis of this book is that the object paradigm is particularly well-suited to solving problems in the real-time domain.

Although a substantial body of recent literature exists on the object paradigm and associated methodologies (for example, [Booch91] [Jacobson92] [Meyer88] [Rumbaugh91]), little of it has focused on the real-time domain. We feel that this deficiency must be addressed, considering the difficulty and the very specific nature of the problems encountered in this domain. Past experience has shown that general-purpose methodologies must be substantially augmented (with additional modeling concepts, for example) before they can be truly useful for application to real time. For example, this was the rationale behind major real-time variants of the basic structured analysis/structured design methodologies that emerged in the past two decades [Ward85] [Hatley87].

The two fundamental drawbacks to using a general-purpose methodology for real-time system development are

- *Inadequacy of the modeling language.* Every design methodology includes a set of fundamental modeling concepts (for example, state machines, concurrent processes) that are used to construct model specifications. These constitute a "modeling language" that, like any language, represents the basic vocabulary used during analysis and design, and that not only defines how we describe things, but also what we can say. Real-time systems have a specific set of modeling requirements that are primarily a consequence of the asynchronous, concurrent, and distributed nature of the real world in which they are embedded. Because these properties are so specific, most general methodologies do not support them adequately. This restricts the ability of development teams to formulate and communicate their understanding and ideas.

- *Implementation difficulties.* The predominance of asynchrony, concurrency, and distribution in real-time systems is reflected in the operating systems and application support libraries that are used in their implementation. For example, some form of concurrent processes and interprocess communication facilities are provided in practically every real-time operating system. In contrast to these are high-level abstractions (such as finite state machines) that are used in analysis and design modeling. If there is no formal linkage between the higher-level modeling concepts and the implementation concepts, developers must resort to error-prone *ad hoc* transformations.

To avoid these pitfalls and to make optimal use of the powerful new features of object-oriented technology, we devised a new real-time modeling language, and a methodology based on this language. We call the modeling language the *Real-Time Object-Oriented Modeling* language, or ROOM for short.

Our approach is based entirely on pragmatic premises. We do not make leaps of faith that assume the inevitability of future technological developments, nor do we base our methodology on rigorous, but daunting, mathematical formalisms (although ROOM models are formal in the sense that they are executable). ROOM is the outcome of the combined practical experience of the authors and their colleagues in developing a variety of real-time systems in different industries (including robotics, aerospace, and telecommunications). In particular, a major impetus for ROOM came from work done on projects that involved the design of the next generation of large distributed telecommunication systems.

One of the overriding concerns in these projects was the ability to capture, validate, and sustain the architecture of software systems. By "architecture" we mean that part of a system that provides the framework on which all other aspects of the system depend. A system's architecture is the principal factor that determines its capacity to evolve and adapt to new requirements. Unfortunately, once an architectural model is transformed into an implementation, it tends to be obscured by implementation detail. As a result, in the process of responding to new requirements, a system typically undergoes "architectural decay." This is the gradual, entropic deterioration of the precise and identifiable boundaries and relationships between system components that occurs when code changes are made. The consequence of architectural decay is that it becomes increasingly more difficult and more expensive to make further changes.

These architectural concerns strongly influenced the ROOM modeling language. In ROOM, high-level architectures are captured explicitly by using a simple graphical notation that facilitates communication between the various groups involved in system development (including customers). To validate and enforce architectural decisions, an architecture specification can be executed with the support of appropriate computer-aided tools. This enables the development team to detect high-level design flaws, as well as inconsistent or incomplete requirements early in the development cycle. This is important, since such fundamental flaws usually are much less costly to fix in the early phases of development than in the later ones.

The executability of ROOM models has a major repercussion on the development process. In contrast to traditional "phased" models, development with ROOM can proceed as a steady sequence of executable system models, progressing from the abstract to the detailed, with each model expressed using the same concepts and notation as its predecessor (thereby ensuring continuity and correctness). To minimize discontinuities in this process, ROOM also incorporates implementation-level concepts provided by traditional implementation languages. (In fact, ROOM allows a broad class of existing programming languages to be incorporated at this level.) Hence, high-level architectural decisions are directly propagated to implementations, thus eliminating the error-laden discontinuities caused by changes in specification formalisms. The final result is higher-quality implementations that are produced in less time than with traditional methods.

In summary, ROOM is distinguished by the following major features:

- It is *inherently object-oriented*, which allows it to fully exploit the advantages of this significant new paradigm.

- It has powerful modeling concepts that are *specific to the real-time domain*, and which facilitate the construction of accurate (yet concise) system models.

- It provides for the *explicit capture and documentation of system architectures*.

- It provides *executable models* at all levels of abstraction, allowing early detection of requirements or design flaws.

- It supports an *incremental and iterative development process* that covers all aspects of development, and that eliminates the error-prone paradigm shifts and discontinuities inherent in traditional development models.

We consider all of these features as key components in a strategy to successfully meet the needs of complex and sophisticated real-time systems. Although other object-oriented methodologies support some of these features to various degrees, it is our view that none of them provides the complete set. In most cases, this a fundamental shortcoming that cannot be rectified by simply adding the missing capabilities. For example, none of the currently popular object-oriented methodologies produce executable models that can be evolved into implementations without a paradigm shift. This requires the modeling concepts to be formally defined and formally related. In general, it is difficult to formalize an informal concept base (in some cases, the informal nature of the modeling concepts is an essential feature of the methodology). Furthermore, the modeling facilities must be broad enough to cover all levels of modeling, from top-level architecture down to implementation detail.

For example, in the methodologies of Coad and Yourdon [Coad91a] [Coad91b] or Rumbaugh, et al. [Rumbaugh91], it is possible to formally validate certain portions of a model, but it is not possible to guarantee that the individually validated parts are mutually compatible since they are not formally related. Several other notable object-oriented methodologies [Booch91] [Wirfs-Brock90] [ESA89] are targeted toward existing object-oriented programming languages that, like most implementation-level programming languages, deal mainly with small-grained objects. This makes them difficult to use for high-level architectural modeling.

At the opposite end are methodologies, such as OOSE by Jacobson at al. [Jacobson92], that address the high-end architectural issues, but have less to say on implementation issues.

The methodology that comes closest to ROOM in its potential for constructing executable models is the one proposed by Shlaer and Mellor [Shlaer92]. However, this methodology (called Object-Oriented Analysis) and the resulting models are intended primarily for the front-end analysis phase of development. Consequently, design and implementation must be realized by alternate sets of modeling and implementation concepts, which inevitably leads to paradigm shifts and mapping errors. This makes it difficult to preserve architectural intent and requirements traceability in the final product.

Target Audience

This book is targeted primarily to those interested in understanding ROOM modeling language in order to *apply* it to system development. This book also can be used by groups responsible for defining the specifications of distributed real-time systems (for example, standards organizations). Finally, this book is useful to those who are seeking just a basic familiarity with real-time system issues and the methodology based on ROOM.

The book is *not* meant as a general or detailed introduction to the object paradigm. Many excellent texts already serve this purpose ([Meyer88] [Booch91] [Goldberg83]) and it seems superfluous to add yet another. What characterizes this book with respect to the object paradigm is that it interprets this paradigm from the specific perspective of distributed real-time systems. Hence, it may also be useful to students and researchers who are interested in the relationship between the object paradigm and concurrent or distributed systems.

Book Layout

The book is divided into four main parts and a set of appendices.

Part One, "General Introduction," contains just a single chapter that describes the requirements for a real-time system methodology. These are used to derive the foundational principles behind the ROOM language and methodologies that are based on it.

Part Two, "Introduction to the ROOM Modeling Language," contains an overview of the ROOM modeling language and the rationale that led to it. It contains the following three chapters:

- Chapter 2, "Characteristics of Real-Time Development," introduces the major characteristics of the real-time problem domain and discusses some general strategies for dealing with its complexity.

- Chapter 3, "Key Elements of the ROOM Modeling Language," describes the strategy used to define ROOM. This chapter describes the object paradigm as adopted in ROOM.

- Chapter 4, "An Overview of the ROOM Modeling Language," is the key chapter in this part of the book and it contains an extensive informal review of the major modeling concepts in ROOM.

The preceding two parts are intended to provide sufficient information for readers who are interested primarily in the central ideas behind the ROOM modeling language, but are less concerned with the finer points of semantics and syntax.

Part Three, "The Definition of the ROOM Modeling Language," contains an in-depth view of the ROOM modeling concepts and their applications. The material in this part is crucial for the practitioner who wants to use ROOM. It consists of the following chapters:

- Chapter 5, "The Conceptual Framework of ROOM," introduces an abstract framework for classifying the ROOM modeling concepts that is used as an aid for navigating through the other chapters in this part.

- Chapter 6, "High-Level Structure Modeling," describes how ROOM combines concurrent logical machines into more complex aggregates.

- Chapter 7, "Layering," deals with a different form of structural modeling that allows complex systems to be constructed as a series of gradually more specialized vertical layers.

- Chapter 8, "High-Level Behavior Modeling," discusses ROOMcharts, a hierarchical state machine formalism that describes the high-level behavior of concurrent logical machines.

- Chapter 9, "Inheritance," describes how this useful technique is applied to high-level structure and high-level behavior in ROOM.

- Chapter 10, "The Detail Level," deals with the fine-grained objects and detailed behavior that are required for building executable models.

- Chapter 11, "Implementing ROOM Models," provides a reference model and implementation heuristics for constructing a virtual machine that supports the ROOM modeling concepts. This is primarily useful for those interested in looking "behind the scenes," as well as for those interested in constructing their own implementation of such a virtual machine. Other readers can safely omit it.

Part Four, "Process Issues," describes various high- and low-level processes for applying ROOM to system development. It has three chapters.

- Chapter 12, "Model Development Heuristics," describes an iterative approach to model construction and validation based on ROOM. These heuristics are useful in any phase of the development cycle that involves building models.

- Chapter 13, "Architectural Heuristics," examines modeling heuristics that pertain to creating the architecture of a real-time system.

- Chapter 14, "Work Organization," discusses major project management issues for organizations that are using or plan to use ROOM. It includes an outline for a project development model that takes advantage of the benefits provided by an operational approach to system development.

In addition, the following appendices include supplementary information:

- Appendix A, "The ObjecTime Toolset," provides an overview of the ObjecTime[1] toolset, a computer-based tool that directly supports the ROOM modeling language and its project development model.

- Appendix B, "An Annotated Implementation Example," contains a detailed and fully worked-out example of the key implementation techniques described in Chapter 11.

- Appendix C, "Rationale for ROOMcharts," describes some of the technical rationale that drove the definition of ROOMcharts, the behavior specification formalism of ROOM.

- Appendix D, "ROOM Graphical Notation Summary," provides a convenient summary of the graphical notation used in ROOM.

- Appendix E, "ROOM Linear Form Representation—Concrete Syntax," contains the formal specification of the concrete syntax (BNF) of the ROOM modeling language.

ROOM and the ObjecTime Toolset

The full benefits of the ROOM modeling language are reaped only if suitable computer-based tools are available to execute the models[2]. This is a departure from tradition, since

---

[1] ObjecTime is a registered trademark of ObjecTime Limited.

[2] Note that it is still possible to use the ROOM concepts for real-time system development without mechanized tools. However, in those cases, the development process becomes much closer to the traditional one, since it is not possible to execute system specifications. It is our view that even in this mode ROOM provides significant benefits stemming from its real-time focus, its support for architectural modeling, and its exploitation of the object paradigm.

most software development methodologies (including some recent ones) are based on the premise that computer-based modeling tools are possibly useful (but not fundamental) "power-boosters." In our view, computing technology has reached a threshold where it offers much more. The history of engineering is replete with examples where new tools have had a fundamental impact on the development process. A prominent recent example can be found in electronics system design: schematic capture and breadboarding are now being replaced by computer-aided design (CAD) tools so that systems are designed entirely using computer-based simulation. This has had a revolutionary positive impact on productivity and design reliability. It is somewhat ironic that this was all made possible through software which is itself, in many instances, still being developed using traditional, pedestrian techniques.

Recent developments in high-powered desktop workstations, object-oriented programming languages, and computer graphics and windowing systems have finally opened up opportunities to create a new generation of computer-based software development tools. One such tool is ObjecTime, created specifically to support the ROOM language and its development process. ObjecTime, along with ROOM, originated in the research and development labs of Bell-Northern Research. The tool has now been in practical use since 1989 and has been applied successfully to a wide variety of large and small industrial projects (including the analysis, design, and implementation of data communications switching equipment, telephony feature processing, protocol standards specifications, and the design of digital signal processing systems).

This book is not intended to be a tutorial on the use of ObjecTime, nor does it deal with the tool itself (except for Appendix A, which provides an overview of its capabilities). However, users of ObjecTime will find it helpful because it describes all the concepts supported by the tool and includes practical guidelines and examples of their usage.

A Note on the Choice of Programming Language

The principal ROOM modeling concepts are independent of the language used to specify detailed behavior and structure. In most of the examples in the book where it was necessary to describe finer detail, we have used the C++ programming language. This should not be construed either as an endorsement of C++ over other object-oriented languages, or as an implication that it is somehow privileged with respect to ROOM. The choice of C++ is because of the following three factors:

- It supports objects and, hence, conforms to one of the central tenets of ROOM.
- It is relatively widespread in the industry and may be familiar to many readers.
- It has a "conventional" syntactical form that even readers with no C++ experience will find familiar.

The book does not include any tutorial material on the language. However, the examples have been formulated in a way that minimizes the use of any idiosyncratic forms of C++. Thus, the text assumes a minimal familiarity with the C/C++ syntax.

Acknowledgments

The authors express their gratitude to their many collaborators who were either directly involved in or who supported the "Telos" project at Bell-Northern Research in Ottawa, Canada. Jim McGee, now president of ObjecTime Limited, was undoubtedly the person without whom none of this would have happened. He initiated the whole undertaking, inspired other team members, sustained and managed both the project and the team during good times and bad. On top of it all, he was, without question, the most important contributor to the conceptual base and the overall philosophy of the ROOM methodology. Raymond Aubin, Ian Engelberg, and Milan Javor were key members of the core team that defined the conceptual base. ROOM would simply not have been possible without their ideas and efforts. We also wish to thank the many highly-talented members of the Telos development group at Bell-Northern Research who designed and built the foundations on which the current work is based. In addition, George Smyth, Robert Pfeffer, Tony Yuen, Jules Meunier, and Frank Mellor, also of Bell-Northern Research, provided the key managerial and moral support to the team when it was most needed. We are also grateful to John Ellis, George Abou-Arrage, Barry Black, Bernard Plourde, Gary Mussar, Jim Coplien, John Herndon, Ron Akers, and Jim Chiampas, who had confidence in us and who risked much to help us prove that the ROOM concepts were indeed pragmatic and effective for industrial system development.

Our colleagues at ObjecTime Limited were indispensable contributors to both the ROOM concepts and their pragmatic realization. In particular, we wish to single out the work of David Daoust, Charley DeSchiffart, Rod Iversen, Joe May, Ray Tigg, Larry Williams, and Peter Epstein, all of whom managed to generate a tremendous amount of innovation and effort under very difficult and highly stressful circumstances, and who produced what we feel is the best tool of its class in the world. We are also indebted to Carol Fairbairn who created order while everyone else around her was busy making chaos and to Gordon Graham who took on a major part of our responsibilities during the writing of this book.

Special thanks are due to Ken Webb of PSC, Inc., in Ottawa, and to Dr. Jernej Polajnar, who braved some of the early drafts of the manuscript and who provided many invaluable and constructive suggestions and comments. We are very grateful to Ray Buhr, Ron Casselman, and Jean-Pierre Corriveau of Carleton University in Ottawa, and to Alan Campbell of Brighton, U.K., for their many useful technical discussions and recommendations. Garth Gullekson would like to thank Professor David Dodds from the University of Saskatchewan, for the inspiration he kindled to adopt a career in the telecommunications industry and for providing an excellent role model of what practical engineering is all about. Paul Ward would like to acknowledge the influence of many technical discussions with Jon Buser and Lloyd Williams on his understanding of the object paradigm.

Needless to say, the authors' families are, perhaps, the biggest victims of such a vainglorious endeavour. It is, of course, impossible to atone for what they had to contend with while this manuscript was in production. Nonetheless, we express our boundless gratitude for their forbearance, understanding, and support to: Lillian, Andrew, Matthew, Sandy, Vladeta, and Sloboda Selic; Ika Pavkovic, Joanne, Ray, and Corinne Gullekson; and Pamela Plate.

PART ONE

General Introduction

In this introductory part, we briefly examine systems development methodologies in general, and then identify an approach to defining a methodology. This approach is the guiding framework for the methodology described in this book.

CHAPTER 1

Elements of a
Real-Time Methodology

It is conceivable that a small real-time system could be developed in a completely *ad hoc* manner, with no particular plan or special facilities other than the wits of the developers and some basic programming tools. However, once a system is beyond a certain level of complexity (a level that is, unfortunately, exceeded by the majority of real-time systems), a more methodical approach becomes essential if we want to increase the likelihood of success. This is the rationale behind systems development methodologies.

One key aspect of a methodical, engineering-oriented approach to the building of systems is the creation of *models*. A model, in our terminology, is a concrete representation of knowledge and ideas about a system to be developed. A model differs from the thing being modeled in that the model deliberately modifies or omits details. For example, a physical scale model of an aircraft often has smaller dimensions than the aircraft itself, may be constructed of different materials, and may omit features of the aircraft such as passenger seats. In fact, a model may be constructed in a completely different medium than the thing being modeled. For example, an aircraft model may consist of a set of parameters that are input to a software simulation.

The critical feature of a model is its ability to concretely represent certain properties of a system. These properties then can be analyzed, understood, and verified prior to investing the resources to create the system itself. As Douglas Ross has stated, "x is a model of X if we can learn about X by asking questions of x." If a small-scale aircraft model (or a software simulation of an aircraft) exhibits aerodynamic properties that mimic those of the final product, then these properties can be systematically modified and analyzed by using the model.

The ultimate *product* of a real-time systems development project is a collection of hardware elements operating under the control of machine instructions to satisfy the system requirements. The final *model* created within the development project is a collection of source instructions. These instructions can be compiled into machine instructions and loaded, or machined into hardware components, or both, to create the desired product. However, the ability to create the final model may be critically dependent on the successful

prior creation of more abstract requirements and design models to verify high-level properties of the system.

This chapter provides an overview of a model-based, real-time systems development
methodology. The material covered here is intended to serve as a frame of reference for the
more detailed and more precise descriptions in the remainder of the book. The treatment is
deliberately kept informal to ensure that excessive detail does not hinder understanding.

1.1   Components of Systems Development Methodologies

Prior to delving into the various aspects of a particular methodology, it is useful to define
what we mean by that term. In its broadest sense, a *systems development methodology* is a
comprehensive and consistent collection of the following three elements:

- A modeling language
- Modeling heuristics
- A framework for organizing and performing development work

If applied judiciously, a methodology increases the likelihood of a successful realization
of the required final product at a cost that is within acceptable limits.

The dependency relationships between the three basic components of a methodology
are shown in Figure 1.1.

Figure 1.1   The Basic Structure of a Systems Development Methodology

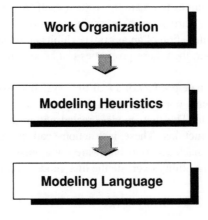

1.1.1 Modeling Languages

A *modeling language* provides the basic vocabulary used to express both domain knowledge and design ideas. For example, conventional programming languages can be thought of as modeling languages because they provide a basic set of concepts (such as conditional statements, procedures, and so forth) that are well-suited to describing different algorithms. However, conventional programming languages cannot express directly the high-level features (for example, state machines) that are the focus of requirements and design models. We will, therefore, use the term "modeling language" to describe a language that can be used to capture high-level system properties in addition to (or instead of) the low-level abstractions captured by conventional programming languages.

Like any language, the modeling language incorporated within a methodology can have a decisive effect on what we can say and the way we think about a problem.

1.1.2 Modeling Heuristics

The *modeling heuristics* of a methodology are informal guidelines on how the modeling language can be used in particular situations. One example of such a heuristic is "First what, then how." This heuristic states that a model builder should capture and understand a particular requirement (the "what") before elaborating a detailed design (the "how") based on that requirement. Heuristics are not rigorous and do not guarantee success, although they often represent modeling approaches that have been successful in the past. Heuristics are by-products of experience and may vary from organization to organization, and even from product to product.

Modeling heuristics occupy a place in a methodology that is a level above the place occupied by a modeling language. This is because they provide a structure for the effective use of a modeling language. Without the guidance of a set of heuristics that define a model-building "style," a modeling language may be used in an ineffective manner. For example, heuristics involving certain forms of the reuse of components based on inheritance may only be appropriate within an object-oriented modeling language, but not within a functionally oriented modeling language.

1.1.3 Work Organization

Work organization deals with the operational and managerial issues involved in software development. This includes issues such as

- How should the development team be organized?
- Which intermediate development products need to be produced?
- In what order should the development activities be performed?

For example, the traditional "waterfall" work organization (see Figure 1.2) prescribes that the building of a substantially complete requirements model should precede the building of a design model [Royce70]. In essence, this framework universalizes the "First what, then how" modeling heuristic and applies it to the development process as a whole.

Figure 1.2   The "Waterfall" Model of System Development

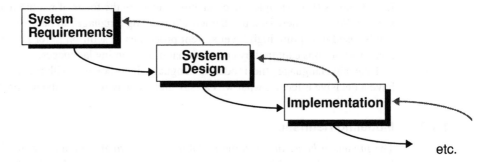

Work organization occupies the highest-level place within a methodology. It provides a structure within which the modeling language and the modeling heuristics can be used effectively. Without an efficient organization of time and work, for example, even an optimal set of heuristics and a powerful modeling language will not result in the creation of the desired product.

Work organization is more flexible than the modeling heuristics and the modeling language. A given organizational framework may be able to accommodate considerable variations in heuristics and languages. However, the modeling language and heuristics are the foundation of any methodology and may have a profound effect on the work organization. For example, if the modeling language and heuristics are based on the object paradigm (described in Chapter 3), the organization of work might be strongly affected by the desire to exploit the capacity for iterative, incremental modeling that is inherent in this paradigm. Thus, a strict "waterfall" approach may not be optimal in this case.

The nature of the development organization, and the nature of the development projects that are undertaken, also may have a strong influence on the work organization. For instance, both a large and a small development project may use the same modeling language and the same heuristics, but the way in which they organize the development process may be radically different.

1.1.4   ROOM

This book introduces a methodology incorporating all three elements just described, albeit at rather different levels of detail. In Part Two, we introduce a modeling language called ROOM (which stands for Real-time Object-Oriented Modeling) and then describe it in considerable detail in Part Three. We also discuss, in depth, a set of model-building heuristics for the effective application of ROOM (Part Four). Also in Part Four, we introduce a framework for organizing development work that incorporates the ROOM modeling language and the modeling heuristics.

Like any system, a methodology (used for developing systems) should also be developed on the basis of rational and structured principles. In the remainder of this chapter, we first examine the most general requirements that drove the development of the ROOM modeling language—the scope of the language and a general constraint on how it impacts the development process. We then briefly examine the other components of the methodology and an automated tool support. In Chapter 2, we describe the characteristics of the systems to which ROOM applies, and the nature of the modeling strategies that it must support. These are, in effect, the detailed requirements that ROOM was developed to meet.

1.1.5   The Scope of the ROOM Modeling Language

It is clearly unrealistic to strive for a modeling language that is equally suited to all possible applications. General-purpose approaches tend to take one of two directions, both of which can be problematic.

One way is to compile an all-encompassing collection of useful concepts from diverse application domains. This approach is often unwieldy, resulting in a bewildering overabundance of concepts. This is compounded by the likelihood that, since the individual pieces were devised independently of each other, the net result will be redundant and lacking in harmony. Perhaps the most notorious example of this is the PL/I programming language [ANSI76]. This language never fulfilled its goal of being the ultimate programming language (perhaps because of sheer bulk), despite being aggressively promoted by the dominant computer manufacturer of the time.

The alternative general-purpose approach lies at the other end of the scale. This approach is based on providing a small number of primitive (but flexible) abstractions out of which it is possible to construct powerful domain-specific concepts. An extreme example of this is a universal Turing machine [Turing36] that can be used to construct any computational system with just a few basic concepts. The disadvantage is that it requires substantial up-front effort (as well as very specialized expertise) to build up the necessary custom abstractions. Moreover, this approach is also prone to a profusion of concepts and redundancy.

We believe that the optimum is somewhere in the middle—a compact set of carefully selected concepts customized to a specific class of systems. This is a compromise that brings about an economy of concepts without sacrificing expressive power. ROOM was, therefore, developed as a real-time modeling language rather than as a general-purpose language. What is lost, of course, is universality. We cannot recommend ROOM for, say, the development of batch-oriented systems that solve large sets of equations. However, we can strongly recommend it for any of the large class of applications loosely referred to as "real-time." We will define this class of systems more specifically in Chapter 2.

1.1.6   A General Constraint—Avoiding the Introduction of Discontinuities

One of the major trouble spots in traditional systems development is the presence of discontinuities that occur within the development process. These discontinuities are caused by the lack of formal relationships between different notations. For example, high-level designs often are formulated in terms of abstract and high-level concepts such as layered diagrams and state machines. This representation is far removed from the concepts supported by standard programming languages. Typically, it is not obvious how such models are to be recast in terms of programming language constructs. Consequently, the process of generating an implementation from such models tends to be extremely unreliable.

These discontinuities also make it difficult to trace the linkages between system requirements and the implementation that is supposed to satisfy them. Maintaining this linkage is important to ensure not only that all the requirements are met, but also that (as the system evolves) the effects of any change can be determined precisely in terms of its effect on the original requirements.

The approach taken in ROOM was to develop the language in such a way as to avoid introducing into the development process any arbitrary or unnecessary discontinuities. Specific features of ROOM were devised to avoid various kinds of discontinuities, as will be seen in Chapter 3 (which discusses the key features of ROOM). Above and beyond this, the overall development process was driven by the constraint that discontinuities, in general, were to be avoided.

1.1.7   A General Constraint—Using Graphical Representation

We believe that graphics-based representations facilitate communication among all parties involved in system development. Therefore, we imposed a general constraint that ROOM provide graphic representation for those aspects that, based on experience, are best communicated by graphical means. For example, state machines are traditionally rendered as graphs, since that representation seems to provide insight faster than equivalent textual or tabular forms. However, one of the traditional shortcomings of graphical representations is their impracticality for capturing detail. A graphic that is overloaded with minutiae loses its synthetic quality and becomes as difficult to digest as an equivalent textual version. (For example, when flowcharts were popular, some experts suggested they should not exceed a page in length.)

1.2   The ROOM Modeling Heuristics

Most systems developers are familiar with a number of general-purpose heuristics (such as "First what, then how") that are independent of the modeling language employed. Therefore, we focused on heuristics that build on the specific characteristics of ROOM and are less widely known. Unlike most modeling languages, for example, ROOM permits the building of fully executable models. In order to take full advantage of this feature, it is necessary to build models that incorporate both the system under development and its environment. This heuristic, along with a number of others, is discussed in Chapter 12 and in Chapter 13.

1.3   The Work Organization Framework

Modeling heuristics tend either to be general in nature, or to be tied to the specific features of the modeling language or the type of system under development. While the work organization component of a methodology is influenced by modeling language and system type, it is also (unlike the modeling heuristics) heavily dependent on the nature of the development organization and on project-specific characteristics (such as the experience level of the developers). Therefore, we are much more cautious about making prescriptive statements concerning work organization. Instead, in Chapter 14 we have provided a number of general suggestions concerning possible changes in work organization that take advantage of the features of ROOM. For example, since ROOM increases productivity and fosters reuse, it might be possible to take account of longer-term requirements concerning the evolution of a system, as well as shorter-term requirements concerning the properties of the initial version.

Our set of suggestions about work organization forms the outline of a ROOM-based methodology. As experience is gained with the use of ROOM in a wider range of products and development organizations, we intend to evolve this into a more detailed form.

1.4   Tool Support for ROOM

A methodology needs automated support at all levels in order to be used most effectively (see Figure 1.3). To this end, the ObjecTime toolset was created. It provides extensive support for the ROOM modeling language, and more limited support for the modeling heuristics and the work organization framework. The limited support for the higher levels of the methodology reflects, not the inherent limits of the toolset, but the limits of our current understanding of how automated support for heuristics and work organization can be provided effectively. Virtually all attempts to provide extensive automated methodology support have been carried out in research and development environments. Little documented experience of methodology support in real-world development situations currently exists.

On a development workstation, the ObjecTime toolset provides a *modeling environment* to support the ROOM language, including model capture and display, model analysis, and model execution. (A model is a program that can be compiled and run.) The toolset also provides facilities for automatic code generation, allowing a model to be ported from the development workstation to the implementation hardware.

The ObjecTime toolset facilities to support model-building heuristics include model reorganization capabilities to support iterative development, execution of partially completed models to support incremental development, and class libraries to support component reuse.

Figure 1.3   The Role of Tools in a Methodology

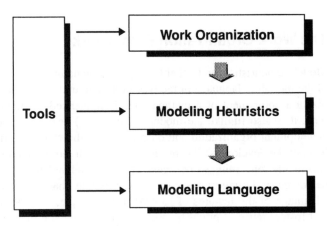

Toolset facilities to support the work organization framework include the publishing of documents based on ROOM models, and version control and networking facilities to support multi-user development.

Appendix A contains more information about the ObjecTime toolset.

1.5   Summary

Software development methodologies have evolved as systematic means for dealing with large and complex software problems. An important category of such methodologies are those based on building models. Model-based methodologies comprise three key elements: a modeling language, a collection of modeling heuristics, and a method of organizing the development process. The modeling language is the foundation of a methodology since it defines what can be modeled and how it is specified. Heuristics are informal techniques which, if applied properly, can increase the likelihood of constructing a correct model. Many heuristics are quite dependent on the modeling language. Work organization deals with managerial issues such as organizing the development team, setting up objectives, and tracking progress. It depends heavily not only on the specifics of individual enterprises, but also on the underlying modeling language and the heuristics used.

The subject of this book is a methodology that is based on the ROOM language. This specialized, high-level, modeling language is intended for the distributed real-time domain in order to provide more effective modeling capabilities (in that domain) compared to general-purpose methods. In devising the language, a key objective was to avoid a variety of error-prone discontinuities that have traditionally been present in the modeling process. This includes discontinuities that occur when moving from a design model (expressed in a modeling language) to an implementation (specified in a programming language). A second key objective for the modeling language was to incorporate the use of graphical representations in order to provide the expressive power required to model and communicate the more abstract levels of a system.

Finally, it was felt that, in order to improve reliability and productivity, a methodology must integrate computer-based tools into its development process. To that end, a computer-based tool called ObjecTime was created specifically to support the methodology based on the ROOM modeling language.

PART TWO

Introduction to the ROOM Modeling Language

This part of the book contains an *overview* of the ROOM modeling language and the rationale behind it. The intent is to provide sufficient information for the reader to gain an overall knowledge of ROOM without dwelling on the finer points of syntax or notation. Readers who are interested primarily in understanding the central ideas behind the modeling language will find the material in this part adequate. For those who are interested in going further and applying ROOM in practice, this part provides a useful primer for the detailed descriptions of the modeling language that follow in Part Three.

This part is split into the following three chapters:

- Chapter 2, "Characteristics of Real-Time Development," introduces the major features of the problem domain for which ROOM is intended, and discusses some general strategies for dealing with complexity. This chapter also includes a specification of a fabric dyeing system, which serves as the primary example throughout this introductory part.

- Chapter 3, "Key Elements of the ROOM Modeling Language," describes the strategic basis used in defining ROOM. Included is a description of a generalized object paradigm that is one of the essential properties of ROOM.

- Chapter 4, "An Overview of the ROOM Modeling Language," contains an extensive informal review of the major modeling concepts of ROOM.

PART TWO

Introduction to the ROOM Modeling Language

CHAPTER 2

Characteristics of Real-Time Development

In what is perhaps the first example of an embedded real-time system, Baron Wolfgang von Kempelen (an eighteenth-century Viennese inventor) constructed a chess-playing automaton that he exhibited with great success in the courts of Europe. The automaton featured a chessboard mounted waist-high on a small rectangular box. Extending from one end of the box was a mechanical puppet, consisting of a torso, a head, and two arms, one of which could move pieces on the board through a special mechanical linkage. To instill a mystical aura to the proceedings and intimidate the opponents, the mechanical figure was made up as a turbaned Saracen with a drooping moustache and a hint of menace in its features. When its opponent made a move, the Saracen would pause briefly and, in a whir of clockworks, slowly raise its mechanical arm, pick up a chess piece, and make its countermove. Not only did this mechanical wonder abide by the complex rules of chess, it almost invariably beat its human opponents!

In the end, this miraculous apparatus proved to be a hoax, undoubtedly to the relief of those who were humiliated by it.[1] The secret of its success, as it turned out, was a diminutive human chess master, who sat hidden in the cramped enclosure underneath the chessboard, and who chose the automaton's moves and operated its controls. Despite the questionable ethics behind it, this eighteenth-century device can serve as an almost perfect illustration of some essential features of today's real-time systems.

The automaton involved a combination of hardware and software (see Figure 2.1). The hardware, used to interact with the environment, consisted of *sensors* (the specialized chessboard through which the moves of the human opponent could be detected) and *effectors* (the Saracen's mechanical hands). The software, in this case consisting of the intellect of the concealed chess master, controlled the actions of the hardware. Like the embedded real-time systems of today, the chess automaton dynamically adapted its behavior to the current state of the external environment and, furthermore, responded within the time interval considered acceptable in chess games.

---

[1] The true story of the infamous baron and his chess-playing automaton is recounted in [Heppenheimer85].

Figure 2.1   The Basic Elements of a Real-Time System

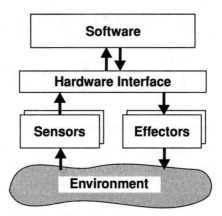

There is no universally accepted definition of what constitutes a real-time system. Systems commonly referred to as real-time span the range from small embedded microcontrollers that drive the operation of a microwave oven to very large systems such as global computer communication networks. A common misconception, even among some computer professionals, is that real-time by necessity implies microsecond response times that impose low-level assembly language programming. While this characterizes one category of real-time systems, it is by no means universal.

The ROOM modeling language was devised to model systems that have a certain set of characteristics, which are described in detail in this chapter. We refer to these systems generically as *real-time systems*. However, the reader should be aware that, given the lack of consensus on what constitutes a real-time system, ROOM may not apply to certain systems conventionally referred to as real-time, and, conversely, ROOM may be applicable to other systems not commonly called real-time (see Figure 2.2). We identify the systems to which ROOM may effectively be applied, not as meeting a precise definition, but as possessing most (or all) of a set of properties.

This chapter first examines these properties, and, in particular, the modeling and design issues that accompany them. The intent is not only to define a particular collection of applications, but also to demonstrate that the problems inherent to these applications are sufficiently complex and unique that their treatment warrants a specialized methodology based on a modeling language such as ROOM. From this we extract the specific requirements that a real-time modeling language must fulfill. This is complemented, in the latter part of the chapter, with a description of more general strategies for dealing with complexity that any effective modeling language must support.

Figure 2.2   The Domain of Applicability of ROOM

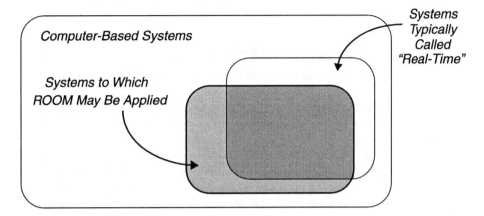

2.1   Properties of Systems to Which ROOM May Be Applied

The salient properties characterizing systems to which ROOM may be applied are

- *Timeliness*. This is, without doubt, the most common attribute of real-time systems of any kind. By definition, a real-time system is required to perform its function "on time," whatever that happens to mean in a particular context.

- *Dynamic internal structure*. Many real-time systems are required to exercise control over an environment whose properties vary with time. This requires that the system components dealing with particular aspects of the environment must be dynamically reconfigured to match the dynamic of external environments. Because of limited resources (memory, processor capacity), this typically entails the dynamic creation and destruction of software components.

- *Reactiveness*. A *reactive system* is one that is continuously responding to different events whose order and time of occurrence are not always predictable.

- *Concurrency*. This is a feature of the real world in which a real-time system is embedded. At any given time, multiple simultaneous activities can be taking place in the real-time system. When this is combined with the need for real-time response, the usual result is that the real-time system itself must be concurrent.

- *Distribution*. A *distributed computing system* is one in which multiple computing sites cooperatively achieve some common function. Distribution is either inherent (as is the case for communications systems) or it may be driven by the need to increase throughput, availability, or functionality. Whatever the reason, distribution introduces an assortment of very difficult problems.

Any one of these properties is sufficient to make modeling and design difficult. Taken in combination, the problems compound each other, requiring considerable ingenuity and resources to be overcome. The following sections discuss in more detail these properties and their ramifications for systems development.

2.1.1   A Sample Application Problem

Before discussing this list of properties in more detail, we introduce a sample application that we use to illustrate these properties, and that also will be the basis for introducing ROOM in Chapter 3 and Chapter 4. In order to keep the essentials of the discussion clear, we have selected a rather elementary example, one that is not necessarily representative of the complexity that typifies real-time problems.

The example is an industrial process-control application, namely *fabric dyeing*. We are aware that only a fraction of our potential readers work in the process-control area. However, because of the nature of the example, anyone who has operated a dishwasher or a washing machine has had experience as a user of a similar application system. Moreover, industrial process-control applications exhibit most of the essential complexities that were originally encountered in the telecommunications arena and that formed the backdrop for the development of ROOM.

The essential nature of the fabric dyeing process is the exposure of fabric to a dyeing solution under circumstances that allow the dye to penetrate the fabric and to change its color. The process is called a dyeing run, and is carried out in a dyeing tank. The essential equipment attached to the tank includes an access hatch to insert and remove the fabric to be dyed, a rack on which the fabric may be stretched out, a dye valve to admit the dyeing solution, and a drain valve to drain the solution (see Figure 2.3). The tank and its associated equipment will be referred to as a *dyeing unit*.

In the simplest possible dyeing run, the dye valve is opened to admit the dyeing solution and then closed when a sufficient quantity has entered the tank. The fabric is allowed to remain exposed to the solution for a time, then the drain valve is opened to drain the solution and is closed when the tank is empty. The parameters for this process are the amount of solution admitted to the tank and the dyeing (exposure) time. If the fabric is stretched on the rack from the bottom up, the amount of solution (measured by the solution level in the tank) is a function of the amount of fabric to be dyed, with an upper limit established by the tank capacity. The dyeing time generally is a function of the type of fabric and the type of dye.

The simple process just outlined is adequate only for a small minority of dyeing runs. The main complication is that most dyes do not penetrate most fabrics effectively at room temperature. Thus, at a minimum, the dyeing solution must be heated to an elevated temperature and maintained at that temperature throughout the dyeing time. This requires a heater within the dyeing tank. The dyeing temperature, and possibly the heating rate, both functions of the fabric-dye combination, are the parameters of the dyeing run.

Figure 2.3 Essential Equipment for Fabric Dyeing

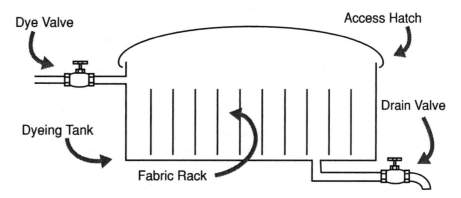

A further complication arises because the optimal exposure temperature is sometimes above the normal boiling point of the dyeing solution. Dealing with this issue requires still more equipment associated with the dyeing unit, namely one or more valves to control the entry of pressurized air to suppress boiling or vaporization of the dyeing solution, and an additional parameter, the air pressure to be applied (which is a function of the dye and of the dyeing temperature).

Finally, it is sometimes necessary to expose a fabric to a succession of dyes or related solutions. This means repeated cycles of solution admission, exposure, and draining, with corresponding multiple dyeing times, heating rates, dyeing temperatures, and pressures.

Equipment of the type just described is almost universally accompanied by some basic safety-related control circuitry that can independently override any computer-based control of the process itself. For example, there is likely to be an interlock between the access hatch and the dye valve, prohibiting the opening of the dye valve while the access hatch is open.

A simple, computer-based control system for a single dyeing run would, on the basis of operator-entered run parameters, control the various valves and the heater. This control would be based on monitoring of both the statuses of these devices and of physical quantities such as tank level, solution temperature, and air pressure. However, just as in the case of the dyeing process itself, the requirements for such a control system are likely to be much more extensive, including

- Detection of, reporting of, and possibly recovery from errors that might occur within the process (for example, failure of equipment such as the heater or of sensors such as the level or pressure sensors)
- Display of run status, process parameters, warnings, and errors to an operator

- Incorporation of a database of process parameters to avoid error-prone manual entry of these parameters

- Recording and statistical analysis of process history information (such as time series of sensor readings), to detect trends that might indicate impending equipment failure or deterioration in product quality

In addition to these requirements for control of a single dyeing run, the industrial nature of the process will impose the following additional set of requirements based on scale:

- It must be possible to concurrently control multiple dyeing units.

- It must be possible to control common resources needed by a set of dyeing units such as a high-pressure air supply and the piping between the units and the dye storage tanks.

- It may be necessary to determine an allocation of dyeing runs to dyeing units that optimizes the use of the units.

Industrial-scale process control often involves multiple computers. A common distribution scheme is to have a relatively primitive microprocessor attached to each collection of equipment to be controlled, and to have these microprocessors connected (by way of dedicated data transmission lines, or by way of a network) to one or more central processors where the control actually is carried out. The local microprocessors, among other tasks, carry out remote data collection. A remote data-collection setup for a dyeing unit is illustrated in Figure 2.4.

Figure 2.4   A Remote Data Collection Unit

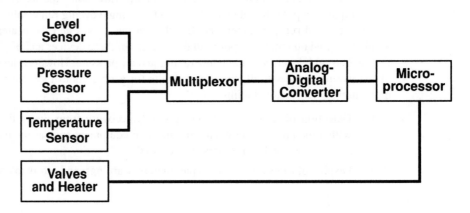

Since the sampling rates for the level, temperature, and pressure are relatively undemanding, a single analog-digital converter (multiplexed to the various sensors) can be used. The data-collection software cyclically collects the various sensor readings, performs some preliminary signal processing (such as linearization and scaling), bundles the sensor readings with the readings of the discrete-state valve and heater devices, and sends the data to the central fabric dyeing processor.

For the sake of this example, we will assume that a systems development project is to be undertaken in a large organization that operates a number of fabric dyeing facilities. The requirement is not for a single system, but for a family of related systems differing in scale, extent of automation, complexity of the process to be controlled, and implementation hardware. The developers are constrained to employ reuse to the maximum possible extent in order to minimize arbitrary variations among the various family members.

2.1.2   Timeliness Issues

In a real-time system, time is clearly a dominant concern. As pointed out in [Ward85], a program that takes 48 hours to predict tomorrow's weather based on today's data is not particularly useful. The timeliness issue boils down to reducing the following two specific time intervals:

- *Service time*. This is the net time taken to compute a response to a given input. It is primarily a function of the algorithm used in the computation and is often deterministic and predictable. For example, consider that the dyeing control system must respond by closing the dye valve when the solution level reaches a predetermined value. The service time is the time required to compare the desired and actual levels, and to decide whether to close the valve.

- *Latency*. This is the interval between the time of occurrence of an input and the time at which it starts being serviced. In the case of the solution level input, it is a combination of a number of different delays. Some of these delays are fixed, such as the delay in cycling through the various sensor readings and bundling the data. Some of the delays are variable, such as queueing delays incurred while waiting for the central fabric dyeing processor to perform calculations for other dyeing units, or the time spent waiting in a scheduler's ready queue. Depending on the nature of the load on the system, the variable delays may lead to significant fluctuations in latency.

The sum of these two intervals for a given input represents the overall *reaction time* for that input. Naturally, this time interval should be shorter than or equal to the deadline specified for this type of input. Ensuring that a system always meets its deadlines is complicated by the presence of variable delays.

Different systems will have different requirements for meeting deadlines. At one extreme are so-called *hard* real-time systems, where missing even a single deadline is considered unacceptable. Examples of hard real-time systems can be found in life-critical systems, such as nuclear power stations, medical equipment, and aircraft control. At the other end of the spectrum are *soft* real-time systems where missing a deadline occasionally is acceptable. For example, telephony systems contain a requirement that a subscriber will receive a dial tone within a certain time period after lifting the handset. However, it is not considered catastrophic if this does not occur in every single case, provided that the number of such failures is below an acceptable threshold. In the fabric dyeing example, the deadline will be determined by the time it takes for the liquid level to exceed the desired level by a sufficient amount to cause problems.

The essential difficulty with achieving timeliness is that usually no direct means of tracking time utilization is available as a system is being designed. The required reaction time for an input defines a "time budget" that must not be exceeded. In the process of design, we must know the precise impact on the time budget of every design decision. Unfortunately, the technology for this does not yet exist, and given the complexity of the problem, we may not see a dramatic improvement in this state of affairs in the near future. For example, in achieving a timely closing of the dye valve, both the scheduling algorithm used to divide the central fabric dyeing processor's time among the various dyeing runs, and the delay across the network to deliver a packet of data from a particular dyeing unit, will have effects on the reaction time that can be quite difficult to determine precisely.

The present techniques for dealing with the timeliness problem fall into the following two main groups:

- *Analytical techniques* are based on constructing a formal mathematical model of the system and extracting the performance characteristics from this model by mathematical means. Queueing theory is one of the most practical analytical methods for this purpose [Kleinrock76].

- *Simulation techniques* are based on the construction of computer-executable models from which performance characteristics are extracted by direct measurement.

However, both of these are statistical approaches and may not be fully satisfactory for hard real-time systems. Furthermore, both are extremely sensitive to the accuracy of the models.

In traditional engineering disciplines, models often can be constructed on the safe assumption that a system can be linearized around its anticipated operating point. Consequently, the model may not be fully accurate, but it is usually close enough that the difference does not matter. Software, on the other hand, is inherently nonlinear. For example, an error in a single (and possibly insignificant) statement of a program can corrupt the entire program and cause it to misbehave in completely unpredictable ways. What this means in practical terms is that we are never quite sure whether a real-time system will be satisfactory until we have actually constructed it (and, sometimes, not even then). Although this is true for most engineering products, what distinguishes software (particularly real-time software) from other systems is that the degree of this uncertainty is much higher.

Based on these considerations, the requirements for a modeling language that effectively deals with the timeliness issue are

- It must explicitly support the concepts of absolute time and time intervals.

- The creation of models with appropriate details must be such that the various elements involved in the reaction time may be estimated.

- The rapid creation of system prototypes is essential so that timing behavior may be measured in the actual implementation environment as early as possible in the development process.

2.1.3 Dynamic Internal Structure Issues

A common source of complexity in real-time systems is the need for reconfiguration of the system as it is running, based on dynamic changes in the external environment. Consider, for example, that the central fabric dyeing processor is responsible for controlling dyeing runs, providing operator displays, analyzing process history information, and possibly scheduling future dyeing runs. A "worst-case" approach to the development of such a system would provide the capability to simultaneously control the most complex type of run in all the dyeing units while analyzing process history data and performing scheduling computations. However, such a worst-case approach is typically not cost-effective, since this maximum load situation is extremely unlikely to occur.

If the worst-case approach is rejected, then some form of resource management is required. In the present case, the system can be designed to deal with varying numbers of concurrent dyeing runs, and to carry out background tasks (such as history analysis scheduling and hardware checking) when the load is lighter. Resource management leads to several difficult problems. Perhaps the most complicated is the need for dynamic creation and destruction of system components and relationships. This not only requires set-up and tear-down scenarios, but also resource management subsystems that control and track the use of shared resources such as memory. Finally, resource management may also require that we devise methods for dealing with error situations. One of the main issues here is that, if an error occurs when the system is near maximum resource utilization, the additional overhead for error handling may require a priority-driven shedding of less-essential tasks.

The requirement on a modeling language that arises from dynamic internal structure is the ability to create models of systems whose internal structures can be dynamically modified at run time.

2.1.4 Reactiveness Issues

One way of classifying computer programs is into transformational and reactive systems [Manna92]. *Transformational* systems start off with some initial data that is transformed by a series of computations into the desired output data. Once the output is produced, the system terminates execution. In contrast, *reactive* systems generally do not terminate. Instead, they are involved in a continuous interaction with the environment. The environment generates input events at discrete intervals through one or more interfaces and the system reacts by changing its state and possibly generating output events.

In this book, we are primarily interested in a subclass of reactive systems that conform to the following definitions:

- *Nondeterminism*. The system has no control over the relative order or time of occurrence of input events.

- *Real-time response*. The system must provide a timely response to all input events.

- *State dependence*. The response of the system to a given input depends on previous inputs and time.

Nondeterminism is simply a reflection of the unpredictable nature of the real world in which such a system functions. For example, data may arrive from various dyeing units in an unpredictable order, and operator inputs may be intermixed arbitrarily with state changes of monitored variables. In some systems, it may be possible to process events in the most convenient order, rather than in the order of occurrence. However, in real-time systems, this generally is not possible because of the timeliness requirement. For example, when a heater or valve in a dyeing unit fails, it may not be acceptable to postpone the recovery action for a later time. In the theoretic framework of Lynch and Tuttle ([Lynch88]), this type of system has been designated as *input enabled*, which means that *any* input can occur at *any* time. Another term commonly used to describe these systems is *event driven*.

The requirement on a modeling language that arises from reactiveness is that system models must have explicit representation of events as drivers of system activity.

2.1.5   Concurrency Issues

Many system requirements involve the specification of a set of sequentially ordered action steps. For example, the requirement to let high-pressure air into the dyeing tank when the solution temperature approaches the normal boiling point can be expressed as follows:

```
if (currentSolutionTemperature >= (boilingTemperature - leeway))
    then {
        reportPressureDemand(desiredPressure);
        controlPressureValve(open, desiredPressure);
        }
etc.
```

This is a simple and effective representation. The overall behavior is broken down into a sequence of more primitive behaviors or steps, each of which can be comprehended individually. Each step transforms the state of the system by executing a specific action. The new state of the system depends on the state of the system at the time that step was initiated, and on the type of action performed by the step. The overall result can be deduced by following the sequence of steps from beginning to end. Such a sequence is called a *thread of control*, since it controls the behavior of a computer. A portion of a system that incorporates a sequential thread of control is often referred to as a *process* or a *task*.

A *concurrent system* contains two or more simultaneous threads of control that dynamically depend on each other in order to fulfill their individual objectives. For example, the thread of control that regulates the central high-pressure air supply must interact with the threads of control for individual dyeing runs that determine when pressure is to be applied. This interaction between threads is at the heart of most difficulties in dealing with concurrent systems. The problem lies in our inability to construct effective mental models of dynamic relationships. Specifying the behavior of concurrent systems requires simultaneous awareness of multiple entities and their progression relative to each other, as well as with respect to absolute time. This is complicated by the fact that threads may progress at different speeds (particularly in distributed systems) so that the number of possible combinations quickly becomes very large and intractable to the human mind. Part of the reason is that time, as humans perceive it, is a continuous quantity with an infinity of values and no recognizable boundaries.

To make this problem more manageable, a variety of techniques has been developed [Andrews83]. Most of them are based on reducing the number of possible interaction points between threads (for example, critical regions, semaphore operations, or message sends and receives). An example of such an interaction point is the reportPressureDemand message sent by a dyeing run thread of control to the high-pressure air supply thread of control. By clustering concurrency issues around interaction points, we can ignore them in the remainder of the thread.

The two primitive forms of interaction between threads are

- *Synchronization.* Synchronization involves adjusting the timing of the execution of an action step in a thread based on the execution state of other threads. For example, the dyeing run thread holds off sending the message to activate the pressure valve until the air supply thread has accepted the reportPressureDemand message. Synchronization may be required either to achieve noninterference between threads (mutual exclusion) or to ensure proper interaction between them.

- *Communication.* It is often necessary to pass information from one thread to another. This can take on many different forms, including global shared memory, message passing, remote procedure calls, and rendezvous. In our example, the desired pressure is passed to the air supply thread as part of the message.

When these two forms of interaction are combined (as they are here) so that synchronization and information exchange occur simultaneously, we talk about *synchronous communication*. In *asynchronous communication*, information exchange does not directly imply synchronization.

By definition, a thread of control is contained within a single task or process. In a system with multiple cooperating tasks, an analogous higher-level concept of an activity "thread" spans multiple concurrent tasks. We refer to this concept as an *action scenario* or, simply, *scenario*. Informally, a scenario is a series of causally chained events typically *spanning multiple tasks* in a system that represent some meaningful high-level operation. In fabric dyeing, for example, a typical scenario might be the sequences of events and actions involved in translating a near-boiling temperature reading in a dyeing tank into the application of high-pressure air to the tank. The difference between a scenario and a control thread is primarily one of implementation. A control thread is a concept that is directly supported by a multitasking operating system within a processor, whereas a scenario may be a purely abstract entity involving (possibly) a set of cooperating control threads spread across multiple processors.

In its simplest form, a scenario can be represented by a concatenation of individual action steps of the following form:

$$step_i : <task_j, input\text{-}event_i, output\text{-}events_i>$$

where $task_j$ is the task involved in executing $step_i$ of the activity, $input\text{-}event_i$ is the event that is the cause of $step_i$, and $output\text{-}events_i$ is a set of zero or more events that are generated by $task_i$ in response to $input\text{-}event_i$. In our fabric dyeing example, the pressure application scenario might be defined as follows:

1: <dataCollectorA, temperatureValueIn, dataBundleReady> // value captured
2: <network, dataBundleReady, dataBundleSent> // value transmitted
3: <RunControllerA,dataBundleSent, reportPressureDemand> // value recognized
4: <airSupplyController, reportPressureDemand, ...> // adjust for demand

A common way of diagrammatically representing scenarios is through *message sequence charts* (see Figure 2.5). These charts show sets of pair-wise message exchanges between entities in a system and the relative order in which they occur. In these diagrams, time is assumed to run downward along the vertical dimension. Messages emanating or terminating on the outside border of the chart are messages that are sent or received by what is referred to as "the environment" (representing any entities not explicitly identified in the chart).

Scenarios are frequently used to specify the functional requirements of a system. Implicit in the definition of each step is the expectation that the destination entity will be in a state that produces the desired output events for the specified input event. In a reactive system, however, the response of an entity to a given input depends on the current state of the entity. For example, the air supply control may not be able to respond to an increase in demand because of equipment problems.

This is an example of a *scenario conflict*.[2] In this case, the scenarios colliding are a pressure-application scenario and an error-handling scenario. Other types of collisions are also possible involving instances of the same scenario. For example, a conflict between two pressure application scenarios is possible if two dyeing run controllers are contending to communicate with the air supply controller. The difficult thing about scenario conflicts is that the scenarios may potentially interfere with each other at almost any step (since they are initiated asynchronously of each other). Hence, to detect a scenario conflict, we

---

[2] We prefer this term over the more common "race condition." In our view, a race condition is just one of the symptoms of a scenario conflict.

Figure 2.5 A Message Sequence Chart for a Scenario

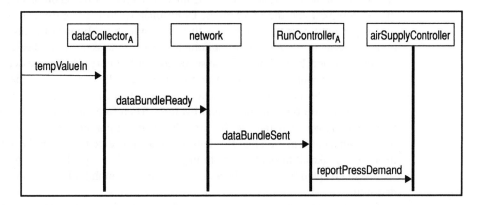

must compare all scenarios with each other step-by-step! This quickly leads to the same type of combinatorial explosion already discussed for control threads.

Scenario conflicts are the result of the concurrent and asynchronous nature of the external environment. It is often unrealistic to try to eliminate scenario conflicts by restricting concurrent inputs to the system. For example, any number of relevant things may be happening at a given time within a complex industrial control environment, and arbitrarily ignoring some of them might be problematic because of timeliness constraints.

The requirement imposed by concurrency on a modeling language is the ability to model a collection of interacting control threads, to model scenarios involving these control threads, and a means to help resolve concurrency issues.

2.1.6 Distribution Issues

Distributed computing systems (consisting typically of a set of computing sites loosely coupled through a communications network) offer a tantalizing view of aggregated computing power capable of dealing with very complex applications. While this promise has been fulfilled in many situations, the benefits do not come without a heavy price. This "dark side" of distributed systems lies in their dramatically increased complexity when compared to centralized systems. We illustrate this with the following parable of the cautious generals.[3]

This story concerns the predicament of two generals of ancient times, Amphilohious and Basileus, whose respective armies are separated by an enemy host. The combined

---

[3] The fable of the generals was originally described in [Gray78].

force of the two armies is sufficient to overwhelm the enemy, but only if both armies start their attacks simultaneously. The problem facing the generals is to agree on a time of attack. Given the historical setting, the only way this can be accomplished is to dispatch messengers between the two armies. Unfortunately, to get from one army to another, a messenger must pass through enemy lines with a high likelihood of being captured in the process. Assume, then, that Amphilohious sends a messenger to Basileus proposing a coordinated attack at dawn. Because of the uncertainty of the messenger's mission, Amphilohious cannot be confident that Basileus actually has received the message. If he attacks under those circumstances and it turns out that Basileus has not received the message, he will lose both the battle and his rank. Therefore, being a prudent sort (which is how generals get their rank in the first place), Amphilohious instructs his messenger to return with a confirmation that Basileus has indeed received the message. Of course, if the messenger makes it through the first time, there is still an equally strong possibility that he will be intercepted on the way back. If that happens, Amphilohious cannot know Basileus' decision.

Even if the messenger gets through on the return trip, so that Amphilohious knows that Basileus knows the time of the attack, the quandary is not necessarily resolved. Amphilohious may still have his doubts that Basileus will indeed attack at the agreed time. Namely, Basileus, perhaps being even more tentative than his peer, might decide to withhold attack until he is certain that Amphilohious has received his confirmation, which, of course, requires another exchange of messages. This chain of reasoning can be extended *ad infinitum*, as one might expect of such prudent types. This leads us to the conclusion that neither of the generals ever will be fully satisfied, that the attack never will occur, and that the opportunity to defeat the enemy will be lost.

The dilemma of the cautious generals is a typical example of a distributed system problem. In fact, several formal proofs demonstrate that it is impossible to define a reliable agreement protocol if communication is not guaranteed.[4] Unfortunately, the probability of losing messages can be substantial in some systems. For example, a message sent to a distant spacecraft can be easily destroyed or corrupted during transmission. And, much as we might condemn the ancient generals for their faintheartedness, if the distributed system for which we are responsible is life-critical, being this cautious may be most appropriate.

Message loss is just one of a collection of truly difficult problems facing designers of distributed systems. In general, the following are sources of major design issues that accompany distributed systems:

- Concurrency
- Unreliable communication media (lost messages, corrupted messages, and so forth)
- Prolonged and variable transmission delays
- Relativistic effects
- The possibility of independent partial system failures

---

[4] See, for example, the paper by Halpern and Moses [Halpern84].

While not all of these necessarily will be present in every situation, even one can cause major complications. We already have examined concurrency and the problems that it causes. We now look more closely at one of the other issues on this list, relativistic effects.

Consider a fabric dyeing system consisting of three physically distributed computers— a data-collection computer, a process-control computer, and a run history computer, as shown in Figure 2.6.

Figure 2.6 A Distributed Fabric Dyeing System

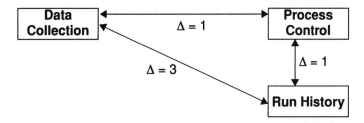

Assume that the transmission delay between individual computers is not equal, so a message from the data-collection computer to the process-control computer (or vice versa) takes a single unit of time ($\Delta = 1$) to arrive, as does a message from the process-control computer to the run history computer. A message to the run history computer from the data-collection computer, on the other hand, takes three time units ($\Delta = 3$).

If the data-collection computer sends a **data error** message at time t_1 to the process-control and run history computers, and the process-control computer sends a **shutdown** message to the data-collection and run history computers one time unit later (that is, $t_1 + 1$ — we assume that the processing time is much shorter than the transmission time), then the order in which the two messages will be received by the run history computer will be different (see Figure 2.7) than the order in which they were sent. The run history computer may thus conclude that the shutdown occurred before the data error.

In other words, the data-collection and run history computers will see a different ordering of events. Note that this effect is *not* caused by any failures of the communication system. That is, it would occur even if the underlying service were fully reliable.

The net result of this phenomenon is that we cannot assume that all sites within a distributed system have a common view of the state of the system and the environment. The effect is exactly the same as that caused by lossy communication: the absence of common knowledge across the distributed sites. This makes any coordinated action by the various sites difficult.[5]

---

[5] For a more in-depth discussion of this problem and methods of dealing with it, refer to the seminal paper by Lamport [Lamport78].

Figure 2.7   The Relativistic Effects of Distribution

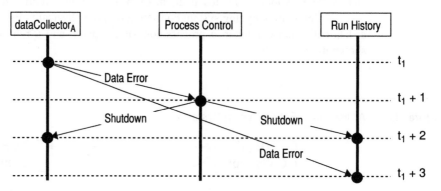

The requirements placed on a modeling language by such distribution issues are the ability to model a system as a collection of independent centers of activity, and the ability to explicitly model those features of interaction among the centers of activity that lead to distribution problems.

2.2   Strategies for Dealing with Complexity

The most common net result of the properties just discussed is complexity. Since complexity has always been part of our environment, humans have devised a set of techniques for dealing with (if not always conquering) complexity. In this section, we examine some of the techniques for dealing with complexity.

2.2.1   Abstraction

The most common and the most effective technique for dealing with complexity is *abstraction*. This is the act of mentally discarding individual aspects of some phenomenon until what remains is small enough for us to comprehend. In the process, we try to retain (as much as possible) those aspects that have a significant impact on the phenomenon under study, while discarding lesser influences. The problem, of course, is that we are not always sure exactly which aspects are significant, particularly if we lack prior domain experience.

Abstraction techniques are a central theme of this book and central to the ROOM modeling language. A methodology encourages abstract thinking, which is why the application of a methodology is useful (if not crucial) for designing large systems. In ROOM, the highest abstraction levels often are referred to as *architectural levels* as a reminder of their fundamental impact on the rest of the system. Analogous to the role of the architecture of a building, the architecture of a system is the framework on which all other aspects of that system depend.

The use of abstraction is clearly not specific to real-time systems development. However, since abstraction is a general strategy for dealing with complexity, any modeling language that aspires to deal with complex systems must support abstraction mechanisms. In the remainder of this section, we first examine several more specific modeling strategies based on abstraction (specifically, recursion, incremental modeling, and reuse) and the requirements placed on a modeling language that supports these strategies. We then examine the problems attendant to applying abstraction-based strategies in the real-time arena.

2.2.2 Recursion

The basic strategy behind recursion is the re-application of a given model structure at successively lower levels of detail within a model. Since the model can thus be as "deep" as desired, it does not have to be "wide." In other words, the top level of a model can consist of a relatively small number of pieces of a highly abstract, easy-to-comprehend character, and each piece can be decomposed into a similar structure at the next lower level of abstraction.

The popularity of top-down functional decomposition, for example, is certainly related to its recursive character. The top level of the model consists of a small number of functions, each of which decomposes into a small number of subfunctions, and so on. As a counter-example, consider the state machine as a modeling tool. Despite the obvious suitability of state machines for representing event-driven systems, the "flat" character of traditional state machines (that is, machines with only a single level of states and transitions) made them unsuitable for modeling complex systems. It was not until suitable formalisms (especially that of Harel [Harel87a]) were developed for extending state machines into hierarchical, recursive structures that it became practical to use state machines as a general systems modeling tool.

The requirement placed on a modeling language by recursion is to provide representation mechanisms whose elements can be expanded into similar lower-level representations, for as many levels as desired.

2.2.3 Incremental Modeling

While recursion provides for the distribution of details among levels of a hierarchy, incremental modeling deals with the aggregation of details within a particular element of a model. The abstraction mechanism involved in incremental modeling is the initial laying aside of most details, followed by successively revisiting the portion of the model in question, and gradually adding new details or correcting existing ones.

Incremental modeling is an alternative to a straightforward linear process, such as that represented by the classical "waterfall" development model. In the waterfall model, development is viewed as a linear progression of phases, each encapsulating just one type of activity. The process typically starts with a specification of the requirements, followed by design, and so on. The products of each phase are passed as input to the next, until the desired system is produced and verified.

The difficulty with this approach is that it assumes all major development problems are anticipated and intercepted during the early phases. For example, any contradictory or incomplete requirements must be detected in the system specification phase. For more complex systems this is not possible. Downstream surprises that result from an imperfect understanding and flawed requirements can have catastrophic consequences requiring, in some cases, major rework at a very late stage of development.

Incremental modeling is based on the observations that it is easier to create a simple structure than a complex one, and that it is easier to modify an existing structure than to create one from scratch. Therefore, instead of trying to create a complete portion of a model in one pass, the initial work is deliberately restricted to incorporating the most critical details (or the details most clearly understood) and then the model is repeatedly incremented until complete.

The requirement placed on a modeling language by the incremental modeling strategy is that the language permit partially complete models to be used effectively to learn about system properties.

2.2.4   Reuse

Reuse is based on comparison of details in multiple parts of a model. Reuse involves laying aside all the details of a part of a model except those that match details of some other part of the model, then segregating the common details so that they are constrained to be consistent across multiple appearances or multiple uses. This extraction of common patterns is just another form of abstraction.

For example, the emergence of the subroutine call mechanism in programming languages, and of abstract models based on this mechanism such as structure charts [Yourdon78], made reuse significantly easier to apply. This was because common portions of a software design could be represented as single subroutines that could be called from multiple places.

Reuse places the requirement on a modeling language of providing mechanisms for representing common details, and constraining these details to be consistent wherever they appear.

2.2.5   Obstacles to the Use of Abstraction in Real-Time Development

Despite the obvious usefulness of abstraction techniques, considerable barriers to their use do occur in real-time systems development. Abstraction is sometimes actively opposed as being too costly to apply to real-time development.

The most painful and obvious cost of abstraction is efficiency. Abstraction involves the placement of impenetrable boundaries around system components and encourages loose coupling between them. For software, this often implies increased memory requirements and less-efficient algorithms. The latter, in particular, is hard to accept in real-time applications characterized by an obsession with efficiency. Yet, for large systems, the benefits clearly outweigh the costs. There is no point in building an efficient system if it does not do what it is supposed to do, or if the cost of operating it and maintaining it is prohibitive.

Much of the resistance to the application of abstraction techniques in real-time applications is based on historical arguments that are increasingly less valid with each new technological advance. For example, the capacity of the latest generation of standard microprocessors has increased manyfold over those of a decade ago. This means that what may have led to an unacceptable performance degradation in the past may be quite acceptable now. That is, rather than utilizing all the capacity improvement brought on by technological advances simply for increasing throughput, it is worthwhile investing a relatively small percentage of it toward improving reliability, controllability, and maintainability of our software.

2.3   Summary

Real-time systems cover a vast domain of diverse applications. The ROOM modeling language is targeted at these systems, which we define as characterized by the following properties:

- Timeliness
- Dynamic internal structure
- Reactiveness
- Concurrency
- Distribution

Each of these properties, in its own way, adds fundamental difficulties to the development problem. Timeliness is inherent to all real-time systems and means that the system must respond to a given input within some acceptable time interval. Guaranteeing that response in all circumstances is difficult to achieve. Systems that, at run time, have a dynamically changing internal structure can significantly complicate the development problem. Reactive behavior implies a system that is event-driven. In other words, the system has no advance knowledge or control of when and which input events will occur next. This means that the traditional known and trusted sequential style of system description (characterized by a single stream of instructions) is not adequate for describing behavior. Concurrency means that the behavior of the system involves multiple concurrent and interrelated threads of control. This leads to major development problems owing to our limited capacity to reason about parallel time sequences. Distribution in a system means that its hardware and software are partitioned among a number of loosely coupled physical sites connected by a communications network. This allows the combined power of multiple computers to be applied to the problem at hand, but also introduces an assortment of inherently difficult problems. Included in this are unreliable communications with prolonged transmission delays that make synchronization difficult, relativistic effects that lead to inconsistencies, and partial system failures that must be handled.

Each of these characteristics of real-time systems places particular requirements on a modeling language.

Abstraction, in various forms, is used to deal with the complexity of large systems. This includes recursion, incremental modeling, and reuse. The support for these abstraction-based modeling strategies also places requirements on a modeling language.

CHAPTER 3

Key Elements of the ROOM Modeling Language

The ROOM modeling language was developed to satisfy the requirements described in Chapter 2, namely, to facilitate the modeling of real-time systems, and to permit the use of effective model-building strategies so that models of large, complex systems can be constructed. To achieve these objectives, ROOM was organized around the following three key elements:

- The *operational approach*
- A *phase-independent set of modeling abstractions*
- The *object paradigm*

This chapter describes each of these key elements in detail. Section 3.1 covers the operational approach, Section 3.2 discusses the phase-independent modeling abstractions, and Section 3.3 describes the object paradigm. Understanding these three elements will make it much easier to absorb the detailed description of ROOM, which is the subject of Chapter 4. Section 3.4 summarizes how, by incorporating these elements, ROOM satisfies the requirements for a real-time modeling language.

A common theme that unites the three elements of the high-level structure is *the elimination of discontinuities in the system development process*. To be sure, discontinuities are intrinsic to the nature of the process itself and cannot be completely removed. For example, the requirements definition, design, and implementation activities are characterized by different thought processes, emphases on different kinds of details, and different verification criteria. However, many of the discontinuities encountered in a typical development project are *artifacts* introduced by the modeling approach. In other words, the choice of particular notations or model-building strategies can introduce unnecessary, artificial discontinuities into a development project. These artificial discontinuities can be eliminated by the use of an appropriate modeling language such as ROOM.

In order to facilitate discussion of discontinuities, we introduce a simple classification scheme for commonly encountered discontinuities. We differentiate the following types:

- *Scope* discontinuities are caused by a lack of formal coupling between the representations of different *levels* of detail.

- *Semantic* discontinuities are caused by a lack of formal coupling between the representations of different *kinds* of related detail.

- *Development phase* discontinuities are caused by a lack of formal coupling between requirements, design, and implementation representations.

Scope refers to the levels of the details encountered in a model, from high-level details (such as the major components of the system and its major functional capabilities) to low-level details (such as primitive data types and the manipulation of data values). Semantic refers to the distinction between details of one kind (such as data structures) and details of another kind (such as functional behavior definitions). Phase refers to the progress of development from concept through design to implementation. Using this scheme, one can differentiate between scope discontinuities (such as the use of different notations for high-level representation and low-level representation), semantic discontinuities (such as the use of different notations for data structure and functional behavior), and phase discontinuities (such as the use of different notations for requirements definition and design).

As in Chapter 2, major concepts will be illustrated by using the fabric dyeing application.

3.1   The Operational Approach

The operational approach eliminates scope and semantic discontinuities in the development process by using a single, integrated, formal set of modeling abstractions to create a given model. The model thus created not only has a formal interpretation, but also has the capability of being *executed* like a program in a conventional programming language. The next subsection discusses scope and semantic discontinuities. The following subsection explains the basic elements of the operational approach.

3.1.1   Problems with Semantic and Scope Discontinuities

Many systems development organizations claim to be using one or another well-defined methodology, which prescribes a thorough model-based requirements definition and design process as a prelude to coding. Nevertheless, a large number of projects within these organizations exhibit the symptoms of the "rush-to-code" syndrome: a pervasive unease during the early development phases, a prevailing attitude among the developers that requirements definition and design models are "just documentation," and a conviction that the "real work" has not begun until code is being written.

Many developers will acknowledge that the modeling approach they are using for requirements definition or design can provide some useful insights into the nature of the system under development. However, the value added by such modeling seems to reach a point of diminishing returns quite rapidly, usually long before the production of a reason-ably complete model. This impatience with the earlier development phases seems to be independent of the particulars of the development method. This problem is not likely to be solved, for example, simply by the substitution of object-oriented requirements definition for functional requirements definition.

Although the "rush-to-code" syndrome may be based in part on a general reluctance to engage in high-level, abstract thinking, it is also based in part on two accurate observa-tions. First, it is possible to get hard, objective evidence that a piece of code is correct and complete, namely from a successful compilation followed by successful execution of a test case. Second, there is no way to get similarly hard, objective evidence that a piece of a conventional requirements analysis or design is correct and complete. To work on a requirements or design model is thus to work under persistent, nagging uncertainty as to the value of the work being done. The causes of this problem are the semantic and scope discontinuities within most modeling methods.

Semantic discontinuities are caused by the fact that different sets of modeling abstrac-tions (that is, different modeling languages or notations) are commonly used to model dif-ferent aspects of a proposed system. Consider, for example, the combined use of *entity-relationship diagrams* and *data flow diagrams* for requirements definition, which is com-mon in methodologies derived from the structured analysis approach of DeMarco [DeMarco78]. A fragment of an entity-relationship model for fabric dyeing is shown in Figure 3.1, and a related data flow diagram fragment is shown in Figure 3.2. The entity-relationship diagram emphasizes structural relationships among the various kinds of data within a system, while the data flow diagram emphasizes functionality (specifically, trans-formations of inputs into outputs).

Figure 3.1   An Entity-Relationship Diagram

The relationships among the elements of the entity-relationship diagram, and among the elements of the data flow diagram, are well-defined. However, no commonly accepted set of relationships exists *between* the entity-relationship diagram and the data flow dia-gram. It is not clear, for example, whether the attributes associated with Dyeing Run Con-troller in Figure 3.1 should be the same as the data elements associated with Dyeing Run Parameters in Figure 3.2, or which elements of Figure 3.2 are associated with the Controls relationship in Figure 3.1. The more time is invested in building such models, the more these uncertainties multiply.

Figure 3.2   A Data Flow Diagram

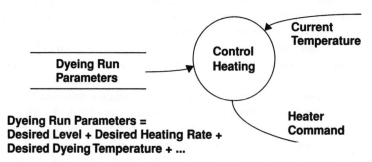

Despite the semantic discontinuities just discussed, the various notations used to represent high-level details are typically well-defined within themselves, and are potentially (or actually) formal languages for system representation. However, the associated scheme for representation of *low-level* details usually follows one of three patterns. No specific representation is provided for such details, the representation provided is informal, or the representation provided is formal but is not formally integrated with the high-level representation. The result in any of these three cases is a scope discontinuity within the modeling method.

For example, consider again the data flow diagram fragment of Figure 3.2. The roles of the various graphic language elements are well-defined. Dyeing Run Parameters represents persistent stored data, Control Heating represents a function, and the labeled arrows represent inputs and outputs of the function and access to the stored data. Structured analysis also provides a textual language for decomposition of complex data structures into simpler ones, as illustrated by the decomposition of Dyeing Run Parameters in Figure 3.2.

However, a complete model of the system fragment of Figure 3.2 also requires a description of the logic carried out by Control Heating. The traditional mechanism provided by structured analysis for this purpose is "structured English," an informal language for logic definition. It is possible to substitute a piece of code written in a conventional programming language for the structured English. However, there is no formal way to integrate the data-manipulation capabilities of the code with the data-decomposition syntax. (For example, how would one refer to a component of Dyeing Run Parameters in the code?) As is the case with structure-behavior discontinuities, the more time invested in modeling, the more the uncertainties introduced by scope discontinuities increase.

We hope it is clear to the reader that we are not proposing the elimination of distinctions between data structures and functions, or between high-level and low-level details. Rather, we are proposing that the relationships among the modeling abstractions that express these different aspects of a model should be defined formally. Figure 3.3 is an attempt to clarify this distinction, for the case of representation of data and function in a hypothetical modeling notation.

Figure 3.3   Formal Relationships versus Representational Distinctions

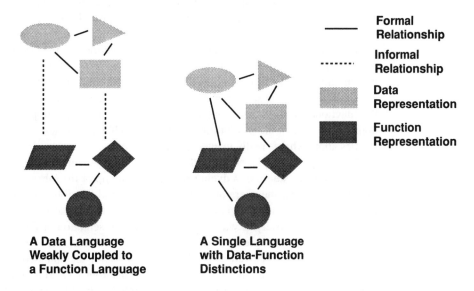

——	**Formal Relationship**
······	**Informal Relationship**
▨	**Data Representation**
▰	**Function Representation**

A Data Language Weakly Coupled to a Function Language

A Single Language with Data-Function Distinctions

To summarize, many modeling approaches suffer from semantic and scope discontinuities among the language elements used to represent a system under development. The existence of these discontinuities is a major factor in the "rush-to-code" syndrome.

3.1.2   Basic Concepts of the Operational Approach

The operational approach recognizes the essential wisdom behind the "rush-to-code" syndrome. Rather than forcing developers to create preliminary development products whose usefulness they mistrust, the operational approach attempts to incorporate the trustworthy properties of code into the creation of these products. The operational approach was originated by a number of researchers in the early 1980s. It has been given its clearest expression by Pamela Zave [Zave84], who also created PAISLey [Zave82], an influential language and environment for the creation of executable specification (requirements definition) models.

The operational approach treats requirements definition models and design models as programs written in a very high-level modeling language. In a full-fledged, executable modeling language, all the elements of the language (those used to represent high-level schematic details as well as those used to represent low-level details, and those used to represent different kinds of details such as structure versus behavior) are formal, compilable, executable parts of an integrated whole.

Verification of an executable model is carried out by compiling it and running it, just as is done with code written in a conventional programming language. Some kinds of verification also may be accomplished by formal analysis. Thus the "rush-to-code" syndrome is avoided, since requirements and design models have the objective verifiability that is absent in conventional models.

More generally, the "executability" of executable models means that they can be used for early prototyping. These models can be used as prototypes in the traditional sense of preliminary versions of the system that are run on the implementation hardware. They are also prototypes in the sense that they can be run on the *development* platform to simulate the functionality and other properties of the system under development. Supported by an appropriate development environment, an executable model can assist in clarifying uncertainties about what is really wanted from a system.

As a simple example, consider that a fabric dyeing control system will be required to track the various stages of a dyeing run: the setting up of the fabric, the filling of the dyeing tank following the operator's start command, and possibly an "aborted" state following the issuance of an emergency stop command by the operator. This requirement can be represented in a variety of ways. However, the representation of Figure 3.4 (in terms of a state machine) has the great advantage of being executable, if it is interpreted as changing state as inputs are received at particular times. Here, the rounded rectangles represent states of the dyeing run, the arrows represent transitions caused by inputs (operator commands, in this case), and the arrow from the circle labeled "I" to the settingUp state shows that settingUp is the initial state.

Figure 3.4   An Executable State Machine

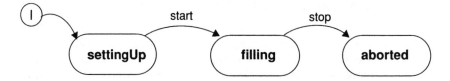

The rules for execution are that the diagram starts in its initial state, and that inputs will cause changes in state only if the input matches a label on an arrow out of the current state. By highlighting the final state, Figure 3.5 shows the results of five different input sequences. Note that it is not possible to reach the aborted state from the settingUp state by issuing a stop command unless the stop command follows a start command. This may not have been clear in a textual statement of the requirement, and even may have been overlooked in a graphical model unless a model execution actually was performed. State machine execution permits such details to be noticed and to be modified if desired. Executable state machines are a feature of the ROOM modeling language.

Figure 3.5 Results of Model Execution

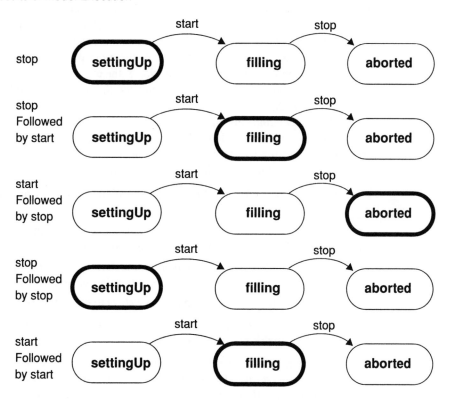

To be effective, executable models must be highly *observable*. That is, it must be possible to clearly convey the semantics of a model as well as its execution. This is an argument for the use of graphical modeling concepts, and for the ability to visualize model execution using the same graphics used for model construction, as illustrated in Figure 3.4 and Figure 3.5. Graphical techniques have a synthetic effect. They convey a considerable amount of information in a compact way. This is why ROOM uses a graphical notation for the higher abstraction levels. Additionally, in order to properly observe and assess the behavior of an executing model, the ROOM model execution environment uses the same graphical representation used to construct the model.

One of the side effects of executable models is that they require more effort in the early phases of development as compared to traditional techniques. In order to make a model executable, it is necessary to fill in some aspects that may be missing in the requirements and to resolve ambiguities. However, detecting such defects in the requirements is precisely one of the major objectives of traditional analysis. This effort usually is well-spent, since the cost of removing such defects increases as development progresses.

The challenge in this is to make the construction of high-level models relatively light-weight. One of the problems with constructing working prototypes of high-level system models using traditional programming languages is that general-purpose languages do not directly support convenient high-level abstractions (for example, state machines). This means that a considerable amount of implementation-level effort may have to be invested to construct the necessary abstractions out of the more primitive facilities provided by a programming language. To make matters worse, the execution of the model is difficult to observe because the working model is formulated through a low-level textual formalism. The features of ROOM are an attempt to make the construction of executable models easy enough that the benefits outweigh the costs.

The details of an executable modeling language for real-time systems, and of the environment provided for its use on the development platform, are dictated by the uses to which the executable models will be put. Such models

- Will be run on the development workstation, as well as on the implementation hardware.

- Will need to operate even when not connected to real sensors, actuators, or other peripheral devices, and thus must be able to simulate these components.

- Will have to provide for stopping and restarting of execution, and thus must be able to run with a simulated real-time clock, as well as with a real one.

- Will be run to collect information, as well as to do real work.

- Will be used to verify high-level, architectural properties of the proposed system, as well as low-level, detailed properties.

The fact that high-level, architectural properties must be verified is a constraint on the modeling language itself—the language must be capable of explicitly expressing such high-level properties. However, the other uses of the model can be accommodated by the model-building environment on the development platform, and thus the modeling language can be defined without any specific features tailored to these uses. For example, information collection can be provided by a software shell between the program and the modeler, and need not be directly incorporated into the language. This usage independence of the language component is extremely important for the phase independence of ROOM, which will be discussed in the next section.

In summary, the operational approach treats early life-cycle models as programs written in a very high-level modeling language. These programs can be compiled and executed to detect errors and inconsistencies in system requirements and design concepts.

3.2   A Phase-Independent Set of Modeling Abstractions

The use of a phase-independent set of modeling abstractions eliminates phase discontinuities in the development process. Section 3.2.1 discusses phase discontinuities, while Section 3.2.2 explains the basic concept of phase independence.

3.2.1   Problems with Phase Discontinuities

Many modeling approaches, in addition to exhibiting the semantic and scope discontinuities mentioned in Section 3.1.1, also exhibit phase discontinuities. In other words, the modeling language used to express the design is different from the modeling language used to model the requirements, as well as from the conventional programming language used to implement the system.

For example, when a data flow diagram is used to model system requirements as illustrated in Figure 3.2, a *structure chart* [Yourdon79] is commonly used to model the associated design. Figure 3.6 shows a fragment of a structure chart corresponding to the data flow diagram of Figure 3.2.

Figure 3.6   A Structure Chart

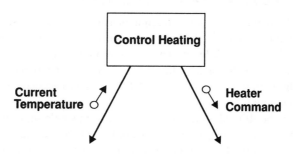

The differences between Figure 3.2 and Figure 3.6 are far deeper than the obvious variations in symbol shapes. The data flow diagram uses an abstract model of communication (with data "flowing" from producer to consumer), while the structure chart uses subroutine calls as the model of communication. One must designate a calling module and a called module for each data exchange, and the direction of the call (shown by the long arrows in Figure 3.6) may or may not be the same as the direction of data movement (shown by the short arrows). Furthermore, the modules on a structure chart typically do not correspond one-for-one with the processes on the data flow diagram from which the structure chart was derived. Procedures to translate a data flow diagram into a structure chart have been devised, but these are of only limited applicability.

A discontinuity between a requirements definition model and a design model is a particularly vexing problem because of the nature of the model-building process. Although a sequential management structure (that is, a "waterfall model") may be imposed on a systems development project, the fact is that the activities as actually carried out by the developers are inherently iterative in nature. Building a design model often exposes problems in the requirements model, which (when modified) leads to a new design model, which may expose further requirements problems, and so on. This iterative process necessitates multiple crossings of the discontinuity.

The problems just discussed often lead to a reaction among systems developers that, by analogy to the "rush-to-code" syndrome, we may call the "single-model" syndrome. Most developers acknowledge that a useful distinction exists between requirements-oriented thinking and design-oriented thinking. However, when faced with the prospect of building two complete, distinct models (each using a different modeling language) prior to coding, many developers decide that the costs outweigh the benefits. Therefore only a single pre-code model is constructed, either by beginning with a design model, or by using a requirements definition language to create a hybrid requirements-design model.

In summary, phase discontinuities in many modeling methods lead to a development process that shortchanges the distinction between requirements definition and design.

3.2.2   The Concept of Phase Independence

The operational approach requires a single integrated set of modeling concepts be used to build a given model. However, this does not necessarily imply that, if different models are to be built in different development phases, the same set of modeling concepts must be used for both models. In other words, the operational approach does not prohibit phase discontinuities. Therefore, ROOM contains a second element that enforces this additional restriction.

The ROOM modeling language uses a single set of modeling concepts across requirements definition, design, and implementation. Note that, as mentioned previously, this does not imply a lack of distinction between requirements modeling and design modeling. A design model almost always requires many components in addition to those present in the requirements model, and often requires reorganization of the requirements model components. However, with an appropriate structuring of the model-building environment, it is possible to have large portions of a design model *that are also portions of the associated requirements model*. This characteristic greatly eases the burden of iterative cycling between the requirements definition activity and the design activity.

As an example, consider the state machine of Figure 3.4, which was used to represent a portion of the requirements for a fabric dyeing control system. If ROOM had phase discontinuities, it might be necessary, say, to recast the state machine into a "case" statement moving from requirements to design. However, ROOM permits the use of the state machine formalism throughout the development process, allowing the state machine of Figure 3.4 to be incorporated directly into the design. Furthermore, a highly efficient, direct translation of the state machine can be incorporated directly into the implemented system.

To devise a single set of modeling concepts that can be used across the development process is, to put it mildly, a difficult task. The language developers must steer a careful course between two dangers. On the one hand, it is possible to create what is, in essence, a conventional programming language, and to claim that it can be used for requirements definition and design. On the other hand, it is possible to create an abstract modeling language that is too limited in flexibility or too inefficient to create useful designs and implementations.

In the case of the ROOM modeling language, this issue was made tractable by carefully limiting its scope in a variety of ways.

- The language was specialized for real-time systems. No attempt was made to create a general-purpose development language.

- The scope was restricted to abstract requirements modeling, abstract high-level design, detailed software design, and software implementation. No attempt was made to cover detailed hardware design.[1]

- Various features to support requirements and design modeling were incorporated into the model-building environment rather than into the modeling language, allowing the language to carry less overhead and thus to execute more efficiently.

In addition, the problem was simplified by the use of the object paradigm (discussed in Section 3.3) as the basis for the set of modeling abstractions. The object paradigm is widely recognized as applying across requirements definition, design, and implementation.

The ROOM modeling language as used on a development platform (workstation) is depicted in schematic form in Figure 3.7. Two interfaces are presented to the modeler: the design (model building) interface and the run-time (model execution) interface.

The design interface allows the modeler to use the ROOM modeling language to create and modify models. A particular model, after compilation, can be executed using the run-time interface. The run-time interface provides for controlling execution, gathering and displaying of information about an execution, tracing of errors, and so on. Another software layer, the ROOM virtual machine, provides basic services (such as communications, timing, and exception handling) to the executing model.

Figure 3.8 shows a ROOM model as installed on a target platform (that is, on the hardware on which the system will be implemented). Note that both the detailed design model and the ROOM virtual machine have been ported from the development platform. This allows the code for the implemented system to use the same services (by way of the same interfaces) as on the development platform. It is assumed that a run-time environment, providing basic services such as an operating system kernel, is available on the target platform. It is also assumed that some components of the application (for example, user interface components) were not developed from ROOM models. This latter assumption requires that the interfaces between the ROOM model and the non-ROOM components were developed on the development platform by installing or by simulating these components.

The situation shown in Figure 3.8 falls short of the nirvana of fully automatic generation of an implemented system from a design, with the development environment somehow supplying missing semantic information. However, it is a significant improvement over the typical situation of having to create an implementation from scratch, with the

---

[1] Note, however, that ROOM *is* intended (and has been successfully used) for *high-level* hardware design and for hardware-software co-design.

Figure 3.7   A ROOM Model on a Target Platform

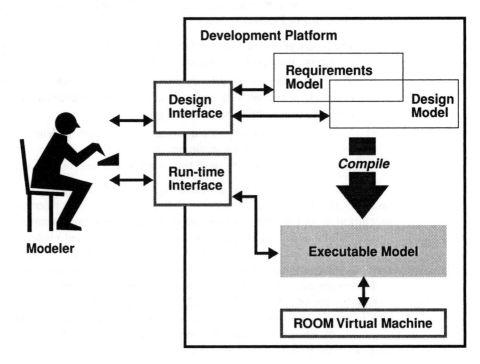

design model merely a guideline, or, at best, the source of a skeletal code framework. ROOM, in fact, allows the final form of the design model to be ported to the target hardware and to *become* the implemented system.

In summary, the use of a single-phase, independent set of modeling abstractions eases many development problems caused by phase discontinuities.

3.3   The Object Paradigm

The optimistic fantasy world of early science fiction featured rosy visions of highly mechanized future societies brimming with ingenious and practical devices. Specialized machines of all kinds were everywhere—housekeeping machines would vacuum and dust the house, intelligent door locks would ensure that only those who should get access do, brick-laying machines would construct houses, book machines would read themselves out loud, medical machines would heal the sick, high-fashion machines would trim our hair and polish our nails, and, to top it all off, machine-making machines would be perma-

Figure 3.8 A ROOM Model on a Target Platform

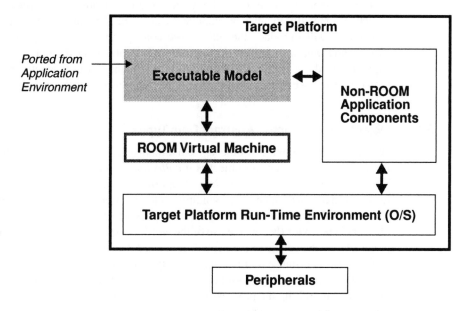

nently busy producing ever-improving models of other machines and themselves. As naive and idealistic as these predictions may seem from today's perspective, they perhaps best capture the spirit of what we call the *object paradigm.*[2]

Using the object paradigm, a system is realized by combining a set of smaller specialized component "machines." These components, called *objects*, are potentially reusable in a variety of different contexts. For example, one of the objects within a fabric dyeing control system is likely to be an operator interface. The same type of operator interface object used here also may be useful in other applications.

The object paradigm originated more than a quarter of a century ago with the Simula programming language, but its roots can be traced back to more mature engineering disciplines, such as electrical engineering and systems theory. The object-oriented approach originally was developed as a programming technique. In the last decade, however, it has been recognized that the basic ideas of object orientation also can be used for software design, for software requirements definition, and even for modeling systems that incorporate hardware as well as software. Thus, the basic concept of what constitutes an object has evolved and broadened over the years. The wide applicability of this concept is the

---

[2] We use this term to encompass a variety of different aspects including object-oriented analysis, object-oriented design, object-oriented programming, and object-oriented testing.

reason that the object paradigm provides a phase-independent set of modeling abstractions, which is an essential part of the structure of ROOM, as discussed in Section 3.2.

The next four subsections will explore the topic of objects by illustrating a series of objects of gradually increasing scope and examining their properties. The following four subsections will introduce the other basic concepts of the object paradigm—*messages, classes,* and *inheritance.* The treatment here is deliberately limited in scope. It seeks to explain only those elements common to most versions of the object paradigm. It is also rather informal. Readers wishing more details should consult the references.

3.3.1   Objects as Instances: Abstract Data Types

We will begin by looking at objects from a relatively low-level programming perspective. From this point of view, an object is *a collection of data and its associated procedures.* This definition can be traced to the concept of an *abstract data type.* Abstract data types were introduced as a means of avoiding some common programming errors [Liskov74]. The essential idea is to describe data not by its internal structure, but by its externally observable behavior (hence, the use of the word "abstract" in the name). This separates the issues of *how* the data is implemented from *what* it achieves.

Consider an instance of an abstract data type as it might be used in the design of a fabric dyeing control system. Assume that a central control processor is concurrently monitoring and controlling the progress of several dyeing runs. The monitored data is provided (by way of a data communications line) by remote data-collection processors attached to each dyeing unit. The data consists of packets, each containing a dyeing unit identifier, a type, and a value. A typical packet might contain the following:

unit id: 18A
type: tankLevel
value: 0.635

Since a single processor is controlling multiple dyeing runs, it is likely that new packets of data will arrive while the processor is still working on previous packets. To handle this situation, the design can make use of a very common abstract data type, the FIFO (first in, first out) queue. An instance of a FIFO queue is illustrated in Figure 3.9. The data is the collection of enqueued packets, and the procedures are Put and Get. The basic idea is that a Put dumps a packet on top of the pile, and that a Get retrieves a packet from the bottom of the pile.

Actually, Figure 3.9 is a bit misleading, since it allows you to look inside the box representing the queue object. The reason that a FIFO queue is an instance of an *abstract* data type is that *you, as the user, cannot look inside.* The physical storage mechanism for the packets is hidden, and is independent of the externally observable behavior. In fact, the packets might well be stored in some compressed form in which they are unrecognizable as packets, and might only be reconstituted as part of the Get procedure. A software component that uses the queue "sees" only the Put and Get procedures, and the data items returned when these procedures are invoked.

Figure 3.9   A FIFO Queue

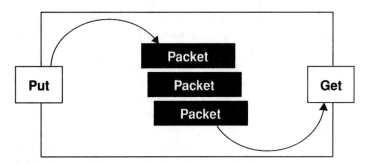

Someone wishing to make use of an abstract type must understand the *interface* (that is, the procedures defined on the type, as well as the input and output arguments of each procedure). The user also needs a description of the externally observable behavior of objects of the type. For example, one property of a FIFO queue is when the queue is empty, a Put of an item X followed by a Get will return X. Descriptions of black box behavior such as this can be precisely formulated as *axioms*. The set of axioms plus the interface definition constitutes, from the point of view of the user, a complete description of the abstract type. (A complete description of a real, concrete data type requires a third element in addition to the interface and the black box behavior—the *implementation*. However, the word "abstract" in the term "abstract data type" is an explicit indication that this third element has been left out deliberately.)

In summary, objects can be thought of as instances of abstract data types (that is, as collections of data with associated procedures whose implementation is hidden from the users).

3.3.2   Objects as Software Machines

The problem with equating the concepts of objects and abstract data types is that it leads to a relatively low-level view of the object paradigm. It conjures images of objects whose level of granularity is exemplified by stacks, semaphores, and record structures.[3] When dealing with large software applications (such as, say, an air-traffic control system), certainly some abstract data types (for example, flight plans) have high-level significance. However, the majority of abstract types that will be used in implementing a large system are not visible from a requirements or high-level design perspective. Conversely, many high-level components of large systems cannot be usefully viewed as abstract data types.

---

[3] This is partly due to the presence of the word "data" in the name "abstract data type." Thus, it would be unusual to think of an air-traffic control system as a data item.

In other words, if the only objects we have available are abstract data types, the benefits of the object model cannot fully be exploited in the earlier development phases.

To overcome this, we can take a different view of the object paradigm. We can define an object as a *software machine*, or as an active agent implemented in software, which is a component of a computer system. The concept of software machines is not inconsistent with the concept of abstract data types—a software machine can encapsulate data and can provide invocable procedures. The concept of a software machine is more general, however, and does not have the connotations of small scope, data-centeredness, and passive nature of the abstract data type. In particular, it is easy to conceive of a software machine as being at a very high level of granularity (scope). An entire system can be pictured as a single machine.

Defining an object as a software machine is feasible because, in essence, any computer is a "machine-building" machine in the sense that it can be made to behave like some desired specialized machine simply by writing and executing an appropriate program. The same computer can be used to implement a range of different machines, from weather-predictors to chess-playing automata.

Programming with objects thus involves constructing different specialized machines in this way, and then interconnecting them in order to achieve the required higher-level functionality. This is analogous to the way that hardware designers combine standard discrete components to construct specialized circuit boards.

We illustrate this idea with a schematic description of a fabric dyeing control system, illustrated by Figure 3.10. The Dyeing Unit Interface provides monitored variable values (tank level, temperature, and so on) to the Dyeing Run Controller and to the Operator Interface, and accepts device commands from the Dyeing Run Controller. The Dyeing Unit Interface takes care of all the issues involving communication with the Data Collector objects associated with the dyeing units, and may provide some level of processing (such as interpolation of missing data values). The Operator Interface isolates the Dyeing Unit Interface and the Dyeing Run Controller from concerns about displaying information to, and accepting commands from, the operator. The Dyeing Run Controller interacts with the Operator Interface and with the Dyeing Specifications object to establish the parameters (for example, temperature and solution-level setpoints) for a particular dyeing run, and then interacts with the Dyeing Unit Interface to carry out the required control actions.

Note that the objects identified in this example are fairly coarse-grained and complex entities. While some of them might be considered as abstract *data* types (such as the Dyeing Specifications object), the majority do not really have a connotation of data. If the monitored data were to arrive slowly and reliably enough, it is even conceivable that the Dyeing Unit Interface could be implemented as a purely functional (that is, stateless) object with no internal data used in its implementation.

The behavior of software machines reflects the fact that they are more complex than abstract data types. An instance of an abstract data type typically "wakes up" when one of its procedures is invoked, carries out the procedure, then "goes to sleep" until the next invocation. In other words, it is active only for the duration of its interactions with its users. A software machine, on the other hand, may be active over extended periods of

Figure 3.10   Schematic View of a Fabric Dyeing Control System

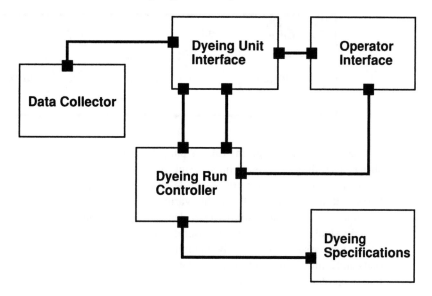

time, even when it is not being invoked, because it has its own thread of control. For example, after receiving a start command by way of the Operator Interface, a Dyeing Run Controller may open the dye valve, periodically poll the Dyeing Unit Interface for values of the solution level, compare these values with the solution-level setpoint, close the dye valve when the solution level reaches the setpoint, and so on. The duration of this activity extends far beyond the initial invocation of the Dyeing Run Controller.

The concept that objects may have a behavior captured by an independent thread of control is directly reflected in the ROOM modeling language. A state machine like the one illustrated in Figure 3.4 can be used to describe the behavior of an object. One can, in fact, picture the state machine as a sort of engine inside the object that drives its activity, as suggested by Figure 3.11.

Software objects, unlike abstract data types, also have the property that they can be (at least conceptually) concurrently active. One can picture, for instance, the Operator Interface accepting an operator command while the Data Collector is delivering a monitored value to the Dyeing Unit Interface and the Dyeing Run Controller is doing a setpoint comparison.

In reality, of course, we do not have the luxury of a dedicated computer per software machine. Instead, many objects typically share the same computer, and operate pseudo-concurrently. However, it is interesting to note that the software object model of computing stands in direct counterpoint to the procedural computing paradigm. In the procedural model, we are encouraged to think of a centralized agent, the computer, executing the

Figure 3.11   A State Machine Incorporated into an Object

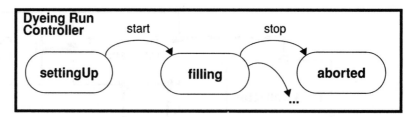

instructions in our program. Like a puppet-master, the computer is in control, pulling strings according to its predefined script. In the object model, on the other hand, the computer takes on a secondary role—a role analogous to that of a power supply in an electronic circuit, which enables the various components to perform their specialized functions. The computer simply provides the raw "computing energy" that is transformed by individual objects into specific useful work.

To summarize, objects can be thought of as software machines (that is, as active agents that can be interconnected to build a software system). This is a more general concept than that of an object as an abstract data type.

3.3.3   Objects as Logical Machines

The idea of objects as software machines is broader and more generally useful than the idea of objects as abstract data types. However, the concept of an object can be made still more general.

For example, consider that many routine, commonly performed tasks originally encoded in software have ultimately been embodied in digital hardware circuits. Functions such as signal processing and pattern recognition are commonly performed by specialized chips. Now consider a system component such as the Operator Interface from Figure 3.10. Portions of this component that require high performance, and that are unlikely to vary, may well be implemented in digital hardware. From the point of view of the other system components, whether the Operator Interface is implemented as software or as hardware, or as some combination of the two, is irrelevant. These details can be hidden in exactly the same way as the physical data organization of an abstract data type can be hidden.

We can thus define an object as a *logical machine*, which is an active component of a system, and which may be implemented as software, as digital hardware, as analog hardware, or even with some nonelectronics-based technology (for example, as a manual procedure).

As an example, consider the partial view of the fabric dyeing application illustrated by Figure 3.12. Unlike Figure 3.10, the scope here is not limited to software. The Heater Error Detector monitors the status of the Heater Mechanism, compares it to the desired status, and issues an error message if a difference in status persists. (The full set of interactions required to do this is not shown on the diagram.) The Heater Mechanism provides its status to the Heater Error Detector, and transforms energy provided by the Power Source into heat applied to the Dyeing Solution.

Figure 3.12 Fabric Dyeing System Components

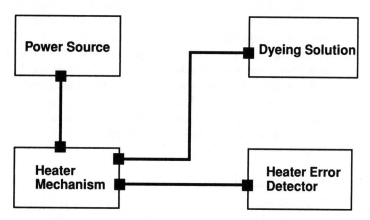

The Heater Error Detector certainly could be implemented as software within the control system, and might be incorporated into the Dyeing Unit Interface shown in Figure 3.10. However, the Heater Error Detector, implemented in digital or analog hardware, also could be realized (external to the control system software) as a component of the heater. Furthermore, the Power Source, Heater Mechanism, and Dyeing Solution cannot be implemented in software. However, all these system components are legitimate objects, if an object is defined as a logical machine.

Note that we are not claiming that the object paradigm can, or should, be used as a general-purpose engineering design approach to the exclusion of others. However, we are claiming that, within the context of developing a real-time system, it is useful to be able to

- Represent a system component (for example, the Heater Error Detector), which may or may not be implemented in software.
- Represent a component that will not be implemented within the computer system at all, but will interact with components of the computer system.

Using the concept of an object as a logical machine, we can incorporate such components into the same framework as components that are unambiguously part of the software system.

Freeing objects from the constraint that they be software components greatly increases the level of granularity at which an object may be defined. A large, complex, system component (whose implementation is a heterogeneous mixture of hardware, software, manual procedures, and so on) can be represented as a single object. Logical machines also are not constrained to be tangible. It is very common, for example, to think of a telephone call as a "thing" that can interact with other "things," even though one cannot point to or weigh a telephone call.

Note that the concept of objects as logical machines is consistent with the natural human tendency to perceive the world as composed of interacting "things," some tangible and some intangible. The claim is sometimes made that the object paradigm imposes an unnatural thought process on developers and end-users. However, if objects are conceived in the most general sense as logical machines, we feel that the claim is patently false.

In summary, the most general version of the object paradigm defines an object as a logical machine (of whatever level of granularity) that may be interconnected with other logical machines to realize a system. It is this most general form of the object paradigm that is the basis of the ROOM modeling language.

3.3.4   Object Encapsulation

We mentioned in Section 3.3.1 that abstract data types hide their implementations from their users. This is also a property of objects defined in a broader sense as software machines or logical machines. ROOM defines objects as having an *encapsulation shell*, through which all interaction with the object must take place. To encapsulate an object is to surround it with a "wall," equipped with "gates" through which all traffic must flow.

It is important to distinguish encapsulation from a variety of other terms that are used to describe the structure of objects.

- *Information hiding* is a general strategy for modular decomposition, originally proposed by Parnas [Parnas71, Parnas72]. Encapsulation is a specific mechanism for achieving information hiding.

- *Aggregation* is a grouping of components into a "package." This does not imply that the components are hidden or inaccessible, merely that they are parts of a whole. Encapsulation is a much stronger form of organization than aggregation.

- *Abstraction* is a view or description that omits certain details. Encapsulation forces the users of an object to deal with it as an abstraction, as a black box with a well-defined interface. However, the designer's view of an object includes the internals.

Figure 3.13 clarifies the distinctions among aggregation, encapsulation, and abstraction as applied to a set of interacting objects.

Note that the encapsulation shell means that objects as logical machines are subject to the same description in terms of interface, black box behavior, and implementation as are objects as abstract data types. Viewed as an abstract entity, a logical machine has an inter-

Figure 3.13 Aggregation, Encapsulation, and Information Hiding

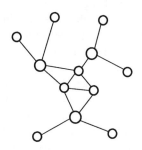

Unstructured Components

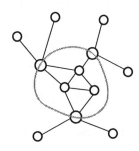

Aggregation

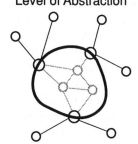

Encapsulation - Designer's
Level of Abstraction

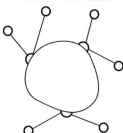

Encapsulation - User's
Level of Abstraction

face and black box behavior. Viewed as a real, concrete entity, a logical machine also has an implementation.

In summary, ROOM defines an object as having an encapsulation shell that defines an interface by which interaction with other objects must take place.

3.3.5 Messages

One of the benefits of the object paradigm is that objects tend to be relatively self-contained and autonomous. This is because objects are specialized, leading to a tendency to incorporate in them most of the elements required to perform their functionality. As a result, an object and its environment are not very tightly coupled. This is highly desirable since, among other things, it enables the object to be reused in contexts other than the one for which it was originally devised. For instance, the Operator Interface object in Figure 3.10 probably can be used in other applications that require interaction with an operator. Loose coupling also reduces likelihood that a change in one component will affect others. Hence, the cost of making changes is reduced.

In order to make the coupling between objects as weak as possible, communication between objects is based on a *message-passing* model. The essential feature of this model is that information between objects is exchanged by means of an intermediate artifact—a *message*. The purpose of the message is to reduce the coupling between the senders and the receivers. The only thing that a sender and a receiver must share is the format and general semantics of the message. They do not have to know anything about each other's implementation. The sender packages the information that it wants to send into a message and then dispatches it to the destination. When the destination receives the message, it responds by performing the activity appropriate to that message. For example, if the control system in Figure 3.10 is required to display the dyeing solution level to the operator, the Dyeing Unit Interface will send a "current level" message to the Operator Interface object and include in it the real number representing the current level. The Operator Interface object responds to this message by displaying to the operator the value in an appropriate format.

A special variant of this type of loosely coupled interaction is known as a *client-server relationship*. In this case, the functionality provided by an object is viewed as a "service" that it can provide to other objects. Sending a message to a server is interpreted as a request by a "client" to have the appropriate service performed on its behalf. The distinguishing feature of this relationship is the very weak coupling between the client and the server. The server does not have any prior knowledge of its clients. The clients, on their part, only must know the identity of the server so that they can direct requests to it. If the request requires a response, the server simply returns a reply to the sender based on the addressing information contained in the original request message. Because of such loose coupling, new clients can be added to, or old ones removed from, the system without requiring any changes in the server.

For example, consider the relationship between the Data Collector and the Dyeing Unit Interface in Figure 3.10. The Data Collector, as a server, does not need to know anything about the recipient of the data or the uses to which the data are to be put. The Data Collector can be constructed so that it can serve a variety of clients in addition to the Dyeing Unit Interface.

Messages directed to instances of abstract data types often have the properties of conventional subroutine calls. In other words, there is a transfer of control to, and a return of control from, the procedure as a result of the invocation, and the user contains a specific reference to the procedure being invoked. However, just as the concept of an object can be made more general than the concept of an abstract data type, the concept of a message can be generalized in a corresponding manner. Neither sequential transfer and return of control, nor identification of the message with the procedure being invoked, are necessary features of the message-passing model. The ROOM modeling language uses a model of message passing in which neither of these features is required.

As an example, consider the interaction between the Dyeing Unit Interface and the Operator Interface shown in Figure 3.10. Assume that the Dyeing Unit Interface periodically sends messages containing monitored variable values to the Operator Interface. It is quite possible for the Dyeing Unit Interface to send such a message and then go about its other business without waiting for the Operator Interface to process the message. Furthermore, the message can be named "Monitored Variable Report" rather than "Operator Display Request." In other words, one can imagine the Dyeing Unit Interface as saying, "Here's a monitored variable value. Do something appropriate with it." The Operator Interface can pass the value to one of a variety of procedures, depending on what display format the operator has requested, or even discard the value if the operator has requested suppression of the display.

Note that the change in name of the message in this example does not change the mechanics—the same data items are passed—but the name change represents an important distinction in how the model builder views the coupling between the objects involved in the interaction.

ROOM, in fact, takes the modularization possibilities of messaging one step further. An object sends a message to *a portion of its own interface*, which is connected by way of a communication channel to a portion of another object's interface, which in turn allows activation of a procedure in the other object. This mechanism is discussed in detail in Chapter 4.

In summary, object communication by messages reinforces the loose coupling introduced by encapsulation by restricting what objects must "know" about one another in order to communicate. This is especially true of the most general form of the message-passing model, which is the one used by ROOM.

3.3.6   Classes

It often happens that two or more object instances in a system have the same set of properties. In the lexicon of the object paradigm, a pattern that describes a set of similar objects is referred to as a *class definition*, and each of the objects is referred to as a *member* of the class. Having a single definition that applies to a collection of objects is clearly advantageous to having to describe each object individually. This not only saves effort and memory, but it also has an advantage in situations where the definition must be modified since the modification need be done just once. A class definition acts like a cookie cutter. It is a *complete* blueprint used to create individual instances of a pattern.

The distinction between classes and objects has important implications for systems development. Actual implemented systems are constructed from objects. A fabric dyeing control system, for example, may contain one or more Operator Interface objects, one or more Dyeing Unit Interface objects, and so on. Executable forms of requirements definition and design models also consist of objects. However, the source from which these implemented systems and executable models are drawn (the original requirements definitions and designs) consists of class definitions. The design for a fabric dyeing control system, while it may specify how many Dyeing Unit Interfaces there will be, defines a single set of properties that apply to all such interfaces. In other words, the design incorporates a class definition for Dyeing Unit Interface.

Since ROOM must facilitate requirements definition and design as well as implementation, it allows the representation of models in terms of class definitions that can be implemented as objects, rather than directly in terms of objects.

3.3.7   The Basics of Inheritance

Strictly speaking, inheritance is simply a relationship between two or more class definitions. That is, it is a means of defining a class by referring to the definition of a different but, presumably, related class. The net result is that objects of the two classes share common attributes. For example, the definition for the class "automobile" can be based on the more general definition of the class "vehicle." In that case, we only must define the differences between the two definitions. This has two major advantages. On the one hand, we get to reuse a previously worked-out definition, clearly a more economical approach. On the other, some of the knowledge we have about the original definition can be applied inductively to the new definition, even though we may not have any direct experience with it as yet. Thus, if we understand that an essential attribute of a vehicle is that it is used to convey things from one location to another, we may be able to infer that automobiles can do so as well without necessarily having to observe one in action.

We will now examine how inheritance might be used in the context of a fabric dyeing control system. The basic control mechanism required for fabric dyeing is to let a dyeing solution into the tank by opening the dye valve until a specified level is reached, to leave the solution in place for a specified time, and then to drain the solution by opening the drain valve. We will give the class of objects capable of carrying out this strategy the name Basic Dyeing Run Controller. Rather than attempt a complete definition of this class, we will simply list the messages that objects of the class receive and send.

Basic Dyeing Run Controller
    Receive: 'Required Level', 'Dyeing Time' (from Dyeing Specifications)
    Receive: 'Start' (from Operator Interface)
    Receive: 'Solution Level' (from Dyeing Unit Interface)
    Receive: 'Timeout' (from Timer)
    Send: 'Start Timeout' (to Timer)
    Send: 'Open Dye Valve', 'Close Dye Valve', 'Open Drain Valve',
                'Close Drain Valve' (to Dyeing Unit Interface)

We will now make the control procedure a bit more elaborate by requiring that the dyeing solution be heated to a specified temperature prior to being left in place for the specified time. Objects capable of carrying out this control procedure are members of the class Elevated Temperature Dyeing Run Controller. We can define its properties as follows:

Elevated Temperature Dyeing Run Controller
    Receive: 'Required Level', 'Dyeing Time' (from Dyeing Specifications)
    Receive: 'Start' (from Operator Interface)
    Receive: 'Solution Level' (from Dyeing Unit Interface)
    Receive: 'Timeout' (from Timer)

> **Send**:   'Start Timeout' (to Timer)
> **Send**:   'Open Dye Valve', 'Close Dye Valve', 'Open Drain Valve',
>   'Close Drain Valve' (to Dyeing Unit Interface)
> **Receive**: 'Dyeing Temperature' (from Dyeing Specifications)
> **Send**:   'Start Heater'. 'Stop Heater' (to Dyeing Unit Interface)

However, this definition fails to take advantage of the fact that we already have defined another class, Basic Dyeing Run Controller, that already has most of these properties. We make use of inheritance by defining a new class, called the *subclass*, in terms of an original class, called the *superclass*:[4]

> Elevated Temperature Dyeing Run Controller
>   **subclass of** Basic Dyeing Run Controller
>   **Receive**: 'Dyeing Temperature' (from Dyeing Specifications)
>   **Send**:   'Start Heater'. 'Stop Heater' (to Dyeing Unit Interface)

Note the simplicity of this definition compared to the previous one. Note also that, since the subclass definition *refers* to the superclass definition rather than *incorporating* it, the relationship is inherently dynamic. Any change to the superclass automatically will be reflected in the subclass.

If inheritance is applied recursively, we end up with an ordered structure of class definitions called an *inheritance hierarchy*. Consider the hierarchy of Figure 3.14 as an example. Here we have defined a subclass of Elevated Temperature Dyeing Run Controller, called High Temperature Dyeing Run Controller. In this case, the dyeing solution is heated above its normal boiling point, requiring pressure to be applied to the solution to keep it from boiling. The hierarchy also contains an additional subclass of Basic Dyeing Run Controller, called Multidye Dyeing Run Controller, which involves applying two different dyeing solutions in sequence.

Note that all the properties of a complex superclass definition, not just the messages, can be inherited by a subclass. For example, a state machine that defines the behavior of a Dyeing Run Controller (as illustrated in Figure 3.4) can be inherited by the subclasses, which can then extend the state machine by adding states and transitions.

In summary, inheritance is a mechanism for creating a new class definition from an existing one by incorporating the properties of the original definition into the new definition.

3.3.8   Multiple Inheritance and Delegation

Consider modifying the inheritance hierarchy of Figure 3.14 by adding a subclass of Multidye Dyeing Run Controller that incorporates heating each of the dyeing solutions. The

---

[4] The definition given here makes use of *strict inheritance* (that is, it retains all the properties of the superclass). It is also possible to modify or delete properties of the superclass, but this topic will be deferred until Chapter 9, which discusses the detailed design of the ROOM modeling language.

Figure 3.14   An Inheritance Hierarchy

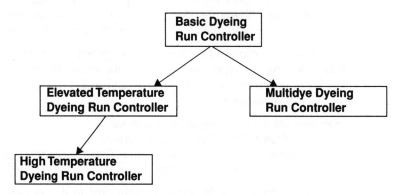

new subclass, Multidye Elevated Temperature Dyeing Run Controller, in addition to its unwieldy name, has another problem. The properties that it adds to its superclass (heating of the dyeing solution) are the same as the properties added by Elevated Temperature Dyeing Run Controller. Yet, nothing in the inheritance structure reflects the commonality of these subclasses, as emphasized by Figure 3.15.

Figure 3.15   Subclass Commonality not Reflected in Structure

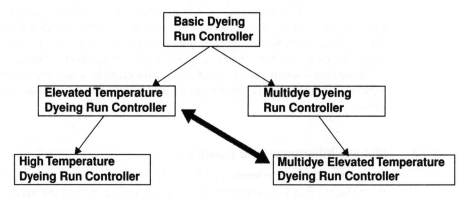

This is merely a specific instance of a more general problem—a set of basic features (in this case, multidye and elevated temperature) that must be combined in various ways within a set of class definitions. One way of dealing with this combinational problem is by

the use of multiple inheritance. This allows a subclass to inherit the properties of two or more superclasses. Figure 3.16 shows a variation of the hierarchy of Figure 3.15 that incorporates multiple inheritance. Here, Multidye Controller is defined as a separate, independent class containing only those properties necessary to deal with multiple dyeing solutions. Multidye Elevated Temperature Dyeing Run Controller inherits from this class as well as from Elevated Temperature Dyeing Run Controller.

Figure 3.16   A Multiple Inheritance Hierarchy

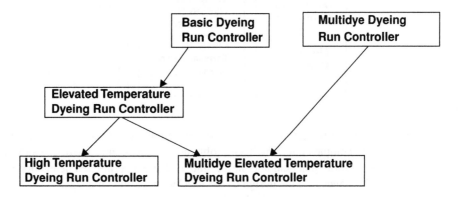

As appealing and intuitive as it sounds, multiple inheritance is not without some serious drawbacks. One of the major problems occurs when attributes from two independently defined specifications clash as a result of being brought together by multiple inheritance. Such conflicts can range from simple name clashes (for example, two attributes in the different parent classes having the same name) to more complicated semantic conflicts. As an obvious (albeit exaggerated) example of a semantic conflict, consider a class that is a subclass of both triangles and rectangles. These and other issues make multiple inheritance complex enough that it has not been universally adopted.

An alternative to multiple inheritance is the use of *delegation*. A class definition using this mechanism acquires a capability by *forwarding the relevant messages to* an instance of a class that has the capability in question, rather than by inheriting the capability from a superclass. Figure 3.17 shows a variation of Figure 3.16 that uses delegation rather than multiple inheritance. Here, Elevated Temperature Controller and Multidye Controller are independent class definitions, whose objects are capable of carrying out the portion of the control procedure suggested by their names. The nested boxes indicate that objects of the class defined by the outer box contain objects of the class defined by the inner box, and pass appropriate messages to the contained objects. Note that delegation does not require containment, although containment is a practical way of providing for delegation.

Figure 3.17   A Hierarchy Using Delegation

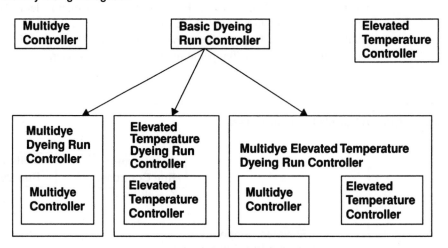

Both multiple inheritance and delegation have disadvantages as strategies for dealing with complex combinational problems. However, our experience indicates that delegation is the more practical alternative, and we have incorporated delegation rather than multiple inheritance into the design of the ROOM modeling language.

To summarize, multiple inheritance and delegation are strategies for dealing with complex combinational relationships among class definitions. ROOM uses delegation, but not multiple inheritance.

3.3.9   ROOM and the Object Paradigm

The ROOM modeling language is based on a version of the object paradigm. This paradigm views a system as an interacting set of objects, communicating by means of message passing. Objects with similar properties are defined as members of a class. Classes can be defined in terms of other classes by the use of inheritance hierarchies. ROOM uses a very general concept of an object, defining it as an independently active logical machine with an encapsulation shell.

3.4   Summary

As discussed in Chapter 2, ROOM was devised for effective modeling of real-time systems and for support of common model-building strategies. The key features of ROOM—its operational character, its use of a single notation throughout the development process, and its use of the object paradigm—give it the required properties to satisfy these requirements.

The key features of ROOM facilitate effective modeling of real-time characteristics, as follows:

- *Timeliness.* ROOM's operational character permits simulation of time-related properties of a proposed system, so that these properties can be estimated from a model on a development workstation. Furthermore, a ROOM model can be ported to the implementation hardware, so that critical time-related properties can be measured directly. Finally, the ROOM modeling abstractions are inherently efficient, so that code generated from a ROOM model will typically be able to meet timing constraints.

- *Dynamic internal structure.* ROOM's support of the object paradigm includes the ability to model explicitly the creation and destruction of system components at run time, and to exercise these properties by way of model execution.

- *Reactiveness.* The combination of discrete message passing and the use of event-driven state machines to model internal object behavior permits effective modeling of reactiveness.

- *Concurrency and distribution.* ROOM supports an extended version of the object paradigm, which represents objects as independent logical machines with separate threads of control that communicate by message passing. Thus, a ROOM model is inherently concurrent and distributable.

The key features of ROOM also support common model-building strategies based on abstraction, as follows:

- *Recursion.* A ROOM object is an arbitrarily complex logical machine; objects may be modeled as being composed of other objects, to any desired depth. ROOM also permits the behavior of an object to be modeled by a hierarchical state machine in which states may be decomposed into substates to any desired depth.

- *Incremental Modeling.* A partially complete ROOM model may be executed. This permits the expression and verification of model properties in an incremental fashion. Furthermore, the fact that a single notation is used throughout the modeling process, and that objects may be components of more than one model, permits repeated cycling among multiple models with relatively low overhead.

- *Reuse.* ROOM support of the object paradigm includes inheritance, which is a powerful technique for capturing abstractions in general, and for supporting reuse in particular.

CHAPTER 4

An Overview of the ROOM Modeling Language

Chapter 3 explained the key elements on which ROOM is based. This chapter describes how these elements are elaborated into a full-fledged modeling language. Although the ROOM modeling abstractions are elements of a formally defined language, the treatment here is deliberately informal. The intention is to convey the basic features of ROOM in an understandable manner, rather than to be exhaustive or rigorous in the presentation. The reader will find a more complete, formally organized description of ROOM in Part Three of this book.

A ROOM model is a complex aggregate of interrelated parts that is difficult to describe in a logical, sequential order. We have, therefore, organized this chapter to present the concepts in an incremental fashion. We first introduce a very simple (but nevertheless complete) ROOM model, then gradually elaborate the model in successive sections.

The effective use of the ROOM modeling language requires not only an understanding of the technical concepts, but also the use of effective model-building heuristics. However, we did not feel that it was practical both to introduce the technical concepts and to discuss good modeling practice in the same chapter. We have, therefore, attempted in this chapter to *illustrate* good modeling practice, but not to *discuss* it. A detailed discussion of modeling heuristics will be found in Part Four of the book. Because of this division of the material, readers may sometimes find themselves wondering why we have made certain modeling choices. To those who find this a problem, we recommend working back and forth between this chapter and Part Four.

As in the previous chapters, we use examples drawn from the fabric dyeing application. However, we will build up a more comprehensive model instead of using examples based on isolated fragments.

4.1   A Simple ROOM Model

We begin our overview of ROOM by constructing a very simple model. This serves to introduce the fundamental concepts of actors and actor classes.

4.1.1   Actors and Actor Classes

Chapter 3 introduced a very general version of the object paradigm, one in which objects were independent, concurrently active logical machines. ROOM refers to such logical machines as *actors*.

Actors are created on the basis of *actor class* definitions. Remember that a class definition is a pattern, a sort of cookie cutter that can be used to "stamp out" objects of a particular class. Although implemented systems (and executable versions of models) are composed of object instances, the base models we will construct are collections of class definitions. This allows us to "stamp out" as many objects of a particular class as are useful to our purposes, while maintaining a centralized definition that applies to all objects of that class and that may be modified as necessary.

Let us begin by identifying a single class definition that is an obvious component of the fabric dyeing domain—DyeingRunController. Clearly, the software control system under development will contain logic that controls a dyeing run. In fact, to a first approximation, the DyeingRunController can be thought of as the software system.

Figure 4.1 shows the class definition for DyeingRunController in its most succinct form, as an entry on a list of such definitions. We will use a standard textual convention for ROOM class definitions, which is to run the words together and use initial capitalization (as in "DyeingRunController").

Figure 4.1   A List of Actor Class Definitions

```
— Fabric Dyeing Actor Classes —

DyeingRunController
...
```

In summary, the basic components of a ROOM model are actor class definitions.

4.1.2   Defining Actor Interfaces—Messages, Protocols, and Protocol Classes

As discussed in Chapter 3, ROOM uses messages as a mechanism for inter-actor communication. In anticipation of introducing other actors that will communicate with DyeingRunController actors, let us begin with the messages that these actors send and receive.

The messages sent and received by the various kinds of DyeingRunController were introduced in Chapter 3 (which discussed the high-level design of ROOM). We will use a very simple version of a dyeing run that requires only introduction of the dyeing solution, exposure of the fabric to the solution for a specified time, and draining of the solution. The messages in this case are

Receive:	runParameters (requiredLevel, dyeingTime)
Receive:	operatorCommand (start, stop)
Receive:	solutionLevel
Receive:	timeout (dyeingTime has elapsed)
Receive:	dyeValveStatus
Receive:	drainValveStatus
Send:	startTimer (for dyeingTime)
Send:	openDyeValve, closeDyeValve
Send:	openDrainValve, closeDrainValve
Send:	runStatus (to operator)
Send:	parameterRequest

Rather than simply attaching these messages to the definition of DyeingRunController, we will follow a more elaborate procedure, which involves

- Grouping the individual messages into sets of related messages
- Using the message sets to create protocol class definitions
- Attaching ports (references to the protocol classes) to the appropriate actor class definition

We can initially group messages on the basis of the *destination* with which the messages will be exchanged. For example, the dyeValveStatus message, the openDyeValve message, and the closeDyeValve message form a natural group. However, further grouping is possible. Notice that the openDyeValve and closeDyeValve messages are both dye valve commands, and could be replaced by a single dyeValveCommand message, accompanied by a data value to indicate which command was given. We can, therefore, define a set consisting of dyeValveCommand and dyeValveStatus that incorporates all the messages to and from the dye valve. Similar grouping strategies can be applied to the other messages.

We can now create a *protocol* called DyeValveControl based on dyeValveCommand and dyeValveStatus. In its simplest form, a protocol defines for each of a set of messages

- A *direction*, either in (received by the actor) or out (sent by the actor)
- A *signal* associated with the message, which is an identifier of that message
- *Data objects* sent or received in conjunction with the message

(A more complete description of protocols is provided in Chapter 6.) We will defer discussion of the data content of messages until later in the chapter (Section 4.1.8), focusing for now on the signals and their directions.

We will use signal names corresponding to the message names, so the signals for the dyeValveControl protocol will be called dyeValveCommand and dyeValveStatus. Since we are taking the point of view of a DyeingRunController actor, the dyeValveStatus message has a direction of "in" and the dyeValveCommand message has a direction of "out."

Note that, just as we may wish to create various actors that have the same properties, we may also wish to create various protocols that have the same properties. For example, the set of messages involving the drain valve has exactly the same properties as the set involving the dye valve. Therefore, instead of defining separate protocols for drain valve and dye valve messages, we can define a single generalized *protocol class* called Device-Control, with deviceCommand and deviceStatus messages replacing the original drain valve and dye valve messages, and incorporate two protocols of this class into the interface of a DyeingRunController actor.

Figure 4.2 shows the DeviceControl protocol class definition added to the class definitions for the fabric dyeing model, and also shows an expanded view of this class definition. The actor and protocol class definitions are grouped into separate lists, and are headed by icons to suggest the nature of the respective definitions.

Figure 4.2   Protocol Class Definitions

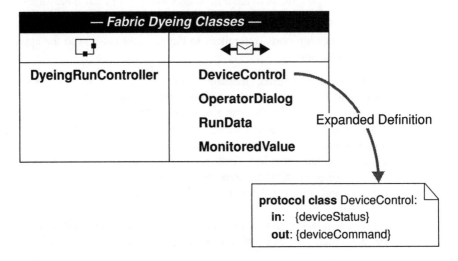

Figure 4.2 also shows several other protocol class definitions derived from the set of messages listed previously. Briefly, the OperatorDialog protocol includes the operatorCommand (start, stop) and the runStatus messages, the RunData protocol includes the parameterRequest and the runParameters, and the MonitoredValue protocol includes the solutionLevel. The startTimer and timeout messages involve a different kind of communication, which is discussed in Section 4.2.8.

In summary, a protocol class definition represents a related set of messages that may be sent and received by an actor.

4.1.3   Defining Actor Interfaces—Ports

Once a protocol class definition has been created, it can be used to define actor interfaces. Interface definition is accomplished by means of *ports*. A port is a declaration that the set of messages defined by a protocol class forms as part of the interface of actors of a particular class.

Figure 4.3 shows a number of ports (filled squares with circular inner regions) attached to the expanded class definition of DyeingRunController. We refer to the interface of an actor, as defined by its ports, as part of the actor's *structure*.

Figure 4.3   Ports as Components of an Actor Class Definition

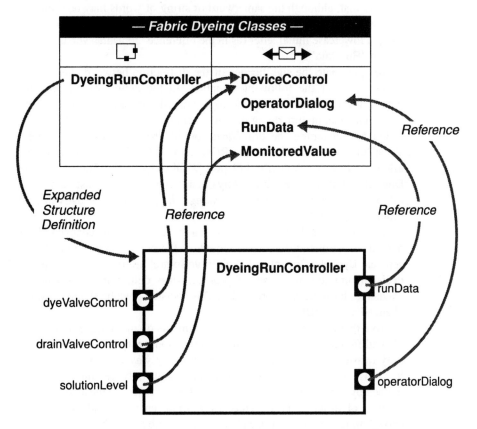

It may not be clear to the reader whether these ports (labeled runData, dyeValveControl, and so on) represent protocols (that is, protocol objects) or protocol classes. Actually, they represent neither. Rather, they are *references*. In general, a reference is a declaration of a

component in some higher class definition. It "refers" to some other class definition that specifies its attributes.

As an example, the port called runData in Figure 4.3 is interpreted as follows. Each actor of class DyeingRunController incorporates a protocol of class RunData (called runData) into its overall interface. As another example, consider the two ports labeled dyeValveControl and drainValveControl, which both refer to the protocol class Device-Control. In this case, the interpretation is as follows. The interface of each actor of class DyeingRunController incorporates a protocol of class DeviceControl that plays the role of drainValveControl, and incorporates another protocol of class DeviceControl that plays the role of dyeValveControl. The significance of "role" here is that the protocols, although they have the same properties, are used differently as parts of the DyeingRun-Controller interface.

Note that, although the same word or string of words may be used for a reference that was used for the class definition, we will distinguish references from class definitions by using a lowercase initial letter (as in the reference "runData" versus the protocol class definition "RunData").

To appreciate the significance of the distinction between class definitions and references, consider the following situation. In the course of building the fabric dyeing model, the modeler may decide to modify the message sequence involving the drain valve. One can picture doing this by reaching inside the DyeingRunController class definition and changing the drainValveControl protocol. However, remember that drain-ValveControl is a reference. In ROOM, modifications at the reference level are not allowed. The drainValveControl port within DyeingRunController is governed by the DeviceControl class definition. Any change in properties must be made to the class definition, *and any such change will change the properties of* dyeValveControl *as well as* drainValveControl.

The modeler is thus confronted with a choice. Either the change will be applied to both dyeValveControl and drainValveControl, or the class structure must be changed to create separate DyeValveControl and DrainValveControl protocol classes. The original modeling decision, implicit in the set of protocol class definitions, was that all valve message exchanges have the same properties. This decision must be changed explicitly. It cannot be changed accidentally.

Note that the use of ports to define segments of an interface, rather than defining a single undifferentiated interface, enhances the modularity of a ROOM model. An actor is not only restricted to dealing with other actors by way of their interfaces rather than their internals, but is also restricted to dealing with only certain segments of interfaces as defined by ports. An actor can present different "faces" to the actors with which it interacts by way of different ports. Thus, even when an actor undergoes a change substantial enough to require an interface change, only those actors that interact by way of the particular ports affected by the change will be impacted.

In summary, a port is used to incorporate a set of messages defined by a protocol class definition into an actor's interface.

4.1.4   Defining High-Level Actor Behavior—ROOMcharts

A system, or a component of a system, is referred to as *having a state* when the effect of
an input depends on the history of previous inputs. Certain system components have no
state—a square root routine, for example, always returns the same root for a given argument independent of the arguments that have been used in previous invocations. However,
actors, which can represent arbitrarily large, complex system components, must be capable of having state.

We refer to the *internal* operation of an actor over time as its *behavior.* When an actor is
required to operate differently during different time periods, we represent the behavior
changes as caused by changes in state. The high-level behavior of an actor is represented
by an extended state machine called a *ROOMchart.* ROOMcharts are based on the statechart formalism of Harel [Harel87a]. As discussed in Chapter 8, we feel that this formalism is particularly useful for real-time modeling. At any point in time, an actor has a state
that determines how it will react when it receives a message through one of its ports. The
set of such states, and the possible sequences in which the states can be visited, is
described by a ROOMchart that is part of the class definition for the actor.

Figure 4.4 is a simplified ROOMchart for DyeingRunController. The states are shown
as rectangles with rounded corners, and the transitions are shown as arrows with states at
their heads and tails.

Figure 4.4   A Simplified ROOMchart for a Dyeing Run Controller

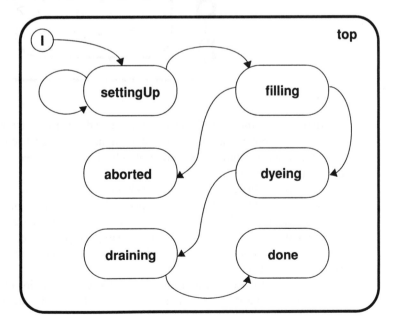

A state represents a period of time during which an actor is exhibiting a particular kind of behavior. A transition represents an allowed path from one state to another. For example, the state labeled filling represents a period of time during which the controller is maintaining the dye valve in the open state to fill the tank, and the transition from filling to dyeing represents the change that occurs when the tank becomes full. The arc from the circle labeled "I" in the upper left-hand corner represents the transition into the initial setting-Up state (that is, the state in which a dyeingRunController actor finds itself when first created). The states are enclosed within a single, all-encompassing state called top.

Graphically, the relationship between behavior and structure can be represented in either of two ways. Behavior can be placed inside an actor's structure, consuming messages received through the ports, producing messages sent through the ports, and performing other activities such as setting values of encapsulated data items. This picture of behavior for DyeingRunController is illustrated in Figure 4.5.

Figure 4.5   Behavior Viewed as Internal to Structure

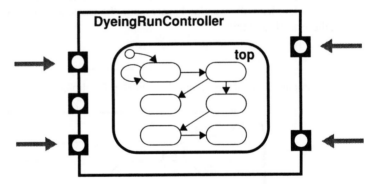

Alternatively, the behavior can be represented separately from the structure, as a distinct, complementary part of the class definition, almost like a separate component embedded within the structure. This picture of behavior is illustrated in Figure 4.6, also for the case of the dyeingRunController.

The view of Figure 4.5, showing behavior situated inside of structure, is intuitively appealing since it integrates the two aspects of a class definition. However, as we shall see later on, the structural definition of an actor ultimately will require other elements that are represented as being "inside" the actor. To simplify graphic representation, ROOM therefore uses the view of Figure 4.6, and represents actor behavior as a separate part of the class definition from actor structure.

To summarize, ROOM represents the high-level behavior of actors of a given class by means of a ROOMchart, which is an extended form of state machine. Actor behavior

Figure 4.6 Behavior Viewed as Orthogonal to Structure

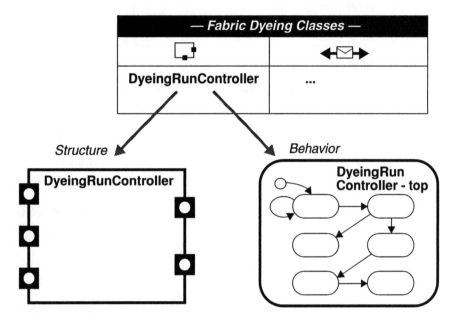

is shown as separate from actor structure, although it can be thought of as a property of the structure.

4.1.5 Defining High-Level Actor Behavior—Triggers

Transitions in ROOMcharts are triggered by the arrival of messages through the interface of the actor whose behavior the ROOMchart defines. Thus, each transition on a ROOMchart (except for transitions into initial states) must have an attached trigger definition. A trigger definition takes the form of a list of one or more port-signal combinations, optionally followed by a call to a *guard function*.

Figure 4.7 shows the transitions among several states of the DyeingRunController ROOMchart, and the trigger portions of the transition definitions.[1] The ellipsis (...) indicates that the figure omits some states and transitions that are parts of the complete model. A trigger definition is of the form **t**: {p, s, g}, where p is the port name, s is the signal name, and g is an optional guard function. For example, the interpretation of the definition

---

[1] ROOM can incorporate any of a variety of conventional programming languages to express low-level behavior details. The syntax of a transition definition will thus vary, depending on the language chosen. The examples in this section use C++ syntax.

t:{start, operatorDialog} on the transition between settingUp and filling is that a transition to filling will occur if the current state is settingUp when a start signal arrives through the operatorDialog port.

Figure 4.7   Transition Trigger Definitions

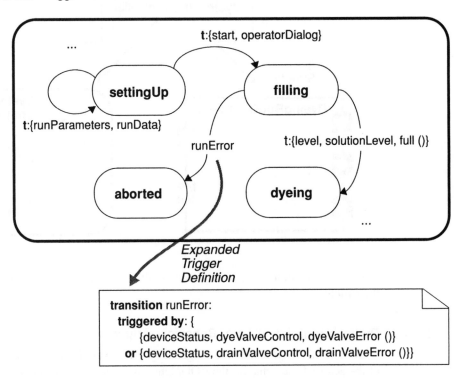

A trigger definition with a function call is a guarded transition. The guard function must evaluate to true or false. When the specified signal arrives, a guarded transition will be taken only if the guard function evaluates to true. For example, the interpretation of the definition **t**:{level, levelInterface, full ()}[2] in Figure 4.7 is that a transition to heating will occur if the current state is heating and the full () function evaluates to true when a level

---

[2] In order to simplify the illustrations in this introductory chapter, we use a slightly simplified syntax for specifying transition triggers and actions as well as for state entry and exit actions. The actual formal syntax for these constructs is defined in Appendix E.

signal arrives through the levelInterface port. The full () function compares the currentLevel value sent with the level message against the desiredLevel, and returns true if the currentLevel is greater than or equal to the desiredLevel.[3] If a guard function evaluates to false, the message is "thrown away" and no transition is taken.

A transition can be given a label and the definition can be shown separately from the ROOMchart. This is useful if a transition is complex (that is, can be triggered by any of a set of port-signal-guard combinations or has long port or signal names). The transition labeled runError, for instance, can be triggered by either of the signal-port-guard function combinations shown in the box labeled runError in Figure 4.7.

In summary, each noninitial transition on a complete ROOMchart must have an attached definition containing one or more port-signal combinations and an optional guard function.

4.1.6 Defining High-Level Actor Behavior—Actions

A *guard function* defines an evaluation that must be performed when a message is received, to decide whether a transition will be taken. Similarly, the various actions that an actor can perform when a transition is taken—sending messages, changing encapsulated data values, and so on—are defined by attaching statements to perform these actions to the ROOMchart. A statement can be an elemental action, or a call to a function to perform a sequence of actions. An action, in the form of one or more statements, may be attached to

- A transition (including a transition to an initial state)
- A state, as an *entry action*
- A state, as an *exit action*[4]

These statements are executable instructions, written in a detail-level programming language incorporated into ROOM. An action attached to a transition is performed when the transition is taken. An entry action is performed when a state is entered by way of any transition. An exit action is taken when a state is vacated by way of any transition. A transition action is suffixed to the trigger definition (if any) and prefixed by **a:**. Entry and exit actions are placed within the state border, with a prefixed **e:** for an entry action and a prefixed **x:** for an exit action. Figure 4.8 shows two similar models of the DyeingRunController filling state and its transitions. The left side of the figure uses transition actions, while the right side uses entry and exit actions.

The result of entering the filling state is the same on both sides of Figure 4.8. However, the result of leaving the filling state will be the same *only* if the statement controlDyeValve

---

[3] In this section, functions will be defined informally. Section 4.3 describes the syntax for the various statements that can be included in a function definition.

[4] State machines are classified as Mealy machines if actions are associated with transitions and as Moore machines if actions are associated with states. ROOMcharts, like statecharts, have characteristics of both Mealy machines and Moore machines.

Figure 4.8   Transition, Entry, and Exit Actions

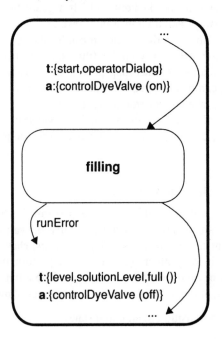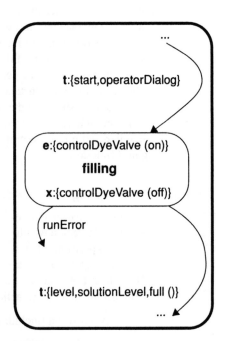

(off) is attached to the expansion of the runError transition on the left side of the figure. If this is not done, exiting the heating state by way of the runError transition will leave the dye valve on. It is more economical to use entry and exit actions if some common activity must be performed whenever a state is entered or vacated.

The effect of transition, entry, and exit actions is cumulative. When a transition from an old state to a new state is made, the exit action of the old state, followed by the transition action, followed by the entry action of the new state, is performed. Thus, in Figure 4.9, a transition from filling to aborted will result in a call to controlDyeValve (off) followed by calls to logError () and reportError ().

Notice that, when a transition definition is replaced by a label and given a separate expansion, the expansion has two sections—one for the trigger and one for the action (as shown for the runError transition in Figure 4.9). Entry and exit actions also may be replaced by labels and may be given separate expansions.

To summarize, the various activities performed by an actor are defined by actions attached to the states and transactions of the ROOMchart for the actor's class definition.

Figure 4.9   Action Definitions

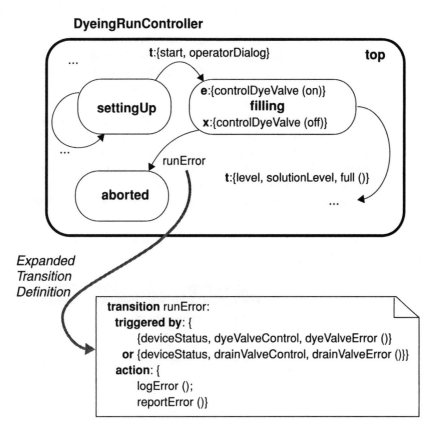

DyeingRunController

transition runError:
triggered by: {
    {deviceStatus, dyeValveControl, dyeValveError ()}
    or {deviceStatus, drainValveControl, drainValveError ()}}
action: {
    logError ();
    reportError ()}

4.1.7   Defining Encapsulated Actor Data—Data Classes and Extended State Variables

As discussed in Section 4.1.1, the actor is the basic unit of structure in a ROOM model. Actors are realizations of the object paradigm in its most general form. They are independently active logical machines of arbitrarily large scope. However, the ROOM model also uses realizations of the object paradigm in its more limited, traditional scope (that is, for objects as instances of abstract data types). ROOM refers to such instances as *data objects* and refers to their types as *data classes*. As in the case of actors and protocols, ROOM models are constructed, not from data objects, but from data classes and references to data classes.

The detail-level programming language incorporated into ROOM provides a fundamental set of predefined data types or classes (for example, integer and real) and associated procedures, which may be used directly or may be the basis for constructing user-defined data classes.

We will start by identifying some data classes that are obvious components of the fabric dyeing application. These are SolutionLevel, DevicePosition, and DyeingParameters. As we did with actor and protocol class definitions, we will represent data class definitions as entries on a list, as shown in Figure 4.10. The figure also shows the details of the definitions for two of the elementary classes, SolutionLevel and DevicePosition. The data class definitions use the syntax and the base types provided by the detail programming language—in this case, C++ syntax is illustrated. For readers unfamiliar with this syntax, data objects of class SolutionLevel are defined as taking on floating point (real) values, constrained to lie within a range defined by maximum and minimum values, and accessed by means of readLevel and setLevel procedures. Data objects of class DevicePosition are defined as taking on character string values and as accessed by get and set procedures.

Figure 4.10   Data Class Definitions

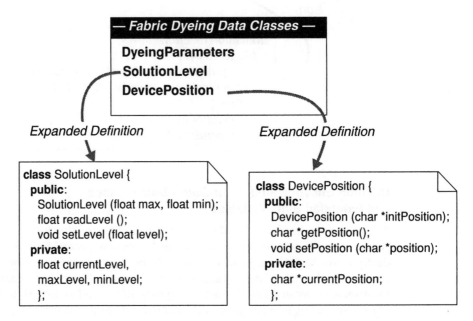

Defining composite data classes requires including references to the classes of included components. For example, consider DyeingParameters. A data object of this class is a composite of a desired solution level and a dyeing time. Figure 4.11 shows the expanded definition of DyeingParameters. It contains references to SolutionLevel and to the pre-defined int(eger) type. The interpretation of such a definition is quite similar to the interpretation of an actor class definition that contains protocol references. In this case, the interpretation is that each object of class DyeingParameters is a composite, consisting of an object of class SolutionLevel playing the role of desiredLevel, and an object of class int playing the role of dyeingTime. Note that we continue to use the convention of an initial lowercase character for reference names.

Figure 4.11 Composite Data Class Definitions

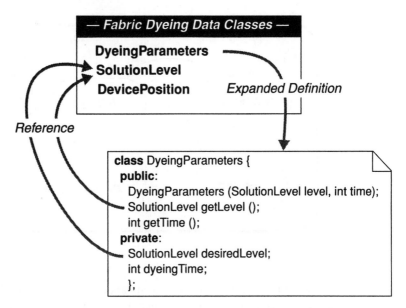

ROOM data classes are used to declare data objects that are encapsulated within actors. Such an encapsulated data object is called an *extended state variable*, or simply a *variable* of the actor. A variable in an actor class definition is a reference to a data class definition, just as a port is a reference to a protocol class definition. Figure 4.12 shows the behavior portion of the DyeingRunController class definition, with an extended state variable called dyeingParameters (referring to DyeingParameters) in addition to the ROOMchart. Note that, since the figure shows both actor and data class definitions, distinctive icons are used to head the respective lists.

In summary, ROOM provides for objects as abstract data types as well as providing for objects as logical machines. Data class definitions are based on a set of fundamental predefined data types or classes provided by the detail-level programming language

Figure 4.12   Extended State Variables as a Component of Behavior

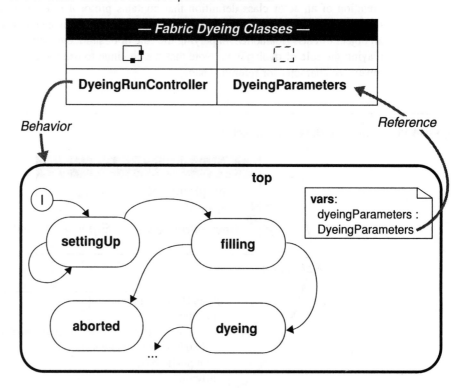

incorporated into ROOM. User-created data classes are defined in terms of these fundamental classes and in terms of other user-created classes. Data objects encapsulated
within actors, called variables, are defined by reference to data classes.

4.1.8   Defining Message Data

Data classes are used to define the data carried in messages, as well as to define actor variables. Each message within a protocol class definition optionally carries a single data
object, which, of course, may be arbitrarily complex. In a protocol class definition, the **in**:
and **out**: portions are of the form {s, d}, where s is a signal name and d is a reference to a
data class definition, when the message in question carries a data object. Figure 4.13
shows the complete form of the protocol class definition for DeviceControl introduced in
Figure 4.2. Note that since a unique data object is within each message, these data objects
need not be named. The protocol class definition simply includes the data class names.

Figure 4.13 Defining Message Data

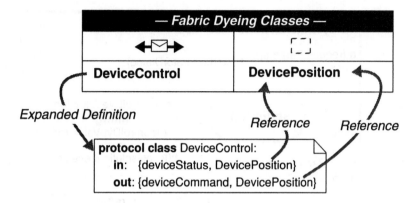

4.1.9   Executing a Simple ROOM Model

The model described in the previous subsections contains only a single actor class definition and thus is very limited in scope. Nevertheless, assuming the statements that comprise the various functions have been filled in, the model contains enough detail to be meaningfully executed.

Any ROOM actor class definition is, in effect, a source program in a very high-level language. An actor class definition can be compiled into an actor object, which is called an *incarnation*,[5] and executed within a suitable ROOM run-time environment. The representation of incarnated ROOM actors is very similar to the representation of actor class definitions. Since the incarnations exhibit the properties defined by the class definitions, and since ROOM makes use of the principle of observability as a feature of model execution (as discussed in Chapter 3), the similarity is to be expected.

We will differentiate graphic representations of incarnated, executable actors from the corresponding class definitions by representing the structural and behavioral details of the executable versions in gray rather than in black. The gray has the significance that the properties in question are exhibited within the incarnation, but are defined elsewhere. The structure and behavior of a DyeingRunController incarnation are shown in Figure 4.14. Note that the settingUp state is highlighted to show that the actor is in this state prior to any activity in the executable model. Note also that the variable declaration has been modified from the one used in model building in order to permit the observation of values assigned to the variables.

---

[5] We have intentionally avoided the more common term "instance" because that term is often used ambiguously to mean either "incarnation" or "reference."

Figure 4.14   An Executable Actor within a ROOM Run-Time System

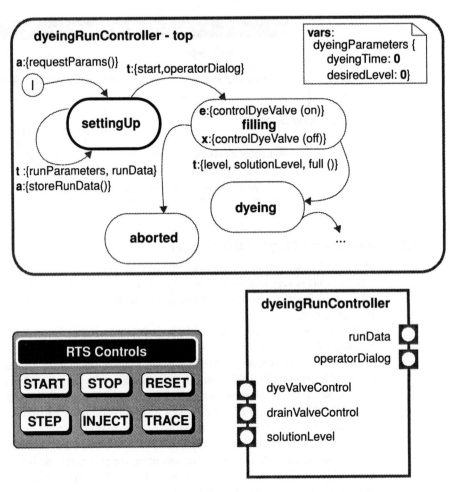

A corollary of the observability of an executable model is controllability. To effectively observe model execution, it must be possible to start and stop the execution, and to inject messages into the ports of the actors. The control panel illustrated in Figure 4.14 provides these functions, as well as the ability to reset the execution, to step through the execution, and to trace the progress of the execution. The progress of the execution is shown by highlighting and de-highlighting ports to show message traffic, by highlighting and de-highlighting states and transition symbols to show state changes, and by displaying the current values of variables.[6] For example, the injection of a runParameters message through the runData port would result in the momentary highlighting of the runData port and a momentary highlighting of the transition from the settingUp state to itself, as illustrated by Figure 4.15. The taking of the transition triggered by the runParameters message would cause the execution of the associated action, namely a call to the function storeRunData (). This function in turn would use the data objects contained in the runParameters message to set the values of the components (desiredLevel and dyeingTime) of the encapsulated dyeingParameters variable as shown in Figure 4.15.

Continuing with the succeeding steps of a typical execution, we might find the following:

1. The injection of a start message through the operatorDialog port. This results in a transition from the settingUp state to the filling state, and the execution of the entry code for filling, which sends an on message through the dyeValveControl port. Graphically, this would be shown by a momentary highlighting of the operatorDialog port, the momentary highlighting of the transition from settingUp to filling, the de-highlighting of the settingUp state, the highlighting of the filling state, and the momentary highlighting of the dyeValveControl port.

2. The injection of one or more level messages through the solutionLevel port, with values assigned to the associated data object that are less than desiredLevel. These messages will cause the evaluation of the full () guard function attached to the transition between filling and dyeing, but will cause the function to evaluate to false, so the transition will not be taken (see the discussion of full () in Section 4.1.5). Graphically, these messages will be shown by a momentary highlighting of the solutionLevel port and of the transition between filling and dyeing.

3. The injection of a level message through the solutionLevel port, containing a value that is greater than desiredLevel. This will cause full () to evaluate to true, will cause the exit code for filling to be executed, will cause an off message to be sent through the dyeValveControl port, and will cause the transition to dyeing to be taken. Graphically, the end result will be that the filling state is no longer highlighted and that the dyeing state is highlighted.

The executability of individual actor class definitions means that a ROOM model can be tested at a very early stage, even though only a small amount of information about the system under development has been included. This permits errors in the representation of requirements to be detected and corrected incrementally. For example, suppose that the full () function had been inadvertently misdefined, so that it evaluated to true when the actual solution level was less than the desired level, and to false otherwise. Errors of this nature are

---

[6] Note that neither the use of gray to distinguish executable actors, nor the particular form of the control panel, nor the use of highlighting and variable value display to trace the progress of the execution, are required elements of ROOM. The requirement is for observability of the execution and for control of the model state. The present discussion is only an example of how this requirement might be satisfied.

Figure 4.15   Injection of a Message

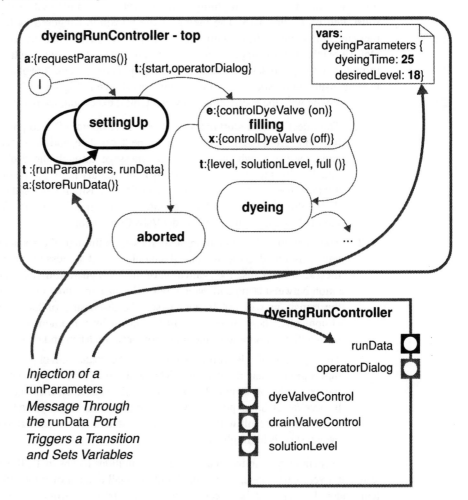

common in requirements definitions, and are often not caught until late in a development project. The simple model execution illustrated previously would have detected this error immediately.

ROOM not only permits the execution of single actor class definitions, but also permits these class definitions to be only partially complete. Consider the transition from filling to aborted in Figure 4.4. The absence of an ellipsis (...) indicates that, rather than omitting model details to simplify a figure, we have deliberately created a model that is missing a transition definition. The model is nevertheless executable. It is simply not possible to cause the transition from filling to aborted to be taken in the course of an execution. A class definition may be missing an arbitrary amount of detail and still be executable. As an extreme example, a class definition that has been given a name but no other properties may be executed—although, in this case, the execution will be singularly uninteresting!

The principle of observability requires that, in addition to being able to follow the progress of model execution in real time, the model builder must be able to collect trace information about the sequence of the execution for later examination. Figure 4.16 illustrates graphic and textual forms that such traces might take. The time references in the figure indicate the elapsed time since the start of execution, as a number of standard time units (say, hundredths of a second).

Figure 4.16 Graphic and Textual Execution Traces

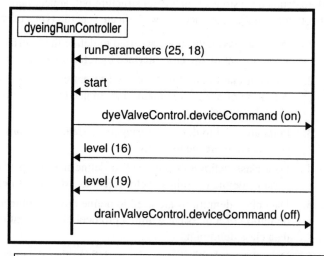

Note that the graphic form uses a message sequence chart (described in Section 2.1.5) to capture the actual message traffic that takes place at run time.

To summarize, a ROOM actor class definition may be compiled to produce an incarnation and executed. Execution of an incarnated ROOM actor can be driven by the injection of messages into the ports of the actor. The graphic representation of an executable actor is similar to the representation of a class definition, and is animated by the highlighting of various features to represent the progress of the execution.

4.1.10   Summary

The basic features of a ROOM model are a collection of actor class definitions, protocol class definitions, and data class definitions. These are interwoven by embedding references to one class definition in another class definition and creating the model structure illustrated in Figure 4.17 (where upward annotation arrows represent references and downward arrows represent expanded definitions). The diagram is titled as preliminary. More detailed versions of the model structure will appear later in the chapter. The numeric annotations on the reference arrows indicate specific types of references, as follows:

1. Protocol class definitions are used to define the interfaces of actors. A port defines a component of an actor interface by referring to a protocol definition.

2. Protocol class definitions are used to define the triggers of state transitions. The definition of a trigger contains a reference to an incoming signal within a protocol class definition.

3. Ports are used to define the triggers of state transitions. The definition of a trigger contains a reference to a port.

4. Data class definitions are used to define the encapsulated variables of actors. A variable defined within an actor refers to a data class definition.

5. Data class definitions are used to define the data objects carried in messages. The definition of a message within a protocol class definition contains a reference to a data class definition.

6. Data class definitions are used to define other data class definitions. A composite data class definition contains references to other data class definitions.

The reference structure allows substantial richness in the model, while permitting the imposition of strong constraints that require consistency among properties that may appear in many places.

4.2   A Multi-Actor Hierarchical ROOM Model

The simple ROOM model described in the previous section illustrates only a fraction of the modeling capabilities of ROOM. In this section, we describe the various features that permit the incorporation of multiple actors and hierarchical structure into a model. These features are critical to building models that can be scaled up to an arbitrary level of complexity.

Figure 4.17   ROOM Reference Organization (Preliminary)

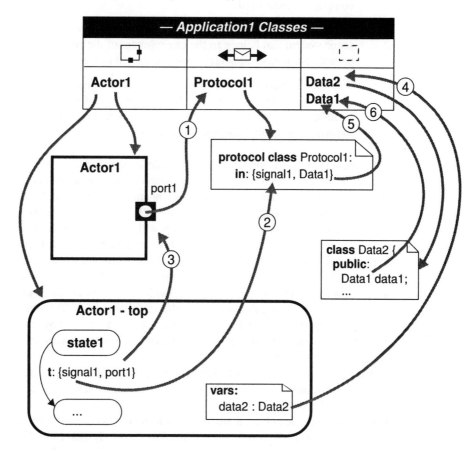

4.2.1   Hierarchical Actor Structure

An actor, as a logical machine, can have as large a scope as desired. One obvious way of creating larger-scope actors is to construct them from other actors. In ROOM, an actor may have other actors as components. These components, in turn, may have components of their own, to any desired depth of recursion.

Returning to the fabric dyeing problem, we will use this technique by defining several class definitions (DyeingSystem, Valve, DyeingSolution, and DyeingSpecifications) in addition to DyeingRunController. These definitions illustrate several categories of actors that commonly appear in models:

- DyeingSystem is a broad-scope actor that is primarily a container for other actors. Note that the term "system" as used in DyeingSystem refers to the larger-scope system within which the computer system (the hardware and software that implements control of the fabric dyeing process) will be embedded, rather than to the computer system itself.

- Valve and DyeingSolution refer to noncomputer-based components of the larger-scope system that belong to the environment of the computer system under development. Such environmental components will turn out to be very useful.

- DyeingSpecifications represents the set of data values from which run parameters (for example, dyeing time) may be selected for individual dyeing runs. A dyeing-Specifications actor is essentially a high-level data object packaged within an actor to permit communication with other actors.

Figure 4.18 shows the updated set of class definitions and also contains an expanded picture of the DyeingSystem class definition, which shows the components of DyeingSystem. The outer, heavily outlined rectangle represents the container, and the nested, labeled rectangles represent the components. (The small filled symbols on the border of dyeingRun-Controller are simplified port symbols, which will be discussed in Section 4.2.3.)

As was done with protocol and data class definitions, we attach component actors to actor class definitions by using references. As an example, the reference labeled dyeing-RunController within DyeingSystem is interpreted as follows: Each actor of class Dyeing-System contains an actor of class DyeingRunController. As another example, consider the two references labeled dyeValve and drainValve, which both refer to the class Valve. In this case, the interpretation is as follows: Each actor of class DyeingSystem contains an actor of class Valve that plays the role of drainValve, and contains another actor of class Valve that plays the role of dyeValve.

The significance of the distinction between class definitions and references is similar to that between protocol class definitions and protocols as actor interface components. For instance, in the course of building the fabric dyeing model, the modeler may decide to modify the properties of the drain valve. In ROOM, such a modification is not allowed at the level of the drainValve reference within the DyeingSystem class definition. The drain-Valve reference is governed by the Valve class definition. Any change in properties must be made to this class definition, *and any such change will change the properties of the dye valve as well as the drain valve.*

The modeler is thus confronted with a choice: Either the change will be applied both to the dye valve and to the drain valve, or the class structure must be changed to create separate DyeValve and DrainValve classes. This protects the original modeling decision implicit in the set of class definitions (namely, that all Valve actors have the same properties). That decision must be changed explicitly (that is, it cannot be changed inadvertently).

To summarize, hierarchical actor structure in ROOM is achieved by including references to contained classes within the definition of the container class.

Figure 4.18   Actors as Components of Actors

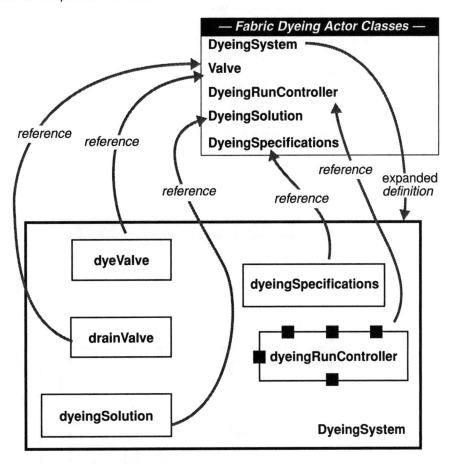

4.2.2   Inter-Actor Communication—Conjugation and Bindings

For communication between two actors to take place, a connection must be established between a port on one of the actors and a port on the other. In general, it is desirable to do this by having both ports refer to the same protocol. However, there is a complication. A protocol, as defined in ROOM, has an imposed directionality—it defines the communication from the point of view of a particular actor, with one subset of the messages as incoming and the complementary subset as outgoing. When two actors communicate, however, the incoming messages for one actor are outgoing messages for the other, and vice versa.

A deviceCommand message, for example, is outgoing for the DyeingRunController, but incoming for the valve to which it is directed.

ROOM deals with this complication by allowing a port reference to be *conjugated*. A conjugated port refers to a protocol, but with the incoming and outgoing directions reversed. Figure 4.19 shows ports defined for DyeingRunController and Valve actors, which reference the DeviceControl protocol. The port symbol for Valve indicates conjugation (the black and white regions are the inverse of those of the port symbol for DyeingRunController) and thus define deviceCommand as incoming and deviceStatus as outgoing. Note that which version of the protocol is defined as unconjugated and which is defined as conjugated is quite arbitrary. It simply depends on which actor's point of view was taken when the protocol was originally defined.

Figure 4.19   Conjugated Versus Unconjugated Ports

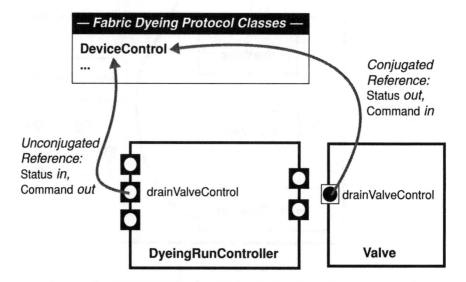

When two ports have been defined so as to permit communication, an additional step is needed. The actors that are to communicate must both appear as references in a common container, and a *binding* must be created between the ports on the respective references. Figure 4.20 shows the DyeingSystem class definition, modified to incorporate inter-actor communication. A conjugated port referencing the DeviceControl protocol has been added to the Valve class definition, as just discussed. This port thus appears on the drainValve and dyeValve references within DyeingSystem. Conjugated ports also have been added to the DyeingSolution class definition to permit sending of level messages. Additional ports have been added to Valve and to DyeingSolution to simulate liquid transfer, and to DyeingSpecifications to permit run parameters to be modified and to be provided to DyeingRunController actors.

Figure 4.20   Bindings Between Actor References

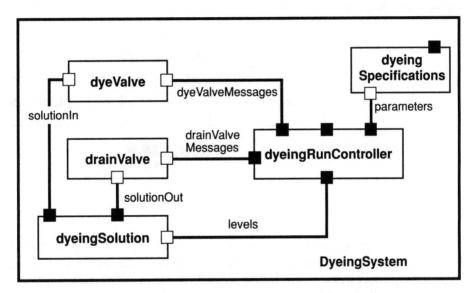

Bindings have been created between appropriate ports to permit inter-actor communication. In ROOM, both ports and bindings are named. Port names are shown in Figure 4.3. Binding names are shown in Figure 4.20, but the port names have been suppressed. Note that, when ports are shown on an actor reference, a simpler graphic form (black squares for unconjugated, white for conjugated) is used than when ports are shown on an actor class definition. This convention is discussed further in Section 4.2.3.

Any property exhibited by an executable ROOM model must belong to an actor class definition. Thus, a protocol must be attached by way of a port to the interface definition of an actor class before its messages can be sent, a data object must be defined as a variable within the behavior definition of an actor class before it can be assigned values, and so on. Inter-actor communication also has this characteristic. The ability of two actors to communicate is a property that must be assigned to an actor class. Inter-actor communication and hierarchical actor structure are thus closely related in ROOM, because a binding is a property of the class whose actors *contain* the communicating actors. In Figure 4.20, the bindings are properties of the DyeingSystem class.

A binding is a communication channel for the exchange of the messages sent through the ports that the binding connects. Figure 4.21 focuses on one of the bindings from Figure

4.20, the one between drainValve and dyeingRunController. The diagram includes annotations to indicate how the port-binding combination is related to the protocol definition (DeviceControl) referenced by the ports.

Figure 4.21   Analysis of a Binding

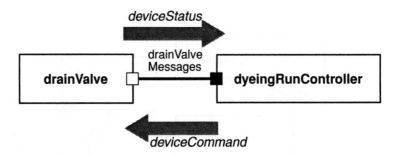

To summarize, communication paths between actors are defined first by attaching ports to the class definitions of the actors and then by creating a binding between the actor references within a common container. Ports are classified as unconjugated or conjugated to reflect the different directionalities imposed on a protocol as an actor interface component.

4.2.3   Relay Ports

All the ports discussed in Section 4.2.2 are *end ports* because the actor behaviors to which they are attached are the ultimate producers or consumers of the messages that are interchanged through them. In ROOM, another kind of port, called a *relay port,* is defined to allow an encapsulated component to safely "export" one of its interface components to the interface of its container.

A relay port, as its name suggests, involves the use of an intermediate interface to relay a message to an actor. In Figure 4.20, assume that the unbound port on dyeingRunController is a reference to the OperatorDialog protocol class. Since messages from the operator originate from outside the system as currently defined, there is no obvious place to attach the other end of a binding to this port. A similar difficulty applies to the unconnected port of dyeingSpecifications. This can be corrected by attaching relay ports to the boundary of dyeingSystem, as shown in Figure 4.22. The relay ports act as intermediaries to pass messages from outside the context of a DyeingSystem actor to the dyeingRunController and dyeingSpecifications components. Relay ports in class diagrams are distinguished graphically from end ports by a rectangular rather than a circular central section.

Figure 4.22 A Relay Port

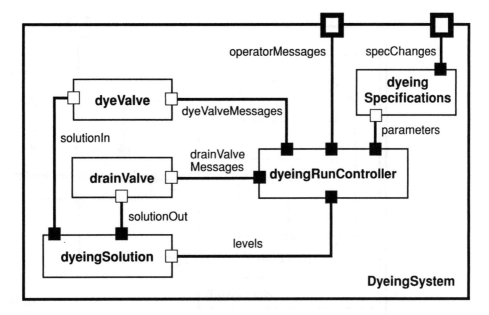

Now consider another variation on the DyeingSystem class definition in which dyeValve, drainValve, and dyeingSolution are components of an intermediate-level dyeingUnit actor, rather than direct components of DyeingSystem. As Figure 4.23 suggests, the original bindings between dyeingRunController and the other components are now illegal, since they violate the encapsulation shell of dyeingUnit.

The appropriate port structure to correct this situation is shown in Figure 4.24. The messages destined for the components of dyeingUnit must pass through ports explicitly declared as part of the interface of the class dyeingUnit. Since these ports are not defined on an actor that is the destination of the messages, they are defined as relay ports.

A message may be passed through any number of relay ports between the producer and the consumer. In Figure 4.25, note that another intermediate-level actor, dyeingSoftware, has been added as a reference within DyeingSystem. This means that, for example, a command sent to dyeValve by dyeingRunController goes from the end port on dyeingRunController through the relay port on dyeingSoftware and through the relay port on dyeingUnit to the end port on dyeValve. However, the figure does not graphically distinguish the relay ports from the end ports, since, from the point of view of a container, it does not matter whether messages terminate at the interfaces of their components.

Relay ports, like end ports, are defined as being either unconjugated or conjugated. Most often, a relay port has the same conjugation status as the port on the contained reference to which it is bound, since it has the same definition of what is meant by incoming

Figure 4.23 Illegal Bindings

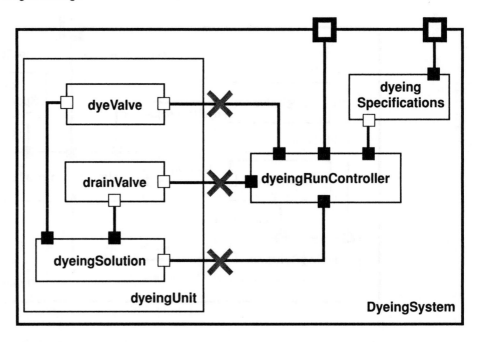

and outgoing messages. In Figure 4.24, for example, the relay ports on dyeingUnit are conjugated because the end ports on dyeValve, drainValve, and dyeingSolution are conjugated. Unconjugated ports on an actor class definition have a light central section and a dark outside section, while conjugated ports have the reverse (see Figure 4.26).

Note that, although it is sometimes convenient to portray two or more levels of containment as in Figure 4.23 and Figure 4.25, only the first-level components of a class definition are its references (that is, the components of a component are hidden). A containing actor does not "know" whether its contained components have lower-level components of their own. Thus, the references of DyeingSystem are dyeingUnit and dyeingSoftware, as shown in Figure 4.25. The lower-level components shown in Figure 4.23 and Figure 4.25 are properties of DyeingUnit and DyeingSoftware, not of DyeingSystem.

To summarize, the mechanism of relay ports allows an actor to provide an intermediary interface for messages directed to other actors.

4.2.4   Replicated References

The preceding examples have been based on single references—a class definition incorporating a single actor playing a specific role as a component, or a single port playing a spe-

Figure 4.24   Conjugated Relay Ports

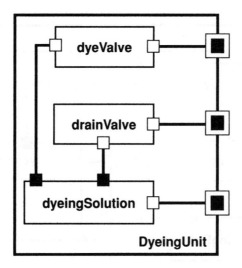

cific role in message passing. ROOM provides a more general reference mechanism, which allows for *replication* in both actor and protocol references. Replication allows for multiple actors or multiple ports playing a single role in a class definition.

We first consider a modification of the class definition for DyeingSystem. The original definition, Figure 4.25, specified that each DyeingSystem actor contains a single DyeingUnit actor and a single DyeingSoftware actor. In other words, we originally defined a dyeing system as composed of a single dyeing unit and a single copy of the control software. A more useful definition, which assumes that a single copy of the software can control multiple dyeing units, is shown in Figure 4.27. (The bindings between dyeingUnit and dyeingSoftware have been removed temporarily, pending a change in the DyeingSoftware class definition discussed later). The replication of the dyeingUnit reference is shown by a doubling of the boundary line. The number of replications is shown by a symbol placed in the upper right-hand corner of the reference. The symbol can be either an integer constant or an asterisk (*) indicating that the replication factor is open-ended as in Figure 4.27.

Replication of an actor reference is simply an economical way of representing a collection of references to the same actor class, all of which are bound in the same way. Thus, the dyeingUnit reference in Figure 4.27, if its replication factor were set to 2, would be a simplified version of the references to dyeingUnit1 and dyeingUnit2 in Figure 4.28. Notice that replication of an actor reference also implies replication of its external and internal ports, and of its contained actors. A copy of each port appears on each instance, and copies of the components occur within each instance. This allows multiplicity to be declared at an appropriate level of abstraction. By introducing a DyeingUnit class definition, we allow the

Figure 4.25   Communication via Relay Ports

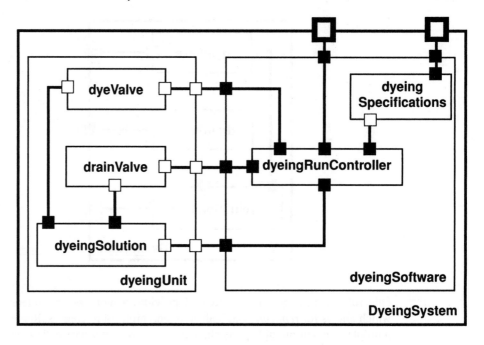

Figure 4.26   References of a Class Definition

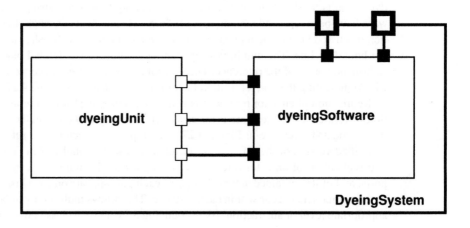

replication property to be attached to the dyeingUnit reference within DyeingSystem. We thus avoid having to attach individual replication factors to dyeValve, drainValve, and dyeingSolution. More significantly, we avoid having to maintain consistency among the multiplicities of the lower-level components. Notice also that replication of an actor reference changes the class definition of the *containing* class, but does not change the class definition of the *referred-to* class. A class definition may thus appear in a variety of situations, with a variety of multiplicities determined by the situation.

Figure 4.27 A Replicated Actor Reference

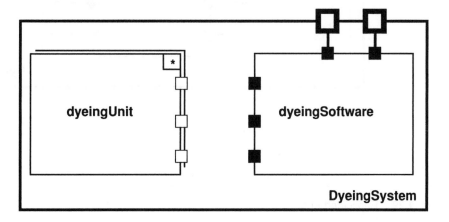

Because of the replication of the dyeingUnit reference in Figure 4.27, there are single ports on the dyeingSoftware reference corresponding to multiple ports on the dyeingUnit reference. This means that legal bindings no longer can be created between the references, because the single ports on dyeingSoftware imply unique sources and destinations for dye valve, drain valve, and level messages. Obviously, it is required that these messages now be associated with one of a set of dyeing units rather than a single dyeing unit.

This communication requirement is represented by replicating *ports*, rather than replicating *actors*, as shown in Figure 4.29. This is a change to the class definition of the referred-to class, as opposed to replication of a reference, which only affects the containing class. As mentioned, replication of a port is shown by a doubling of the boundary, as it is for an actor reference. The number of instances of a replicated port is governed by the number of ports to which it is bound, subject to an optional limit associated with the class definition containing the replicated port. The dyeingSoftware ports that are bound to the dyeingUnit reference, for example, will be replicated according to the number of dyeing units.

Figure 4.28   Replication as Equivalent to Duplicated References

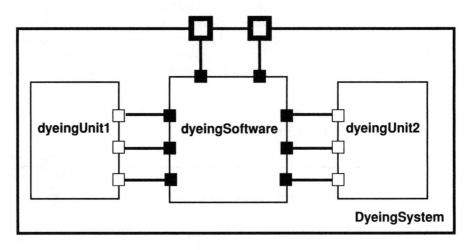

Figure 4.29   Replicated Ports

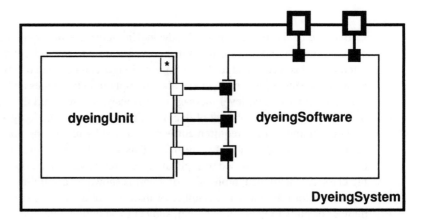

In summary, actor references and ports may be declared as replicated, which allows sets of contained actors to be bound in the same way within a containing actor.

4.2.5   Optional References

Figure 4.30 shows the class definition for the revised, replicated-port version of DyeingSoftware. Since a single software system now controls multiple dyeing units, it is necessary to replicate the dyeingRunController component. This can be done simply by declaring an unspecified number of replications, as was done in the case of dyeingUnit. However, there is no requirement for a fixed number of controllers. The requirement is that each dyeing unit in which fabric dyeing is being carried out must have a controller. This means that the requirement is for a variable number of controllers. This requirement is represented in Figure 4.30 by showing dyeingRunController as replicated and *optional*. The replication is shown, as before, by doubling the boundary, and the optionality is shown by shading. Optionality, like replication of a reference, changes the containing class definition but not the referred-to class definition. The class definition for dyeingRunController is unchanged. The symbol in the upper right-hand corner of an optional reference represents the upper limit on the number of replications.

Figure 4.30   An Optional Actor Reference

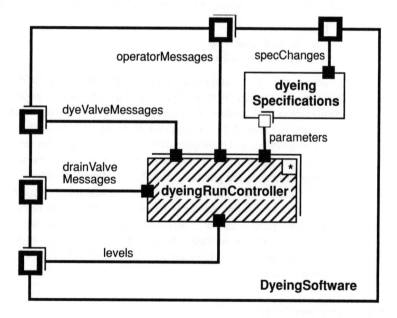

Optionality and replication may appear in any combination as properties of an actor reference. A reference that is optional but not replicated permits either no actors or exactly one actor of the referred-to class.

Although ports may be replicated independently of the replication of the actor to which they are attached, ports have no independent optionality property. In other words, a port cannot be declared to be optional. When a port is attached to an optional actor reference, there will be a port for each actor created. Thus, the number of ports will vary with the number of actors.

To summarize, ROOM provides for the varieties of communication among multiple actors by allowing actor references to be optional.

4.2.6   Actor State and Behavior

Before completing the discussion of inter-actor communication, it is necessary to revisit the topic of an actor's state, and the relationship of actor state to behavior as described by ROOMcharts.

In Section 4.1, we examined the internal makeup of DyeingRunController actors in some detail. These actors are of an intermediate level of complexity. They have a high-level state, described by a ROOMchart. For example, at a specific point in time a Dyeing-RunController actor might be in the filling state. These actors also have an extended state, described by the combination of the ROOMchart state and the values of their encapsulated data objects. For example, the extended state of a DyeingRunController actor might be

```
filling:
     desiredLevel = 18
     dyeingTime = 25.
```

Actors that have component actors are potentially at the other end of the complexity spectrum with respect to state. The state of an actor with components is, at a minimum, the combination of the states of its components. Consider, for example, the DyeingUnit actor illustrated in Figure 4.24 and Figure 4.25. Its state includes the states of the contained dye-Valve, drainValve, and dyeingSolution actors. Since an actor can have any number of direct components, and since the components of an actor can themselves have components, there is no upper limit to the potential complexity of such an actor.

The state of a DyeingUnit actor is determined totally by the states of its components. This is because all the messages received are passed on to components by way of relay ports. DyeingUnit actors are mere containers, with no capability for behavior above and beyond the behavior of their components. It is possible, however, for an actor to have components and also to have its own high-level behavior. This topic is discussed in the following section.

4.2.7   Internal Ports

One situation where the need for both component actors and high-level behavior arises is when a component is optional. Optionality of a component implies that the logic necessary to create component instances exists somewhere in the model. In ROOM, creation of an optional component is initiated by the behavior of the container actor. In Figure 4.30, for example, the ability to create dyeingRunController actors must reside in the behavior of DyeingSoftware, which we have not yet defined.

When an actor has both components and its own high-level behavior, another variation on actor-to-actor communication (one involving messages sent between a contained actor and its container) is possible. Consider Figure 4.31, a modified version of the class definition for DyeingSoftware shown in Figure 4.30. In this modification, we assume that the set of messages sent by way of the OperatorDialog protocol class definition has been augmented to include a create message, as well as start and stop messages. The create message is sent before a given dyeingRunController exists, and thus must be delivered to the behavior of the DyeingSoftware actor so that the controller can be created. However, the start and stop messages involve existing dyeingRunControllers, and must be passed through to these controllers. This is shown by connecting the appropriate port on dyeing-RunController to an *internal port* of dyeingSoftware (called operatorInOut) and by replacing the operatorDialog relay port of DyeingSoftware with an external port. An internal port has the same graphic representations as an ordinary (external) port. However, the port symbol for an internal port is placed *within* the actor boundary, rather than on the boundary.

Figure 4.31   An Internal Port

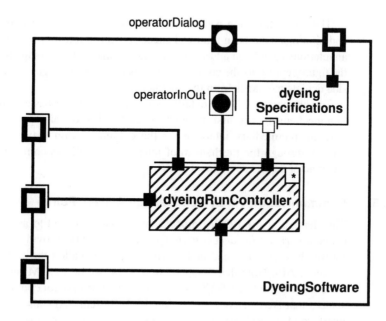

The behavior of a DyeingSoftware actor is illustrated by Figure 4.32. A start or stop message triggers a transition whose action passes the message to the dyeingRunController by way of the operatorInOut port. A create message triggers a transition whose action creates a dyeingRunController. A runStatus message, entering by way of the operatorInOut port, triggers a transition whose action passes it to the operator by way of the operatorDialog port.

Figure 4.32   Dyeing Software Behavior

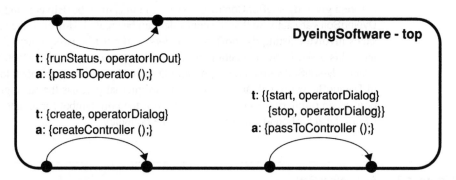

The communication pattern just discussed is repeated in Figure 4.33. Here, all ports and bindings have been removed except for those relevant to the present discussion, and annotations have been added to show the details of the message handling. The left side of the figure represents the communication pattern for messages to the operator, and the right side depicts messages from the operator.

To summarize, ROOM entails two variations on the basic actor-to-actor communication mechanism. The first, through the mechanism of relay ports, allows an actor to provide an intermediary interface for the communication between two other actors. The second, through the mechanism of internal ports, allows communication between a container actor and its component actors.

4.2.8   Communication via System Service Access Points

The element of the ROOM model that we have referred to as a port is, more precisely, called a *port service access point* (port SAP). ROOM provides an additional mechanism by which actors can send and receive messages, called the *system service access point* (system SAP). Note that "system" here refers to the ROOM run-time system, not to the system being modeled. SAPs can be used for actor-to-actor communication, under circumstances that are discussed in Section 4.5.1. System SAPs also are used for accessing the interface of the ROOM virtual machine (a software layer that underlies a ROOM model) in order to obtain services such as timing and exception handling. As suggested by Figure 4.34, one can visualize communication by way of ports as occurring horizontally, and communication by way of a system SAP as occurring vertically.

Figure 4.33 Internal Port Communication Patterns

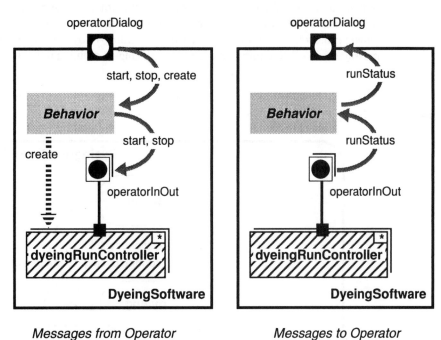

Messages from Operator

Messages to Operator

Figure 4.34 Communication via Ports Versus Communication via SAPs

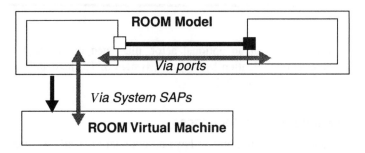

The ROOM virtual machine provides predefined protocol definitions for its various service interfaces. For example, the Timing protocol, defined on the Timing Service, includes a predefined timeout message sent when a timer expires.

Consider, for example, the communication necessary for a DyeingRunController actor to leave the fabric exposed to the dyeing solution for a specified time interval. This requires a system SAP that references the Timing protocol. Figure 4.35 shows this system SAP, which is called timer. The figure also shows the use of the Timing Service (via the Timing protocol) by a message sent when the filling-to-dyeing transition is taken, and a message received in return that triggers the dyeing-to-draining transition.

Figure 4.35   A Timing SAP and Its Use

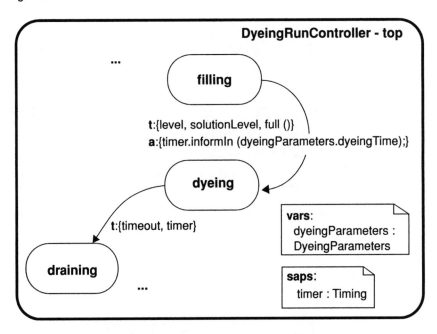

The creation of an optional actor, illustrated in Figure 4.32 and Figure 4.33, also involves communication by way of a system SAP. The details of this communication are discussed in Section 4.3.2.

4.2.9   Internal Message Sequences

An actor class definition can have an optional *internal message sequence* specification.[7] An internal message sequence declares the expected sequence of a set of messages among

---

[7] We anticipate that future versions of ROOM will incorporate more elaborate and powerful descriptions of message sequences. This is currently an active research topic.

the various components of an actor. Figure 4.36 shows an internal message sequence for the DyeingSystem class definition.

Figure 4.36   An Internal Message Sequence

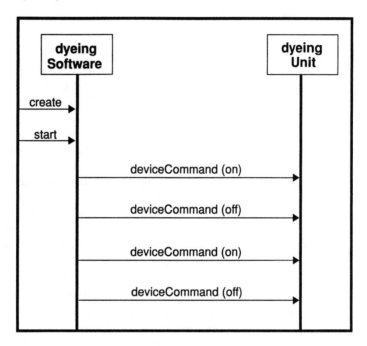

A full description of a message in a message sequence may include values of the data objects that are included in the message. For example, an "on" command sent to a device is represented as a message containing a deviceCommand signal and a data object with the value on. The message deviceCommand thus refers to any message containing the signal deviceCommand, while the message deviceCommand (on) refers to a message containing both the deviceCommand signal and a data object with a value of on.

Message sequences are used in ROOM to specify scenarios (defined in Section 2.1.5)—that is, the expected results of executing a model. When an actor is compiled and executed, an execution-time sequence of messages that violates an internal message sequence for the actor's class will generate a warning (described in Section 4.1.9).

Message sequences are important because they can directly reflect requirements on the system being developed. Any requirement of the form "When the system receives an x, it must produce a y" can be translated into a message sequence that is applied to the actor representing the system. Thus, since model execution will detect violations of these sequences, it can be used to verify the faithfulness of the system model to the requirements.

To summarize, message charts represent expected orderings of messages exchanged through a port or across the set of ports that comprise an actor's interface. Message sequences are used to verify the implementations of actors, by checking that the sequences of messages produced by compiling and executing an actor are consistent with the actor's message sequences.

4.2.10   Hierarchical State and Transition Structures

All the ROOMcharts discussed in Section 4.1 have a single "flat" state machine within the all-encompassing top state. It is also possible to define hierarchical state machines, and much of the modeling power of ROOM is because of this capability.

Consider Figure 4.4, and in particular the aborted state. The only transition shown to this state is from the filling state. However, a more realistic model, shown in Figure 4.37, permits transitions from any of the other states to the aborted state. We will assume that all these transitions have the same trigger, as defined by runError (Figure 4.7). This change significantly increases the complexity of the model, but it only increases the amount of provided information by a small amount. Increases in complexity of this nature are common in "flat" state models like the one shown in Figure 4.4.

The complexity of Figure 4.37 is a symptom of a more fundamental problem—an opportunity to introduce a significant abstraction into the model has been overlooked. The settingUp, filling, dyeing, draining, and done states all can be considered as substates of a higher-level, more abstract state. This state, which might be called running, has the significance that the dyeing run is proceeding as planned, and that no errors have occurred.

The hierarchical state modeling capabilities of ROOM can be used to express this abstraction by nesting all the states that have the runError transition inside a higher-level running state. This change is reflected in Figure 4.38. The new high-level state has a single *group transition* to the aborted state. The semantics of Figure 4.38 are the same as the semantics of Figure 4.37—the occurrence of the runError trigger will cause a transition from any of the other states to the aborted state. However, Figure 4.38 increases the understandability of the model by emphasizing the equivalence of the substates of the running state.

The existence of hierarchies of nested states changes the characteristics of a ROOMchart. For example, Figure 4.38 has two initial state transitions, indicating that, of the two highest-level states, running is the initial state, and, of the substates of running, settingUp is the initial state. In general, the state of a ROOMchart is a complex entity, consisting of the set of states at various levels that is active at a given time.

Hierarchical state organizations also make the effects of transitions more complex. If a transition traverses multiple levels of a hierarchy, multiple exit and entry actions may occur. For example, if a transition from the filling state to the aborted state occurs in the model of Figure 4.38, the following sequence of events will occur:

- The exit action for filling

Figure 4.37 A Complex Flat ROOMchart

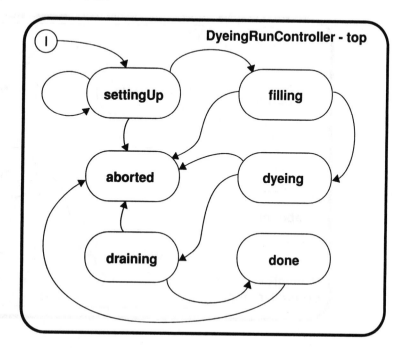

- The exit action for running
- The action for the runError transition
- The entry action for aborted

This additional structure permits greater expressive power for representing high-level requirements. For example, an exit from the running state means that things are no longer normal, and may have safety implications. Requirements for actions such as putting devices into a "safe" state can, therefore, be attached as exit code to the running state. Changes to the details of which substates constitute the running state will have no impact on this expression of the requirement.

The group transition from the running state to the aborted state in Figure 4.38 connects two states at the same level of the hierarchy. It is also possible for a transition to connect states at different levels. For example, Figure 4.39 shows an abandon transition indicating that the dyeing run cannot be salvaged. This connects the aborted state to the done substate within the running state.[8]

---

[8] The notation in Figure 4.39 and Figure 4.38 has been simplified somewhat from the true formal syntax in order to reduce the complexity of the diagrams in this introductory chapter.

Figure 4.38   A Hierarchical ROOMchart

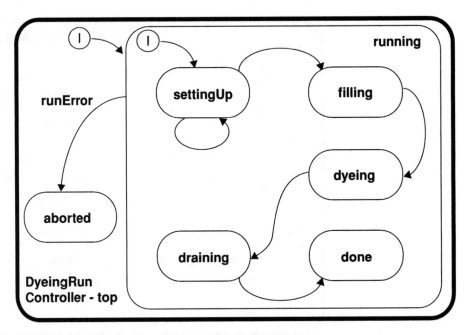

Figure 4.39 also depicts another ROOM feature involving hierarchical states. The transition in which recover connects the aborted state to the hierarchical running state is called a *history* transition. This transition will cause a re-entry to the most recently visited substate of running. For example, if the transition to aborted happened while the filling substate was active, a subsequent recover transition would return control to the filling state. The advantage of this construct is that it significantly reduces graphical clutter (imagine if we had to draw an explicit transition from the aborted state to every individual substate of running).

To summarize, ROOM provides for hierarchical state models to any desired depth, making it possible to capture behavioral abstractions in an easy-to-understand form.

4.2.11   Another Look at Model Execution

Although it is possible (as discussed in Section 4.1.9) to execute a single-actor ROOM model, the true power of model execution derives from the execution of complex, multi-actor models. This is true because any interesting system under development will need to be modeled in terms of multiple actors. It is also true because models that incorporate the environment of the system under development, as well as the system itself, allow for more elaborate kinds of testing.

Figure 4.39 Transitions to Specific Lower-Level States

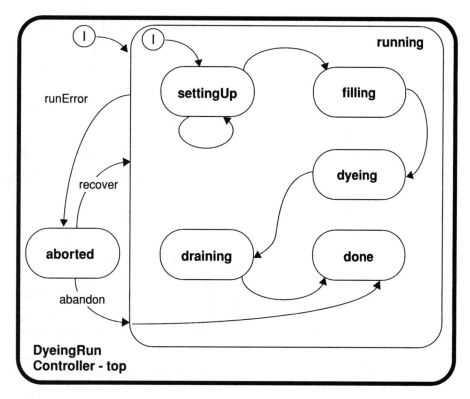

Figure 4.40 shows the structural view of an executable dyeingSystem actor, and also shows the behavior of one of the component dyeingSolution actors. When the dyeingSolution actor is initialized, it sets a timer upon entry to its initial state. The corresponding timeout causes it to report its currentLevel and to reset the timer. The actor thus broadcasts its level on a periodic basis, simulating the availability of the monitored value to the dyeingSoftware. A message from the drainValve or dyeValve will cause the currentLevel to be adjusted, mimicking the effect of valve opening and closing on the liquid level. The drainValve and dyeValve behaviors contain similar mechanisms, allowing them to broadcast their statuses and to send messages to the dyeingSolution, as well as to respond to commands.

At the point in the execution shown in Figure 4.40, one of the two possible dyeingRunController actors has been created (indicated by the number "1" in the lower right-hand corner and the fact that the actor reference is no longer shaded) and the start command has been given.

Figure 4.40   An Executable Multi-Actor Model

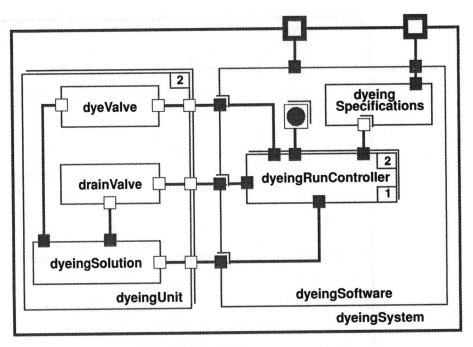

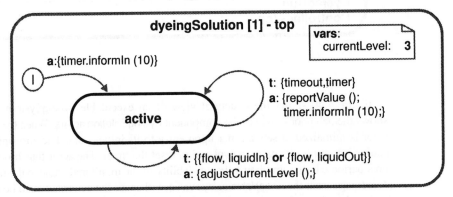

Now consider a time interval following this point, within which the following occurs: the dyeValve, drainValve, and dyeingSolution actors send their timer reset messages, the corresponding timeouts occur, the actors broadcast their level or status, and the receipt of these messages causes the dyeingRunController to take some action. This set of events is shown in Figure 4.41, projected onto a time line that shows the actual use of processor time to execute the events. The assumption here is that the model is executing on a single multitasking workstation that uses timeslice-based process swapping to simulate concurrency. It is also assumed that each event represented takes two "slices" to complete, except for the receipt of the messages by the scheduling component of the ROOM run-time system, which takes only a small fraction of a "slice."

Figure 4.41 Event Handling During Model Execution

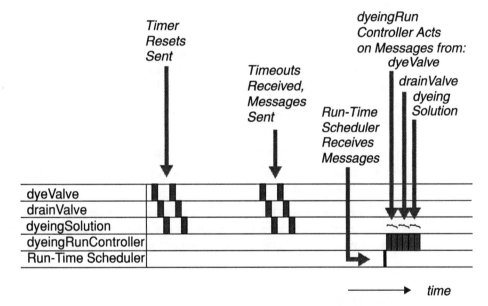

Notice that the processing of timer resets and the timeouts for different actors can overlap. This is because the actors within a ROOM model are executed as independent, concurrent centers of activity. The only sequence imposed on the activity of a ROOM actor is caused by message passing. In other words, actors act only in response to receiving messages. Otherwise, any number of actors can be operating within the same time interval.[9] Hierarchical structuring does not constrain concurrency. The components of an actor all can be concurrently active, and the components of those components, to any depth of recursion. In the present example, all the components of a dyeing unit are shown to be

---

[9] The fact that the actors do not literally operate in parallel in this example is because of the limitations of the workstation rather than any property of the model. If the workstation were capable of multiprocessing, or if the model were distributed over a network and executed, the actors actually would operate in parallel.

concurrently active. In fact, since the model of Figure 4.40 contains two dyeingUnit actors, all the components of both dyeingUnit actors are concurrently active.

Now consider the right-hand side of Figure 4.41. Notice that, even though the scheduler within the ROOM run-time system receives all three messages for the dyeingRunController at essentially the same time, there is no intermixing of the responses to the messages. Messages destined for a single actor are processed sequentially, and the response of an actor to a message is treated as an atomic, (logically) uninterruptible activity. A ROOM run-time system must handle messages for an actor (for example, by queueing) to enforce this sequencing. This property of executing a ROOM model is referred to as *run-to-completion semantics*.

Before leaving the subject of model execution, we must consider the implications of the more complex model with regard to the principles of observability and controllability. These principles require that, when a model with hierarchical actor or state structure or other kinds of complexity is executed, it must be possible to trace the execution and control the model state in a fine-grained manner. In particular,

- It must be possible to start and stop individual actors within a model, as well as to start and stop the model as a whole.

- It must be possible to trace the messages sent through a particular port.

- It must be possible to trace the activity of a particular state transition within a ROOMchart.

To summarize, ROOM handles the execution of complex, multi-actor models by treating the actors as concurrent centers of activity with run-to-completion semantics. ROOM also provides for fine-grained tracing and fine-grained control of model state.

4.2.12 Summary

Figure 4.42 extends the diagram of Figure 4.17 by adding the features of ROOM that deal with hierarchical actor and state structure. The numeric annotations 1 through 6 on the reference arrows are as discussed in Section 4.1.10. The additional annotations are

7. Actor class definitions are used to define the components of actors. The components in an expanded actor class definition are references to other actor class definitions.

8. A port may refer to a protocol class definition with a reversed sense of incoming and outgoing messages by being conjugated.

9. A detail-level language statement may refer to a system SAP (an internal interface component), which in turn refers to a predefined protocol for accessing the ROOM virtual machine.

10. A state on a ROOMchart may be associated with a lower-level state machine whose states are considered as substates.

Figure 4.42   ROOM Reference Organization (with Hierarchical Actor and State Structure)

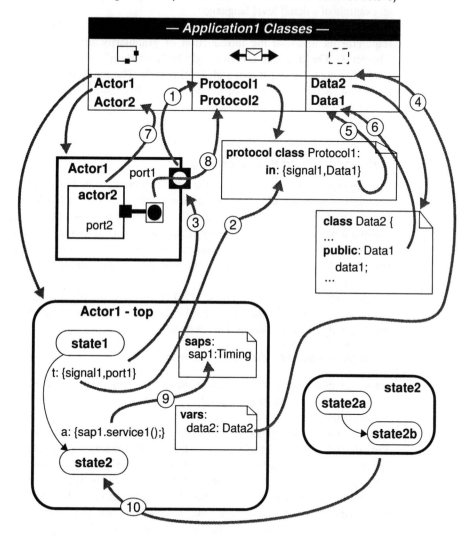

4.3   The ROOM Detail Level

As mentioned previously, ROOM was devised to incorporate a conventional object-oriented programming language (referred to as the detail-level language) to express low-level model details. Most of the types of low-level detail within a ROOM model, such as data value manipulation and decision making, are identical to types of detail encountered in conven-

tional programming. Therefore, it was decided to refrain from inventing yet another variation on the syntax for expressing such details. As in the previous examples, we use C++ as
an example of a detail-level language.

The incorporation of a programming language into ROOM involves some special
requirements to avoid the introduction of granularity discontinuities (as discussed in
Chapter 3). The language cannot simply be "pasted on" to the portion of the ROOM modeling language that expresses high-level details. The mechanism of attachment involves
providing (within the syntax of the detail-level language) facilities for accessing the services of the ROOM virtual machine.

4.3.1   Message Sending and Receiving

The sending of messages is one of the activities incorporated into a transition, state entry,
or state exit action, and thus must be expressible within the detail-level language. This is
handled by treating a port as an object from the point of view of the detail-level language.
Passing a particular kind of message is thus treated as invoking an appropriate procedure
(or "member function" in C++ parlance) on a specific port object. The parameters to this
procedure include a signal and an optional data object containing the data to be trans-
ported in the message. Figure 4.43 contains a variation on the behavior of a Dyeing-
Solution actor as shown in Figure 4.40. Here, instead of attaching the reportValue ()
function call to the transition triggered by the timeout, we attach the code for reporting the
level directly to the transition. This code is

   solutionLevel.send (level, currentLevel);

where solutionLevel is the port name, send is the member function being invoked, level
is the signal name, and currentLevel is a data object, a copy of which is to be included in
the message.

Invoking the send procedure ultimately results in accessing the services of the ROOM
virtual machine. The virtual machine identifies that the dyeingRunController actor is at the
other end of the binding attached to the solutionLevel port, and delivers the message to its
behavior. The arrival of a message eventually causes the receiving actor to be allocated
processor time by the run-time scheduler, which activates the code associated with the
appropriate state transition within that actor's behavior. In Figure 4.43, for example, we
show the case where the dyeingRunController actor is in the filling state. When the solution-
Level message arrives on the level port, that will trigger the transition that takes the actor
into the dyeing state (provided that the guard condition evaluates to TRUE).

A special default extended state variable called msg is used to access the message that has
just been received by an actor. Formally, this variable is declared as a pointer to a system-
defined message class object (ROOMMessage*). It is used to extract the signal and the data
object of the incoming message. In the example in Figure 4.43, we see this variable being
accessed in the code for guard function (full ()) to determine if the solution has reached the

Figure 4.43   Sending and Receiving a Simple Asynchronous Message

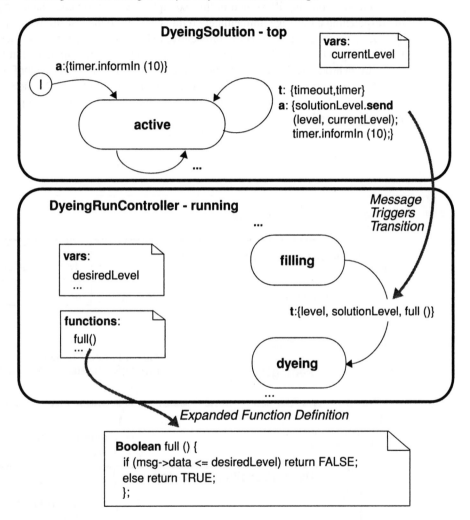

desired level. The expression msg->data returns the value of the data object (in this case, the current level) inserted into the message by the sender.[10] Note that a function is defined

----

[10] Strictly speaking, this is incorrect since the expression msg->data actually returns a *pointer* to the data inside the message rather than the object itself. However, given the introductory nature of this chapter, these and other finer points of C++ syntax have been omitted. The precise syntax and usage of the various system primitives are discussed in Chapter 10.

within the scope of the behavior of an actor class, so that it has direct access to the variables and the messages of its actor.

The message passing illustrated in this example is *asynchronous*. The send procedure, after dispatching a message, immediately returns control to the transition code, which then continues executing (or terminates completely) independently of the subsequent handling of the message. The interchange of messages involving the run parameters in Figure 4.44 also is asynchronous. On entry to the initial settingUp state of a DyeingRunController actor, the action code uses send to pass the parameterRequest to the DyeingSpecifications actor, and then "waits" in the settingUp state for this actor to pass an independent runParameters message in response.

Figure 4.44   Asynchronous Message Exchange

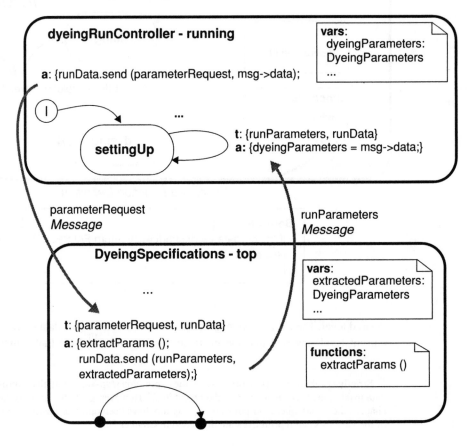

(On the initial transition in Figure 4.44, the reference to msg->data in the send state-ment returns the data (the fabric and dye type) that is contained in the initialization mes-sage sent when the dyeingRunController actor is created. This is explained further in the discussion of Figure 4.46.)

Figure 4.45 is a variation on the run parameters interchange and illustrates *synchronous* communication. Here, the action code on the initial transition uses the synchronous proce-dure invoke rather than the asynchronous procedure send. The exchange of messages hap-pens *within* the state transition, and the transition blocks until a reply is returned by the DyeingSpecifications actor (using the reply procedure).

Figure 4.45   Synchronous Message Exchange

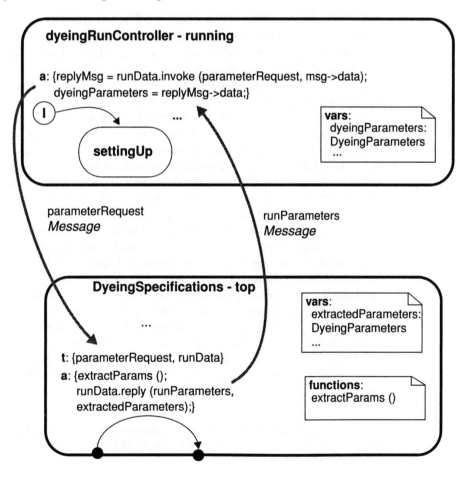

Note that a protocol defining an exchange of messages is independent of whether the message exchange is synchronous or asynchronous. The change from Figure 4.44 to Figure 4.45 requires no change in the RunData protocol.

In summary, message passing is implemented in ROOM by providing facilities to access the services of the ROOM virtual machine in code written in the detail-level language. Both synchronous and asynchronous communication are supported.

4.3.2   Access to Other ROOM Services

Communication by way of ports is only one of the ROOM services that can be accessed from the detail-level language. It is also possible to access the Timing Service in this way, as illustrated by Figure 4.34 and Figure 4.35 and the associated discussion. System SAPs, such as timer in Figure 4.35, are treated as objects by the detail-level language. Thus, the expression

timer.informIn (dyeingParameters.dyeingTime)

is the invocation of the informIn procedure on the timer object. The dyeingTime component of the dyeingParameters variable (that is, encapsulated data object) is passed as a parameter. The invocation of this procedure causes a timer to be initialized within the ROOM virtual machine, and, upon expiration of the timer, causes a default timeout message to be sent to the DyeingSoftware actor that invoked the Timing Service.

As a final example of access to ROOM services from the detail-level language, consider the Frame Service,[11] which, among other facilities, provides for the creation and destruction of actor incarnations at run time. A preliminary example of this service is shown in Figure 4.32, where a create message from the operator triggers a DyeingSoftware actor to call the createController () function. Figure 4.46 is a variation that replaces the createController () function with the actual code. Here, the incarnate procedure is invoked on the frame object (a SAP). Parameters are passed to indicate the actor reference to be incarnated (dyeingRunController) and the initialization data to be passed to the incarnated actor (createData, which was the data object, containing the dye and fabric types, passed from the operator in the create message). Figure 4.46 also shows the connection between the initialization data and the action attached to the initial state of the DyeingRunController actor. The data is passed in a message that may be used during the transition into the initial state. Here, the data is used to send a message to a DyeingSpecifications actor, requesting the runParameters corresponding to the dye and fabric type (see Figure 4.44 and Figure 4.45 and the associated discussion for more details).

To summarize, the detail-level language incorporated into ROOM must provide for access to all the services of the ROOM virtual machine, including Timing and Frame Services.

---

[11] A container actor provides a "frame" for its component actors, and controls properties such as the number of actors corresponding to an optional, replicated reference. The Frame Service provides services to a container actor.

Figure 4.46 Invoking the Frame Service

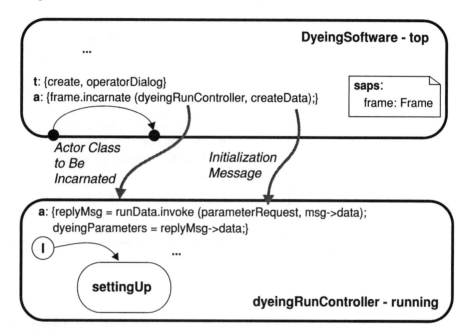

4.3.3 Source-Level Debugging and Model Execution

The principle of observability requires that status of an executing model be made as easy as possible to interpret. Clearly, this is best achieved if this status is reported in the same form in which the model was originally specified (that is, using the same graphical notation that was used to specify the model in the first place). Thus, the modeler need not learn and understand the form of the compiled output, which is not only difficult to follow, but also is highly prone to change with each release of the compiler. (This is the high-level equivalent to the so-called "source-level" debugging in traditional programming environments.)

An example of such a facility is shown in Figure 4.47. Here, it is assumed that the modeler has made an error in defining the behavior for a DyeingRunController actor, by encoding an illegal port-signal combination as the action on the transition from filling to dyeing. (As illustrated in the previous discussion, deviceCommand messages are sent through the drainValveControl and dyeValveControl ports, but not the solutionLevel port.) In Figure 4.47, the run-time system has detected the error and has responded by showing the code in the context in which it appears in the model.

Figure 4.47   Source-Level Debugging

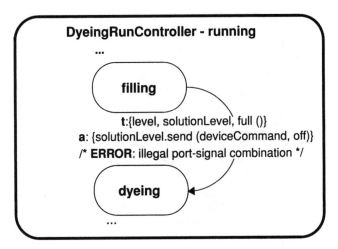

4.3.4   Summary

Figure 4.48 extends the diagram of Figure 4.42 by adding the features of ROOM that are associated with the detail-level language. The numeric annotations 7 through 10 on the reference arrows are as discussed in Section 4.2.12. The additional annotations are

11. Code attached to transitions and states may incorporate function calls. A call is a reference to a function defined as part of the behavior of the actor class.

12. Functions have the same scope as the behavior of the actor class to which they are attached. They may refer to variables of the actor class (shown), and also to ports, SAPs, and messages (not shown).

4.4   A ROOM Model with Inheritance

As discussed in Chapter 3, inheritance is a mechanism for incorporating features of one class definition (the superclass) into another (the subclass). ROOM allows inheritance among actor, protocol, and data class definitions. ROOM permits nonstrict inheritance—in other words, features of a superclass may be redefined or deleted in a subclass definition.[12]

---

[12] The rationale for this is provided in Chapter 9.

Figure 4.48   ROOM Reference Organization (Complete)

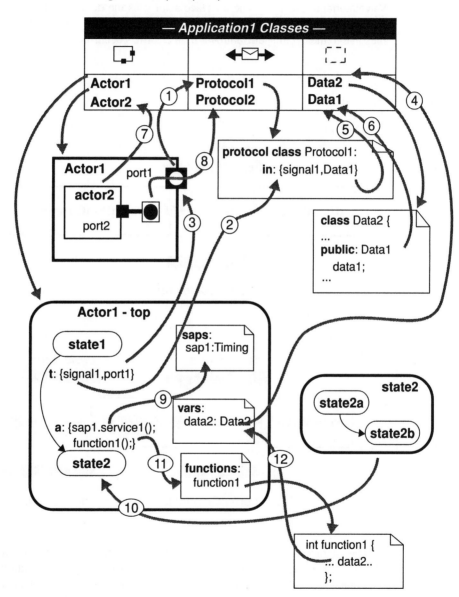

4.4.1   Inheritance among Protocol Classes

As a simple example of the use of inheritance, consider a modification of the fabric dyeing model to separate the detection of device errors from the control of the dyeing run. In Figure 4.49, the top part of the figure shows the message passing in the original model, and the bottom part shows the message passing in the revised model by way of the new drain-ValveInterface reference. The interface actor uses the device status and device command information to determine whether there has been a device error, and then passes an error message to the dyeingRunController if an error has occurred.

Figure 4.49   Revision of Drain Valve Message Passing

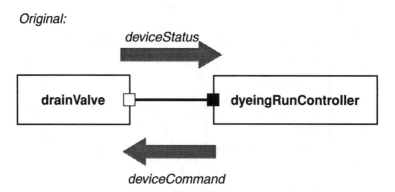

Original:

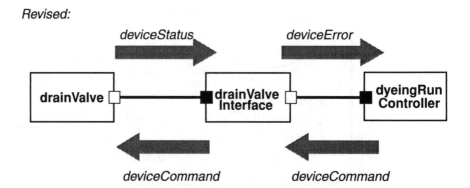

Revised:

The interaction between drainValve and drainValveInterface involves the message interchange defined by the DeviceControl protocol. However, the interaction between drainValveInterface and dyeingRunController is different. This could be handled by defining a new, separate protocol for the interface-to-controller message passing. However, to do so is to ignore a significant abstraction—the deviceCommand message should have invariant properties across both interfaces. This abstraction can be captured by the use of inheritance.

Figure 4.50 shows the revised set of protocol class definitions and their expansions. The superclass, DeviceControlBasic, captures the invariant property (the presence of the message containing the deviceCommand signal and its associated data object). The subclasses, DeviceControlPhysical and DeviceControlVirtual, inherit the deviceCommand message, and add the deviceStatus and deviceError messages, respectively. Within the list of protocol class definitions, subclassing is shown by indentation.

Figure 4.50   Inheritance among Protocol Classes

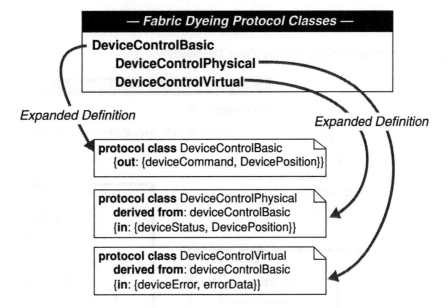

4.4.2   Inheritance among Actor Classes

The example just discussed illustrated the use of inheritance to capture a property that is invariant over multiple appearances within a single model. Inheritance also can be used to capture properties that are invariant across models. Consider a variation on the simple fabric dyeing model discussed so far, in which the dyeing unit contains a heater, and in which the dyeing solution is heated and maintained at an elevated temperature within a dyeing run. This model, while it has some new features, retains the features of the model we have been discussing so far. Therefore, the components of the new model can be derived from the components of the original model by using inheritance.

Figure 4.51 shows a subclass of DyeingUnit called ElevatedTemperatureDyeingUnit and shows the expanded structures of both the superclass and the subclass. Inherited features of the subclass definition are shown in gray. This indicates that the feature in question is defined elsewhere, and is analogous to the use of gray to depict incarnated actors in an executable model.

Note that *all* the features of an actor class definition are inheritable. In particular, since the existence of component actors is a property of the class definition of the container actor, the references within a class definition are inheritable by its subclasses, as shown by drainValve, dyeValve, and dyeingSolution in Figure 4.51. The subclass definition has been extended by the addition of a new actor reference (heater) and a new relay port to provide for an interface to the heater.

Figure 4.51   Inheritance among Actor Class Definitions

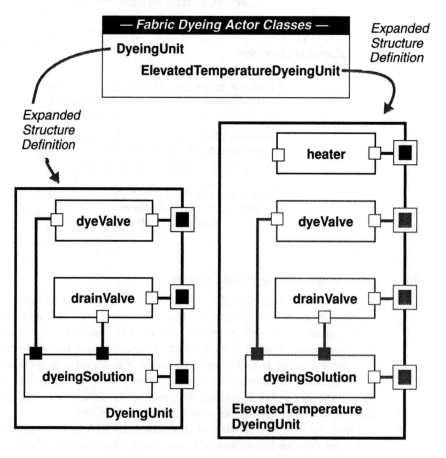

Notice that there is no interaction between the heater and dyeingSolution references within the ElevatedTemperatureDyeingUnit class definition. In order to simulate the effect of the heater on the solution, such an interaction must be added. However, remember that the dyeingSolution reference is governed by the DyeingSolution class definition. Modifying this class definition (to add an extra port for simulating the effects of heating) is workable, but will result in a superfluous port on the dyeingSolution reference within the original DyeingUnit class definition. Another solution is to create an inheritance hierarchy for DyeingSolution that parallels the hierarchy for DyeingUnit. This alternative is shown in Figure 4.52. Note that this alternative requires the overriding of the dyeingSolution reference within the ElevatedTemperatureDyeingUnit class definition. The reference is no longer gray, indicating that the existence of the heatableDyeingSolution reference is not a property of the superclass.

Figure 4.53 is another illustration of the use of inheritance in class definitions. In this case, the focus is on the inheritance of behavior. We have created a subclass of Dyeing-RunController, called ElevatedTemperatureDyeingRunController, to control dyeing runs that involve the heating of the solution. All the states of the ROOMchart for the super-class (some of which are omitted in the diagram) can be inherited by the subclass. The behavior can be extended (as desired) by adding states, transitions, and so on. In the case of ElevatedTemperatureDyeingRunController, the dyeing state has been extended by the addition of a set of substates to distinguish the various stages of the application of heat to the solution.

4.4.3   Inheritance among Data Classes

Data classes within ROOM are defined by using the facilities of the detail-level language. Therefore, the precise details of inheritance among data classes will depend on the language chosen. As in previous examples, we will continue to use C++ notation to illustrate the detail-level language.

In creating the version of the fabric dyeing model that deals with heating of the dyeing solution, it will be necessary to have at least one additional run parameter—the dyeing temperature to be maintained. This will require a modification of the DyeingSpecifications class definition to provide this parameter, and also a more complex data structure associated with the runParameters message. The data structure can be defined by creating a subclass of the DyeingParameters data class definition, as shown in Figure 4.54.

4.4.4   Summary

ROOM provides a comprehensive implementation of inheritance for actor, protocol, and data classes. In particular, all the class properties implemented by references (such as ports and component actors) and all features of behavior definitions may be inherited among actor classes.

Figure 4.52   Parallel Inheritance Hierarchies and Overriding

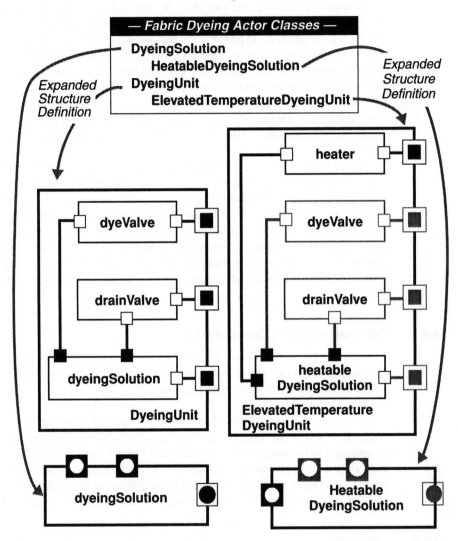

4.5   Some Advanced ROOM Features

This chapter is not intended as an exhaustive description of all ROOM features. Such a treatment will be found in Part Three of this book. However, we mention here a few features of

Figure 4.53 Inheritance of Behavior

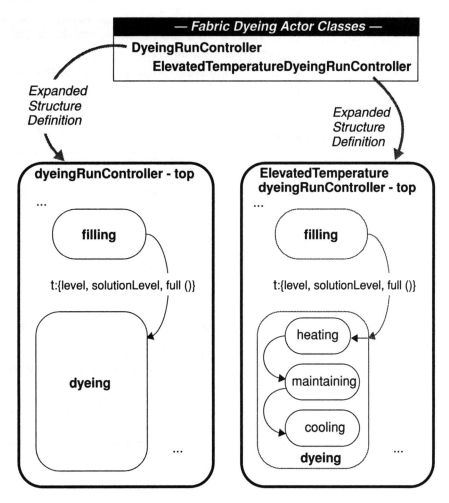

ROOM that enhance its modeling power and that extend the conventional limits of the object paradigm. These features are

- The ability to create models composed of independent layers
- The ability to have a single actor incarnation present at multiple places in a model
- The ability to substitute actors of various classes for a generic actor reference

Figure 4.54   Inheritance among Data Classes (for C++)

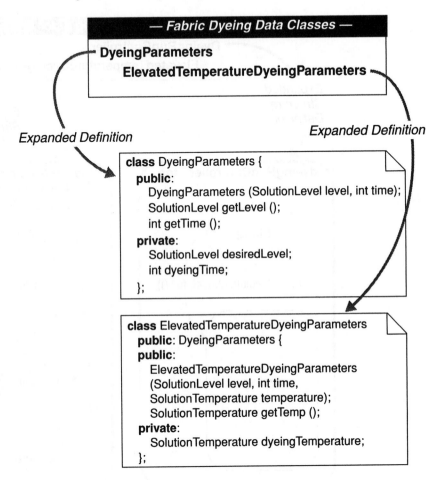

4.5.1   Layering

We have previously discussed (Section 4.2.8 and Section 4.3.2) the use of SAPs to provide communication between an actor and the services of the ROOM virtual machine. ROOM also includes a generalization of this mechanism to provide communication between an actor and a *user-defined service layer*. Such layers consist of high-level actors with properties identical to those discussed in this chapter. The differentiating factor is simply the existence of an internal interface component called a service provision point (SPP). An SPP is the conjugate of a SAP. The existence of a SAP in one actor paired with an SPP in another permits interlayer communication between the actors. The actor containing the

SPP, or an actor that contains this actor, is defined as the service layer. The actor containing the SAP, or an actor that contains this actor, is defined as the layer using the service. The mechanism is shown schematically in Figure 4.55.

Figure 4.55 Interlayer Versus Intralayer Communication Mechanisms

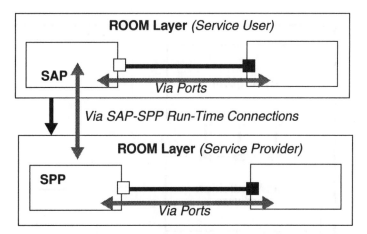

Interlayer communication differs from standard inter-actor communication in that there are no bindings involved. The dependency between layers is indicated by directed arcs called *layer connections* (shown by heavy arrows like the one in Figure 4.55), which are not bound explicitly to individual component actors. However, interlayer communication in all other ways behaves the same as communication by way of ports. The same send and invoke statements are used to pass messages, and the messages are defined by protocol classes.

In ROOM, as in computing in general, layers are used to model centralized, widely shared, implementation-level services. Centralization is important because, if the service can be segmented into a set of disjoint instances, then these simply can be incorporated individually into each client as internal components and layers are not required. This topic is covered in detail in Chapter 7.

As an example, consider Figure 4.56, which is a version of the fabric dyeing model that contains considerably more implementation detail than the previous models in this chapter. The DyeingUnit class definition is the same as previously discussed, and the dyeing-Software class definition is substantially the same. However, the simple, abstract bindings between the dyeingUnit and dyeingSoftware references have been replaced by a set of components that more closely resemble the actual connections.

Within the components of Figure 4.56 are a number of actor references whose class definitions were developed as independent layers, and that provide direct or indirect services to the dyeingSoftware actor. These are the networkSoftware, dataCollectionSoftware, and dataCollectionInterface references. The layer connections indicate interlayer communication paths.

Figure 4.56   Network and Data Collection Layers for Fabric Dyeing

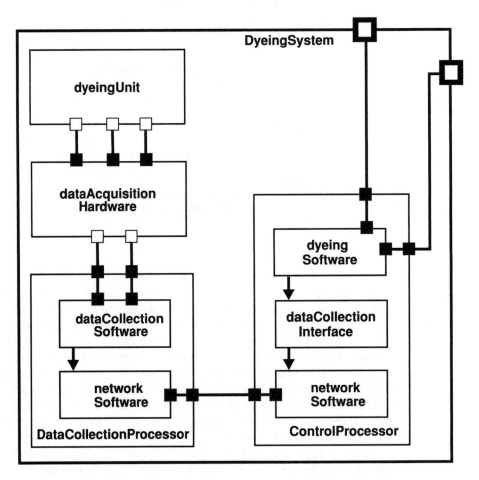

Figure 4.57 shows the DyeingSoftware class definition. The dyeValveInterface, drainValveInterface, and dyeingSolutionInterface references have been added to separate error detection from run control, as discussed in Section 4.4.1. A dyeingUnitInterface reference also has been added, so that the multiplicity of the interface components can be declared at the appropriate level of abstraction. However, the relevance of this class definition to the

present example is that the ports and bindings that originally provided direct connections to the dyeing unit have been removed, and have been replaced by SAPs that connect the dyeingSoftware layer to the dataCollectionInterface layer.

The change in an actor class definition to convert from port-to-port communication to interlayer communication is simple. In addition to removing the unneeded ports and bindings, it is necessary to declare a SAP that is a reference to a protocol defined on the service layer (the corresponding SPP is a reference to the same protocol but with the opposite conjugation), and to replace the name of the port with the name of the SAP in the appropriate send and invoke statements.

Figure 4.57   Ports Replaced by SAPs

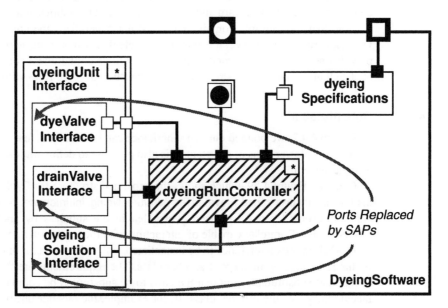

To summarize, interlayer communication provides for message passing between actors without the need for explicit bindings. It thus allows high-level actors that represent centralized, widely shared, implementation-level services to be developed independently as layers, and integrated at run time.

4.5.2   The Multiple Containment Construct

We mentioned in Section 4.2.10 that a number of similar transitions on a flat ROOM-chart may be an indication that an opportunity for an abstraction has been missed. A similar situation holds when a number of similar relay ports connect an actor reference to components within another reference. This is the situation in Figure 4.57, where the relay ports on dyeingUnitInterface connect dyeingRunController to the various interface components.

The interpretation of this situation is that dyeingRunController operates within the model in two distinct contexts: it operates as a direct component of dyeingSoftware; and, via the relay ports, it operates as though it were a component of dyeingUnitInterface. ROOM provides a construct, called *multiple containment*, to express this feature of a model in a more direct way than Figure 4.57 expresses it. In Figure 4.58, the *same* dyeing-RunController reference appears twice, along with a property (called an *equivalence*) attached to the dyeingSoftware class definition. The equivalence states that the pair of references indicates single dyeingRunController actors that appear at multiple places in the model. In other words, a particular dyeingRunController actor is simultaneously a direct component of dyeingSoftware and also a component of dyeingUnitInterface.

Note that the multiple containment construct generalizes the concept of a reference. Using an ordinary reference, it is possible to state that two or more actors of the same class play distinct roles within a model. Using the multiple containment construct, it is possible to state that the same actor simultaneously plays two or more roles within a model.

4.5.3   Substitutability

In Section 4.4.2, we pointed out that inheritance can be used to define components that can model multiple versions of a system. It is also possible to define multiple configurations of a single system.

Consider Figure 4.59, which shows the expanded structure for DyeingUnitInterface and also for a subclass called ElevatedTemperatureDyeingUnitInterface. Note that the dyeing-RunController reference has been overridden in the subclass by an ElevatedTemperatureDyeingRunController capable of interacting with the heaterInterface.

ROOM permits a reference to be instantiated with either an actor of the class pointed to by the reference, or an actor of another class. The requirements are that the reference be declared as substitutable, and that the class to be substituted be compatible with the interface definition of the original class. If, for example, the dyeingRunController and dyeingUnitInterface references in Figure 4.58 are declared as substitutable, it is possible to modify the behavior of dyeingSoftware so that, based on the data in the create message, either the basic or elevated-temperature versions of the controller and the interface are incarnated at run time.

4.5.4   Summary

ROOM provides a number of features that extend the object paradigm to give a model increased expressive power. These features are the ability to create actors that can be used as layers, the ability to allow an actor to appear at multiple places within a model by way

Figure 4.58   The Multiple Containment Construct

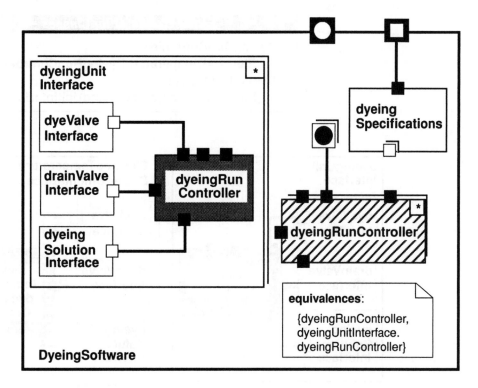

of the multiple containment construct, and the ability to declare a reference as substitutable with either an actor of a given class or an actor of an interface-compatible class.

4.6   Summary

ROOM can be used to create an executable, object-oriented model of a real-time system, and to support commonly used model-building strategies.

The primary component of a ROOM model is an actor class, which represents a set of objects, using the broadest definition of an object as a logical machine of arbitrary scope. An actor interface is defined in terms of protocols, which represent sets of related messages. Actors have a behavior, which is described by a state machine called a ROOMchart and by extended state variables defined in terms of data classes.

Figure 4.59   An Inheritance Hierarchy Suitable for Run-Time Substitution

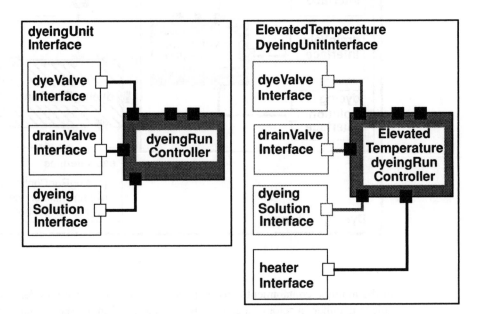

A ROOM actor can have an arbitrarily complex internal structure, defined by references to other actor classes whose actors are its components. The behavior of an actor can also be described hierarchically, by defining substates of states on the ROOMchart.

ROOM incorporates a conventional programming language. Statements in the syntax of this language are used to represent low-level details such as message passing and manipulation of data values.

ROOM provides for a comprehensive implementation of inheritance. In particular, all the properties of a complex actor class may be inherited by its subclasses.

A number of advanced modeling features are provided by ROOM, including timing and dynamic instantiation services, multiple containment, and substitutable generic classes.

ROOM models are executable. The execution environment provides for observability and controllability of the model state.

PART THREE

The Definition of the ROOM Modeling Language

In this part, we take a detailed look at the concepts supported by the ROOM modeling language. This material is aimed at the practitioner who wants to build ROOM models for analysis, design, or implementation purposes.

Despite the fact that the ROOM concepts are formal, most of the descriptions in this part are informal. Our principal objective is to convey the essential pragmatics of modeling with ROOM. For example, concepts are introduced and described along with an assortment of heuristics for their practical application. Nevertheless, formal descriptions of the *abstract* syntax of the most important modeling concepts also are included (their corresponding *concrete* syntax is provided in Appendix E).

The material is organized into the following chapters:

- *Chapter 5,* "The Conceptual Framework of ROOM," introduces an abstract framework for classifying the ROOM modeling concepts that is then used as an aid for navigating through the other chapters in this part of the book.

- *Chapter 6,* "High-Level Structure Modeling," describes the ROOM facilities for assembling concurrent logical machines into more complex aggregates.

- *Chapter 7,* "Layering," discusses a different form of structural modeling that allows complex systems to be constructed as a series of gradually more specialized vertical layers.

- *Chapter 8,* "High-level Behavior Modeling," discusses ROOMcharts, a hierarchical state machine formalism for describing the high-level behavior of concurrent logical machines.

- *Chapter 9,* "Inheritance," describes how this useful technique is applied to high-level structure and high-level behavior in ROOM.

- *Chapter 10,* "The Detail Level," discusses the fine-grained objects and detailed behavior that are required for building operational models.

- *Chapter 11,* "Implementing ROOM Models," provides a reference model and implementation heuristics for constructing a ROOM virtual machine that supports the concepts described in the preceding chapters in this part of the book. This is useful primarily for those interested in looking "behind the scenes," as well as for those interested in constructing their own implementation of such a virtual machine. Other readers can safely skip this chapter.

CHAPTER 5

The Conceptual Framework of ROOM

A formal language such as ROOM, which is designed to span a significant portion of the overall development cycle, abounds in a variety of concepts, rules, and guidelines. On first encounter, even the most determined reader might be overwhelmed by a glut of detail unless some navigational assistance is provided. As the details of this conceptual space are described piece by piece, no matter how systematic the traversal, there is a danger that the forest will be obscured by the trees. It is, therefore, useful to lay out some type of reference grid, or *framework*, over this space that then can be consulted on occasion (like a map) to re-establish a sense of direction.

Once such a framework is in place, it can serve not only as a teaching aid, but also as a guide to the experienced practitioner. In the latter case, it acts much like a compass, helping the development team pinpoint where it currently stands, which directions have been covered, and which ones still remain to be explored.

In ROOM, this conceptual framework is, in essence, a classification of the set of modeling concepts. It consists of the following two paradigms:

- The *abstraction levels paradigm*
- The *modeling dimensions paradigm*

In this brief chapter, we examine these two paradigms and how they relate to each other. The framework is then used as a basis for describing the detailed syntax and semantics of the ROOM language in subsequent chapters.

5.1   The Abstraction Levels Paradigm

In dealing with the intricacies of the natural world, modern science uses different models to represent phenomena at different levels of granularity. For example, the concepts and notation used for describing particle physics are radically different from those used in chemistry. Yet, the phenomena they deal with individually both can be traced to a common cause—the properties of matter. Needless to say, it would be unreasonable to try to describe chemistry using the language of particle physics (since that would produce an excess of detail) just as it would be impractical to do all of our computer programming using the instruction set of a Turing machine. Conversely, the language of chemistry is inappropriate for describing particle physics, since it is lacking some of the concepts fundamental to particle physics.

This stratification of notations and languages in natural sciences is a consequence of the complexity of the physical world and of our inability to comprehend that complexity in its entirety. More and more, however, we are facing a similar predicament in the artificial world of computer-based systems. A modern computer network, for instance, is a complex system by almost any definition of the term. It contains many levels of complexity, from hardware and various operating systems to network-level distributed applications.

The increase in complexity of software systems was gradual, so the shift to a higher scope was not always obvious. As a result, there have been many attempts to cover the higher levels by simple extension of existing programming languages, rather than through qualitatively new paradigms. In some ways, this is like trying to extend the language of particle physics to deal with chemistry.

The approach taken in ROOM is to separate the concepts and notation used for different *scopes*, or *levels of granularity* of a software system. The picture that emerges is of a vertical stack of "concept bases," each with its own notation, and each dealing with a different scope (see Figure 5.1). (Note that this tiered structure does not represent the structure of some system, but is just a way of classifying modeling concepts.) The concepts defined at one level are complemented by the concepts provided in other levels, so a larger software system is described by concepts from a number of levels.

Currently, ROOM covers only two of these abstraction levels—the *Detail Level* and the *Schematic Level*. Other levels, above and below these two, are not only conceivable, but already exist. For example, machine languages or languages for modeling hardware (such as VHDL) belong in levels below the ROOM Detail Level. However, they have not yet been integrated into the ROOM modeling language.

The Detail Level includes concepts for modeling the structure and behavior of passive data objects such as strings, numbers, or record structures. This is the level of granularity encompassed by traditional machine-independent programming languages such as C, Pascal, or Smalltalk. Although no programming language is perfect, it is fair to say that most current languages provide at least adequate conceptual support for modeling phenomena at this level. As a pragmatic approach, therefore, it is simpler to utilize existing programming languages here rather than to devise yet another programming language. This is the strategy adopted in ROOM.

The Schematic Level provides concepts for dealing with higher-level phenomena (including concurrency and distribution), as well as for modeling large-scale software systems. Included at this level are high-level concepts for modeling structure (such as actors, ports, and bindings), as well as concepts for describing high-level behavior found in ROOMcharts.

Figure 5.1 The General Abstraction Levels Paradigm

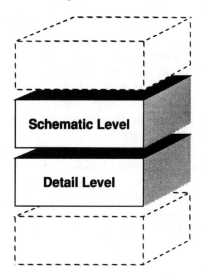

Despite this separation of concerns, the concepts at different abstraction levels in ROOM still are formally interrelated. This ensures that, for any given model, specifications at lower levels are constrained by and consistent with specifications at the higher levels. As a result of this formal linkage between concepts, even the most abstract ROOM models are executable. This is consistent with the approach of utilizing executable models for development.

5.2 The Modeling Dimensions Paradigm

A system model created during development generally must answer at least the following two fundamental questions:

- What are the major components of the system?
- How does it function?

The answers to these questions are tightly intertwined, since the workings of a system are determined by the interactions between its components. From the answer to the first question, we derive the *structure* of the system. This describes the components in the system and their mutual relationships. The answer to the second question specifies the *behavior* of the system.

Structure is topological and primarily static, and is naturally represented by graphs. The most common relationships captured by structure are communication relationships between the components of a system (modeled in ROOM by bindings) and containment relationships. Containment relationships capture the decomposition of higher-level components into lesser components and are, therefore, key to the modeling of large and complex systems. The structure of a data record, for example, defines the set of component fields of the record (the container) and, possibly, the relative ordering of the fields.

Behavior is dynamic and describes the changing of the state of a system over time. Traditionally, behavior has been the starting point for most software modeling with the result that structure often was neglected. Early software systems usually involved simple structures that did not require deep insight to be understood. With the introduction of larger software systems, it became obvious that structure and behavior should be treated as concerns of equal importance.

This separation of structure from behavior provides a convenient framework for organizing modeling activities. Structure captures primarily the static aspects of a system, whereas behavior addresses the dynamics. The two aspects can be thought of as two separate dimensions in some abstract "modeling space" (see Figure 5.2). A particular model represents a point in this space. For example, the models identified by points labeled Model 1 and Model 2 in Figure 5.2 are two different models that have common behavior, but different structures. The two dimensions, Structure and Behavior, provide a framework for modeling. That is, to fully specify an operational model, we must specify both its structure and its behavior.

Figure 5.2   The Dimensions of the Modeling Space

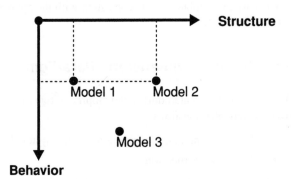

One aspect that is unique to the object paradigm is the presence of an inheritance hierarchy. Our first instinct might be to treat inheritance as an element of structure. However, this can lead to confusion since inheritance relationships, in contrast to other structural relationships, are relationships between classes and not between object incarnations. Since it seems better to separate inheritance from structure, and since experience with applying inheritance has indicated that obtaining a well-formed class hierarchy often requires the same type of painstaking development effort as normally is spent on behavior and structure ([Johnson88]), it seems justifiable to represent it as a third independent modeling dimension (see Figure 5.3).

Figure 5.3   The Modeling Dimensions Paradigm

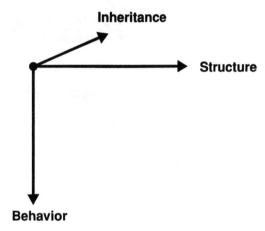

It can be argued that inheritance is of lesser significance than the other two modeling dimensions. After all, it is quite feasible to model a system without touching on inheritance, whereas the same cannot be said for the other two dimensions. This view, however, disregards the evolutionary nature of most large systems. These systems constantly are subjected to new and unforeseen requirements, which means that they are continuously changing and extending their functionality. When this is taken into account, abstraction and reuse become just as vital to a system as the structural and behavioral aspects.

5.3   Complementarity of the Framework Paradigms

Note that structure is manifested both at the Detail Level and at the Schematic Level. For example, the composition of a C++ class with component objects and pointers to objects of other classes exemplifies structure at the Detail Level. An actor class diagram with component actor references and bindings between them represents structure at the Schematic Level. The only difference is that the form of structure (its detailed semantics and notation) is different in the two levels. The same conclusion holds for the other two modeling dimensions. This means that the Modeling Dimensions paradigm applies equally to all modeling scopes. This complementarity of the two paradigms is rendered symbolically in Figure 5.4.

Figure 5.4   The Conceptual Framework of ROOM

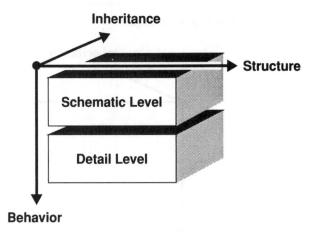

One of the interesting consequences of combining these two paradigms is that it provides new insights. For example, the notions of classes and inheritance, traditionally applied almost exclusively to the Detail Level, also can be applied to the higher abstraction levels. This allows complete system architectures or subsystem structures to be captured as class specifications that are embedded in an inheritance hierarchy.

5.4   Summary

The modeling concepts of ROOM can be classified in either of the following two ways:

- According to the scope or granularity of objects that are under consideration
- According to the modeling aspect that they address

The first classification scheme leads to the Abstraction Levels paradigm, in which concepts are classified as addressing either low-level detail concerns (the Detail Level) or higher-level distributed system concerns (the Schematic Level). The second classification decomposes the modeling space into three independent dimensions representing different degrees of freedom in modeling: Structure (which deals with the static aspects of a system), Behavior (which deals with the dynamic aspects), and Inheritance (which covers abstraction and reuse characteristics).

The combination of the two paradigms is referred to as the *conceptual framework of ROOM* and is the basis for the organization of subsequent chapters in this part of the book. This same framework also is useful during development as a navigational aid that helps drive modeling activities.

CHAPTER 6

High-Level
Structure Modeling

When we talk about the "structure" of a system, we are referring to the set of entities that comprise that system, as well as to the relationships between those entities. In an object-oriented software system, for instance, structure is defined by the objects in the system and their communication, encapsulation, and similar relationships.

In the early days of computing, structure received scant attention, with most of the emphasis placed on the behavioral or algorithmic aspects of software. Structure was typically limited to describing relationships between relatively fine-grained data items (such as the association between the elements of an array or a record structure). However, as software became more complex, it necessarily became more modular. That, in turn, required the ability to specify and manage the relationships between modules. Subsequently, with the advent of concurrent and parallel computing systems (characterized by their inherent modularization boundaries), the specification of structure became a first-level concern, on par with the specification of behavior. The highly modular nature of object-oriented software might suggest that structure inherently plays an important role in these systems. Until recently, however, this has not been the case, as initial work on the object paradigm focused much more on the properties of modules (objects) rather than on the patterns in which such modules are combined.

In ROOM, high-level structure appears in two basic forms. Layering captures "vertical" hierarchical structures, whereby the overall functionality of a complex systems is partitioned into multiple layers with each successive layer constructed out of the generic facilities provided by the layers below. The second type of structure defines the structural relationships between objects that occur within the same layer. In this chapter, we examine this second category. In terms of the ROOM modeling framework, this topic lies primarily along the structural dimension of the Schematic Level as shown in Figure 6.1. Layered structures are discussed in Chapter 7.

Figure 6.1   The ROOM Conceptual Framework: High-Level Structure

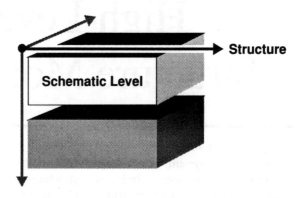

6.1   High-Level Structural Classes

In current practice, the term "software reuse" often is interpreted as the use of language-specific program libraries containing utility functions and data type definitions. While the value of this form of reuse is self evident, the problem is that it takes place only at the most detailed of scopes. The potential payback of reuse at higher levels (sometimes referred to as *design* reuse) is much greater. For example, if we had the ability to reuse a carefully crafted high-level architecture of an existing complex system for a new system of a similar nature, much effort could be saved and the new system likely would be more reliable than if it were designed from scratch.

It can be argued that this is nothing new and that such reuse has always been practiced. New designs almost invariably mimic the form of earlier successful designs. However, this type of reuse usually was achieved by some form of "cloning" (that is, by manual or mechanical copying of the original pattern). Cloning has two major drawbacks. The first of these occurs if cloning is done manually, which can lead to errors in transcription so that the copy does not quite match the original. The second problem is one of maintenance and evolution. The result of cloning is that there are two or more instances of the same pattern. If that pattern must evolve (to respond to new requirements, for example), then each copy must be updated individually. This not only requires duplication of effort, but also increases the likelihood of further transcription errors.

The object paradigm overcomes this problem by way of the mechanisms of abstract classes, inheritance, and polymorphism. If these are supported by appropriate mechanization tools (such as compilers), transcription errors are avoided and maintenance effort need not be duplicated. Support for reuse is automated.

The ROOM concepts used for high-level structural modeling were formulated with the objective of exploiting this automated reuse support. Thus, the concept of reusable components is formally extended to cover complete structural frameworks of concurrent cooperating objects of the highest scope. This is achieved by extending the concept of a class, as defined in the object paradigm, to cover logical machines, as discussed in Chapter 3.

The potential for reusing a class specification increases the more it is decoupled from the context of the particular application in which it is first defined. This is best accomplished through a combination of two mechanisms: encapsulation, and explicit interfaces between an object and its environment. Encapsulation is necessary to ensure that the coupling is indeed restricted to only the interactions across the interfaces. The interface definitions should be formal in order to clearly and unequivocally specify all the elements involved in the coupling between the object and its context. To maximize reuse, the interface specifications also should be generic in order to abstract away the particulars of one application-specific context.

In accordance with this approach, a general principle adopted in ROOM is that *a class specification should minimize the restrictions that it imposes on its reuse.* For example, to illustrate the impact of this approach, consider the case of an operating system in which there are multiple occurrences of a disk controller, one for each disk device in the system. Assume that all disk controllers are references to the same class. In that situation, should the property of "multiplicity" be an attribute of the disk controller class or of the operating system application? If it is attributed to the class, then the same disk controller class would not be usable in other applications where a single disk controller is sufficient. In ROOM, the principle of maximizing reuse suggests that the multiplicity attribute should *not* be associated with the class, but rather with the reference.

6.2　　Actors and Actor Interfaces

ROOM is an object-oriented modeling language and it is natural that its basic modeling concept is a special kind of object. In this section we look at the actor concept.

6.2.1　Actors

The fundamental concept for modeling high-level structure in ROOM is that of an *actor.* Actors model functionally significant components in a reactive system, which gives them a fairly broad scope, since functional significance is a relative term. Significant components occur at many levels in a system starting from the basic units of concurrent execution all the way up to complete systems consisting of multiple layers distributed over a wide physical domain. This is to be expected, since practically any system can be considered as a component of some greater system.

In general, a ROOM *actor* represents an active object that has a clearly defined purpose. It may be used to model physical objects (such as a disk drive or a human operator) or abstract objects (such as a software task). In this context, the term "active" means that an actor may have its own execution thread and can, therefore, operate concurrently with other active objects in its domain. The precise semantics of actor concurrency are described in Chapter 8.

In contrast to actors are passive *data objects*. The functionality of these objects is activated only in the context of some actor's execution thread. In order to eliminate a class of difficult concurrency problems (discussed in Chapter 8) as well as to facilitate modeling of physically distributed systems, passive objects in ROOM are restricted to the context of a single execution thread. This means that an individual data object can be accessed only by the single actor that encapsulates it. That is, there is no sharing of data between concurrent threads in a ROOM model. If the information contained by a data object in one actor must be conveyed to another actor, a copy of that object is made and embedded in a message that is then sent to the destination actor. This means that data objects in ROOM do not appear as part of the high-level structure of a system, but are relegated to a lesser, auxiliary role.

It is worth stressing that actors need not be based exclusively on "real-world" entities, particularly when modeling software. In the fabric dyeing example described in Chapter 2, the Dyeing Run Controller actor represented a software entity rather than a physical component.

The key to identifying an actor is its *purpose*. Like any object, each actor should have a definite purpose that it fulfills and that justifies its presence in a larger system. As a good rule of thumb, the purpose of an actor should be expressible in a single sentence. For example, in case of the fabric dyeing application, the Dyeing Run Controller was responsible for the progress of an individual dyeing run.

6.2.2 The Encapsulation Shell of an Actor

The purpose of an actor is an abstraction, or distillation, of its various functional capabilities. This is both implied and enforced by the encapsulation shell of the actor. This shell suggests that the contained functionality is to be viewed as a conceptual unit. In line with the principle of maximizing reuse, the encapsulation shell of a ROOM actor is opaque both from without *and from within*. That is, the shell not only hides the internal structure of an actor from outside viewing, but also prevents the internal components of the actor from viewing the environment. Although this may seem obvious, it is not always the case. For example, in most block-structured programming languages (such as Pascal or Algol), information hiding extends in only one direction—a nested block can access the context of its containing block (but not vice versa). As a result, the nested block only can be used in the context imposed by all of its containing blocks, which makes reuse impractical.

In summary, the encapsulation shell of an actor serves multiple purposes. First, it is an abstraction mechanism that enables the potentially complex functionality of an actor to be comprehended as a single conceptual unit. Second, it is a decoupling mechanism that shields the environment from implementation changes within the actor, and vice versa. Finally, it can serve as a basis for security mechanisms since it prevents any external access to objects within an actor.

6.2.3 The Interface Components of an Actor

To communicate with other entities in its environment, an actor provides one or more openings (or *interface components*) in its encapsulation shell. These interface components allow the exchange of messages between the actor and its environment. Each interface component is formally typed to ensure that only expected information can flow through it. ROOM defines three different forms of actor interface components: ports, service access points, and service provision points. In this chapter, we limit our discussion to ports that are used for communications between actors within the same layer. Service access points and service provision points are described in Chapter 7 when we examine layered structures.

Note that an actor can have more than one interface component, each (potentially) of a different type. This means that there can be many different views of the same actor depending on which component is accessed. This is extremely useful in real-time systems in which most concurrent objects simultaneously collaborate with two or more other actors. A useful heuristic relating to this is based on the principle of separating internal control from function (described in Chapter 13). In this approach, control ports are distinguished from functional or service ports. Control ports are used for interactions with the controller of the actor. Through this type of interface component, an actor receives control signals and sends out status information. Service ports are used either to provide access to the functionality of the actor to other actors or, conversely, to access the services of other actors. This separation ensures that only control entities will have access to control functions. An alternate way of viewing multiple interface components is that an actor can simultaneously take on multiple *roles* [Pernici90].

6.2.4 Graphical Notation for Actor References

The graphical notation for an actor *reference*, appearing as a component in some actor class definition, is a labeled rectangle (as illustrated in Figure 6.2). The label corresponds to the name of the reference and must be unique in its context.[1] If the corresponding actor class has ports, then these are represented by small squares on the perimeter of the rectangle. These may be filled in black depending on whether their type is based on the unconjugated or conjugated protocol, respectively. The names of the ports correspond to the names of appropriate ports in the actor class definition. (In subsequent diagrams, on occasion, the port labels may not be shown in order to reduce the visual clutter in the diagrams.)

---

[1] The context of an actor reference is described later in this chapter.

Figure 6.2   Graphical Notation for an Actor Reference with Multiple Ports

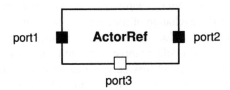

6.3   Messages and Protocols

Communication with actors in ROOM is based exclusively on message passing. This permits the sender and receiver to be physically separate, making it suitable for distributed system modeling. In this paradigm, the information to be communicated between actors is first transferred to an intermediate *message* object that is then conveyed from the sender to the receiver by virtue of an underlying *communication service*. It is important to keep in mind that message passing does not necessarily imply that communications must be asynchronous. In fact, ROOM allows both synchronous (blocking) and asynchronous (nonblocking) communication.

6.3.1   Messages

Syntactically, a ROOM message is a special type of data object that incorporates a mandatory *message signal* attribute, a *message priority* attribute, and an optional *message data object* attribute (see Figure 6.3). The message signal is a symbolic value that captures the application-specific meaning of the event that the message represents. For example, a message that indicates confirmation of the receipt of a previous message might be tagged with an "acknowledgment" signal. The information conveyed by the signal optionally may be supplemented with a *single* data object. Since the type of this data can be arbitrarily complex, there is no theoretical limit on the amount of information that can be conveyed in a single message. The priority of a message determines its significance relative to other messages that may be in transit between actors. (This and other aspects of the ROOM communication model are discussed in greater detail in Chapter 8 and Chapter 10.)

Messages in ROOM are typed. Each *message type* is defined by a combination of a unique signal literal and an optional data type. Textually, this is represented by an ordered pair,

{sig, data-type}

where sig specifies a signal name and data-type the name of a data type. As a pragmatic measure, a special "universal" data type, called null, can be used when the type of the data to be embedded in a message is not known in advance.

Figure 6.3 ROOM Messages

(a) No Data Object

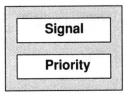

(b) With a Data Object

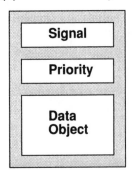

6.3.2 Protocols

The set of messages exchanged between two parties in a concurrent system typically conforms to a dynamic pattern or *protocol*. This pattern defines not only which messages comprise the protocol, but also the direction and relative order in which the messages are sent and received. In essence, a messaging protocol is like a contract that constrains the behavior of both parties in a communication.

For example, consider the case of a standard two-phase commit protocol partially[2] specified by the message sequence chart diagrams in Figure 6.4. In this protocol, the first message carries the PrepareToCommit signal from the Control entity to the Database entity. This message includes an embedded transaction identifier (trId) data object, followed by a Ready message, and so on.

More formally, a protocol class in ROOM is defined as

- A set of *incoming message types*
- A set of *outgoing message types*
- An optional specification of *valid message exchange sequences*
- An optional specification of the expected *quality of service*

The terms "incoming" and "outgoing" in this definition imply that a ROOM protocol specification has a "sidedness," or *polarity*. That is, a protocol is specified *from the perspective of one of the participants*. The reason for this is that a protocol is used to specify the type of an actor interface component. Thus, incoming and outgoing are defined with respect

---

[2] The specification in Figure 6.4 does not account for the possibility of an aborted commit. A full protocol specification would include this as well.

Figure 6.4   A Two-Phase Commit Protocol

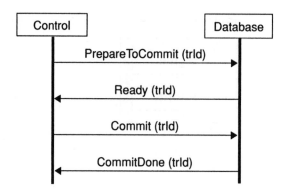

to the actor to which the interface component is attached. A protocol is considered *symmetric* if its set of incoming message types is equal to its set of outgoing message types.

At first, this approach may appear to force us to define each protocol twice (once for each side). However, this can be avoided by introducing the concept of a *conjugated* protocol. A conjugated protocol for a protocol P (denoted as P*) has the same definition as protocol P except that the incoming and outgoing message sets are interchanged. In other words, the outgoing message set of protocol P is the incoming message set of P*, and vice versa. The ROOM graphical notation uses a white square (as opposed to a black one) to indicate that a port reference is conjugated.

As a practical guide to choosing a side when defining a protocol, it is recommended to define a protocol from the perspective of the clients. This means that only the server must conjugate the types of its interface components.

In addition to defining valid input and output message sets, a protocol specification includes an optional specification of valid message sequences. Message-exchange specifications can be provided by using a variety of formalisms. For example, Figure 6.5 shows a finite-state machine specification for the valid message-exchange sequences of the two-phase commit protocol introduced previously. At present, this attribute is defined as *optional* since the theoretical basis for such dynamically defined types has not yet been fully developed.[3] For this reason, in the remainder of the book we will overlook the message-sequences attribute of protocols.

---

[3] Some promising work in this direction has been reported in [Nierstasz90].

Figure 6.5   Valid Message Sequences for a Two-Phase Commit Protocol

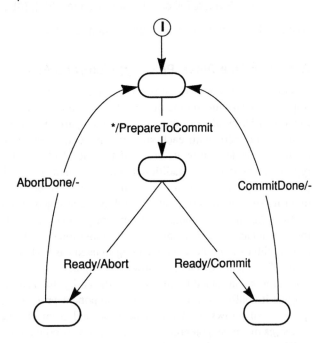

The last component of a protocol definition is a specification of the expected quality of service. The service referred to here is the underlying communications service that is used to convey the protocol. Namely, each protocol is defined with some expectations concerning the reliability of the communications facilities available. For example, if we suspect that the underlying service cannot guarantee delivery, then we would include positive acknowledgment signals in our protocol specifications. Service quality is defined by a complex set of attributes, including reliability and propagation delay characteristics. To avoid excessive technical detail, we will omit this attribute from further consideration, and simply assume that the quality of service of a protocol is defined implicitly.

In this text, we primarily will use a textual representation to specify the protocols used in the examples. The generic format of this representation is

protocol class P:
    in: {{sig_1, data-type$_1$}, {sig_2, data-type$_2$}, ...}
    out: {{sig_m, data-type$_m$}, {sig_n, data-type$_n$}, ...}

where P is the protocol class name, and the pairs {sig_i, data-type$_i$} specify individual message types. For example, the two-phase commit protocol, defined from the perspective of the database user, is specified as

> **protocol class** TwoPhaseCommit:
>   **in**:   {{Ready, trId}, {CommitDone, trId}, {AbortDone, trId}}
>   **out**: {{PrepareToCommit, trId}, {Commit, trId}, {Abort, trId}}

where trId is the type name of a transaction identifier data object.

6.3.3   Actor Interface Types, Polymorphism, and Actor Types

Typing prevents inconsistent design specifications. Traditionally, typing achieves this by imposing constraints on the ranges of values that can occur at run time. ROOM uses typing to restrict the flow of messages across a particular actor interface component by associating a protocol with each such component. In other words, the *type* of an interface component is defined by its *protocol* attribute. Note that this is a broader definition of the type concept than the traditional one in which a type is equated to a set of values [Cardelli85]. This is because, in addition to values, protocol types may include a temporal ordering specification (the set of valid message sequences) [Nierstrasz90].

Note that interface component types or protocols are independent of the actors to which they are attached. This means that the same interface type can appear on many different actors with exactly the same meaning in each case. This is a form of *polymorphism*.[4] The value of this feature is that it allows a strong decoupling of an actor from its collaborators. The actor is unaffected by the class of the entity that is at the other end of the interface, as long as it conforms to the interface component protocol. This has two beneficial consequences—it allows an actor to be protected from changes in the environment, and it increases the reuse potential of an actor class specification.

The provision of interface component types leads us to actor types. The *type of an actor* is defined by the set of the types of all its interface components. (Note that the same interface component type can appear more than once in an actor type. This happens if an actor has multiple interface components of the same type.) The type of an actor captures its semantics from the perspective of external observers. It is important to note that, in ROOM, the concept of an actor type is distinct from the concept of an actor class. Briefly, an *actor class* is a specification that incorporates the actor's type, as well as its implementation.

6.4   Actor Composition

Object composition, and its inverse, object decomposition, are at the very heart of all structural modeling. A structure is a combination of parts that are connected according to

---

[4] Based on the taxonomy provided by Danforth and Tomlinson [Danforth88], the polymorphism of interface types can be classified as *functional* polymorphism, which is a variant of universal polymorphism.

some pattern. Composition is the process of creating a structure of actors, and consists of selecting which parts to use and defining the relationships between them.

The two primary types of structural relationships considered in this chapter are

- Object interaction, or *communication*, relationships
- Object containment relationships

In this section we look at communication relationships. Containment relationships are discussed in Section 6.4.2.

6.4.1 Communication Relationships and Bindings

Most *causal* relationships between objects require an exchange of information. This means that we can obtain a basis for understanding causality linkages between the components of a system by identifying the paths of communication between them. For instance, Figure 6.6 is an informal block diagram of some hub system with the arcs representing communication channels. From this diagram, we can observe that the central coordinator component can directly influence each of the peripheral agents, and vice versa. We also can see that the agents cannot directly affect each other since they have no direct interconnections.

Figure 6.6   A System Topology with Explicit Communication Relationships

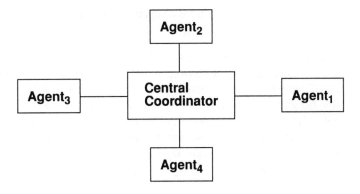

Pictures such as this are immensely useful in helping us understand the operation of a complex, concurrent system. For this reason, ROOM uses a notation that explicitly identifies communication paths between objects. These paths are called *bindings*. The graphical notation for a binding is a continuous line that interconnects two ports. An example of a formal ROOM diagram with a binding is shown in Figure 6.7. Here the binding B connects two ports, a1 and b1, on actors ActorA and ActorB, respectively.[5]

Figure 6.7   A Binding

6.4.1.1   Protocol Compatibility Rules

To ensure consistency of specifications, only ports with compatible protocols can be bound to each other. Clearly, two ports are compatible if one of them is a conjugate of the other. This is the most common case in practice. However, port compatibility is defined more broadly. Two ports are considered *compatible* if the following conditions hold:

- For each port, every message type in the outgoing message set of one port protocol is a member of the incoming message set of the other port protocol. This means that any outgoing message sent by either port can be received by the other. On the other hand, a port protocol may be capable of receiving additional messages that are not available in the outgoing set of the other end.

- The two protocols have compatible message sequence sets.

- The two protocols have equivalent qualities of service.

Until a more rigorous theoretical foundation is established for dealing with message sequences and quality of service, we will disregard the last two conditions and settle for a simplified working definition of port compatibility that is based solely on the first condition listed. This condition can be expressed more formally as the *compatibility of protocols*. If P_1 is a protocol class with a set of incoming message types I_1 and a set of outgoing message types O_1, and P_2 is a protocol class with a set of incoming message types I_2 and a set of outgoing message types O_2, then protocol classes P_1 and P_2 are said to be *compatible* if O_1 is a subset of I_2 and O_2 is a subset of I_1. That is, if

---

[5] In Figure 6.7, as well as other diagrams in this and subsequent chapters, the names attached to model components (such as ports and bindings) tend to be terse and cryptic. This is a consequence of the physical limitations on the size of diagrams imposed by the standard book format and definitely does not reflect a style recommended by the authors. Common sense dictates that, in practical situations, the names chosen to identify the components of a model should be far more descriptive.

$$P_1 = <I_1, O_1> \text{ and } P_2 = <I_2, O_2>$$

then P_1 and P_2 are compatible if and only if

$$O_1 \subseteq I_2 \text{ and } O_2 \subseteq I_1$$

Note that the compatibility relationship is *transitive*, which means that, if P_1 is compatible with P_2 and P_2 is compatible with P_3, then P_1 and P_3 are also compatible. However, in the general case, it is a nonreflexive relationship—a protocol is not compatible with itself unless it happens to be a symmetric protocol.

6.4.1.2   The Semantics of Bindings

In essence, a binding is a graphical abstraction for an underlying communication channel whose function is to convey messages from one port to the other. In ROOM, the precise semantics of these channels are *neither idealized nor predefined*. Instead, they are determined by the protocols that are associated with the ports at the ends of the binding. Different bindings can, therefore, have very different characteristics. For example, if the associated protocol provides only outgoing signals (which means that its conjugate only allows incoming signals), then the binding represents a unidirectional (simplex) channel. In all other cases, it represents a bidirectional (duplex) channel. Similarly, the communication properties of channels (such as the probability of loss, duplication, or reordering, as well as transmission delays and similar characteristics), are determined by the quality of service associated with the protocol.

A port that is not bound cannot receive messages (such as port a2 on ActorA in Figure 6.7). Conversely, messages sent out through an unbound port are lost and cannot have any effect on other actors.

6.4.1.3   Contracts

An actor often has multiple ports. The significance of individual ports may depend on the specifics of the application in which the actor appears (recall that actor specifications are potentially reusable in multiple applications). It is quite possible that in some applications, one or more ports of an actor may be intentionally left unbound. This indicates that the activities normally undertaken through those ports are not relevant for this application. On the other hand, if a port is bound, that means that the interaction achieved through that port is critical to this application. In other words, the set of bound ports of an actor identify its "contractual" obligations in a particular application context.

We formalize this notion by introducing the auxiliary concept of contracts. A *contract* consists of a binding and the two interface components that it connects. We say that an actor *satisfies* a particular contract if it has an interface component that is part of the contract.

If we abstract out the mechanics of communication (but not necessarily its effects), we can think of bindings as representing relationships between objects. The "meaning" of these relationships is defined by the protocols associated with a binding and can be indicated by choosing suitable names for the bindings and the actors. For example, simple relationships (such as the relationship between a database server and a client) can be modeled by an actor structure diagram such as the one shown in Figure 6.8.

Figure 6.8   A Simple Entity-Relationship Model Represented as Two Actors and a Binding

In other words, actor structure diagrams can be interpreted as entity-relationship diagrams [Codd70] with the actors representing the entities and the bindings modeling the relationships. This isomorphism is not surprising since the majority of relationships between entities ultimately require direct communication. Furthermore, since the protocols associated with the ports specify expected behavior, ROOM structural diagrams can provide much clearer insight into the semantics of a relationship than is possible with traditional entity-relationship models.

We will return to this topic later in the chapter and show how even more intricate relationships between objects can be modeled with structure diagrams.

6.4.2   Actor Structures

Bindings and ports provide the means to assemble arbitrarily complex aggregates of actors or other high-level structures. The graphical representations of these aggregates clearly and explicitly identify all the components that constitute a system, as well as all their relationships. Perhaps equally important as showing which relationships exist, is showing explicitly which relationships do *not* exist (indicated by the absence of a binding between two actors). One of the major causes of architectural decay is the introduction of *ad hoc* couplings between the elements of an architecture that were meant to be kept separate. For example, in the centralized system shown in Figure 6.6, it may have been the intent to keep the individual agents decoupled from each other in order to simplify their implementation.

Assuming the availability of a suitable library of standard parts, creating actor structures is similar to assembling toy blocks. The required parts are picked out of a library of actor classes and then connected together with bindings. If an appropriate block does not exist in the library, a new one is defined. Figure 6.9 illustrates a typical actor structure: a database manager that manages two separate databases (the databases may be duplicated for fault tolerance). Note that even this simple structure captures several important architectural decisions. First, clients accessing the database through port a on the database manager need not be aware of the redundancy in the database system, since they never access the databases directly. In addition, if the individual databases have different access protocols, the clients are not affected. Finally, the databases themselves are unaware of each other or the need to synchronize their contents, since all the coordination is handled by the manager. This simplifies their implementation by allowing them to focus purely on database issues.

Figure 6.9 A Simple Actor Structure

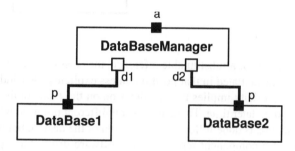

6.4.3 Generic Actor Structures

Genericity is a feature that allows a single specification to represent a set of individual specifications [Meyer88]. This usually is achieved through some form of parameterization so that individual specifications are obtained from the generic one by substituting different values for the parameters. One of the primary mechanisms for implementing genericity in ROOM is through the concepts of actor types and contracts.

Consider the structural specification in Figure 6.9. In this case, the responsibilities (obligations) of any component (actor reference) in the structure are determined by its contracts. For example, the database manager must satisfy the contracts involving its ports d1 and d2. On the other hand, in this application, the manager has no responsibilities regarding port a since that port is not contracted. The *contracted type* of a component actor in an application context is defined by the subset of all of its external interface components involved in contracts. Since the interface of an actor defines its externally observable behavior, in principle, any actor class that satisfies the contracted type of an actor reference could be put in its place without affecting the overall functionality of the aggregate. From this perspective, any structure specification can be considered as generic.

In general, this may be too flexible. To control the use of genericity, in ROOM it is necessary to explicitly designate an actor reference in a structure as being *substitutable*. A reference marked in this way can be replaced by an incarnation of an actor of another class that can satisfy the contracted type of the component. This substitution takes place when the actor is instantiated. The graphical notation for substitutability is a "**+**" icon placed in the upper left-hand corner of the actor reference (see Figure 6.10).

Figure 6.10   Graphical Notation for a Substitutable Actor Reference

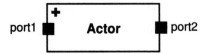

In case of a substitutable reference, the class of that reference specifies the *default* class to be instantiated in that position unless explicitly overridden.

Genericity implies that the decision on the final configuration of the model is deferred for some later time. There are several different points at which this can be resolved. In one case, this is done following completion of the design, but prior to its execution. For example, if a component represents the software driver for a printer, it may be designated as substitutable since different installations may have different types of printers. At any given site, the type of printer is known so that the information can be specified and the software modified appropriately before starting up the program. In ROOM, this customization of software during installation is referred to as *configuration*.

In other situations, the appropriate class will depend on some dynamic circumstances established only after the program has started executing. In that case, genericity must be resolved at run time when the actor component is instantiated. Details of how this is done are discussed in Chapter 10.

6.5   Hierarchical Structures

In many situations, it is useful to treat a particular actor structure (such as the database assembly in Figure 6.9) as a single conceptual unit that is part of some larger system. This allows us to abstract out the particulars of the relationship between the components of a structure. Such abstraction can be achieved with the standard technique of enclosing the desired subassembly within an abstraction shell. However, this seems to have the unpleasant consequence of introducing yet another type of object (an aggregate) into the modeling process. As in the case of actors and data objects, this new object type should conform to some formal semantics and syntax. Furthermore, it is reasonable to assume that, at some point, we will need to combine such aggregate objects into yet higher-level aggregates, and so on. This raises the spectre of an ever-expanding spiral of different object types until the whole thing becomes intellectually unmanageable.

The approach taken in ROOM is to circumvent this problem by taking advantage of the simple, yet effective, idea of recursion.

6.5.1 Composite Actors

The entire assembly in Figure 6.9 can be encapsulated by a single *composite actor* as shown in Figure 6.11a (the database "system" actor). This new actor has the usual actor semantics. It has an opaque encapsulation shell and it can even have its own interfaces (such as port rp) through which it can communicate with other actors. Like all actors, it is defined by a class specification that includes, as one of its attributes, the specification of the contained structure. Viewed from the outside, a composite actor reference is not visibly different from any other actor (Figure 6.11b). Consequently, it can be incorporated as a part of the structure of some other composite actor. This process of actor encapsulation can be applied to any depth, allowing the construction of arbitrarily complex hierarchical structures.

Since the actor concept is defined recursively, there is no need to define a separate concept to represent some top-level "system." A system is simply an incarnation of some actor class. This approach yields flexibility in allowing arbitrary application-specific decomposition strategies. It also opens up the possibility of easily embedding any given system within a greater context.

Composite actors represent reified abstractions and are the basis for formalizing the abstraction process. This ability to formally specify abstract entities is key to the ability to express and retain high-level design intent throughout the development process. In ROOM, all abstractions are explicit and are retained even in the implementation.

Figure 6.11   A Composite Actor

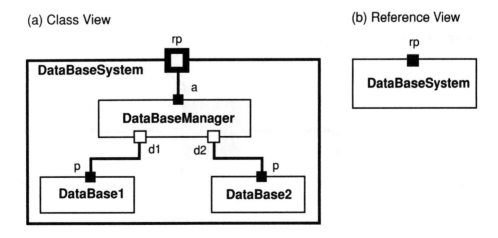

The space enclosed by an encapsulation shell is referred to as a *decomposition frame*. All component actors that appear in the same decomposition frame are called *peer* actors, since they are all at the same level of abstraction. These actors represent part of the implementation specification of the class of the composite actor.

6.5.2   Relay Ports

Port rp, which appears on the outside of the composite actor, is known as a *relay port* since it relays incoming external messages to a contained actor and also relays outgoing messages from the contained actor to the outside. A relay port has two sides: an "outward" side that faces the environment and an "inward" side that looks within the actor (Figure 6.12). The protocol P that is associated with a relay port is always defined with respect to the *outward* side. That is, incoming messages for the relay port are defined to be messages that flow into the actor. Note that on the inward side, the polarity of the protocol is reversed so that the inward side uses the conjugate protocol. Consequently, the binding compatibility rules remain unchanged for relay ports.

6.5.3   Customized Functional Combinations

Relay ports and their associated internal bindings are mechanisms by which an actor can selectively export the capabilities of its components. This, in turn, allows the defining of components that can combine almost arbitrary functional capabilities in a fairly straightforward manner. For example, assume that we have in some library a component that implements a functional capability S1, which it provides through a port interface component, and another component in the same library that provides a different capability, S2, also through a port interface component (Figure 6.13). We can now easily construct a new component that simultaneously provides both capabilities by combining them in a common composite actor, as shown in Figure 6.13. (The "coordinator" actor ensures that the

Figure 6.12   The Two Sides of a Relay Port

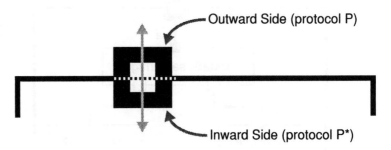

operation of the two independent server actors is synchronized and may not be necessary in all cases.)

Figure 6.13 Combining the Functionality of Different Actors

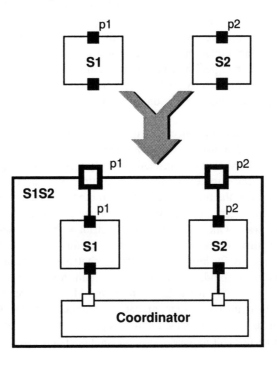

Note that this ability to mix and match actor components to create new functional composites practically removes the need for multiple inheritance. Another way of viewing relay ports is as a special form of *delegation*, a mechanism by which an object delegates responsibility for performing an operation to some other object [Wegner87]. The run-time cost of delegation in this case is negligible, since messages are delivered directly to the target actor without being intercepted by the containing actor. This technique is similar to the notion of mixins [Stefik86]. Mixins are "ancillary" classes with very specialized functionality that can be combined with another class to augment its functionality.

6.5.4   Complex Relationships as Composite Actors

In Section 6.4.1.3, we noted that bindings can be used to model simple relationships between objects. However, *one of the most common uses of composite actors is to model complex relationships between two or more objects.* This is based on the simple observation that components encapsulated in a common composite actor must be related in some way. The nature of this relationship usually can be determined from the stated purpose of the encapsulating actor.

For example, consider the situation in which two telephone subscribers are involved in a telephone call. It is quite natural to imagine this relationship as a distinct object that "incorporates" the two parties. (The degree to which this matches our intuition is revealed by the fact that we use the word "call," a noun, to describe this situation.) The advantage of modeling a relationship as an object is that it makes it feasible to operate on the relationship as a logical machine. For instance, we can add a third party to an existing telephone call by directly "asking" the telephone call object to include the new subscriber within itself. This "reification" approach to modeling relationships can significantly simplify the models.

The relationship object provides a common focus for dealing with the individual members of a relationship and allows them to be decoupled. In our example, to add another party to an existing call, instead of notifying each individual party already involved in the call, it suffices to contact the relationship object (a much simpler task). This, of course, assumes that the relationship actor is more than just an encapsulation shell and that it has innate intelligence that captures the semantics of the relationship. This can be done in one of two ways. One possibility is to distribute the necessary behavior among the member objects themselves (see Figure 6.14a). In this approach, each object takes on part of the responsibility for implementing the semantics of the relationship. The number of bilateral relationships (bindings) required to sustain this grows with the square of the number of members ($O(n^2)$). If another member is added to the relationship, then all the other members must change to accommodate it. Another problem with this arrangement is that the knowledge of one specific relationship is so deeply imbedded within the members that it becomes difficult to reuse the same components in different relationships.

Figure 6.14 Two Ways of Modeling Complex Relationships as Actors

(a) Distributed Model   (b) Centralized Model

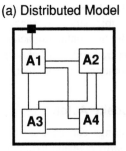
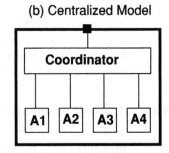

A second way of dealing with complex relationships is to connect each member to a central *coordinator* (or "moderator") object, as shown in Figure 6.14b. This not only simplifies the topology (the number of bindings grows linearly $(O(n))$ with the number of members), but it also completely decouples the members from each other for greater reuse potential. The individual members must only synchronize with the coordinator, which is usually simpler. Finally, the responsibility for the semantics of the relationships are concentrated primarily in a single object, the coordinator, for easier comprehension and modification.

The use of composite actors and coordinator objects is a common heuristic technique for modeling complex application-specific relationships in ROOM.

6.6   The Linkage Between Structure and Behavior[6]

The structural view we have described up to this point makes no mention of behavior. If actors are just hollow shells that contain other actors, where is the source of behavior? One obvious location for behavior is in the "leaf" actors, actors that are not decomposed into component actors. The simplicity of this approach is appealing, but has one serious drawback. This is because an actor is strongly encapsulated, so that any entities outside its encapsulation shell are not visible in its context. (Recall that this was imposed by the objective of maximizing reuse.) Since a leaf actor has no internal components, its behavior cannot reference other actors. However, in real-time systems it is frequently necessary to reference other actors to dynamically create and destroy them as the need arises. This means that some behavior, somewhere, must be able to reference these actors.

6.6.1   The Behavior Component

ROOM resolves this dilemma by introducing behavior through a special optional component called the *behavior component* (or simply, the "behavior") of an actor. In contrast to other components in a composite actor, the behavior is not a reference to some other actor class, but is an attribute of the actor class that contains it. Leaf actors, by definition, only include behavior.

The behavior of an actor has the following distinguishing properties:

- It is created and destroyed automatically with its containing actor.
- It is "pure" behavior and has no internal high-level structure.
- It can share interface components with its containing actor.
- It can directly reference all its peer actors in its decomposition frame.
- It is not rendered explicitly in the graphical ROOM notation for actor structures.

---

[6] This section only discusses the structural aspects of behavior. A detailed description of how behavior is specified in ROOM is provided in Chapter 8.

Figure 6.15   The Behavior Component of an Actor (Informal Representation)

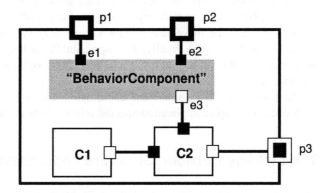

Ignoring the last point for the moment, consider an actor that, in addition to two other components (C1 and C2), has a behavior component represented by the shaded rectangle in Figure 6.15. In this informal diagram, the behavior is viewed as another component in the structural decomposition.

The ROOM graphical notation uses several shortcuts in order to minimize the visual clutter of structure diagrams. These are illustrated in Figure 6.16.

Figure 6.16   The Behavior Component of an Actor (Actual Representation)

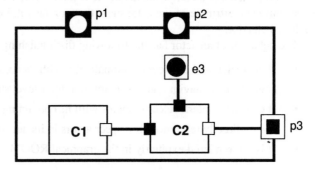

6.6.2   End Ports

The most obvious difference between the two representations is that in the second diagram (Figure 6.16), the behavior component is not shown. This is because it is implicit. Its presence can be inferred from the presence of special ports in the diagram called *end ports*. These ports are identified by a special graphical symbol: a circle within a square (ports p1, p2, and e3 in the diagram). The distinguishing feature of end ports is that they can be directly referenced by the behavior. In fact, *end ports are the link between structure and behavior* since they are visible in both modeling dimensions. (Relay ports, on the other hand, are purely structural elements that lie outside the scope visible to the behavior.)

The entire white space representing the actor's decomposition frame can be used to access the implicit behavior component simply by placing an end port in the desired spot (for example, port e3).

The second graphical shortcut in Figure 6.16 is the removal of the trivial bindings that link relay ports p1 and p2 to the corresponding ports on the behavior (e1 and e2, respectively). These are replaced by end ports that appear on the border of the encapsulation box (which makes them part of the interface of the actor).

6.6.3   Classification of Ports

At this point, it is worth reviewing the different kinds of ports that we have encountered. The three different kinds are as follows:

- *Relay ports* appear on the interface of the actor and may be connected to a component actor. Messages coming through a relay port are *not* seen by the behavior component. For example, messages arriving on port p3 in Figure 6.16 are funneled directly to component C2 without disturbing the behavior component. If a relay port is not connected to an internal component, all messages arriving on that port are lost.

- *External end ports* are ports that are part of the interface of the actor and that are connected directly to the behavior (for example, ports p1 and p2).

- *Internal end ports* are ports that are used to connect the behavior component to an internal component actor (port e3, for example). These ports are not visible from the outside of the actor since they are part of the internal decomposition of the actor.

Relay ports and external end ports are called *interface ports*, since they appear on the interface of an actor. Note that the distinction between relay and external end ports is not discernible from the outside.

6.6.4   Behavior as the Coordinator

In Section 6.5.4, we discussed a convenient modeling heuristic that recommended the use of common coordinator objects in situations where it was required to synchronize the activities of a number of peer actors (see Figure 6.14b). The function of the coordinator can be performed by the behavior component of an actor, as shown in Figure 6.17.

Figure 6.17   The Behavior as a Coordinator

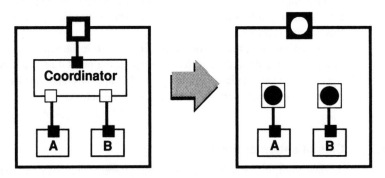

This approach has the advantage of reducing the number of actor classes by one, since the coordinator and the encapsulating actor are the same actor. However, this technique applies only if the function of the coordinator can be realized as a single actor.

6.7   Multiple Containment

Depending on the perspective chosen, the spark plugs in an internal combustion vehicle can be considered either as part of the electrical system or as part of the engine system. Both views are equally valid and equally useful. Multiple views are crucial in constructing and understanding large systems that are too complex to be comprehended in their entirety. In a physical system such as a vehicle, this apparent conflict is of little concern, since both the electrical "system" and the engine "system" are purely intellectual aggregations of parts. In ROOM, however, abstractions are reified as composite actors that encapsulate other actors. In order to support such overlapping abstractions, it is necessary to allow actors to simultaneously belong to more than one composite actor. This feature is called *multiple containment* (or "multiple part of").

Consider the case of the simple database system introduced previously in Figure 6.11. If we examine either of the database actors in more detail, we may find that it consists of two component actors, as shown in Figure 6.18. The first of these is a file system comprising one or more files (encapsulated within the file system actor), while the second is a device driver. The driver component is the software interface to the physical storage device (not shown, since it is in a separate architectural layer) and performs basic internal control functions on it (such as diagnostic testing, initialization, and fault recovery). The file system communicates with the interface to perform the standard data read and write operations through port d.

Figure 6.18 A Database Actor

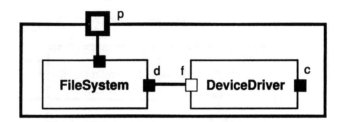

Each device driver has two ports—port f is used to accept requests from the file system and port c is used to accept signals from an external controller (for example, control inputs such as start, stop, and reset). Let us assume that all the device drivers in the system are controlled by a single devices controller and that this controller, along with the device drivers, comprises a distinct devices subsystem (Figure 6.19). This new subsystem is generic and independent of any particular file system or database application.

Figure 6.19 The Devices Subsystem

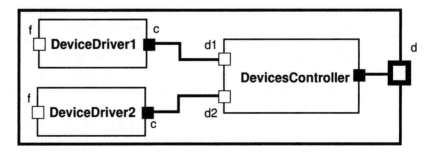

This an example of *multiple containment*. The overlapping structures are shown in Figure 6.20. (Note that this diagram is informal and is included for illustrative purposes. Such overlapping representations are not part of the formal ROOM graphical syntax.)

Figure 6.20   A Multiple Containment Structure

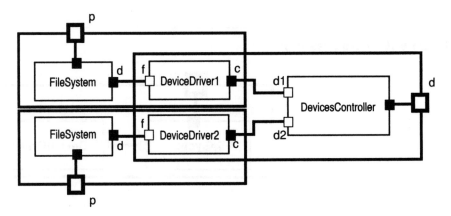

Each device driver is simultaneously part of the devices subsystem, as well as part of the appropriate database actor. However, in spite of the apparent overlap of the devices subsystem and the database actors (since they share common components), the two abstractions are still independent of each other. The database actors are completely unaware of the devices subsystem, and vice versa. For example, we may decide at some point to restructure or even eliminate the devices subsystem, and this will have no effect on the database actors. This is precisely the type of separation of concerns that we want to achieve through abstraction and encapsulation. Of course, the device drivers still must deal with the potentially conflicting demands of the different worlds, but this is no different than the case of any actor that has multiple ports.

Notice that the device driver actors are connected by way of different ports in the two views. Each view can be considered as a different role that an actor must fulfill. In the database actor view, a driver is accessed through its client port f, whereas in the devices subsystem view it is connected by way of its controller port c. The provision of multiple interface components on an actor provides a formal basis for the concept of multiple containment. Each port of an actor can be connected in at most one view (composite actor).

The specification that an actor reference is involved in multiple containment relationships is an attribute of the reference and not of the class specification of that actor. For example, it is quite possible to devise a system in which neither the database actors nor the devices subsystem abstractions exist, so the base component actors (file systems, device drivers, device controller, and the database manager) are directly interconnected in a complex nonhierarchical structure.

Since the devices subsystem and the individual database actors also are unaware of each other, the question then is, in what scope is the multiple containment specification defined? To understand this, let us look at a hierarchical view of a larger system (called the "storage system") that contains both the devices system and the complete database system from Figure 6.11. A graph-based notation of the complete decomposition hierarchy is more convenient for this purpose and is depicted in Figure 6.21. The shared components are underlined.

Figure 6.21 The Containment Hierarchy of the Storage System

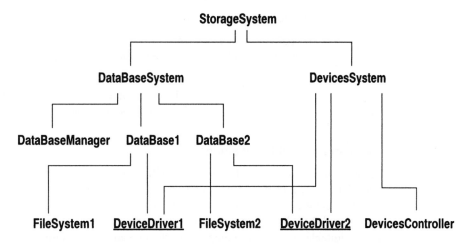

The multiple containment specification is an attribute of the *first common containing actor*. Placing it at any level below that would result in an undesirable coupling between two or more distinct actor specifications, since at least one would have to reference the others. This would reduce the reuse potential of the actor specifications. For example, if the multiple containment specification was to be associated with the device subsystem actor and the database system actors, then these two actor specifications would become mutually dependent and could not be used independently of each other. On the other hand, placing the specification at a level higher than the first common container class would unnecessarily couple the higher levels to the internal structures of their components.

6.7.1   Equivalences

In order to understand the mechanisms behind multiple containment, we first must examine how to distinguish individual actors in a hierarchy. In a decomposition hierarchy graph, each actor is uniquely identified by a directed path taken from the root of the graph to that actor. For example, the path leading to the devices controller component is specified as

/StorageSystem/DevicesSystem/DevicesController

Multiple contained actors can be reached by more than one path. Each separate path is called an *aspect,* and it represents one view, or role, of the actor. The set of all aspects that lead to a given component actor is called an *equivalence.* For example, the equivalence for component DeviceDriver1 is defined by

E_{DD1} = {/DevicesSystem/DeviceDriver1,
        /DataBaseSystem/DataBase1/DeviceDriver1}

while the equivalence for the second device driver component is defined by

E_{DD1} = {/DevicesSystem/DeviceDriver2,
        /DataBaseSystem/DataBase2/DeviceDriver2}

These equivalences are part of the class specification of the storage system actor.

It is important to keep in mind that the different aspects of an equivalence are not different objects, but just different "identifiers" for a single object.

6.7.2   The Semantics of Equivalences[7]

Consider the situation depicted in Figure 6.22. Actor A has a component A1 with a port a. Actor B has a component B1 with a port a and a port b. Assume that port a on actor A1 and port a on actor B1 are of the same type (that is, the same protocol). The question is, if actors A and B are both components in some common container and actor A1 is designated as substitutable, can the two component actors A1 and B1 be equivalenced? At first glance, it may seem that this should not be feasible since the two actors are obviously of two different types. On the other hand, if we look at this issue from the viewpoint of roles then the answer is different. From the perspective of actor A, all that is required of component A1 is that it fulfill the contract specified by the protocol on port a. Similarly, in actor B, the only expectation of component B1 is that it conform to the behavior implied by the protocol associated with port b. Clearly, a component that meets both contracts simultaneously (for example, B1) is, in principle, compatible with both sets of expectations.

If actors A1 and B1 can be placed in an equivalence, what is the class of the actor that is actually created when the model is executed? In this case, it must be the class of B1 (as

---

[7] This section contains advanced material and may be omitted on first reading.

Figure 6.22   Equivalence Drawn Between Actors of Different Classes

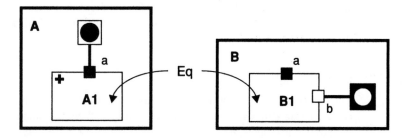

opposed to the class of A1) since only actors of this class can simultaneously meet both contracts.

To summarize the rules that control the semantics of equivalences, we first introduce the auxiliary concept of a contracts set. Previously, we formally defined a contract as a binding and its associated ports. The *contracts set* of an equivalence is the complete set of contracts satisfied by all its members. The rules that must be met for a valid equivalence are as follows:

- Each contract in the contracts set of an equivalence must be satisfied exactly once (that is, an interface component cannot be bound in more than one "view").
- At least one of the members must be of an actor class such that it has an interface component for every protocol in the contracts set. This class is called a *common compatible class* of the equivalence.
- Components whose classes are not the same as the common compatible class must be designated as substitutable.

The common compatible is the class of the object that is actually created when the system executes. It is possible for more than one common compatible to exist for a given equivalence.

6.8   Dynamically Modifiable Structures

We now turn our attention to the temporal properties of structures.[8] The primary purpose of actor structures is to specify explicitly which object relationships are valid. However, up to this point, all of the structures discussed were static. In Chapter 2, we noted that

---

[8] In this section we only look at the *representational* aspects of dynamically modifiable structures. This is complemented by a description of the *operational* aspects of these structures in Section 10.2.3.

most real-time systems are highly dynamic. In these systems, objects are being continually created and destroyed, and the relationships between them keep changing. What is needed then is to enhance the graphical structural specifications to allow modeling of dynamically changing structures. That is, we must make the pictures move.

The two primary forms of dynamic structure in ROOM are dynamic actors and dynamic relationships.

6.8.1   Dynamic Actors

The component actors shown in previous actor structure diagrams were examples of *fixed* actors. These actors are created simultaneously with their containing actor. In order to deal with dynamic objects, ROOM introduces the concept of *optional* actors. These are *not* created with the creation of their containing actor, but may be created subsequently. Furthermore, once it has been created, an optional actor can be destroyed. The graphical notation for an optional component actor is shown in Figure 6.23 (actor reference OptActor).

Figure 6.23   A Composite Actor with an Optional Actor Reference

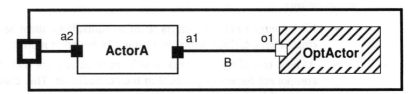

Note that the optionality of an actor is an attribute of the actor reference, rather than an attribute of the actor class. This conforms to the principle of maximizing the reuse potential of class specifications.

When an optional actor is created dynamically, all its fixed component actors automatically are created along with it. (Note that this implies, from a global perspective, that a fixed actor is not necessarily always present. Its existence is tied to the existence of its containing actor.)

Creation and destruction of optional actors is driven by the behavior component of the containing actor, since it is the only component that can reference other components in its decomposition frame. For this reason, it is not possible to destroy the behavior component.

When an optional actor is created, any bindings that are structurally linked to it (for example, binding B) are activated, so the underlying communication channels are ready to accept messages as soon as the actors are created.

When an optional actor is destroyed, all its component actors are destroyed along with it, unless they are part of a multiple containment relationship.

6.8.2 Dynamic Actor Relationships

A second form of dynamic structure occurs when an existing actor must enter into a dynamic relationship with another actor. For example, consider a prototypical client-server system in which a single server is shared among a number of clients. Assume that the server only can serve one client at a time, and that the need for service occurs unexpectedly. We can model this relationship by a "service usage" actor that incorporates the server and the current client, as shown in Figure 6.24. The problem, however, is that we do not know in advance which particular client will be involved in the relationship at a given time.

Figure 6.24 Imported Actor Reference

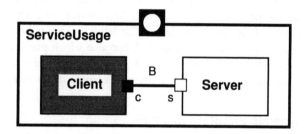

6.8.2.1 Imported Actor References

This situation is covered by the concept of an *imported* actor reference. An imported actor reference is a typed "placeholder" into which it is possible to *dynamically* insert an actor that already exists in some other decomposition frame. The graphical notation for imported actors is illustrated by the Client actor in Figure 6.24. To use a programming language analogy, an imported actor reference can be compared to a typed pointer declaration.

A particular actor incarnation can be placed into the imported actor slot by the behavior component of the containing actor. This operation is known as *importing*. The reverse operation is called *deporting*.

6.8.2.2 The Semantics of Importing

An actor can be inserted into an imported reference *only if it has a defined equivalence* (multiple containment) with respect to the imported actor reference. In other words, only components that have been explicitly designated can be imported into a given slot. Based on the rules of multiple containment (described in Section 6.7.2), the actor that can be inserted must not be of the same class as the class of the imported actor reference. Any class that is type-compatible with the contracts specified for the imported actor reference can be used. For example, the contract imposed on the imported actor reference in Figure 6.24 is defined by the binding B and ports c and s. Any component actor that can satisfy this contract (that is, it has an *unbound* port of the same type as port c) at the time the importing takes place, is a candidate that could be inserted in place of the client, provided that the appropriate equivalence has been defined.

Note that a separate equivalence must be defined for every actor that can be imported into an imported actor reference. This means that an imported actor reference can be part of many separate equivalences.

6.8.2.3   The Genericity of Importing

Like any component actor in a structure, an imported actor reference can be designated as substitutable. However, note that the restrictions imposed on imported references through equivalences allow a more refined control over parameter substitutability than most traditional polymorphic languages [Cardelli85]. This is because equivalences not only limit which classes can be substituted, but also which particular *references* can be substituted. This is crucial if architectural integrity is to be preserved, since architectural relationships usually are defined between object references rather than between object classes.

6.8.3   Dynamic Structure Example

To illustrate the pragmatics of dynamic structure, consider the example of a small four-line intercom system (see Figure 6.25). This system consists of four intercom sets attached to four independent voice-grade lines that are connected to a central switch. On demand from a user, the switch can establish a voice path between any two lines. To simplify the problem, we assume that the switch can handle only one call at a time.

Figure 6.25   A Simple Four-Line Intercom System

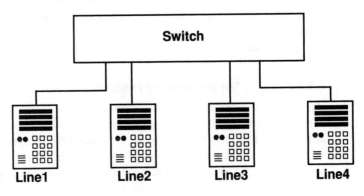

A user initiates an intercom call by activating the intercom and dialing the number of the desired party. The switch receives this information and determines the line to which the called party is attached. If the called line is idle, the switch sends a signal to the terminal to notify it of the incoming call. If the user at the other end answers the call by activating the set, the switch establishes a voice channel between the two lines. Either party can terminate the call by deactivating their set.

For our present purpose, we are only interested in modeling the structural aspects of the software inside the switch component of the system. This is depicted in Figure 6.26.

Figure 6.26 The High-Level Structure of the Intercom Switch Software

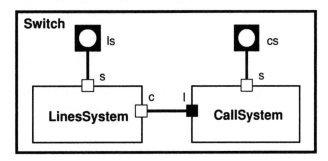

At this most abstract level, a switch is decomposed into two main subsystems: a "lines" system (responsible for controlling the operation of the physical communication lines) and a "call" system (responsible for processing intercom calls). This high-level separation is the result of the desire to decouple the two sets of concerns. Ideally, call processing should be independent of the particulars of the actual devices attached to the switch, since those are likely to change over time with evolving technology. A second reason is to control complexity. Namely, interacting with physical equipment (such as communication lines and intercom sets) can get quite complex and includes a plethora of low-level functions (such as detecting when a set has been activated, accumulating dialed digits, or ringing a set to warn of an incoming call). As much as possible, such mundane detail should be kept separate from the call-processing aspects that are already surprisingly complex. The two systems do communicate with each other to synchronize their activities.

The two subsystems are controlled by the behavior component of the switch. This component is primarily responsible for ensuring that the two systems are properly synchronized with each other (for example, following a power-up sequence).

The lines system has a simple structure shown in Figure 6.27. Each line is controlled through a software handler. Each handler has a port for communicating with the lines system whose behavior component acts as the coordinator for all lines.

The high-level structure of the call processing system is shown in Figure 6.28.

Figure 6.27   The Lines Subsystem of the Intercom Switch

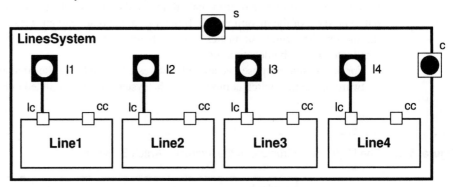

Since the system supports only one call at a time, there is only one call actor. The call actor is optional and is instantiated only if a call is in progress. Its internal structure is shown in Figure 6.29. It contains two imported actor references representing the two parties involved in a call. The class of these imported references is the same as the class of the line handlers.

Figure 6.28   The Calls Subsystem of the Intercom Switch

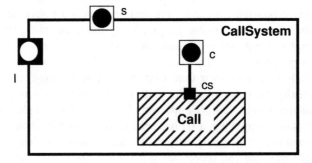

Notice that the imported references have been designated as substitutable (indicated by the "+" icon in the top left-hand corner). This accounts for possible system evolution in which, at some point, different intercom set types may have to be accommodated.

To complete the structure, we must establish equivalences between the imported actor references in the call and the individual line handlers in the lines subsystem. Since we do

Figure 6.29 The Structure of the Call Actor

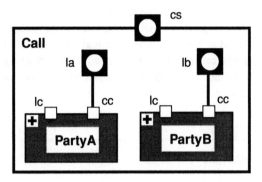

not know in advance the order in which the lines will become involved in the call, we must create an equivalence between each line handler and each party in the call. This yields a total of eight separate equivalences. These equivalences are specified as part of the switch actor class.

6.9   Replication

The example just described exposes a practical limitation of the graphical formalism as described so far: When the number of elements becomes large, the graphics get unwieldy. For example, if the number of lines attached to the switch grows to several dozen, representing each individual line as a separate actor is impractical. A second problem is that, in some cases, we may not know precisely how many elements will be required. The number may vary from case to case, or it may vary in time. In these situations, we would like to be able to express generic specifications in which the exact number of objects is a parameter.

If the graphical notation is intended to be used only during analysis and design, large numbers may be less of a concern. In analysis or design, large numbers often can be approximated by as few as two or three instances. However, since we require that the ROOM notation be capable of expressing actual implementation models, this information must be both explicit and precise.

For this purpose, ROOM provides the concepts of *replicated actors* and *replicated ports*. These are used for models in which multiple references to an actor or protocol class are included repeatedly *based on some regular pattern*. The regularity of form is exploited to provide a practical and compact way of representing large populations graphically. Replication is, in fact, a special form of abstraction. We ignore the differences between individual instances in favor of their common aspects in order to deal with the instances in a uniform way.

6.9.1   Replicated Actors

A replicated actor component in some structure is a shorthand way of representing multiple references of actors of the same actor class. The *replication factor* of a replicated actor is an integer value that specifies the maximum number of incarnations of that actor that can be created at run time. The graphical notation for a replicated actor is shown in Figure 6.30. The replication factor is indicated in the upper right-hand corner of the actor. In the diagrams, the actual literal can be replaced by a symbolic name that is defined as an integer constant.

Figure 6.30   A Replicated Actor

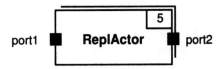

Replication is an attribute of an actor reference and not an attribute of an actor class. Thus, the decision whether to create one or more incarnations of a class is not limited by the class, but can be based on the needs of the application.

Replication semantics are a function of the type of actor that is replicated.

*   All incarnations of a *fixed* replicated actor are created automatically when the containing actor is instantiated. The number of incarnations is equal to the value of the replication factor.

*   Incarnations of an *optional* replicated actor are created dynamically and their number can vary from zero up to the number specified by the replication factor.

*   *Imported* actor references are filled in dynamically, as required, at run time. However, the maximum number of incarnations that can be imported in the slot reserved by a replicated imported actor is limited to the size of the replication factor.

If the replicated actor is substitutable, any compatible actor class can be inserted in place.

6.9.2   Replicated Ports

Replicated ports are collections of ports on a single actor that share the same protocol and name. They commonly are used to connect to replicated actors. The replication factor of a replicated port is an integer value that determines the number of incarnations of a port. The graphical notations for the replicated versions of different port types and views are shown in Figure 6.31 (including the direct and conjugated versions of each). The actual replication factor is not shown in the diagram but is specified along with other textual information that supplements the diagram.

Figure 6.31   Notation for Replicated Ports

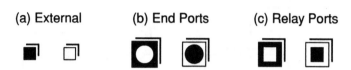

(a) External   (b) End Ports   (c) Relay Ports

A replicated port can be viewed either as a collection of individual ports, or as a single compound object. In the first case, sending and receiving messages through any particular incarnation has the usual port semantics. In the second case, the replicated port is considered as a single interface component that can participate in multiple, simultaneous contracts. Messages sent out through a replicated port (as opposed to messages sent through just one particular incarnation) are *broadcast* to all the destinations bound to the replicated port.

Both views are equally accessible. The choice of perspective is made within the behavior components based on the needs of the moment. The exact mechanisms involved in this are described in Section 10.2.4.

6.9.3   Common Replicated Structures

Replicated ports and actors can be combined to model standard architectural configurations. In Figure 6.32a, we see an example of one of the most common structures, the "star" configuration in which a set of components are connected to a common central node or hub. Figure 6.32b shows the equivalent structure without using replication.

The star configuration is used in the case of the so-called coordinator components (described in Section 6.5.4) in which the hub acts as a central intelligence that coordinates the activities of the agents. In many instances of the star configuration, the function of the hub component can be undertaken by the behavior component of the encapsulating actor. For example, the lines subsystem in the simple intercom system shown in Figure 6.27 can be modeled as shown in Figure 6.33.

Another common structure that can be represented easily with replication is the "bus" structure (Figure 6.34) in which two actors are interconnected through a series of parallel connections similar to the interconnection patterns between integrated circuits.

A third type of common structure involving replication is the so-called "array" structure in which a single interconnection pattern of two actors is repeated (Figure 6.35) multiple times.

Figure 6.32   A "Star" Structure Modeled with and Without Replication

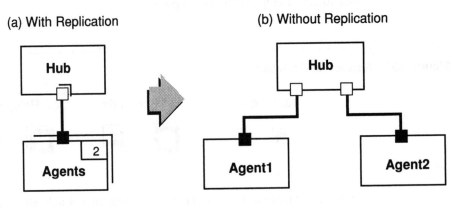

Figure 6.33   The Lines Subsystem of the Intercom Modeled with Replication

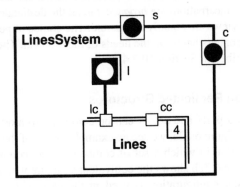

Figure 6.34   A "Bus" Replicated Structure

Note: A Replication Factor of 2 Is Defined for the Ports

Figure 6.35 An "Array" Replicated Structure

Finally, more complex regular structures also can be modeled with replicated ports and actors, as shown in Figure 6.36. The only restriction here is that these relationships hold between the various replication factors

$$n_A * p_A = n_B * p_B$$
$$p_A = k * p_B \quad k = 1, 2, 3,...$$

where n_A and n_B are the replication factors of actors A and B, respectively, and p_A and p_B are the replication factors of their corresponding ports.

Other, more complex combinations of replicated ports and actors also are possible, but are beyond the scope of this book. More information on this topic can be found in [ObjecTime92a].

Each binding connected to a replicated port is a distinct contract.

Figure 6.36 Complex Regular Structure Modeled with Replication

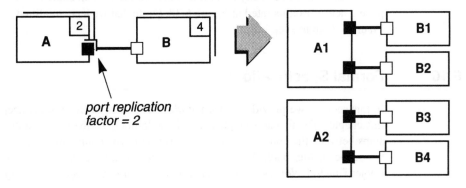

6.9.4   Replicated Port Splitting

In some cases, it is necessary to partition a replicated port among actors that are not repli-cated. This usually is done when the nonreplicated actors are not related to each other in any way (for example, they are of different classes). This can be achieved as shown in Fig-ure 6.37, as long as the protocols on the ports are compatible and the number of connected actors does not exceed the replication factor of the port.

Figure 6.37   Splitting of a Replicated Port

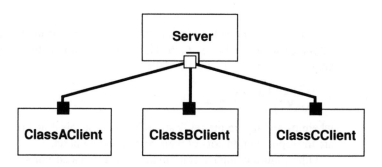

6.9.5   Replication and Multiple Containment

The semantics of replication can become quite complex when replication is combined with multiple containment and dynamic structure. A complete discussion of this issue can be found in [ObjecTime92a]. In this section, we limit our description to the most common situation.

In the intercom system (Section 6.8.3), we must indicate that any of the lines in the lines subsystem can call any other line. This is done with an equivalence between the com-ponent actors, as illustrated in Figure 6.38. (Note that we have modified the call actor from Figure 6.29 to use replication.)

6.10   Formal Specifications

In this section, we provide the formal *abstract syntax* of the main concepts introduced in this chapter. The formalisms presented here do not describe the semantics of the relation-ships between the concepts (such as the rules of type compatibility), since that is beyond the scope of this book. For readers interested in this level of detail, we refer them to [ObjecTime92]. *Note that the material in this section may be skipped on first reading.*

Figure 6.38 Multiple Containment and Replication

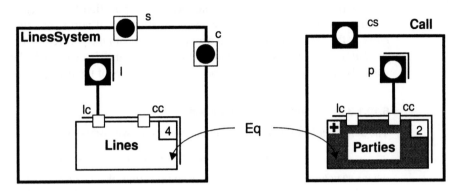

6.10.1 Actor Classes

An actor class is defined as a 4-tuple,

$$actor\text{-}class = <class\text{-}name, parent\text{-}class, actor\text{-}type, actor\text{-}implementation> \qquad (6\text{-}1)$$

where *class-name* is the symbolic name of the class and *parent-class* is the immediate parent class from which this class was derived. If this is a root class, then this component can be empty.[9]

6.10.1.1 Actor Interface

The type of an actor is defined by its interface,

$$actor\text{-}type = actor\text{-}interface \qquad (6\text{-}2)$$

where *actor-interface* is defined as,

$$actor\text{-}interface = <peer\text{-}interface, sp\text{-}interface, impl\text{-}interface> \qquad (6\text{-}3)$$

The latter two components (*sp-interface* and *impl-interface*) pertain to layering relationships and are defined in Chapter 7. The *peer-interface* of a class is defined as a set of zero or more *port references* representing the ports that appear on the outside of the actor,

$$peer\text{-}interface = \{port\text{-}ref_1, port\text{-}ref_2, ...\} \qquad (6\text{-}4)$$

6.10.1.2 Port References

Each port reference is defined as a composite of four elements,

---

[9] The topic of inheritance is discussed in Chapter 9.

$$port\text{-}ref_i = <port\text{-}ref\text{-}name_i, replic\text{-}factor_i, protocol\text{-}class_i, conjug\text{-}ind_i> \qquad (6\text{-}5)$$

The *port-ref-name$_i$* is the name of port reference i and it must be unique with respect to other port references in the peer interface. The replication factor *(replic-factor$_i \geq 1$)* is a positive integer that indicates how many incarnations of port i are defined. The *protocol-class$_i$* is the basic class of the protocol associated with the port reference. Finally, the *conjug-ind$_i$* is a Boolean *(conjug-ind$_i \in \{true, false\}$)* that indicates whether port i is conjugated. Both end ports and relay ports can be members of the peer interface set.

6.10.1.3   Actor Implementation

The *actor-implementation* of an actor consists of two components,

$$actor\text{-}implementation = <structure, behavior> \qquad (6\text{-}6)$$

where *structure* defines the internal decomposition of the actor and *behavior* defines the behavior component of the actor and may be an empty specification (for actor classes representing pure encapsulations). The formal definition of behavior components is provided in Chapter 8.

6.10.1.4   Actor Structure

The structure component of an actor's implementation is defined as the following 4-tuple,

$$structure = <behavior\text{-}interfaces, components, contracts, equivalences> \qquad (6\text{-}7)$$

The set of interface components that are directly accessible by the behavior component is defined by,

$$behavior\text{-}interfaces = <end\text{-}ports, saps, spps> \qquad (6\text{-}8)$$

where *saps* and *spps* are service access points and service provision points, respectively. These concepts are defined in Chapter 7. The ports that are directly accessible to the behavior component are defined by the following set:

$$end\text{-}ports = \{port\text{-}ref_a, port\text{-}ref_b, ...\} \qquad (6\text{-}9)$$

This set can be empty. Note that some of the port references in the *end-ports* set also can appear in the *peer-interface* set. These are the so-called external end ports,

$$external\text{-}end\text{-}ports = \{port\text{-}ref \,|\, (port\text{-}ref \in end\text{-}ports) \wedge (port\text{-}ref \in peer\text{-}interface)\} \quad (6\text{-}10)$$

From this we can define the set of relay ports of an actor as

$$relay\text{-}ports = \{port\text{-}ref \,|\, (port\text{-}ref \in peer\text{-}interface) \wedge (port\text{-}ref \notin external\text{-}end\text{-}ports)\} \qquad (6\text{-}11)$$

The full set of ports of an actor is defined by

$$ports = end\text{-}ports \cup relay\text{-}ports \qquad (6\text{-}12)$$

6.10.1.5 Actor Components

The set of component actors that form part of the implementation of an actor are specified by a possibly empty set of *actor references*,

$$components = \{actor\text{-}ref_1, actor\text{-}ref_2, ...\} \qquad (6\text{-}13)$$

where each actor reference is defined by the 5-tuple,

$$actor\text{-}ref_i = <actor\text{-}ref\text{-}name_i, replic\text{-}factor_i, actor\text{-}class_i, dyn\text{-}ind_i, subst\text{-}ind_i> \qquad (6\text{-}14)$$

where *actor-ref-name$_i$* is the name of actor component i, *replic-factor$_i$* is its replication factor, and *actor-class$_i$* is its actor class. Note that the name of the component must be unique for every component in the components set. The *dyn-ind$_i$* specifies the dynamical attribute of the component and can take on a symbolic value from the following set:

$$dyn\text{-}ind_i \in \{fixed, optional, imported\} \qquad (6\text{-}15)$$

Finally, the *subst-ind$_i$* ($\in \{true, false\}$) indicates whether component actor i is substitutable.

6.10.1.6 Contracts

The contracts within the structure part of an actor class are partitioned into contracts involving bindings and contracts involving layer connections.

$$contracts = <binding\text{-}contracts, connection\text{-}contracts> \qquad (6\text{-}16)$$

Contracts involving layer connections are defined in Chapter 7. Binding contracts are defined by the set

$$binding\text{-}contracts = \{b\text{-}contract_1, b\text{-}contract_2, ...\} \qquad (6\text{-}17)$$

where binding contract i is defined as

$$b\text{-}contract_i = <binding\text{-}name_i, end\text{-}point_1, end\text{-}point_2> \qquad (6\text{-}18)$$

Note that binding names do not have to be unique. The end points of a contract are specified by

$$end\text{-}point_i = <port\text{-}id_m, actor\text{-}id_n> , i = 1, 2 \qquad (6\text{-}19)$$

which can specify either a port reference on the actor itself,

$$port\text{-}id_m \in port \qquad (6\text{-}20)$$

$$actor\text{-}id_n = self \qquad (6\text{-}21)$$

or a port reference to an interface port on component actor,

$$actor\text{-}id_n. \in components \qquad (6\text{-}22)$$

$$port\text{-}id_m = peer\text{-}interface\text{-}name(m, class(actor\text{-}id_n)) \qquad (6\text{-}23)$$

where function *class(r)* returns the class of actor reference *r* and *peer-interface-name(k, c)* returns the port reference name of the *k*th interface port of actor class *c*.

6.10.1.7   Equivalences

The final components of the structure of an actor are the equivalences which are defined by the following set:

$$equivalences = \{equival_1, equival_2, ...\} \qquad (6\text{-}24)$$

An equivalence *equival$_i$* is defined by a name and a set of two or more path specifications,

$$equival_i = <equival\text{-}name_i, \{path_1, path_2, ...\}> \qquad (6\text{-}25)$$

The name of the equivalence must be unique for every equivalence in the equivalences set. A path specification can consist of a catenation of actor component identifiers at different decomposition levels,

$$path_i = actor\text{-}ref\text{-}name_m \, . \, actor\text{-}ref\text{-}name_n \, . \, actor\text{-}ref\text{-}name_p \, ... \qquad (6\text{-}26)$$

where "." is the catenation operator. The first element in the path, *actor-ref-name$_m$*, is the name of an actor reference that is part of the components set of this actor. The next element in the path must be the name of an actor component the class specification of *actor-ref-name$_m$*, and so on. A path must have at least one element.

6.10.2   Protocol and Message Classes

A protocol class is defined by the following 5-tuple:

$$protocol\text{-}class = <class\text{-}name, parent\text{-}class, messages, service, sequences> \qquad (6\text{-}27)$$

Components *class-name* and *parent-class* have the same meaning as equivalent components for actor classes (with the provision, of course, that the parent class of a protocol must be either empty or another protocol class). The valid messages of a protocol class are defined by the following two sets:

$$messages = <incoming\text{-}messages, outgoing\text{-}messages> \qquad (6\text{-}28)$$

Both the incoming and outgoing message sets consist of zero or more message types,

$$\{message\text{-}type_1, message\text{-}type_2, ...\} \qquad (6\text{-}29)$$

where each message type is defined by

$$message\text{-}type = <signal, data\text{-}class> \qquad (6\text{-}30)$$

The *data-class* attribute can be null, which means that messages of that type do not include any data in addition to the signal.

The quality of service specification (*service*) and the specification of all valid message sequences allowed by the protocol *(sequences)* will not be refined further (refer to Section 6.3).

6.11   Summary

The primary concepts introduced in this chapter (actors, protocols, ports, and bindings) are used to model architectures consisting of hierarchies of communicating concurrent objects. To support reuse, all specifications are captured in the form of classes. Since these are high-level specifications, they provide a level of reuse that has a much larger potential payback than simple code reuse.

An actor is a concurrent active object that hides its implementation from other actors in its environment. Each actor can have multiple interface components, called ports, through which it can communicate with other actors by exchanging messages. A message is a composite object consisting of a signal, a priority, and an optional message data attribute. Each port has an associated protocol that restricts the types of messages flowing through the interface component. The linkage of protocols with interface components means that a protocol is defined from the perspective of one of the ends involved in the protocol. In order to deal with asymmetric protocols, the conjugation operation is defined over protocol specifications. The separation of protocol specifications from the objects that they serve allows a strong form of polymorphism and increases the potential reuse of specifications. For example, the same protocol specification can be used for many different actor classes. The type of an actor is defined by the set of interface components (and their respective types) that appear on the outside of the actor.

Actors can be assembled into complex structures by interconnecting their ports with communication channels called bindings. In a more abstract view, these networked structures can be interpreted as entity-relationship models. Such aggregations of actors always are encapsulated within a higher-level composite actor specification. Through the concept of relay ports, such actors can selectively export the interfaces of their components. This means that the actor concept is recursive so that arbitrarily complex hierarchical actor structures can be constructed.

The ability to encapsulate actor structures with a containing actor means that an actor can be used as an abstraction facility that replaces the underlying aggregate with a single conceptual unit. This makes it suitable for modeling complex inter-actor relationships. In these cases, internal coordinator components are extremely useful, since they can capture all the essential semantics of such relationships and thereby reduce the need for tight coupling between the components involved in the relationships. This increases the flexibility and reuse potential of component actors.

A component of a structure can be designated as substitutable, which means that, when the actor is instantiated, that component can be replaced by a functionally equivalent component of another class. This feature means that actor specifications can be generic. A generic specification permits many different variants to be constructed, all of which preserve the design intent expressed in the original.

Each actor can optionally have a behavior component. This component can initiate activities by sending messages as well as respond to external messages. The ports of this component are called end ports and can be shared with the containing actor.

Complex systems can be viewed in many different ways. A single component can participate in two or more abstractions simultaneously. Since actor encapsulation is used as an abstraction mechanism, this means that an actor may have to be part of more than one decomposition. The multiple containment feature is used for this purpose. In this case, the ports of an actor are partitioned out among different "views" in the sense that a port can be bound in only one decomposition.

To model dynamic structures, ROOM provides two utilities. Optional actors are actors that can be created dynamically based on current needs. Imported actor references are used to allow an actor to dynamically enter into complex relationships. In this latter case, an actor reference in a decomposition acts as a placeholder into which some actor can be imported. Through the multiple containment feature, it is possible to explicitly specify which actors can be imported into an imported reference slot.

Finally, actor components in composite actors can be replicated. This allows graphical representation of complex systems involving a large number of actor incarnations. It can also be used to model situations in which the precise number of incarnations is not known at design time.

CHAPTER 7

Layering

Layering is a common form of abstraction that is used to reduce the apparent complexity of large systems. It is a variant of the traditional "divide-and-conquer" approach in which some complex functionality is dissected into a progression of layers, each of which can be understood independently of the layers above, and with only minimal knowledge of the layers below. In ROOM, layering represents the highest form of *structural* organization in a system. This simply means that, when we peel away the outermost encapsulation shell of a complex software system, the first thing typically revealed is a structure consisting of one or more layering hierarchies.

In this chapter, we describe the ROOM model of layering and investigate various practical techniques related to its application. The relative position of vertical structure within the ROOM conceptual framework is the same as high-level horizontal structure (see Figure 7.1). This is because, in ROOM, the concepts used to represent vertical structures overlap significantly with those used to model horizontal structures. In fact, a layer is simply a ROOM actor with some specialized interface requirements.

7.1 The Semantics of Layering Relationships

The top-level structure of many of today's complex software systems (such as operating systems or large distributed applications) is represented by layered diagrams (for example, Figure 7.2). Yet, despite its undeniable usefulness, layering is not directly supported as a first-class concept by any current mainstream programming language or modeling formalism. Layering seems to be one of those elusive concepts that is understood intuitively by almost everyone, but is quite difficult to pin down in a formal sense. A *semiformal* model of layering was developed in conjunction with the *open systems interconnection* (OSI) model under the auspices of the International Standards Organization (ISO) [Zimmerman80]. However, the scope of that work is limited to communications services.

In this section, we analyze the essential characteristics of layering with particular focus on its use in software systems. Our objective is to obtain enough insight to be able to provide

Figure 7.1   The ROOM Conceptual Framework: Layering

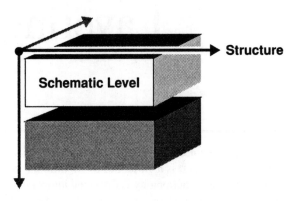

Figure 7.2   The Top-Level Structure of a Typical Operating System

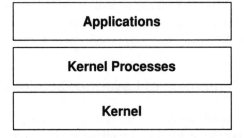

a formal model of layering. With formal support for layering, layered system architectures become not only more explicit and semantically precise, but also enforceable.

7.1.1   The Characteristics of Layering

Layers of the type that we are discussing here do not occur naturally in the physical world. They are just abstractions, mental aids devised to promote understanding. A layer boundary occurs at the point where we decide to perform a mental shift of focus. This usually happens when the amount of detail that we must track exceeds our capabilities. In order to make progress, some of the underlying detail is abstracted out, so that what remains becomes intellectually manageable.

As an example, consider the distinction made in physics between the "molecular" and "atomic" perspectives of matter. At the atomic level, we see complex structures composed of orbiting electrons and tightly packed bundles of nuclear particles. As we move above the threshold to the molecular level, these intricate subatomic structures are substituted by almost monolithic abstract particles, representing individual atoms.

What gets abstracted out (and how) depends very much on what we wish to accomplish. In quantum physics, for instance, an electron can be modeled either as a waveform or as a particle. These two models are different abstractions of the same underlying entity, and the choice of models is determined by the needs of the higher levels. Clearly, no detail that is relevant to the higher level needs should be eliminated, or as Albert Einstein put it, "The problem should be made as simple as possible, but no simpler."

As we move from a layer to the next higher one, we invariably introduce some qualitatively new concepts. Thus, at the molecular level, we see the concept of structured aggregates of atoms, or molecules. The basic mechanisms for this concept are provided by the lower level, although the concept itself is not defined there. One of the characteristics of layering, therefore, is that the abstracted lower-level entities serve as a ubiquitous "raw material" out of which we construct the higher-level objects and relationships. Usually, this material can be molded in many different ways. For example, we can construct a wide assortment of molecules out of a collection of atoms. This flexibility to use a common base to achieve a variety of different objectives is one of the key advantages of layering.

The concepts introduced in higher levels are usually more application specific than those of the lower levels. As a result, layer hierarchies tend to be quite specific on top and more general at the bottom.

Layering is a strictly *hierarchical* relationship. An upper layer's implementation depends on the lower layer (but not the other way around). This distinguishes layering from horizontal structural relationships (such as the peer relationship between two communicating actors that are bound in a common decomposition frame).

This hierarchical nature of layering sometimes leads to confusion with containment, a different form of hierarchical relationship. The principal difference is that, in layering, the upper layer does *not* contain the lower one (see Figure 7.3). The semantics of containment in software systems are usually such that the existence of a component is predicated by the existence of its container. When a container is destroyed, all its components are destroyed with it. This is not true for layers. If a higher layer is destroyed, the lower layer normally remains.

In many cases of layering (but not all), an upper layer's existence is critically dependent on the presence of its underlying layers. For example, an application program executing on top of an operating system would be destroyed if the underlying operating system were to fail. As noted previously, the lower layer provides the basic building blocks for constructing the objects of the upper layer. When those building blocks are destroyed, the upper level also is dissolved.

In summary, layering has enough singular properties to qualify as a fundamental type of relationship along with other fundamental relationship types that are explicitly modeled in ROOM (communication relationships, containment, and inheritance).

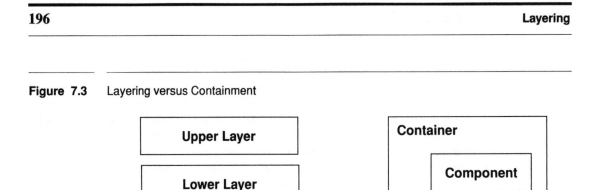

Figure 7.3   Layering versus Containment

7.1.2   Layering in Software Systems—Virtual Machines

In most software systems the layering relationship takes on a specific form. The lower layer can be viewed as a component of an abstract "virtual programmable machine" ([Allworth87]), while the upper layer represents the "program" that drives the operation of this virtual machine (see Figure 7.4). In this paradigm, the programmable facilities of virtual machines are called *services*.

The virtual machine concept often is applied recursively so that the desired machine is constructed through a series of two or more layers. For example, a program written in the BASIC language usually runs on top of an interpreter that is itself a program written to execute on some physical processor. Ultimately, all virtual machine hierarchies bottom out with some real (hardware) machine.

Note that virtual machine services need not be packaged together into a single monolithic entity. A virtual machine could be an aggregate of an assortment of services that may have been developed independently. Figure 7.4 shows an example of a virtual machine in which the services are spread across three modules.

Figure 7.4   Layering of Software: The Virtual Machine

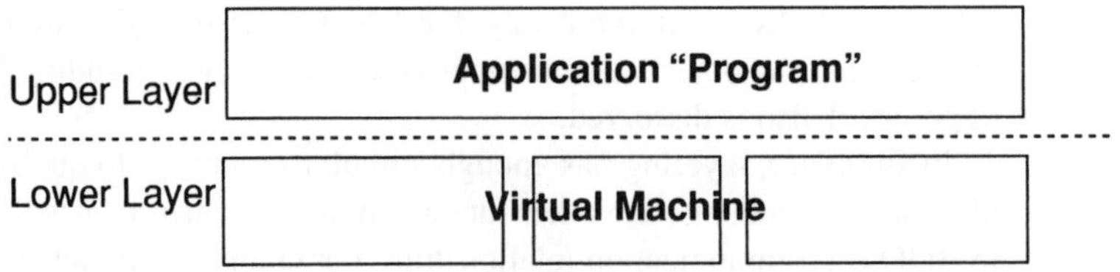

Upper Layer | **Application "Program"**

Lower Layer | **Virtual Machine**

7.1.3   The Dimensionality of Layering

Consider the layered diagram of a typical layered system shown in Figure 7.5. This system contains two cooperating application programs (Application1 and Application2). Assume that both of these programs use the same basic services—a user interface for interaction with human operators, a database service for persistent data storage, and a communications service. Assume further that all communication between the components of this system is achieved by way of the communication service. That includes communication between the database and its clients, as well as between the applications and the user interface. Naturally, all of these components also make use of the services of the underlying operating system (for example, to obtain dynamic memory).

Figure 7.5   A Complex System Layered in Two Dimensions

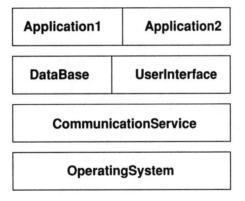

At first glance, the diagram in Figure 7.5 may seem to be a faithful rendering of the relationships between the layers, and, indeed, such diagrams are frequently encountered in the literature. However, one of the central tenets of layering is that a layer is dependent only on the interface of the layer immediately below and *not* on the layers further down the hierarchy.[1] Thus, in Figure 7.6, Layer (N + 1) depends on the interface of Layer (N) but has no access to Layer (N - 1).

---

[1] This is motivated by the desire to minimize coupling between layers. The dependency of Layer (N) on Layer (N-1) is part of the implementation detail of Layer (N). Hence, coupling Layer (N + 1) to anything but the interface of Layer (N) would constitute a violation of encapsulation [Zimmerman80].

Figure 7.6   Decoupling of Layers

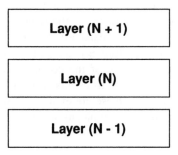

If we adopt the usual graphical convention that interaction is represented by the adjacency of layers, then Figure 7.5 is misleading, since it implies that only the Communication Service layer has access to the operating system. This is wrong, since we stated previously that all three upper layers make use of the operating system services. Furthermore, we must show that the two applications also have direct access to the Communication Service layer and are not separated from it, as suggested by Figure 7.5.

We can attempt to resolve this dilemma by resorting to a three-dimensional diagram, such as the one in Figure 7.7.[2] Here the diagram is closer to the actual structure, but is still inadequate. In this case, we had to leave out the operating system layer, which lies beneath all the other components, since it is not clear how to draw this in a meaningful way. If we maintain the common convention that only adjacent layers interact, graphical renderings are restricted to two dimensions so that the most we can represent in one diagram is a three-dimensional layering relationship by using perspective projection. Unfortunately, this is insufficient for most practical systems.

One alternative is to represent each individual layering relationship (or *service dimension*) by a separate diagram, as illustrated in Figure 7.8. For example, each of the two applications in Figure 7.5 has four service dimensions (the database dimension, the user interface dimension, the communication service dimension, and the operating system dimension). The complete layering structure for one application in this example requires four diagrams. This means that the virtual machine for the application consists of four modules. Another alternative, which we use in ROOM and which is discussed later, is to represent interaction by explicit arcs between layers, rather than by adjacency.

Note that the services also may have their own virtual machines. For example, the database service has a virtual machine comprising the communication service and the operating system.

---

[2] This particular structure is known as the "toaster" model because of its peculiar form.

Figure 7.7   A Multidimensional Layering Diagram

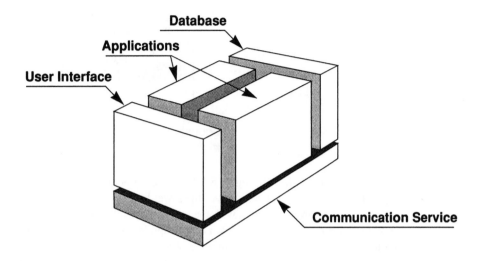

Figure 7.8   A Service Dimension

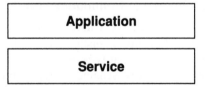

7.2   The ROOM Model of Layering

In ROOM, we are interested in formal models that can serve as a basis for executable specifications. The work done on the OSI layered system architecture mentioned previously represents the most extensive treatment of layering to date, and is used as the basis for the ROOM model. However, the OSI model focuses exclusively on communication services and must be generalized to be applicable to a wider domain.

A fundamental property of the OSI model is that all interactions between adjacent layers take place through discrete points on the interlayer boundary called *service access points*, or *SAPs* (see Figure 7.9).

Figure 7.9   The OSI Layer Interaction Model

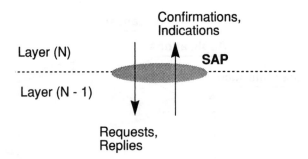

Information can flow through a SAP in either direction. In the downward direction, the upper layer makes *service requests* of the lower layer by invoking any one of a set of *primitives,* or operations associated with the service beneath the SAP. A typical service request might consist of a request to deliver a message to some remote peer entity, or to reply to requests made by a remote peer. In the upward direction, the lower layer notifies the upper layer of the arrival of messages originated by the remote peer (called *indications*) or of the results of processing a previous service request (*confirmations*).

Each of these elementary information exchanges also can carry data. The data is packaged into discrete message-like blocks called *interface data units*. The OSI model is general enough to accommodate both synchronous and asynchronous communications.

7.2.1   The ROOM Interlayer Communication Model

If we abstract away the specialized semantics of the OSI model (such as the notions of requests and confirmations, which imply communications between two peer entities), we can see considerable similarity between it and the message-based communications model used between peer actors. Sending messages corresponds to invoking primitives, message signals can be matched to primitive names, and message data objects are reminiscent of interface data units. The association of a set of service primitives with a SAP is similar to the concept of a typed port.

This symmetry is exploited in ROOM to provide a homogeneous communication model that is consistent for both vertical (interlayer) interactions and horizontal (peer) interactions. That is, the definitions of messages and protocols for interlayer communications are identical to the ones already specified in Chapter 6.

7.2.1.1   Service Access Points and Service Provision Points

To allow the individual layer entities to be decoupled from each other and treated as independently reusable objects, it is necessary to "split" the layer interface points into two parts so that each layer gets half of this interface. The upper part of the interface (a SAP) is attached to the upper layer. The bottom part is attached to the lower layer and is called a *service provision point* (SPP). This model is depicted in Figure 7.10. Note that this diagram does not represent the formal ROOM graphical notation.

Figure 7.10 Service Access Points and Service Provision Points

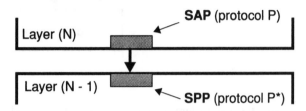

Each SAP and SPP has an associated communication protocol that determines its type. By definition, in ROOM, *the protocol of an SPP is conjugated*, whereas the protocol of a SAP is not.

7.2.1.2   Layer Connections

Since the upper and lower layers are distinct objects, it is necessary to explicitly connect a SAP in an upper layer to an appropriate SPP. Similar to the manner in which two ports are bound, this is achieved by a communication channel (similar to a binding) called a *layer connection*. This interaction model is general enough to allow the layers to be physically separated if so desired.

The graphical notation for a layer connection is a labeled, directed[3] arc between the two layers, as shown in Figure 7.11. The arrow points from the service user to the service provider. By convention, we will always attempt to draw the service user above the service provider but, strictly speaking, this is not necessary.

The graphical form of a layer connection does not explicitly specify which SAP connects to which SPP. (This information is specified by a complementary textual declaration as explained later.) In fact, ROOM does not use an explicit graphical notation for representing SAPs or SPPs. The reason for this is that, in most applications, the number of individual interlayer connections tends to be very large. This is because layers often are used to model shared services (as the raw material out of which the upper level objects are constructed). For example, assume that the lower layer in Figure 7.11 provides a generic file service, and that the upper layer is composed of a large number of objects, each of which

---

[3] This reflects the hierarchical nature of layering.

Figure 7.11   The Graphical Notation for a Layer Connection

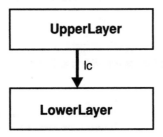

uses the file system as a service. If every individual usage link were to be explicitly defined, the resulting visual clutter could yield an almost useless graphical representation.

In order to get around this difficulty, we allow a single layer connection to represent a collection of individual SAP-to-SPP links. By definition, links that share a layer connection must have a common protocol and are all bound to the same SPP. If a layer connection represents multiple links, then the SPP must be replicated with a replication factor that is large enough to accommodate all the links in that connection.

To avoid having to explicitly specify every single link that is part of a layer connection, by default, any SAP in the upper layer (whose protocol is the same as the protocol class of the layer connection) is automatically included in that layer connection. In the file service example, all SAPs using the file-service access protocol will be bound automatically to file service SPPs in the lower layer with a single layer connection associated with this protocol. The complementary textual declaration might have the form

    connection lc **isa** FileAccessProtocol

where FileAccessProtocol is the name of the protocol class of the service.

If more than one layer connection is defined for the same protocol, then the corresponding protocol links are partitioned randomly between them. As a general guideline, we prefer to use only a single layer connection per protocol. At the service provision end, if more than one SPP exists with the same protocol as the layer connection, the default mechanism will choose the SPP that has the largest replication factor. If more than one SPP has the same replication factor, then a random choice is made.

Should this default mechanism be inappropriate, it is possible to override the default by explicitly anchoring a layer connection to a particular SAP or SPP. For example, a layer connection could be defined as

    connection c **isa** servProtocol : {someSAP/AppActor **to** someSPP/serviceX} where servProtocol is the name of the protocol class associated with the layer connection, someSAP/AppActor is a SAP on an actor reference (the AppActor), and someSPP/serviceX is an SPP on some other actor reference (the ServiceX actor).

Defaults should be overridden only in very special situations. Otherwise, the diagrams may become unreadable.

The semantics of replicated SPPs are the same as the semantics of replicated ports (see Section 6.9.2). This means that a service layer can either broadcast to all its clients or communicate with individual ones as needed. Replicated SPPs are the most common form of service provision in practical usage.

To prevent circular usage dependencies, the graph of all layer connections must not have any cycles in it.

Figure 7.12 shows the use of layer connections to model the "toaster" structure. One layer connection exists for each distinct service used by an upper layer. Note that layer connections allow the flattening out of the original multidimensional picture.

Figure 7.12 The Use of Layer Connections for Multidimensional Layering Structures

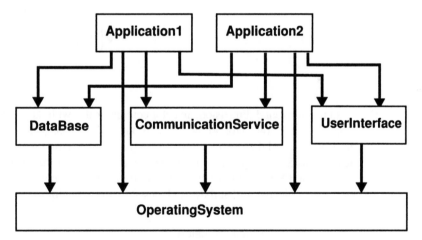

Despite the graphical compaction caused by layer connections, it is clear that diagrams still can get quite complex. In the following section, we revisit this example and show how it can be simplified.

7.2.2   Layers and Actors

The boundary between layers is similar to the encapsulation shell of an actor. Both serve as abstraction and information-hiding mechanisms. When this is combined with the homogeneity of the horizontal and vertical communication models, it suggests that *layer objects can be modeled by actors*. To achieve this, we only need to slightly extend the semantics of the actor model already introduced. In essence, these extensions consist of adding a "vertical" dimension to actors in addition to the horizontal one already defined. This is shown in Figure 7.13.

Figure 7.13   The Dimensions of an Actor

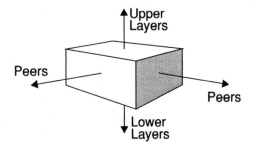

In the horizontal dimension, an actor communicates with its peers through ports. On the "top" surface of the actor are its SPPs, through which it provides service to the upper layers. This is called the *service provision interface* of the actor. Finally, on the "bottom" of the actor are its SAPs, through which it obtains the services of the layers directly below it.

SAPs and SPPs are directly available to the behavior component of an actor, just like end ports. This means that they can be used by the behavior to send and receive messages.

7.2.2.1   Service Provision

Section 6.5.3 discussed the ability to construct custom combinations of specialized actors. In that case, the component actors were combined into a single actor that *selectively* exported the interfaces of its components through relay ports and bindings. The same type of facility is useful in the vertical dimension. It is possible for a composite "layer" actor to selectively pass on the services of its components as part of its own service provision interface. This allows the construction of customized virtual machines that combine a variety of services into a single object.

This effect is accomplished with a special form of layer connection called an *export* connection. An export layer connection "exports" an SPP of a component actor to the interface of the containing actor, effectively making it part of the containing actor's service provision interface. The graphical notation for an export connection is shown in Figure 7.14. It has the same graphical form as a regular layer connection, except that it originates from the actor boundary and terminates on a component actor.

Figure 7.14 An Export Connection

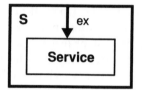

An export connection can be defined only if the component actor provides an SPP with the appropriate protocol. Formally speaking, an export connection implicitly defines a new "relay" SPP that has the same name as the export connection and has the same replication factor as the SPP to which it is attached. This new SPP can then serve as a target for other layer connections (see Figure 7.15).

Figure 7.15 Accessing an Export Connection

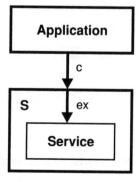

7.2.2.2　　　Service Access

SPPs define which services an actor *provides* to other actors. SAPs, on the other hand, specify which services an actor *requires* for its implementation. A SAP is said to be *fulfilled* if it is matched against an SPP by a layer connection. When a composite actor encapsulates another actor, all the component actor's unfulfilled SAPs become part of its own implementation requirements. The transitive closure of all such unfulfilled SAPs within an actor class is called the *virtual machine specification* of that class.

Since all service accesses are considered fundamental, there is no selective exporting of SAPs. All unfulfilled SAPs of an actor (that is, its virtual machine specification) are exported *automatically* and are part of the interface of the actor. This means that there is no need for an explicit export connection for SAPs.

Consider, for example, the hypothetical system shown in Figure 7.16. In this case, three component actors (each of which might be a composite actor) require various services for their implementations. Assume that component S1 provides service *s1* but requires service *s0*. Component C1 requires service *s1* (which is fulfilled by component S1 by way of layer connection c) and service *s2* (which is not fulfilled by any other component in the class). In addition, component C2 requires service *s3* and has an internal component C21 that requires service *s4*. Finally, the behavior of the container actor X requires service *s5*. The virtual machine of this class is defined by a combination of all unfulfilled SAPs and the ROOM virtual machine (discussed in Section 7.3).

Figure 7.16　　The Virtual Machine Specification of an Actor Class

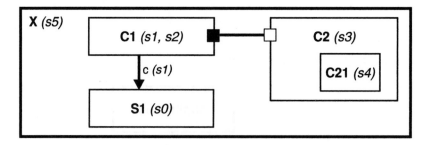

*Virtual Machine (**X**) = {s0, s2, s3, s4, s5} + ROOM VM*

7.2.2.3　　　Service Interfaces and Replication

We have noted already that a single SPP may need to support multiple clients simultaneously, and that this situation is handled through replication. SAPs also can be replicated.

Replicated SAPs have the same dual semantics as replicated ports. That is, a message can be sent to the compound replicated SAP, resulting in a broadcast to all attached SPPs, or it can be sent to an individual instance of a replicated SAP. However, given the nature of service usage, within a given application it is rarely necessary to define multiple instances of service usage for any given service. This means that replicated SAPs rarely are encountered in practice.

7.2.2.4   The Type and Interfaces of an Actor Class (Revisited)

In Section 6.10.1.1, we mentioned that the interface of an actor consists of three distinct parts. The *peer interface* is defined by the set of interface ports that appear in the horizontal dimension. The *service provision interface* consists of the set of all SPPs defined on the behavior component or exported from component actors. Finally, the *implementation interface* is defined by the virtual machine specification of the actor. These three interfaces together define the *type* of an actor. That is, they specify what an actor provides to an environment, as well as what it expects of the environment. Finally, the *behavior interface* of an actor consists of the service provision interface, the implementation interface, and the set of end ports.

7.2.2.5   Examples

We first demonstrate the use of layer and export connections by way of the multidimensional example introduced in Section 7.1.3. In this case, we can aggregate all the individual services into a single layer actor, as illustrated in Figure 7.17. In this case, there is just a single layer for all the services representing a complex virtual machine for the applications. The two applications are combined into a separate layer. Four layer connections emanate from the applications layer, one for each service used by the applications.

Figure 7.17   An Alternative Layering Structure to Figure 7.12

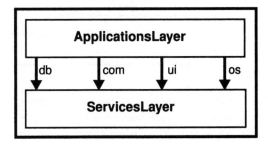

The internal structure of the services layer uses export connections to export the services of the various components and is shown in Figure 7.18.

Figure 7.18   The Internal Structure of the Service Layer

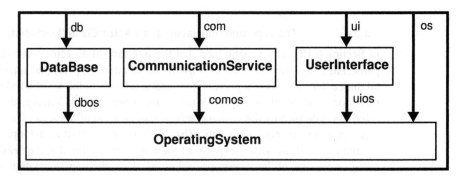

It is common to combine the horizontal and vertical dimensions of an actor in single diagram. Consider the case of a system with three layers, as shown in Figure 7.19.

Figure 7.19   A Three-Layer Structure with a Coordinator

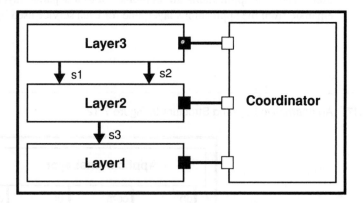

The Coordinator actor views the three layers as its peers. Typically, the coordinator ensures that the layers are initialized in the proper order by initializing the lower layers before the upper ones. Thus, when a layer is initialized, it is assured that all its services are

operational. This can significantly simplify the initialization behavior of the individual layers, since it eliminates the need for complex handshaking protocols between layers.

7.3   The ROOM Virtual Machine Layer

We mentioned previously that all software hierarchies ultimately bottom out on a hardware layer. In ROOM, that common "bedrock" layer is set above the hardware, since hardware systems do not directly support high-level ROOM abstractions (such as bindings or actors). For example, when instructions are issued to create an optional actor, some underlying run-time system must interpret and carry out this activity. This is done by the *ROOM virtual machine* (which is implemented by a ROOM run-time system). The relative position of this layer with respect to an executing ROOM model is depicted in Figure 7.20.

Figure 7.20   The ROOM Virtual Machine Layer

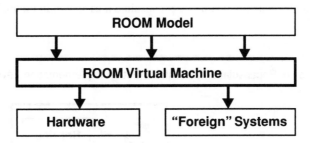

Since this layer is present in every design, it is implicit and is not shown in any ROOM structure diagrams.

7.3.1   System Services

In addition to executing ROOM specifications, the virtual machine also provides a set of elementary *system services* that are common to most real-time applications and that are included in the virtual machine for convenience. Examples of system services include timing services and communication services. These and other primitive services are discussed in more detail in Chapter 10. System services are accessed through SAPs like all other services. However, since they are part of the ROOM virtual machine, their SPP declarations are implicit.

7.3.2 Interfacing to External Environments

The ROOM virtual machine also is the gateway to other non-ROOM environments such as specialized hardware or "foreign" software systems. For example, the ROOM virtual machine is responsible for providing a message-based SAP interface component to some hardware device controlled by a ROOM design. The issues involved in providing such an interface are discussed in Chapter 11.

7.4 Identifying Layers

The issue of when and how to use layering is a complex one and, similar to the problem of identifying actors, often depends on intuition and personal preferences. As usual, a good guide in such situations is to emulate similar existing models.

As a rule, layering is used to model relationships with *implementation-level* services that are *unified* and *widely shared*. By "implementation-level," we mean that these services are used by the behavior of an actor or by the behaviors of some of its components. Since they are part of the implementation detail, we would prefer not to see them in a higher-level structure diagram that includes that actor. Normally, when we want to hide implementation detail, we encapsulate it as shown in Figure 7.21.

Figure 7.21 Use of Encapsulation to Abstract Out an Implementation-Level Service

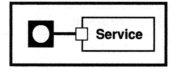

However, if a service is shared by multiple actors, this approach cannot be used unless we resort to multiple containment. If we ignore the latter alternative for the moment, then we must "pull out" the service, as shown in Figure 7.22. In this example, a low-level service is shared by a number of other higher-level actors (A, B, C, and D).

This has two undesirable consequences. First, an implementation detail of the individual actors now becomes visible at the higher conceptual level. Thus, if we needed to change the implementation of one or more of these actors to use some other service, the high-level structure of the container X might need to change as well. Second, the visual clutter can be quite substantial. The high-level binding-based relationships between components are obscured by a "forest" of low-level implementation relationships. Clearly, if the number of clients of a shared service is large, then the value of a graphical representa-

Figure 7.22 A Shared Service Represented by a Peer Actor Reference

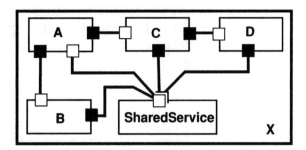

tion becomes dubious. In a large real-time system, for example, hundreds of actors could share a single timing service. Not only would it be tedious to specify each of these relationships individually, but the resulting diagram would be practically unreadable.

For the same reason, multiple containment also might be impractical, since it requires that each individual service access relationship be specified by a separate equivalence. Another disadvantage of using multiple containment for widely shared services is that it can hide the extent to which a high-level model depends on the service. This is important, since services that are used ubiquitously can have a significant impact on a high-level model, even though they are part of the implementation detail.

Underlying this discussion is the assumption that all the individual instances of service usage must be interrelated for some reason. If this is not the case, then we simply can partition the service into a set of disjoint relationships, such as the one shown in Figure 7.21. The need to correlate service instances usually occurs when their activity must be coordinated, or if the shared service provides interconnectivity between actors (communication services). A shared timing service, for instance, may have to be synchronized from a common master clock. We refer to this type of shared service as *unified*. Note that this does not mean that the service must have a central control point, but only that, for some purposes, it must be treated as a unit.

The simplification that results from layering can be seen in Figure 7.23, which is a layered version of the system shown in Figure 7.22. The top structure shows the "pure" application, stripped of implementation detail and thereby making the significant relationships between the components more noticeable. On the other hand, the fundamental dependency of this higher application layer on the shared service can be clearly seen from the layered structure of actor X.

A common situation where layering is applied occurs when there is a paradigm shift in the environment such as occurs at the interface between hardware and software.

Figure 7.23   The Effect of Layering for the System in Figure 7.22

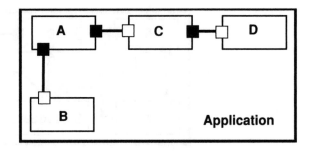

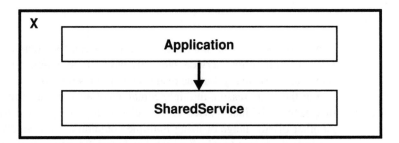

7.5   Formal Specifications

We now continue our formal specification of the abstract syntax of actor classes started in Section 6.10.[4]

7.5.1   Service Provision Interface

Recall that the interface of an actor class is defined by

$$actor\text{-}interface = <peer\text{-}interface, sp\text{-}interface, impl\text{-}interface> \qquad (7\text{-}1)$$

and that we had deferred the formal definition of the last two parts. The service provision interface consists of the following two sets of SPPs:

$$sp\text{-}interface = <spps, exported\text{-}spps> \qquad (7\text{-}2)$$

The first set,

$$spps = \{spp\text{-}ref_1, spp\text{-}ref_2, ...\} \qquad (7\text{-}3)$$

---

[4] This section contains advanced material and can be omitted on first reading.

consists of the SPPs defined on the behavior component. Each SPP in this set is defined by

$$spp\text{-}ref_i = <spp\text{-}ref\text{-}name_i, replic\text{-}factor_i, protocol\text{-}class_i> \qquad (7\text{-}4)$$

where $spp\text{-}ref\text{-}name_i$ is the name of SPP reference i, $replic\text{-}factor_i$ is the replication factor, and $protocol\text{-}class_i$ is its protocol class. In contrast to port references, SPP references do not have a conjugation indicator since they are conjugated by default.

The set of exported SPPs is defined by the following set of export layer contracts:

$$exported\text{-}spps = \{exp\text{-}contract_1, exp\text{-}contract_2, ...\} \qquad (7\text{-}5)$$

Each exported contract is defined as a pair,

$$exp\text{-}contract_i = <conn\text{-}name_i, conn\text{-}end\text{-}point_i> \qquad (7\text{-}6)$$

where $conn\text{-}name_i$ is the unique name of the export connection and $conn\text{-}end\text{-}point_i$ is an SPP on a component actor defined by either

$$conn\text{-}end\text{-}point = <spp\text{-}id_m, actor\text{-}id_n> \qquad (7\text{-}7)$$

with

$$actor\text{-}id_n \in components \qquad (7\text{-}8)$$

$$spp\text{-}id_m = sp\text{-}interface\text{-}name(m, class(actor\text{-}id_n)) \qquad (7\text{-}9)$$

The function $sp\text{-}interface\text{-}name(k, c)$ returns the name of the kth SPP reference on the service provision interface of actor class c.

7.5.2 Implementation Interface

The implementation interface refers to the set of SAPs required by the actor class and has the following two components:

$$impl\text{-}interface = <saps, component\text{-}saps> \qquad (7\text{-}10)$$

The first component consists of all the SAPs defined for the behavior component

$$saps = \{sap\text{-}ref_1, sap\text{-}ref_2, ...\} \qquad (7\text{-}11)$$

where the ith SAP reference is defined by the following two elements:

$$sap\text{-}ref_i = <sap\text{-}ref\text{-}name_i, replic\text{-}factor_i, protocol\text{-}class_i> \qquad (7\text{-}12)$$

Note that we do not include conjugation indicators for SAPs since a SAP cannot be conjugated.

7.5.3 Layer Connection Contracts

Connection contracts are part of the specification of the internal structure of a component and consist of the set of exported SPP contracts and the set of layer connections between components.

$$connection\text{-}contracts = <exported\text{-}spps, layer\text{-}contracts> \qquad (7\text{-}13)$$

The exported SPP contracts are defined by Equation (7-6).
    Layer contracts are specified by the set,

$$layer\text{-}contracts = \{c\text{-}contract_1, c\text{-}contract_2, ...\} \qquad (7\text{-}14)$$

with the ith contract consisting of,

$$c\text{-}contract_i = <conn\text{-}name_i, srce\text{-}end\text{-}point_i, conn\text{-}end\text{-}point_i> \qquad (7\text{-}15)$$

The first end point, $srce\text{-}end\text{-}point_i$, represents the source of the layer connection, and is a SAP on a component actor defined by

$$srce\text{-}end\text{-}point = <sap\text{-}id_m, actor\text{-}id_n> \qquad (7\text{-}16)$$

where $sap\text{-}id_m$ is a SAP belonging to $actor\text{-}id_n$ The second end point of the connection, $conn\text{-}end\text{-}point_i$ represents a destination SPP and is defined by Equation (7-7).

7.6   Summary

This chapter introduced the concept of layers and layering. Layering is a hierarchical relationship between objects that also involves abstraction and encapsulation (information hiding). The upper layers have a greater conceptual significance with respect to a particular application than lower layers. Because of this hierarchy, layering is different from peer relationships between objects. It is also different from containment, since an upper layer does not contain the lower ones.

In software systems, layering can be viewed as the relationship between a virtual computer and a program for that computer. The lower layers represent a virtual machine that has a basic "instruction set" composed of services and that can be combined in various ways to realize the functionality of the desired application.

In most interesting cases, layering is a multidimensional relationship that extends beyond just two dimensions. Consequently, complex systems can be considered as having a separate layering dimension for every service.

The ROOM model of layering is a generalization of the well-known OSI model. The interface between two layers is split into two parts to allow each layer to be specified independently of the other and also to maximize the reuse potential of each. This leads to a communication model that is very similar to the communication model between peer actors. Communication takes place by exchanging messages through explicitly defined interface components. The message exchanges are constrained by the protocol specifications associated with the interface components. The portion of the interface in the upper layer is called a service access point (SAP), while the interface component in the lower layer is called a service provision point (SPP). By definition, the SPP protocol is conjugated. SAPs and SPPs are interconnected by communication channels called layer connections. A single layer connection can represent multiple SAP-to-SPP links that can significantly reduce the visual clutter in graphical representations.

Layers are modeled by actors that can extend in the upward and downward directions, as well as horizontally. In the upward direction, an actor can provide service to other layers (actors) through its SPPs. This defines its service provision interface. In the downward direction, an actor uses the services of one or more lower layers through its SAPs. The set of SAPs that are used by an actor defines its virtual machine specification.

An actor can encapsulate component actors that have a service provision interface. In that case, it is possible (through the mechanism of export connections) to selectively export the service provision interface of the components and make them part of the service provision interface of the containing actor. This allows construction of arbitrary but formal virtual machine specifications by combining (and reusing) more primitive components. On the opposite side, all the SAPs of all the containing component actors are automatically exported in the downward direction. Consequently, an actor has three categories of interfaces: peer interfaces represented by ports, service provision interfaces through SPPs, and the service usage interfaces represented by the virtual machine specification. The composite of these three categories defines the type of an actor.

The bottom layer in every ROOM layering hierarchy is always defined by the ROOM virtual machine. This layer provides a standard set of services useful in real-time designs and also acts as the interface to hardware and other "foreign" environments.

Layering generally is used to model unified implementation-level services that are shared by a large number of actors.

CHAPTER 8

High-Level
Behavior Modeling

In this chapter, we explore that portion of the conceptual space identified by the behavior dimension of the Schematic Level (see Figure 8.1). This domain is characterized by the presence of two complex and difficult phenomena, concurrency and distribution. As explained in Chapter 2, these two are the source of much tribulation in software design and must be addressed with adequate tools on hand.

Figure 8.1   The ROOM Conceptual Framework: High-Level Behavior

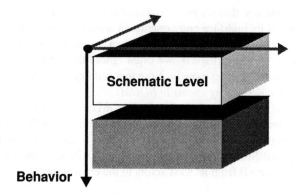

The structural concepts at the Schematic Level, which were described in the preceding chapters, impose few constraints on the model of behavior. As a result, it is possible to combine them with a variety of behavior description formalisms. Stimulated by the development of the computer and the study of algorithms, many different techniques for describing behavior have evolved over the last four decades. For example, this is reflected in the diversity of available programming paradigms, including imperative programming, functional programming, and logic programming.

The behavior formalism that is described in this book is called *ROOMcharts* and is based on the concepts of event-driven behavior and hierarchical extended state machines. This is a variant of *statecharts* (a hierarchical state machine formalism invented by David Harel [Harel87a]) that has been defined with the objective of meeting the needs of the real-time domain in a way that also takes advantage of the object paradigm. Some of the rationale behind this choice is provided in Appendix C.

8.1   The ROOM Event-Processing Model

Before we look into the ROOMcharts formalism and its notation, it is useful to examine the dynamic properties of the ROOM environment. Recall from Section 6.6 that the behavior of actors is concentrated in special "behavior" components. These components interact with their surroundings by exchanging messages that pass in and out through special behavior interfaces. The discrete nature of this interaction naturally suggests an event-driven paradigm.

8.1.1   Events

In ROOM, we say that an *event* is generated whenever a message is sent by an actor through one of its interface components. In addition, we say that an event occurs when a message is received by an actor. Strictly speaking, an event is a temporal concept, whereas a message is not. Nevertheless, we often ignore the difference and use the terms "message" and "event" synonymously. Note that *sending and receiving messages are the only mechanism for generating events in ROOM*.

Events that are generated outside the ROOM environment (for example, timing signals, low-level interrupts), and that need to be conveyed to ROOM actors, are translated by the ROOM virtual machine into messages and then introduced into the ROOM environment through special SAPs. These same or similar SAPs also can be used to relay messages (suitably converted) from ROOM actors to the environment.

8.1.2   Run-to-Completion Event Processing

When a message is received by an actor, some response by the behavior usually is required. This typically involves performing some calculation to formulate the appropriate response, followed by the sending of one or more messages. The behavior, therefore, alternates between two modes: It is either idle "listening" for the arrival of the next event or it is busy responding to the most recent event. This model of behavior is illustrated in Figure 8.2.

What happens in this model when a high-priority event occurs while we are still busy processing the current one? For example, in Figure 8.2, event e_2 may arrive at time t_q while the behavior is still busy handling the previous event (e_1). There are two possible

Figure 8.2   Event-Driven Model

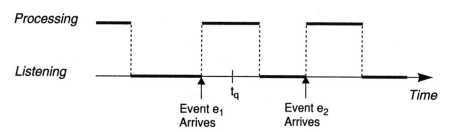

courses of action. We can immediately suspend processing of the current event and commence with the new high-priority event (we refer to this as the *preemptive* model). Alternatively, we can queue up the new event until processing of the current event has completed and then process the new event (this is called the *run-to-completion* model).

The problem with the first approach is that it introduces internal concurrency within the scope of a single behavior. If preemption is allowed, handling of the high-priority event might modify some internal variables that were in the process of being modified as a result of the previous (low-priority) event. When the low-priority handling is resumed, some of these variables might be changed, leading to errors. This is a standard concurrency problem and it requires some form of mutual exclusion. The complexity of such mechanisms often leads to significant reliability problems ([Andrews83]).

In the run-to-completion approach, handling of the current event cannot be "interrupted" by a higher-priority event, thereby completely avoiding the internal concurrency issue. The advantage of this model is simplicity. Its biggest disadvantage is that the processing of events cannot take too long to ensure a timely response to a higher-priority event. In order to achieve this, protracted event-processing sequences must be broken up into a number of shorter chunks. This can significantly complicate the implementation.

Note that run-to-completion does not mean that an actor can monopolize the processor. The preemption restriction only applies to actors that are already busy handling events. High-priority events destined for *other* actors can still preempt a currently executing actor. This situation is illustrated in Figure 8.3.

Assume that actor A is handling some event when a high-priority event e arrives for actor B. We also assume that actors A and B share the same physical processor environment so that they cannot run in parallel. In this case, the underlying scheduling system may suspend actor A and switch the processor to execute the high-priority handler of actor B. When B finishes its event handling, actor A resumes its processing. Since ROOM does not allow shared data between actors, there are no mutual interference problems between the two event handlers.

Figure 8.3   Preemption and Run-to-Completion

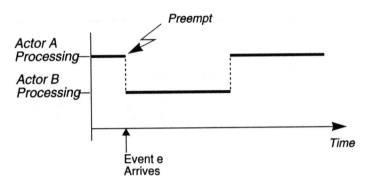

8.1.3   Event Priorities

In the preceding discussion, we have implied that *events have priorities*. In most multi-tasking operating systems, priorities traditionally are assigned to tasks instead of events. This is a reasonable choice if we assume that each task is responsible for just a single activity. However, in an event-driven system, we often find that actors are exposed to two or more simultaneous scenarios.[1] For example, an actor normally responsible for high-priority events may be asked periodically to perform an internal audit, usually a background type of activity. If the priority is assigned to the actor, then even this relatively minor activity would be executed at the priority ascribed to the actor, possibly at the expense of some truly important activity. To use an analogy from everyday experience, an airline pilot is far more "important" (at least as far as the passengers are concerned) when flying an airliner than when sitting at home watching television. The point here is that, in a reactive system, the relative significance of objects is determined by the activities in which they are involved.

Note that it is possible to emulate an object-priority system with an event-priority system simply by ensuring that all events directed at a particular object (task) are of the priority corresponding to the desired priority of the object. The inverse generally is not possible.

The semantics of event priorities in ROOM are such that events of higher priority get *some* precedence in terms of delivery promptness over events of lower priorities. Promptness of delivery is determined by the quality of service attribute of the underlying communication services, as well as the scheduling system. Since both of these tend to be highly system-dependent, we intentionally avoid defining any specific guarantees regarding priorities. In some systems, for instance, it is important to ensure that background activities

---

[1] The issue of scenario conflicts was discussed in Chapter 2.

are not completely squeezed out even during the busiest periods. One example of this can be found in large telecommunications switches. In these systems, handling telephone calls is the most important activity. As a background activity, the switching computer system also may handle interactions with the system operator. In times of heavy traffic, the operator may be required to intervene in order to redistribute the load and, therefore, must be allocated at least some processing time.

Since the semantics of priorities are not guaranteed, it is generally a good idea to avoid models that are critically dependent on priorities. That is, it should not be taken as a rule that a high-priority event will be processed before a concurrent lower-priority event on all occasions. Designing in this "priority-insensitive" way protects systems from race conditions.

Another difficulty with event priorities is that they enable messages to overtake each other. This can cause confusion on the receiving side. For example, suppose that actor A in Figure 8.4 sends a normal priority message to actor B informing it that event e_1 has occurred, and then follows that up with a high-priority message specifying that event e_2 has happened. Actor B may receive these messages in reverse order and, consequently, reach an incorrect conclusion about the relative ordering of events e_1 and e_2. To minimize the likelihood of this problem, messages sent between peers normally should all be of the same priority.

Figure 8.4 Overtaking of Events

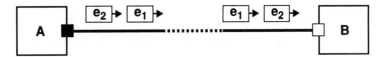

The advantage of priorities is that they allow some level of urgency to be provided in the majority of situations. With all the problems described previously, it may seem best to avoid them altogether and just to have a single universal priority for all events. However, as discussed in Section 2.1.6, event overtaking is an inevitable aspect of many distributed systems so that eliminating event priorities will not necessarily eradicate the problem. From the perspective of the designer, the design effort required to deal with event overtaking is the same, regardless of the cause.

8.1.4   Event Queueing and Scheduling

The scheduling of events for processing is handled by the scheduling system within the ROOM virtual machine. Since ROOM models can be distributed, the scheduling system may be spread across multiple physical processing sites. Each site represents a distinct *scheduling environment* with its own local scheduling and dispatching mechanism. A given behavior component always exists within a single scheduling environment, even though its encompassing container actor may span multiple physical sites. In general, we cannot assume that the multiple scheduling environments are synchronized. Each scheduling environment can operate at different speeds and might even be using different policies for handling priorities. This reflects the inherent relativistic nature of distributed systems. Imposing a global ordering of event processing in a distributed system introduces significant performance overhead and, therefore, should not be a default policy.

The run-to-completion model requires that events arriving while a previous event is being handled must be queued. Each interface component of a behavior component (end port, SAP, or SPP) has a separate set of priority queues for incoming events. Whether these queues can overflow (and the discard policies used if they can) is determined by the quality of service attribute associated with the interface component protocols.

A behavior component may have multiple events queued simultaneously on different interface components. Within a particular priority level, events are dispatched for processing in the order of *arrival*, first-come first-serve, regardless of which interface component they arrived on. (Recall that the arrival order does not necessarily match the sending order.) This is illustrated in Figure 8.5 in which the message queues are shown explicitly (this is not part of the formal notation). For simplicity, we assume that only two event-priority levels are defined with priority P1 being the higher of the two. The diagram depicts a particular instant in which a set of ten events are queued at the various port queues.

Assume that the relative order of arrival of each event is specified by its index so that the arrival times of the events are ordered as follows:

$$t(e_1) < t(e_2) < ... < t(e_{10})$$

In this example scenario, for priority level P1, the order of event processing will be

$$\textbf{P1}: e_1, e_3, e_7, e_9, e_{10}$$

and, for priority level P2:

$$\textbf{P2}: e_2, e_4, e_5, e_6, e_8$$

The interleaving of event processing at levels P1 and P2 is system-dependent. In general, however, we can expect that the higher-priority messages will be handled before any lower-priority ones.

8.2   State Machine Models

Another important characteristic of real-time reactive systems is that their response to an event is often determined by past events in which the object was involved. A very common and straightforward way of modeling this type of behavior is through *state machine* specification techniques.

Figure 8.5 Event Handling

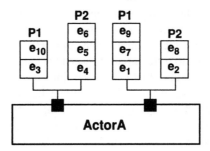

8.2.1   The Essentials of State Machines

State machines, or *automata*, are suitable because a "state" captures the relevant aspects of the history of an object in a very compact way. For example, when a key is struck on a typewriter, the character actually printed will be either an uppercase or a lowercase character, depending on whether the SHIFT key is depressed at the time. Therefore, we can say that the typewriter is either in the "shifted" state (if the SHIFT key is depressed) or in the "default" state (if the SHIFT key is not depressed).

Formally, a state machine (or automaton) is defined by the 6-tuple

$$<I, O, S, Y, F, s_0>$$

where

- I is a set of input events
- O is a set of output events
- S is a set of states[2]
- Y is a function that maps states and inputs to outputs $(S \times I \rightarrow O)$
- F is a function that maps states and inputs to states $(S \times I \rightarrow S)$—this is the state transition function
- s_0 $(s_0 \in S)$ is a specification that identifies the initial state

Informally, a *state* is a static condition of an object during which the object is receptive to new events. When an event occurs, the object responds by changing its state to reflect the new history of the object. The new state depends on the event that occurred, as well as

---

[2] If set S is finite, then the state machine is called a *finite-state* machine. The state machine formalism used in ROOM is based on finite-state machines.

on the previous state. This transfer from one state to another is called a *state transition*. In our typewriter example, if the typewriter is in the "default" state when the SHIFT key is pressed, it will enter the "shifted" state. However, if the typewriter is already in the "shifted" state, then depressing the second SHIFT key will not cause a change of state. Notice that in this case we chose to represent the situation when one SHIFT key is depressed and the situation when both SHIFT keys are depressed by the same state. Also, we chose not to differentiate between the individual occurrences of the typewriter being in the "shifted" state (that is, the first time, the second time, and so on). This is because, no matter how many times the typewriter had been in the "shifted" state previously, for a given state, it will always respond to input events in exactly the same way. This leads to the conclusion that the concept of a state is, in essence, an *abstraction* mechanism that can be applied to the history of an object. Namely, a state symbolizes the set of all possible event sequences that can lead to it. The relevance of a state lies in its capacity to determine how a dynamic event will be handled by an object.

The event that causes a state transition is called a triggering event or, simply, a *trigger*. When a transition is triggered by an event, the object may perform some *action* that can generate new events. There are two interpretations of this activity. In one case, the action is associated with the transition. This type of state machine is known as a *Mealy* automaton. Since actions always take a finite amount of time, there is a conceptual difficulty with a Mealy automaton because it implies that, while an object is executing a transition, it is not in any state. This seems to clash with the intuitive view that every object is always in some state, even if that state is dynamic. This problem is avoided in the alternative model in which the action is associated with the state so that the transitions can be considered as instantaneous. This is known as a *Moore* automaton.[3] However, the Moore model introduces a different problem. If two or more different events force a transition to the same state, then the same action will be performed regardless of which event caused the transition. This makes it difficult to associate different actions with different events.

The behavioral model of state machines consists of a series of alternating pauses (modeled by states) and actions (modeled by the transitions). This is, in fact, the very same event-driven behavior described previously. The run-to-completion model seems better suited to the Mealy approach, since it implies that an object is unresponsive during event handling (state transition). This means that, during the transition interval, the state of the object has no practical significance.

State transition diagrams are graphical renderings of state machines. In our diagrams, we use the convention that a state is represented by a rectangle with rounded corners and a transition is represented by a directed arc from the source to the destination state. The arcs are typically labeled with the event that triggers the appropriate transition. The state transition diagram for the typewriter example is depicted in Figure 8.6.

---

[3] More formally, the output of a Mealy machine depends on the current state and current input, whereas the output of a Moore machine depends only on the current state [Harrison65].

Figure 8.6 A State Transition Diagram for a Typewriter Keyboard

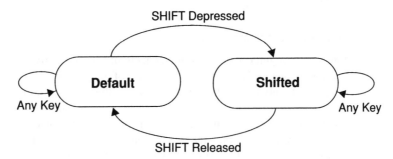

The main value of the graphical notation is that it provides a compact (and yet complete) view of all possible behaviors of an object. Ironically, this is also one of the main weaknesses of the state machine models. When we view the state transition diagram as a directed graph, there usually are many valid traversal paths through the graph. (If the graph is cyclic, like the one in Figure 8.6, then the number of traversals can be infinite.) In most systems, however, not all traversals are equally likely. There are so-called "main paths" through a state transition diagram that are taken in the great majority of cases, while the remaining paths might only be taken in pathological or exceptional situations. The problem is that it is not possible to discern which are the main paths by simple inspection of a state transition diagram. Thus, to the uninitiated observer, the state transition diagram does not reveal which behavior is common and which is exceptional.

This can be contrasted with the sequential model of behavior in which the main path is obvious. In this model, behavior that deviates from the main path usually is handled by the mechanism of exceptions and exception handlers. Unfortunately, in most imperative programming languages, exception handlers typically are secondary mechanisms with very restricted capabilities and built-in assumptions about how recovery is to be performed. For example, many programming languages restrict their exception handlers to the context in which a failure is detected, and that may not be the proper context to perform recovery. On the other hand, abandoning this context in order to handle recovery at a higher level means losing any intermediate information established in the abandoned contexts.

The uncertainty and unpredictable nature of reactive systems (where failures and asynchronous demands can occur at any time) may mean that the bulk of the specification may be in the exception handlers. Furthermore, the exception handlers themselves are likely to be nested since further "exceptions" can occur while handling previous ones. The result can be a complex structure of handlers that is even less comprehensible than the event-driven model because of all the nesting of contexts. This simply reaffirms our previous conclusion that the event-driven model of behavior, as embodied in state machines, is more appropriate than a sequential one for reactive real-time systems. In this case, the argument is made that, once we are past the point of dealing with only the main paths, a specification based on an event-driven model actually is more easily understood than a sequential one.

8.2.2   Extended State Machines

One common interpretation of the concept of state for software systems is that each state represents one distinct set of valid values of all program variables. Even for simple programs with only a few elementary variables, this interpretation leads to a very large number of states. For example, a single 16-bit integer variable can have more than 65,000 states. This interpretation clearly is not interesting for practical purposes. Therefore, we dissociate variables from states. States are abstract views of an object that determine the *qualitative* aspects of its behavior, while variables (and their values) pertain to its detailed *quantitative* aspects. In this interpretation, a change in the value of a variable does not always imply a change of state.

Consider, for instance, a state machine that is an abstract model of the life cycle of an automobile (see Figure 8.7). Associated with this description is an integer counter variable (ctr) that indicates how many times the vehicle has been sold. On the very first sale, the counter is set to 1 and is subsequently incremented each time the vehicle is sold.[4]

When a state machine specification is supplemented with variables, its complete (or *extended*) state is determined by the combination of the (qualitative) state and the values of all its variables. For this reason, the variables are called *extended state variables*, while state machines with extended state variables are called *extended state machines*.

The value of extended state machines is that they enable the underlying formalism (and its graphical rendition, in particular) to be applied to much more complex systems than is realistically possible with basic state machines.

8.2.3   State Machines and Complexity

Despite the additional range achieved with extended state machines, state machines can still become unmanageable when confronted with the complex reality of real-world systems. We illustrate this with a relatively simple example.

8.2.3.1   The Traffic Light Control System

The Traffic Light Control System (TLCS) is responsible for ensuring the smooth flow of traffic through an intersection of two streets. Its central component is a Traffic Direction Controller (TDC) that is responsible for deciding when to change the direction of traffic

---

[4] In this diagram, we employ a convention in which each transition is labeled with the name of the event that triggers it and an optional expression (separated from the event name by a "/") specifying the action performed by the state machine in response to that event. Note that this is just a temporary convenience and is not representative of the actual notation adopted in ROOM.

Figure 8.7   An Extended State Machine

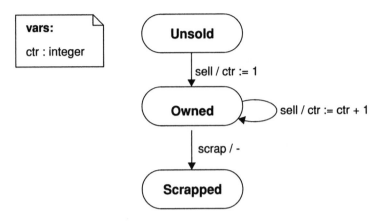

flow. For this purpose, the TDC is connected to specialized traffic sensing systems that notify the TDC when a vehicle has reached an intersection. There is a separate sensing system for each street. The TDC is also connected to a light controller. The light controller is responsible for the timing details involved in switching lights from one direction to another (including the transition from green through yellow to red, and vice versa), as well as for low-level maintenance and diagnostics on the lights (for example, detecting the failure of a bulb). Finally, the TDC also is connected to an external control system that is responsible for synchronizing the operation of this controller with the operation of a larger traffic control system. The structure diagram of this system is depicted in Figure 8.8.

Our first naive attempt at describing the state machine of the TDC is to have just two states as shown in Figure 8.9. The state AEnabled means that street A has the green light and state BEnabled means that the green light is on for street B.

This may be sufficient for a very abstract model, but it is inadequate when more detailed requirements are introduced. Consider the following additional requirements for the operation of the TLCS:

1.   The switchover of lights is not instantaneous and requires an interval during which the yellow light is displayed. In order to simplify the TDC, we assume that the switchover sequence is handled by the lights controller. The TDC simply instructs the lights controller that it must initiate a switchover sequence (with a switch signal). When the switchover is complete, the lights controller responds to the TDC with a switchDone signal.

2.   In order to optimize traffic flow, once the lights have been changed, they cannot be changed again until some minimum time interval T_{min} has expired.

Figure 8.8   The Traffic Light Control System

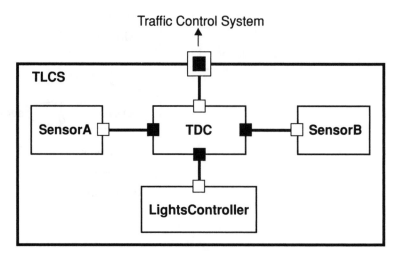

3. The lights cannot stay set for one direction longer than a maximum time interval,
    T_{max} $(T_{max} > T_{min})$.

4. If a vehicle is waiting for a green light at the intersection when T_{min} has expired,
    the lights switchover sequence must be initiated immediately (that is, without wait-
    ing for T_{max} to expire).

5. If a car arrives at a red light during the interval between T_{min} and T_{max} the switch-
    over sequence must commence immediately.

Notice that the TDC only needs to be told of the arrival of the first vehicle at a red light.
Therefore, we will assume that the sensors report the arrival of vehicles only when
enabled by the TDC. The TDC enables a sensor only after the red light is set for the corre-

Figure 8.9   First Attempt at Defining the Behavior of the TDC

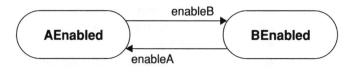

sponding street. As soon as the first waiting vehicle is reported (by an arrival signal from the sensor), the sensor is disabled by the TDC.

The resulting state transition diagram, shown in Figure 8.10, is surprisingly complex. In either of the "switching" states (SwitchingA or SwitchingB), the lights are in the process of being switched by the lights controller. When the switch is complete (indicated by a switchDone signal from the lights controller), the TDC sends an enable signal to the appropriate sensor and enters an "open" state (AOpen or BOpen). In this state, the TDC is waiting either for T_{min} to expire or for a signal from the sensor. If a vehicle is detected, the sensor sends the arrival signal and the TDC enters a "pending" state (BPending or APending) in which it is still waiting for T_{min} to expire. As soon as T_{min} expires, a switchover is performed, since it is known that a vehicle is waiting. If no vehicle arrives in the "open" state prior to the expiration of T_{min}, the TDC moves into a "timing" state (TimingA and TimingB). In this state the TDC is waiting for the maximum time interval T_{max} to expire in order to initiate a switchover. However, if a vehicle arrives at a red light during this time, the switchover will be initiated without waiting for T_{max} to expire.

In spite of the complexity of this diagram, our specification is far from complete. Consider the following additional requirement:

6.   If any light bulb burns out, the lights must automatically switch to a mode in which the red lights are flashed periodically in all directions.

Figure 8.10   A More Detailed Model of the Behavior of the TDC

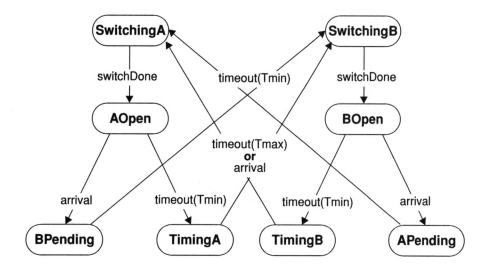

The possibility of a light bulb failure introduces a "failed" state into the diagram. Since a failure can occur at any time, this means that there will be a separate transition from each of the states in Figure 8.10 to the failed state (a total of eight new transitions). In that situation, the diagram becomes a tangled web of states and transitions that is difficult to interpret. The value of a visual representation is significantly diminished.

To complicate matters even more, additional requirements normally would be defined for a system such as the TLCS. For instance, we might require that, prior to start of normal operation, the TDC should run through a diagnostic sequence to validate that the lights controller and the sensors are operational. Also, the TDC may need to respond to control signals from the higher-level traffic control system that might force it into an externally controlled switching mode. The final state transition diagram would contain many states and would be almost unreadable.

8.2.3.2   Hierarchical State Machines

If the diagrammatic representation for a relatively simple system such as the TDC can become so cumbersome, how can we hope to apply graphical state machine models to larger and more complex systems? To answer that question, we compare the detailed state machine in Figure 8.10 with its more abstract equivalent in Figure 8.9. The relationship between the two is represented by the composite diagram shown in Figure 8.11.

Figure 8.11   High-Level and Detailed State Machine Representations

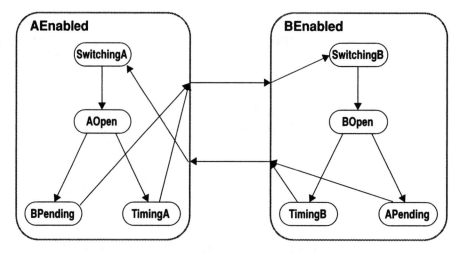

The significance of the diagram in Figure 8.11 is that it actually points to a partial solution to the complexity problem. Not surprisingly, it is a solution based on the traditional approach to reducing complexity: the use of hierarchy and abstraction. That is, we can aggregate states into composite states similar to the way in which we aggregated actors into composite actors. When we also apply abstraction to hide the details of a composite state, we end up with the simple abstract diagram in Figure 8.9. By doing this, we have decomposed the overall complexity of the behavior into a set of simpler units, each of which can be comprehended individually. (We will revisit this example in more detail later in this chapter.)

Clearly, any state machine formalism that needs to be applied to implementations should be capable of handling the complexity of systems such as the TDC. This means that, at the very least, it must be hierarchical. Hierarchical state machines have another advantage—they allow flexibility in selecting the level of detail that can be specified. This means that a state machine description can be initiated as a relatively simple abstract machine in the early phases of development and gradually evolved toward an implementation by refining states over time into more detailed contained state machines.

We now turn our attention to the specific hierarchical state machine formalism used in ROOM to describe the behavior of actors.

8.3   ROOMcharts

The technique used in ROOM to specify behavior components was inspired by the *statecharts* formalism [Harel87]. In recognition of this key influence, the formalism is called *ROOMcharts*.

8.3.1   Basic Notation and Concepts

We introduce ROOMcharts using the example of a simple "name server" actor whose structural form is shown in Figure 8.12. The purpose of this actor is to handle requests from clients to map a symbolic name into a communication address. The actor can handle up to two clients through its client service ports (clientA and clientB). It also interfaces to a controller, through port master. The controller is responsible for supplying the server with the initial version of the name mapping table and for subsequent table update requests.

We assume that the service protocol on the client ports is defined by

```
protocol class NameServiceRequest:
    in:   {{address, Address}, {error, ErrorCode}}
    out:  {{addrReq, Name}}
```

Figure 8.12   The Structure of the Name Server Actor Class

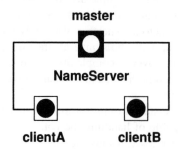

where Address, ErrorCode, and Name are the names of the appropriate data types. The protocol for the master port is defined as follows:

protocol class NameServiceControl:
    in: {{initialTable, Table}, {addEntry, Entry}, {removeEntry, Name}}
    out: {{ack, null}, {error, ErrorCode}[5]}

The state machine diagram for the behavior of this system is depicted in Figure 8.13. (In this diagram, transition labels match the names of the signals that trigger them. As we shall see later on, this is just a convention.) During its lifetime, the name server progresses through two basic phases. On creation, it enters the Uninitialized state, during which it waits to receive the initial version of the name table. Once it has received that data, the server stores it in an extended state variable (nameTable) and enters the Operational state in which it processes service requests in the order in which they occur. For simplicity, we assume that the nature of the requests is such that each one can be handled by a single action.

8.3.1.1   States and Transitions

When an actor is resting in a state, it is ready to process external events. (There is no explicit "receive" primitive. It is automatically assumed whenever the behavior enters a state.) If an event is scheduled for this behavior, it *may* trigger a transition. An event will trigger a transition only if it satisfies the trigger specification of any of the outgoing transitions attached to the current state. If it does not, then the event is discarded and there is no effect on the state. For example, if the initialTable event occurs in the Operational state, it is simply ignored.

---

[5] For simplicity, we have assumed that the same error codes are used for both protocols.

Figure 8.13　　The Behavior of a Name Server Actor

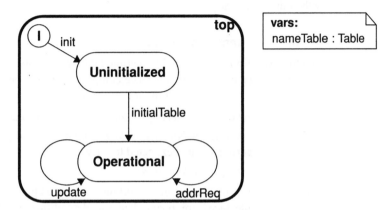

A transition takes the behavior from one state to another. Each transition may have an *action* associated with it. An action consists of a set of *action steps* that are limited to operating over any of the following types of objects:

- Extended state variables
- Temporary variables that are used to store intermediate results during the execution of an action
- Behavior interface objects (end ports, SAPs, and SPPs) that are accessed to communicate with other actors

The message that caused the current event is automatically stored in a predefined extended state variable so that it can be accessed if necessary. In our C++ examples, we will call this variable msg and assume that it contains a pointer to the message object just received.

8.3.1.2　　Initial Point and Initial Transition

When an actor is created, it does not start off in a state, but instead takes an *initial transition*. In our example diagram, this is the transition labeled init. The initial transition is the start of a new concurrent execution thread and is one of the features that distinguishes an active object from a passive one. Like all transitions, an initial transition can have an action associated with it. The typical activities performed in an initial transition include initialization of extended state variables and the dispatching of messages for synchronization with other actors.

The anchor point for the source of the initial transition is called the *initial point*. The initial point is not a state since the behavior cannot persist in the initial point. The ROOMchart icon for the initial point is a circle with the letter "I" in the middle. There can be at most one outgoing transition from each initial point: the initial transition.

In effect, the initial transition is triggered by the "creation" event on its actor. When an actor is created dynamically, it can optionally be given an initial message to be processed by the initial transition.

8.3.1.3   Transition Triggers

With the exception of the initial transition, all other activity in an actor is triggered by the arrival of events at one of the interface components of the behavior component. A *simple trigger specification* consists of the following three elements:

- The name of the *triggering signal* of the event that causes the transition
- The name of the *behavior interface component* (end port, SAP, or SPP) on which the triggering event is expected to arrive
- An optional *guard condition*

The triggering signal must be a valid input signal as prescribed by the protocol associated with the interface component. The *guard* condition is a Boolean expression that is evaluated dynamically when the event is scheduled for processing. The trigger is satisfied, and the associated transition taken, if and only if the expected signal arrives at the specified interface component *and* the guard condition evaluates to "true." For example, the guard might check if a particular component of the incoming message has a desired value, or it may determine whether an extended state variable is set appropriately. Guards are just a pragmatic feature that allows the specification of refined triggering conditions. This type of refinement is most frequent in the later phases of development when such detail becomes relevant. If no guard condition is specified, it defaults to "true."

A single transition can have more than one simple trigger. For example, the addrReq transition is triggered by an addrReq signal on either of the client ports. The semantics of such compound triggers are such that satisfying *any* one of the simple triggers will cause the transition. That is,

simple-trigger$_1$ **or** simple-trigger$_2$ **or**...

Recall that the run-to-completion event-processing model offers only one message at a time to the behavior so that it is not possible to construct trigger conditions based on a conjunction ("and") of two or more simultaneous events. Compound triggers can be considered as a notational convenience that reduces visual clutter by combining two or more transitions with common actions into a single transition.

A special compound trigger is the so-called *universal* trigger that provides a shorthand form for specifying that a transition is triggered by any valid input signals on any interface component. A universal trigger still can have a guard associated with it. The specification for a universal trigger has the following generic form:

{*, *, guard}

The usual convention for labeling transitions in a state transition diagram is to automatically assign a transition the name of the signal that triggers it. This is clearly impractical if compound transitions are allowed. Therefore, the transition label is not formally linked to a particular signal, but is an arbitrary user-defined identifier. Common sense tells us that it is wise to name transitions in a manner that will in some way symbolize the underlying causes. If there is just a single simple trigger, this is usually the name of the signal. However, if the trigger is a compound one, then the name should be chosen to reflect the common feature of all triggers. An example of this is provided by the update transition in Figure 8.13 that is triggered by the arrival of either an addEntry or a removeEntry message on the master port. Transition labels do not have to be unique. Although, to avoid confusion, two transitions emanating from the same state cannot have the same name.

The presence of dynamically evaluated guard conditions in the trigger specifications makes it impractical to prevent overlapping triggers. This situation occurs when more than one trigger in a given state is satisfied by the current event. When that happens, the state machine will select an arbitrary transition and take it. In general, such ambiguous specifications should be avoided if at all possible.

8.3.1.4 Detail Level Action Code

We use the following generic textual form to specify the details of a transition:

transition T:
    triggered by:{{signal$_1$, interface component$_1$, guard$_1$}
               or {signal$_2$, interface component$_2$, guard$_2$}
               or ...}
    action: { ...action code...}

The triggered by clause is optional since some transitions (such as the initial transition) do not have triggers. The action code may be empty or it may contain detailed code. In the case of the name server example, and assuming that the detailed language is C++, the transition that handles service requests might be defined as

```
transition addrReq:
    triggered by: {{addrReq, clientA, true} or {addrReq, clientB, true}}
    action:     {
        // extract the desired name from the incoming message
        // and ask the name table to translate it for us:

        Address* addr = nameTable.translateName (getName ());

        // if the translation was successful return the result,
        // otherwise respond with an error message:

        if (*addr == invalidAddress)
            msg -> reply (error, BadName)
        else
            msg -> reply (address, addr);
    };
```

where getName() is a function that extracts the name component out of the current event, translateName() is a member function of the Table class that returns a pointer to an instance of the class Address, msg is a pointer to the message that triggered the transition, and reply() is a special member function on message objects that is used to send a new message through the same interface component through which that message was received. The first parameter of the reply function is a message signal and the second is an optional data object. We discuss this and other communication facilities in greater detail in Chapter 10.

The variable addr, which holds a pointer to an instance of a Detail Level data class Address, is an example of a *temporary variable* that is used to store an intermediate result. This object is created dynamically when the transition is triggered and is destroyed when the transition completes. It is equivalent to a local variable of a function in a block-structured language.

8.3.2   Advanced Modeling Concepts

The state machine model described up to this point is quite conventional. We now look at some more sophisticated features in the ROOMchart model that allow specification of more complex systems.

8.3.2.1   Composite States

In the example of the Traffic Light Control System in Section 8.2.3, we saw that the apparent complexity of a large state machine can be reduced by chunking it into separate sub-machines and packaging these within composite states (Figure 8.14). Composite states serve to abstract away detailed behavior. The internal state machine of a composite state can be viewed as its "implementation" much like the decomposition of a composite actor. By applying this idea recursively, we can specify almost arbitrarily complex behavior using the basic building blocks of states, events, and transitions.

A *composite* or *hierarchical state* is a state in some state machine that contains a lower-level state machine or *sub-machine*. In Figure 8.14, we have an example of a state machine with two composite states S1 and S2. The current state of such a system can be described by a nested chain of states called a *state context*. For example, if the system is in state S12, then its context is defined by the chain S12-S1-top. (The topmost state machine is always given the default name top.) The behavior is simultaneously "in" all of these states, depending on the level of abstraction under consideration.

States that are not decomposed into finer state machines are called *leaf* states (for example, state S11).

Figure 8.14 A State Machine with Composite States

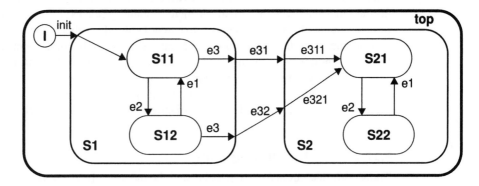

The diagram in Figure 8.14 depicts a "flattened" view in which composite states are shown along with their decompositions. While this representation is useful in some circumstances, there is clearly no complexity reduction in the diagram over a nonhierarchical state machine. An alternative representation is one in which each state machine is drawn separately. In that case, the state machine in Figure 8.14 would be modeled by three related diagrams: one for the entire state machine (that is, the top state), one for state S1, and one for state S2. The state transition diagram for the top-level state machine is shown in Figure 8.15.

Figure 8.15 The Abstract View of the Top-Level State Machine in Figure 8.14

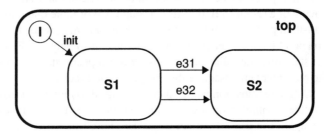

8.3.2.2 Scoping Rules

In ROOMcharts, the nesting of lower-level state machines within more abstract composite states is analogous to the nesting found in block-structured procedural languages and follows the same scoping rules. That is, each nesting level represents a distinct lexical scope with its own extended state variable declarations. The semantics of abstraction do not permit higher levels to access (that is, "be aware of") lower-level scopes. Lower-level scopes, on the other hand, can access all of their containing scopes. As we shall later see, this nested scoping of states provides a convenient facility for subclassing.

One important difference between nested states and nested block contexts is that states are *static* entities, whereas blocks are created and destroyed dynamically as a program executes. This means that the extended state variables of a nested state are not destroyed automatically when the state is abandoned. That is, upon returning to a state, we encounter the same values in the extended state variables that were left there during the last visit.

8.3.2.3   Transition Segments

Transitions that cut across composite state boundaries obviously change contexts on the way from source to destination. Therefore, they must be partitioned into multiple *transition segments* with each segment belonging to a separate context. Each transition segment has a distinct name. For example, the transition from substate S11 to substate S21 in Figure 8.14 is composed of three segments. The first (or *originating*) segment is in the context defined by the chain top-S1. The middle segment is only in the top context and the last segment is in the top-S2 context. Naturally, only the originating segment has a trigger defined.

8.3.2.4   Transition Points

Transition points provide a formal basis for correlating the different segments of a transition that spans multiple contexts. Transition points are located on the boundary of a state, and represent either the source or destination of a transition segment. For convenience, a transition point is labeled with the name of the external transition segment. This allows the tracing of a segmented transition through two or more diagrams. The icon for an incoming transition point is a circle enclosing a diagonal cross, while the icon for an outgoing transition point is a circle enclosing a diamond-shaped polygon. Figure 8.16 depicts the individual state transition diagrams for the two composite states of our example, and also shows the placement and usage of the transition point icons.

Outgoing transition points also can be used to *join* two or more transition segments that are then continued through a common outgoing transition segment. In Figure 8.14, for example, it is possible to converge the two e3 transition segments in S1 by terminating both segments on transition point e31, and then continuing with a shared outgoing transition to state S2. Of course, this would be done only if the same action is performed in both cases.

Figure 8.16   Transition Point Icons

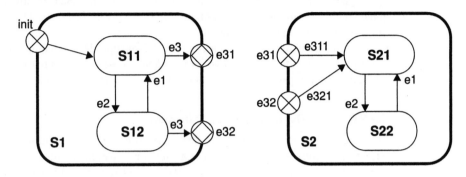

8.3.2.5   Group Transitions

It is not unusual for all substates of a composite state to respond to the same event in exactly the same way. This commonality suggests that the behavior associated with these transitions should be attributed to the enclosing composite state rather than to each of the individual substates. In the ROOMchart notation, such common transitions (called *group transitions*) are indicated by a transition that originates from the composite state. This is illustrated in Figure 8.17.

Figure 8.17   A Group Transition

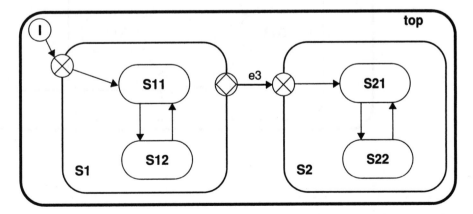

The meaning of a group transition is that it applies equally to all substates. That is, regardless of whether we are in substate S11 or S12, the arrival of the event that satisfies the trigger of transition e3 will result in a transition to state S21. In effect, the event associated with a group transition is a higher-order event when compared to events that trigger transitions within the sub-machines.

A group transition acts like a high-level interrupt. The behavior of the nested state machine is suspended as we move away to a new state.[6] For this reason, group transitions often model high-priority events that cannot be left untended for too long.

8.3.2.6   Overriding Group Transitions

In some circumstances, it may be necessary to exempt one or more substates from the effects of a group transition. Consider a situation in which all substates but one respond to a given signal in exactly the same way. We would like to take advantage of the group transition concept for all substates except the one that handles the event differently. For this purpose, ROOMcharts allow a group transition to be *overridden*. This is accomplished by specifying an explicit transition from the nonconforming substate that is triggered by the same event as the group transition. This is illustrated in Figure 8.18.

Figure 8.18   Overriding Group Transitions

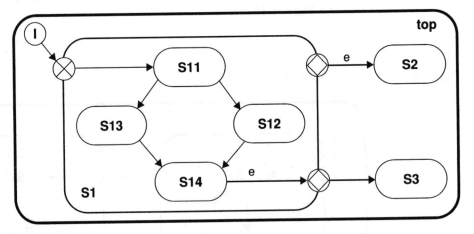

---

[6] In contrast to hardware interrupts, however, there is no preemption (because of the run-to-completion model). The "interrupt" occurs only while the nested state machine is waiting in a state.

In this example, if the behavior is in any of the three substates S11, S12, or S13, and event e arrives, the group transition to S2 will be taken. However, if the system is in substate S14 when e occurs, then the transition from S14 to S3 will take place.

8.3.2.7 Event Triggering Rules

The implication behind overriding group transitions is that triggers are evaluated in a predefined order. When an event arrives, a search of candidate triggers takes place to determine which one will fire. This search order is specified by the following rules:

1. The search starts with the scope defined by the *innermost* current state.
2. Within a given scope, triggers are evaluated sequentially. If a trigger is satisfied, the search terminates and the corresponding transition is taken. The search order is arbitrary, but deterministic. If two or more triggers in the same scope are satisfied by an event, we cannot predict during design which one will be evaluated first. However, during execution, the search order will not change over time. This means that, under equal circumstances (that is, the same state), repeat occurrences of the same event always will trigger the same transition.
3. If no trigger in the current scope is satisfied, the search is repeated for the next higher scope (state) in the current state context.
4. If no triggers are satisfied even at the topmost scope, then the event is discarded and the state of the behavior remains unchanged.

The topmost scope is the top-level state machine, which is given the default name top. The triggering algorithm described previously allows group transitions to be defined for this scope as well. Such top-level transitions are very convenient for dealing with events that are handled the same way regardless of the current state. Figure 8.19 shows two common applications of this technique.

Figure 8.19 Top-Level Group Transitions

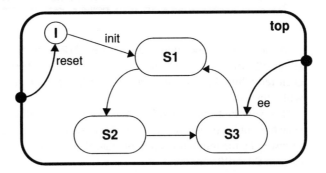

Transition ee will force the behavior into state S3, regardless of which state was current at the time. A special case of this is illustrated by the reset transition that forces the behavior back through the initial point and the initial transition to state S1. (Recall that the initial point is not a state.) If the initial transition is used to initialize all the extended state variables, this can be used to effectively reset a behavior back to its "pristine" initial state without the overhead of destroying and re-creating its actor.

8.3.2.8   History

As noted previously, group transitions often are used to interrupt the behavior of a nested state machine to process some higher-level event. Once the emergency has been dealt with, it may be required to return to the interrupted behavior at the point where it was suspended. This point is represented by the relative state context that was current at the time the group transition was taken. This context is called the *history* of a state.

The graphical notation for a transition that returns to the history of a composite state is a transition segment that terminates on the outer border of a composite state, as shown in Figure 8.20 (transitions e21 and e2).

Figure 8.20   Transitions to History

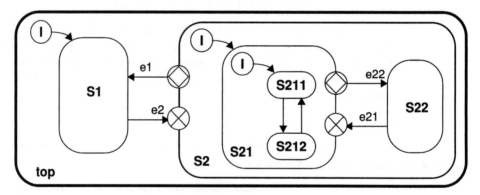

Assume that the behavior was in state S212 when event e1 occurred. In that case, transition e2 will force the behavior back to the context S212-S21-S2-top. If event e22 occurred while the behavior was in state S212, followed by event e21, the system again will return to state S212.

The very first time transition e2 is taken, there will be no history for state S2 since the state has not been visited before. In that case, the initial transition in state S2 will be taken, followed by the initial transition of state S21, and the system will eventually end up in the context S211-S21-S2-top.

It is possible for a composite state to not have an initial transition. In that case, the first time the state is visited by a transition to history, the internal state machine is not activated and its scope is not entered, since the state at that time has no history. For example, in Figure 8.20, if there had been an initial transition within state S21, the first entry into state S2 simply would leave the behavior in state S21 without penetrating into its sub-machine.

One of the most common applications of the history mechanism is depicted in Figure 8.21. In this case, transition **ee** is a self-transition that occurs at the topmost level. Since it ends on the border of a global state (top), it automatically reverts to history. The effect is to perform event handling without changing the state of the system. This type of transition is used to model events that are always handled the same way, regardless of the current state. A special case of this is a *catchall transition*, a top-level self-transition with a universal trigger. This transition provides a default handler for all possible input events. Since it is defined at the topmost level, a catchall transition automatically is overridden by other transitions.

Figure 8.21   A Global Event Handler

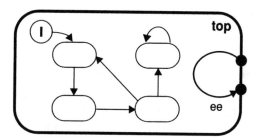

8.3.2.9   Choicepoints

Sometimes it is necessary to split a transition into multiple, mutually exclusive branches, each one terminating on a different destination state. This is appropriate when the decision about which state is going to be the next state can only be determined after some preliminary calculations are performed. The ROOMchart facility through which this is achieved is called a *choicepoint* and is shown in Figure 8.22.

Each branch of a choicepoint is associated with a Boolean predicate (called a *branch condition*) that is evaluated dynamically when the choicepoint is reached. The choicepoint behaves like a "case" statement in procedural programming. If the condition associated with a particular branch evaluates to "true," the transition connected to that branch will be taken. It is possible for more than one branch condition of a choicepoint to be true simultaneously. In that case, the branch taken will depend on the order in which the individual

Figure 8.22   A Choicepoint

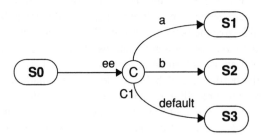

branch conditions are evaluated. With the exception of the default branch, the order of evaluation is not predefined, but does not change dynamically. As a rule, it is good practice to avoid overlapping branch conditions.

Each choicepoint must have exactly one *default branch*. This branch is taken *only* if no other branch condition has evaluated to "true." The default branch does not have an associated branch condition. The default branch ensures that a transition will be completed in all situations.

8.3.2.10   State Entry and Exit Actions

A *state entry action* is an action that can be optionally associated with a state (like the Moore state machine model). This action is executed whenever the corresponding state is entered. Note that *this applies to self-transitions as well*. A state entry action provides a convenient mechanism for executing a common action, regardless of which transition was taken into the state. The action is performed *after* the action that is associated with the incoming transition.

Similarly, a *state exit action* is an action that can be optionally associated with a state, and that is executed whenever a transition is taken out of that state. Once again, this applies to self-transitions. The exit action is executed *before* the action associated with the outgoing transition segment. If state S in Figure 8.23 has both an entry action entry(S) and an exit action exit(S) defined, then the action execution sequence for self-transition ee1 is

```
exit(S);
transition(ee1);
entry(S);
```

The transition execution sequence for the transition from S2 to Sa is

```
transition(ee3);
exit(S);
transition(t1);
```

If we want to avoid the automatic execution of exit and entry actions for self-transitions, we can use so-called "internal" self-transitions (such as transition ee2 in Figure 8.23). Formally, since an internal transition occurs within the scope of the state, it never leaves the state, so neither the exit nor the entry actions will be executed. Another difference between the two types of self-transitions is the scope that they can access. The internal transition can access the extended state variables within the state, while the external one cannot.

Figure 8.23 The Effect of Entry and Exit Actions

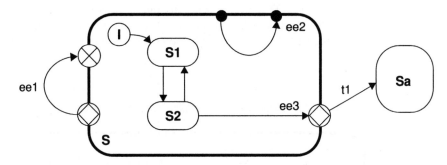

Entry and exit actions must be used with caution if group transitions and history also are present. To demonstrate this, assume that the behavior in Figure 8.23 is in state S2 and that this substate has its own entry and exit actions. In that case, when event ee1 occurs, the action execution sequence is

```
exit(S2);
exit(S);
transition(ee1);
entry(S);
entry(S2);
```

The difficulty here is that a high-level event also triggers actions in the lower nested scopes (in this case, the exit and entry actions of state S2).

8.3.2.11 Example

We now illustrate the application of some of the advanced modeling concepts introduced in this section. For this purpose, we will return to the Traffic Lights Control System introduced in Section 8.2.3. In that first attempt, we ignored some of the practical issues in order to simplify the examples. In reality, of course, many of these cannot be ignored even in the preliminary phases of analysis. We will now consider the following additional requirements:

- The system can fail because of the failure of a light bulb. We will assume that the business of flashing yellow and red lights will be handled by the lights controller. However, the TDC still must account for this situation.

- Prior to start of operation, the system must go through a proper initialization sequence in which a series of self tests are performed on the equipment to ensure that it is functional. Any failures must be reported to the higher-level control system.

- It must be possible to force an external reset of the entire system at any time. A reset may need to be issued following a failure and recovery of the global traffic control system, or following some cataclysmic event such as a power failure.

- It must be possible to drive the operation of the light control system from an external source. This may be necessary during peak traffic hours when the operation of multiple traffic lights must be synchronized. In this case, the entire system simply acts as a light controller and ignores inputs from its own sensors.

Figure 8.24   The Control State Machine for the Traffic Direction Controller

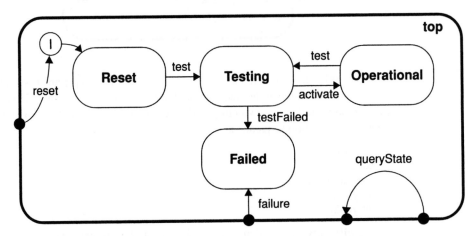

We start with the topmost level of the TDC behavior. At this most abstract level, there are four main "control" states (see Figure 8.24). In the Reset state, the system has completed its reset sequence and is awaiting further instructions from an external source.[7] The system is then instructed to perform a series of tests on itself and its attached equipment. For the TDC, this means asking the sensors and the lights controller to test themselves and

---

[7] For those who are concerned about what is happening to the traffic during this time, we assume that the lights controller is autonomously flashing the red lights in both directions.

report back the results. This is done in the Testing state. If any of the tests fail, the system will enter the Failed state and report back to the central control system. If all the tests have passed successfully, the TDC is activated by the external control system upon which it finally enters the Operational state. While in the Operational state, the TDC may be forced back into the Testing state by its controller. Also, the queryState transition is invoked by the central control whenever it needs to know the current state of the TDC and its lights. Since this may be required at any time, it is handled at the topmost level as a group self-transition.

One of the interesting aspects of the state machine in Figure 8.24 is that it is almost generic. Few facets directly imply a traffic light application. For example, the same top-level state machine might also describe the top-level behavior of the lights controller and the individual sensors. In Chapter 13 we see that this is a characteristic of most real systems—the functional aspects tend to be contained within the control aspects.

The state transition diagram for the Testing state is depicted in Figure 8.25. We are assuming that the testFailed transition has a compound trigger specified by

{{testFailed, sensorA, true} **or**
{testFailed, sensorB, true} **or**
{testFailed, lightsController, true}}

Figure 8.25   The "Testing" State Machine

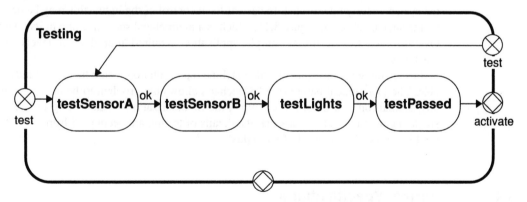

where sensorA, sensorB, and lightsController are the names of the appropriate end ports on the TDC behavior. This eliminates the need to specify individual transitions from the internal states to the testFailed transition point, and thus simplifies the diagram.

Next, we look at the internal structure of the Operational state in Figure 8.26. The default substate here is the LocalControl state. In this state, the timing of the lights is controlled directly by the TDC based partly on the information supplied by the sensors. In the ExternalControl state, the whole system is under control of an external system and the TDC simply acts as a relay between that system and the lights controller. The transition between the two is driven by the external source through appropriate control signals (externalControl and localControl).

Figure 8.26   The "Operational" State Machine

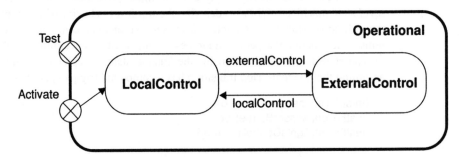

Finally, we get to the "functional" part of the system: the operation of the lights when the system is fully operational. In case of local control of the lights, this may be described by the state machine in Figure 8.11, which is a hierarchical state machine in its own right. Overall, even this relatively simple application required four distinct levels of state machines!

In such circumstances, a flat state machine representation would have been indecipherable. The hierarchical nature of ROOMcharts allows the problem to be addressed gradually, a small bit at a time. For example, the modularization of the testing process into a single hierarchical state means that the details of testing are decoupled from other behavioral issues (such as control of the lights).

8.4   Formal Specifications

We now continue with the formal definition of the abstract syntax of the concepts introduced in this chapter. The material in this section is of reference nature and may be omitted on first reading.

Recall that the definition of the implementation of an actor is specified by

$$actor\text{-}implementation = <structure, behavior>$$ *(8-1)*

and that the set of behavior interface components was defined by the following ordered triple:

$$behavior\text{-}interfaces = <end\text{-}ports, saps, spps> \tag{8-2}$$

The formal definition of *structure* was given in Section 6.10.1.4. In the current section, we look at the formal definition of *behavior*

$$behavior = <detail\text{-}definitions, functions, state\text{-}machine_{top}> \tag{8-3}$$

where *detail-definitions* are language-specific definitions of Detail Level elements (such as class and type definitions, macros, library functions, and the like) that are required by the Detail Level code within the state machine. For example, in C++ this might consist of a list of header files that contain declarations of various classes and types. *functions* is the set of zero or more language-specific procedures or functions that can be invoked within the detailed code of the state machine,

$$functions = \{function_1, function_2, ...\} \tag{8-4}$$

These functions are fully encapsulated by the behavior and cannot be accessed from other behaviors. Within the behavior, however, they can be accessed by any code segment.

The state machine aspect of a behavior is specified by the pair

$$state\text{-}machine_{top} = <variables_{top}, state\text{-}graph_{top}> \tag{8-5}$$

where $variables_{top}$ is a set of extended state variables of the top-level state machine ($i = top$),

$$variables_i = \{variable_{i1}, variable_{i2}, ...\} \tag{8-6}$$

and $state\text{-}graph_{top}$ is a specification of a top-level state transition diagram. Each variable is defined by a unique variable identifier and a class representing the detailed data class of that variable,

$$variable_k = <variable\text{-}name_k, data\text{-}class_k> \tag{8-7}$$

In general a state graph at any level of decomposition is a composite entity specified by

$$state\text{-}graph_i = <transition\text{-}points_i, substates_i, transition\text{-}segments_i> \tag{8-8}$$

where $transition\text{-}points_i$ is a set of points for anchoring individual transition segments, $substates_i$ is a possibly empty set of substates, and $transition\text{-}segments_i$ is a possibly empty set of transition segments.

The set of transition points in the top-level state graph consists of the initial point and a possibly empty set of choicepoints,

$$transition\text{-}points_{top} = <initial\text{-}point_{top}, choicepoints_{top}> \tag{8-9}$$

The set of choicepoints at any level of decomposition is defined by a set,

$$choicepoints_i = \{choicepoint_{i1}, choicepoint_{i2}, ...\} \tag{8-10}$$

and each individual choicepoint is defined by the ordered pair,

$$choicepoint_k = <choicepoint\text{-}name_k, choicepoint\text{-}branches_k> \qquad (8\text{-}11)$$

The branches of a choicepoint are specified by a set of zero or more branch specifications and a default branch,

$$choicepoint\text{-}branches_k = \{ch\text{-}branch_{k1}, ch\text{-}branch_{k2}, ...\} \cup \{default\text{-}branch_k\} \qquad (8\text{-}12)$$

Each branch of a choicepoint is defined by

$$ch\text{-}branch_n = <ch\text{-}branch\text{-}name_n, condition_n> \qquad (8\text{-}13)$$

where $ch\text{-}branch\text{-}name_n$ is the name of the branch and $condition_n$ is a language-specific Boolean expression that evaluates to either "true" or "false." The default branch has no condition associated with it and is labeled with the default name *default*.

The set of substates of a state graph at any level is simply a set of states,

$$substates_i = \{state_{i1}, state_{i2}, ...\} \qquad (8\text{-}14)$$

Each state in this set is defined by the following 4-tuple:

$$state_k = \{state\text{-}name_k, entry\text{-}action_k, exit\text{-}action_k, state\text{-}machine_k> \qquad (8\text{-}15)$$

where $state\text{-}name_k$ is the unique name for the state, $entry\text{-}action_k$ is a possibly empty entry code segment executed whenever the state is entered, and $exit\text{-}action_k$ is a possibly empty code segment executed whenever the state is exited. Finally, if the state is a leaf state, then $state\text{-}machine_k$ is an empty state machine specification. Otherwise, it is a specification for yet another state machine,

$$state\text{-}machine_k = <variables_k, state\text{-}graph_k> \qquad (8\text{-}16)$$

with $variables_k$ defined already by Equation (8-6) and $state\text{-}graph_k$ by Equation (8-8). However, because of the singularity of the top-level state machine, the definition of the set of transition points in a state graph is different for the general case than for the top level (i.e., $i \neq top$),

$$transition\text{-}points_i = <initial\text{-}point_i, incoming\text{-}tr\text{-}points_i, outgoing\text{-}tr\text{-}points_i,$$
$$choicepoints_{i>} \qquad (8\text{-}17)$$

where $incoming\text{-}tr\text{-}points_i$ is the set of incoming transition points, $outgoing\text{-}tr\text{-}points_i$ is the set of outgoing transition points, such that,

$$incoming\text{-}tr\text{-}points_i = \{incoming\text{-}tr\text{-}pt_{i1}, incoming\text{-}tr\text{-}pt_{i2}, ...\} \qquad (8\text{-}18)$$

and

$$outgoing\text{-}tr\text{-}points_i = \{outgoing\text{-}tr\text{-}pt_{i1}, outgoing\text{-}tr\text{-}pt_{i2}, ...\} \qquad (8\text{-}19)$$

The singularity is because the top level does not have transitions that extend beyond its own scope. Both outgoing and incoming transition points have just a single attribute, an identifier that uniquely identifies them within their context,

$$transition\text{-}pt_k = <tr\text{-}id_m> \qquad (8\text{-}20)$$

where *trans-id$_m$* is the identifier that uniquely identifies the *external* transition segment connected to the transition point in the next higher scope. (Each state machine defines a distinct *scope*.)

Finally, we define the set of transition segments in a state machine,

$$transition\text{-}segments_i = \{tr\text{-}segment_{i1}, tr\text{-}segment_{i2}, ...\} \qquad (8\text{-}21)$$

A transition segment is specified by a 5-tuple,

$$tr\text{-}segment_k = <tr\text{-}name_i, tr\text{-}source_i, tr\text{-}destination_i, tr\text{-}trigger_i, tr\text{-}action_i> \qquad (8\text{-}22)$$

where *tr-name$_i$* is the name of the transition segment, *tr-source$_i$* is the entity in the state graph from which the transition emanates, *tr-destination$_i$* is the entity on which the transition segment terminates, *tr-trigger$_i$* is an *optional* trigger specification (that is, a transition segment need not have a trigger defined), and *tr-action$_i$* is the possibly empty code segment that is executed as the transition segment is taken.

ROOM stipulates that the combination of the transition name and its source must be unique in a given context. Hence, the combination of these two uniquely identifies a transition in that context,

$$tr\text{-}id = <tr\text{-}name, tr\text{-}source> \qquad (8\text{-}23)$$

Given its uniqueness, this pair can be used to identify a transition point at the next scoping level (Equation (8-20)).

The source of a transition (*tr-source$_i$*) can be any of the following:

- The initial transition in its scope
- Any incoming transition point in its scope
- Any branch of a choicepoint in its scope
- Any state in its scope
- The inside border of the containing state

The last possibility occurs when the transition is a group transition within the scope of the state. The target or destination (*tr-destination$_i$*) of a transition segment can be any of the following:

- The initial point in its scope
- Any outgoing transition point in its scope
- Any choicepoint in its scope
- Any state in its scope
- The inside border of the containing state

The last case represents an internal transition to history.

Only the first transition in an end-to-end chain of transition segments can have a trigger defined. A transition trigger is defined by a set of one or more simple trigger specifications, any of which can trigger the transition,

$$tr\text{-}trigger_i = \{simple\text{-}trig\text{-}spec_{i1}, simple\text{-}trig\text{-}spec_{i2}, ...\} \qquad (8\text{-}24)$$

where each trigger specification is defined by an ordered triple,

$$simple\text{-}trig\text{-}spec_k = <signal_k, \ interface\text{-}component_k, \ condition_k> \qquad (8\text{-}25)$$

The signal that triggers the event is identified by $signal_k$ and must be defined as an incoming signal with respect to the protocol of the receiving interface component. The receiving interface component is specified by $interface\text{-}component_k$ (note that $interface\text{-}component_k \in behavior\text{-}interfaces$). $condition_k$ is a Boolean predicate, which evaluates to either "true" or "false," and represents the guard condition.

8.5   Summary

The behavior of actors in ROOM is specified by a variant of the extended state machine formalism. This formalism was chosen based on its capability to effectively model asynchronous event-driven systems and also because of its relative widespread use in the modeling of real-time systems. In addition, it has the potential for being directly transformed into efficient programming language implementations, which is critical to meeting real-time requirements.

In the chosen model, the behavior component of an actor is always in one of two modes—it is either waiting for an event to occur ("listening" mode) or it is busy processing an event. All events in this model are represented by the arrival of messages. When an event is received, it may cause a transition of the behavior from one state to another. While executing the transition, the behavior may undertake a set of Detail-level actions, including the sending of messages to other actors. A transition that has been initiated is guaranteed to complete even if higher-priority events occur while it is in progress. This is referred to as the "run-to-completion" processing model and its main advantage is that it significantly simplifies the specification of behavior. Applications need not be concerned with being disrupted in the middle of some complex event-handling sequence. However, it means that the time taken to process any single event should not exceed the maximum latency requirements of the actor. Fortunately, relatively short processing times are the norm for most real-time systems so that this restriction is not a significant impediment.

In keeping with the view that most actors are simultaneously exposed to multiple and possibly independent activities, ROOM ascribes priorities to events and not to actors. The semantics of priorities are intentionally loosely defined in order to allow custom scheduling policies to be defined for individual applications. In general, a high-priority event has a high likelihood of being delivered and processed before a lower-priority one. As a result, it is possible for events to overtake each other. For this reason, event priorities must be used with caution.

The behavior formalisms chosen for describing the behavior of actors is a variant of extended state machines. Extended state machines are characterized by the fact that, in addition to states, they include auxiliary detail-level objects whose values generally do not affect the control state of the behavior. In the ROOM model, these extended state objects are completely encapsulated within their behavior components and cannot be shared.

In order to deal with the complexity of the environment in which event-driven systems operate, it is necessary to introduce some facility to control complexity. In the ROOM behavior model, this is achieved primarily through hierarchy. Namely, a state at one level of abstraction may turn into a complete state machine at the next level down. This allows gradual specification of complex behavior by multiple levels of abstraction. The hierarchical state machine formalism in ROOM is based on statecharts and is called ROOMcharts. Consequently, the current state of a behavior component may, in some cases, be described by a nested chain of states called a state context. Each nested state represents a lexical context with its own optional set of extended state variables. The scoping rules for such contexts are similar to those of block-structured procedural languages. Each context can access its own variables, plus the variables in all the enclosing (nesting) scopes. However, it is not possible to access variables in nested scopes. One major difference is that extended variables are not destroyed when a context is vacated. Thus, if the same context is revisited, the local extended state variables will be unchanged from the last time. A state that is not decomposed further is called a leaf state.

In addition to hierarchical states, ROOMcharts provide a set of modeling concepts that simplify the modeling of complex systems. Initial transitions can be used whenever a new behavior context (state machine) must be initialized. At the topmost level of behavior, the initial transition represents the start of a new concurrent thread of activity. Initial transitions are rooted in initial points.

With the exception of the topmost initial transition, all other transitions are triggered by events. The trigger specification of a transition may include an optional guard condition that can be used to refine triggering specifications to very precise detail. Some transitions can have multiple simple triggers defined so that any of a set of simple triggers can initiate the same state transition. When this feature is combined with guard conditions, it allows very flexible and complex triggering to be defined.

A single transition may cut through a series of different state contexts as it moves from its originating state to its target state. Such transitions are composed of a set of transition segments with each successive segment in a different context. This allows each segment to deal with only those variables that are valid in its context. Incoming and outgoing transition points are defined in order to provide formal connectivity between two successive segments of a transition.

Group transitions are an efficient way of modeling common behavior that is independent of any substate at the next conceptual level. If it is necessary to make an exception for one or more substates, then a group transition can be overridden with an explicit transition that has the same trigger specification as the group transition. The order in which triggers are evaluated starts with the innermost state in the current state context. If no transitions are found at this level, the next level is searched and so on until either a transition is triggered or the topmost level is exhausted. If no trigger is satisfied in this search process, the event simply is ignored and will have no effect on the state of the behavior.

The history of a hierarchical state represents the state context that was active the last time the state was current. It is possible to specify a return to the history of a state with a transition that terminates on the border of a hierarchical state. Like group transitions, this can significantly simplify the specification of complex behavior. The need to return to the history of a state is a common requirement in event-driven systems where a high-priority sequence may often interrupt a less important one. A return to history allows easy resumption of the interrupted sequence. This is frequently used at the topmost level of behavior to implement event handlers that are independent of the current state.

Choicepoints are used to split a single transition into two or more branches, each potentially terminating on a different target state. This is useful when modeling situations where the target state is dependent on computations done after the transition has been triggered. A default branch is always defined to ensure that a transition always terminates on some state.

State entry actions are optional detailed actions that are executed whenever the associated state is entered, regardless of which transition was taken into the state. Similarly, state exit actions are executed whenever a state is exited, no matter which outgoing transition was taken. Entry and exit actions must be used with caution since they are implicitly executed in case of group transitions and the returns to state history.

CHAPTER 9

Inheritance

In the most general sense, inheritance is the passing on of intrinsic properties from progenitors to offspring. In earlier tribal societies, for example, it was common to form initial opinions of strangers on the basis of their genealogy. However we may judge this custom from the perspective of present-day ethics, we cannot condemn the pragmatic principle underlying it: the reuse of prior knowledge. The advantage gained is that we only need to learn what the *differences* are between a parent and the offspring and not bother with those things that are the same.

The desire to reuse knowledge and experience in this way leads naturally to a concept that is, in some ways, the inverse of inheritance: *generalization* or *induction*.[1] Faced with a set of particular cases, we may, over time, identify certain common patterns between them and then imagine an abstract case that possesses only the common aspects, while leaving out those aspects that are case-specific. Of course, such generalized cases are purely conceptual constructs. The benefit is that, by considering only the *single* abstract case, it is possible to automatically subsume all the *multiple* individual cases, at least for those aspects where they are the same. This can significantly reduce the conceptual load one has to face. Consequently, in addition to reuse, the notion of inheritance is tightly bound to the concept of abstraction. This is particularly important for architectural modeling where abstraction plays a primary role.

In this chapter we examine how inheritance is manifested and exploited in ROOM at the Schematic Level (see Figure 9.1).

---

[1] Strictly speaking, there is nothing in the inheritance mechanism dictating that ancestors are more general than their descendants. Nevertheless, this is the accepted practice so that inheritance hierarchies are typically abstraction hierarchies. We will have more to say on this later in the chapter.

Figure 9.1   The ROOM Conceptual Framework: High-Level Inheritance

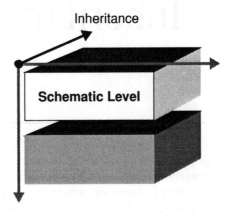

9.1   Toward a Theory of Using Inheritance—Issues, Guidelines, and Heuristics

The initial impetus for work on inheritance is said to have come from research in artificial intelligence. Whatever its origins, inheritance is a relatively new concept in software and is, to a degree, still unexplored. Just as it took decades of experience with programming before structured programming techniques were finally formulated, it may take many years before we know the optimal ways in which inheritance is to be defined and exploited.

In this section, we summarize some of the general issues pertaining to inheritance, as well as various practical techniques and guidelines (developed mostly by empirical means) that address some of these issues and that may someday serve as a basis for a future theory of inheritance. These are discussed in a general context, but they can be applied directly to ROOM.

9.1.1   The Meaning of Inheritance Hierarchies

In previous chapters, we have made a point of distinguishing between types and classes. In the broadest sense, a class definition consists of a type specification and an implementation specification. The type specification part captures the externally observable behavior of an object. Consequently, if a subclass modifies the type specification of its superclass, then it cannot be guaranteed to behave in the same way as its superclass under equivalent circumstances. This has led many to the rather extreme view that inheritance is purely a mechanism for reusing implementations. This is rarely true in practice. The fact that, in the majority of cases, a class and its subclasses share common attributes (including some that are part of the type specification) usually means that the relationship between them is more intimate than purely utilitarian code reuse. Inheritance hierarchies based exclusively on this approach would not be much better than traditional code libraries consisting of shared routines and macros.

A more pragmatic view (adopted in ROOM) is to assume that, with rare exceptions, subclasses are *semantically related* to their superclass, even when they are not fully behaviorally compatible in the type-subtype sense. The benefits of this approach are those inherent in any classification scheme: a structured and graduated means for dealing with what would otherwise represent overwhelming complexity. To reap these benefits, *inheritance hierarchies should be based primarily on semantic relationships between classes and not on implementation reuse*. Note that, in the majority of cases, the reuse of implementations still occurs as a natural consequence of semantics-based inheritance.

9.1.2 Inheritance and Inclusion

Inheritance hierarchies based on implementation reuse often lead to absurd class relationships. As an extreme (but revealing) example, consider the following hypothetical situation. Assume that we are required to define a new class that represents all automobiles and that there already exists, in the class hierarchy, a class that represents motors. Since most automobiles incorporate a motor, they generally exhibit many of the properties of motors. Motivated by the desire to reuse the effort that went into defining the motor class, we may be seduced into declaring that automobiles are subclasses of motors. Unfortunately, most people would find this conclusion unnatural, regardless of how rational a decision process led to it. This is because an automobile has many more significant properties in addition to those that it shares with motors (for example, it has wheels and can carry passengers, it can be steered, and so on).

In such situations it is more appropriate to achieve reuse through inclusion rather than through inheritance. Namely, the automobile class can incorporate an instance of the motor class. This not only avoids absurdities in the class hierarchy, but also corresponds more closely to reality. This technique of including instances of other classes (as opposed to subclassing) is particularly useful in ROOM where the run-time cost of such inclusion is practically negligible.

9.1.3 The Definition and Use of Abstract Classes

In essence, classification is just another form of abstraction whereby we equate a set of different things by ignoring (abstracting) their differences. From that viewpoint, any class that has subclasses can be considered an abstraction. More generally, we use the term *abstract class* for a class that does not have all the detail filled in[2] (regardless of whether or not it has subclasses). Conversely, classes that have all their (implementation) detail filled in are called *concrete* classes.

Since abstract classes model abstractions, it is reasonable to require that an abstract class should be meaningful, as opposed to being a mere collection of shared attributes brought together simply for convenience. This is generally not as difficult as it may first seem, since, in the majority of cases, common attributes are an indication of an underlying abstraction. In fact, it is one of the best ways of discovering good abstractions. As a basic validity check when defining an abstract class, it should be straightforward to devise a descriptive name for it that clearly conveys the meaning of the abstraction. Conversely, the inability to come up with a suitable name may be a sign that the abstraction is not fully understood. The importance of meaningful abstractions is that they facilitate understanding and also encourage reuse.

It is appropriate to define an abstract class in situations where there are two or more variants of a common pattern. In those cases, the abstract class should capture the common pattern, while each of the variants would be a separate subclass of the abstract class. The purpose of an abstract class should be to define the "envelope" within which all its subclasses should fit. In order to preserve this generic quality, an abstract class should not depend in any way on information specific to any of its subclasses. Viewed from this perspective, abstract classes are an architectural tool since they capture essential, unchanging properties.

In circumstances where future variations are anticipated, it may be useful to define an abstract class even if only one subclass exists. The abstract class provides the framework for future system evolution. For example, the first version of a disk controller may be constructed to work only with one type of disk drive. However, in designing the software for the controller, it may be useful to introduce an abstract class that would capture the characteristics common to all anticipated drive types that the system is expected to support in the future. One of the challenges in this is to not overspecify the abstract class, since system evolution often confounds even the most experienced designers.

An alternative to subclassing as a method of representing variants is parameterization. In that case, a single class specification is used to capture all the variants, while the differences are captured through internal variables. The final specialization usually takes place at run time when values for the variables are supplied to an instance of the class. If inheritance is available, this method of representing variables should be used for only the most trivial cases, since parameterization has some undesirable side effects. The most unpleasant of these is that it complicates the implementation of the class. Additional mechanisms

---

[2] This is a departure from the more widely held view which states that an abstract class is a class that is not executable since it is incomplete. Standard programming practice states that a class should have either subclasses (that is, it is an abstract class) or instances (a concrete class), but not both. We find this definition unduly restrictive. The ability to execute abstract classes and validate high-level system models early in the development cycle is a key feature of the methodology described in this book.

are required to initialize the parameter variables and extra code is required to perform "case analysis," (that is, conditional statements that dynamically adjust the behavior of the object based on the parameter value). These mechanisms typically introduce a performance overhead that often is incurred in the "main" path of execution.

Another reason for introducing abstract classes is to capture some convenient level of abstraction. This is done primarily for its documentational value in order to promote understanding of some complex object. In this case, it is of secondary import whether the abstract class will resolve into multiple variations (subclasses). What is key is how well the abstraction captures the essential properties of the concrete system. Fortunately, the points where convenient abstractions are located typically coincide with the points where variants are abstracted away, so the two criteria lead to a common inheritance structure.

Ready-made class hierarchies often can be misleading in their simplicity. In practice, as noted by Johnson and Foote [Johnson88], good abstractions are typically "discovered, not invented." This means that common patterns that lead to abstract classes may not be detected until after two or more distinct class specifications incorporating that pattern have been defined. In other words, we do not always work top-down. (However, the end result, as pointed out by Parnas and Clements [Parnas86], should look as if it were developed that way. This simplifies the task of the people who are responsible for subsequent evolution and maintenance of the system.) This means that the design of a good class hierarchy requires special and dedicated effort. One of the problems with this is that the payback for this investment mostly comes in *subsequent* development projects. In an enterprise that is strictly project-oriented, it may be difficult to justify prolonging a project (with concomitant cost extensions) for the benefit of future, possibly undefined projects. In such organizations, substantial cultural change may have to take place if the full benefits of the object paradigm are to be reaped.

9.1.4 Subclassing

Concrete classes are typically found at the bottom of a class hierarchy. Most inheritance schemes have no restrictions to prevent subclassing from a concrete class. However, as a rule, this should be avoided since it couples the subclasses to the specifics of the concrete class. Thus, if it becomes necessary at some later time to add some very specific attributes to the concrete class, these automatically will be propagated to the subclasses.

In order to illustrate the difficulties caused by subclassing a concrete class, we will consider the simple case of queue and stack objects. A cursory examination reveals that there is a great deal of similarity between these two types of objects. Both keep an ordered collection of objects with the relative position of the elements determined by the temporal order in which they were added to the collection. Given this, and assuming that we already have in our inheritance hierarchy the specification for a queue class, we might be tempted to define the stack class as a subclass of the queue class,

```
class queue (type T)
      operations
            addFirst     :      T, queue -> queue;
```

```
            removeFirst :        queue -> T;
        implementation
            ...
        endclass queue;
```

and

```
    class stack
        inherits queue
        adding operations
            top     :       stack -> T;
        implementation
            ...
        endclass stack;
```

In this highly simplified example, the stack class inherits the addFirst (push) and removeFirst (pop) operations, including their implementations, and adds another operation (top) to return the topmost element on the stack without removing it. Assume that, after having done this, we belatedly realize that we need to modify our definition of the queue class to allow the addition and removal of elements at the end of the queue (operations addLast and removeLast, respectively). Since these new operations are automatically propagated to the stack class, we will violate the fundamental last-in-first-out property of stacks unless we explicitly exclude these new attributes in the definition of the stack class.

This interdependency between the two concrete classes can be avoided simply by defining a common abstract class, orderedCollection, as follows:

```
    class orderedCollection (type T)
        operations
            addFirst     :       T, orderedCollection -> orderedCollection;
            removeFirst :        orderedCollection -> T;
        implementation
            ...
        endclass orderedCollection;

    class stack
        inherits orderedCollection
        adding operations
            top           :       stack -> T;
        implementation
            ...
        endclass stack;

    class queue
        inherits orderedCollection
        adding operations
            addLast     :       T, queue -> queue;
            removeLast :        queue -> T;
```

implementation

...

endclass queue;

The abstract class, orderedCollection, decouples the two concrete classes. If there are any attributes that have to be added that are common, we simply add them to the abstract class and they will be inherited by both subclasses. Conversely, if a specific change must be made to a particular concrete class, then the change can be made directly to that class without affecting the other one.

A direct consequence of this recommendation is that *all superclasses are abstract classes*. Note that the reverse does not always hold. It is quite possible to define abstract classes that (at least initially) have no subclasses, but have been defined to capture architectural intent. Also, not every subclass is a concrete class, since there may be many levels of abstractions before concrete classes are reached.

Subclassing should be undertaken only if there is a clearly defined objective. That is, there should be an obvious and justifiable explanation for the difference between a class and its superclass. This should be carefully documented for each subclass.

9.1.5   Excluding Attributes

The abstract nature of superclasses leads to an ordering in the class hierarchy in which the most abstract classes are at the top, and the concrete classes are at the bottom. In this order of things, we would expect to see more and more detail as we descend the class hierarchy. This raises an interesting question. Should a subclass be allowed to exclude an inherited attribute? If it can, then this seems to subvert the essence of inheritance where we expect the superclass to be more abstract than the subclass. Indeed, it is often argued that the need to delete an inherited attribute is a sure sign of an improperly organized inheritance hierarchy. While this argument is valid in a general sense, practical considerations dictate that *it should not be applied dogmatically*.

It sometimes happens that, when trying to define a new class, there may already exist an almost ideal abstract class for it, except that there are one or two "nuisance" attributes that do not belong in the new class. If we try to reorganize the existing hierarchy to rectify this, we may find that the required reorganization can be quite drastic, especially if the offending attributes happen to be defined very high up in the hierarchy. If the attributes are relatively minor, it may not be justified to undertake a serious and far-reaching reorganization of a large class hierarchy since that can have repercussions on many existing products. This is particularly true if the hierarchy is extensive and deep, and if classes are complicated objects with very many complex attributes (as is the case with ROOM actor classes). For such systems, it is very hard (if not infeasible) to devise fully consistent class hierarchies. This can be compared to attempts to classify natural phenomena where exceptions invariably occur. (The platypus, a mammal that lays eggs, is a notorious example of just such an exception.) Despite such exceptions, classifications are still extremely valuable.

In summary, excluding attributes should be avoided except in situations where doing so implies a major reorganization of the class hierarchy.

9.1.6   Overriding Attributes

Overriding superclass attributes is somewhat less dramatic than exclusion. Formally, overriding is equivalent to excluding a superclass attribute and then defining a new one with the same name, but a different specification. In this case, however, the intent should be not to remove detail, but to refine it further while preserving the original semantics. This usually means replacing an abstract version of an attribute specification with one that is semantically related, but more detailed. For instance, in an actor class, we might replace a port based on an abstract protocol with a port with the same name, but with a more concrete version of the protocol. Any other form of overriding should be avoided.

9.1.7   Inverted Inheritance

A frequent misuse of inheritance when attribute exclusion is permitted is so-called "inverted inheritance." In this situation, a superclass contains a merge of the attributes of all of its subclasses. A subclass is produced then by excluding all the attributes of the superclass except those pertinent to the subclass. This practice should be avoided. First, it violates the informal rule that abstract classes should be meaningful and not just conglomerates of attributes. Second, it reverses the expected direction of inheritance that naturally flows from the general to the specific. This implies that we would expect to find more detail further down in the hierarchy. Inverted inheritance can be the source of confusion since it runs counter to expectations.

9.1.8   Issues in Generating an Inheritance Hierarchy

In their excellent treatise on class-based design, Johnson and Foote ([Johnson88]) make the important point that "useful abstractions are. . .discovered, not invented." This is simply a reflection of the way in which the human mind derives generalizations, which are usually the outcome of reflection on and experience with one or more special cases. Direct experience allows us to build up an intuitive understanding of which features are dominant within some complex system. With that realization, it becomes much easier to extrapolate or identify the relevant common patterns across a number of variants.

This, of course, is nothing new and is common to all design activities. Our abilities improve with experience. Having done something one or more times, we usually can think of ways of doing it better the next time around. Work on an inheritance hierarchy, therefore, should proceed as a series of refinements.

There are several common situations that arise in the course of refining the class hierarchy. Perhaps the most frequent of these occurs when a common pattern is detected in two or more formerly unrelated classes. This requires that an abstract class be created and inserted into the class hierarchy with all the appropriate classes defined as its subclasses (see Figure 9.2).

This operation involves some complicated manipulations. One way of proceeding is as follows.

Figure 9.2   Inserting a New Abstract Class

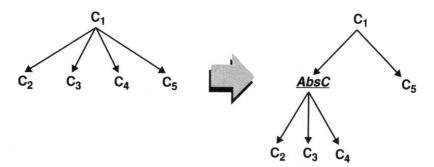

First, we must identify those attributes that are common to all cases. If a proper abstraction is being done, then these attributes should be present in all the candidate classes. This collection of attributes defines the abstract class. Unfortunately, the shared attributes likely will be defined differently in each case, since the candidate classes were developed independently of each other. For instance, they may have different names and different specifications. Next, we select the candidate class that is semantically closest to the desired abstract class (that is, it has the fewest differences) and make it the abstract class by renaming it appropriately. This new class has some of the common attributes and also includes some attributes specific to the selected class. To eliminate the latter, we create a new subclass of the abstract class and move the specialized attributes into it (by cutting them out of the abstract class and pasting them into the new subclass). After that, we must create new subclasses for each of the remaining candidate classes and copy over the specialized attributes from the candidate classes into the respective subclasses. Once the subclasses are created, the original candidate classes are eliminated from the class hierarchy.

Clearly, this type of manipulation can be quite complex and, hence, error-prone and inefficient if it is performed manually. In spite of that, few object-oriented development environments provide specialized support for this type of manipulation, relying mainly on the cut, copy, and paste capabilities of the underlying graphical interface. This seems to bear out our earlier claim that experience with inheritance is still inadequate.

The inverse transformation, the removal of an abstract class, may also be required on occasion (see Figure 9.3). This type of transformation is less frequent and usually happens when an anticipated abstraction did not materialize. The situation is deduced from the fact that the abstract class is practically devoid of attributes. This should be done, however, only if the abstraction is truly inappropriate and does not promote understanding.

In this case we must first move any shared attributes in the abstract class down into the individual subclasses. (Strictly speaking, there should be no such attributes, or else the

Figure 9.3   Removing an Existing Abstract Class

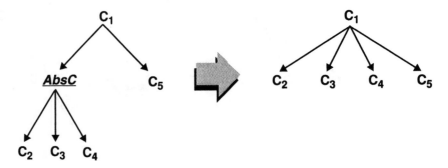

abstract class may be justified.) Next, we must relink the subclasses to the parent class of the abstract class. As a last step, we must delete the redundant abstract class.

Another common transformation of the inheritance hierarchy is illustrated in Figure 9.4. In this case, we must move a class from under one abstract class to another. This is necessary when a class has initially been classified under the *wrong* abstraction. This can be detected by noting that a class shares few, if any, attributes with its current abstract class, but shares many more attributes with the other abstract class. This is perhaps the most complicated transformation since it requires the most complex manipulation of attributes.

Figure 9.4   Moving a Class to a Different Abstract Class

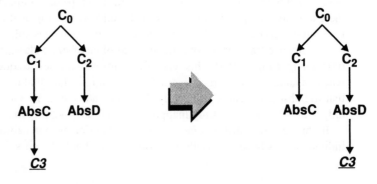

The first step is to decide which attributes the class needs to bring along to its new position. Note that, even though it may not share any attributes with its immediate superclass, it may need some of the attributes that it inherited from higher ancestor classes. This means that all ancestor classes up to, but not including, the first common ancestor of the two abstract classes[3] may have to be visited, and the appropriate attributes collapsed into the class. Next, we need to decide which attributes it needs to inherit from its new superclasses. Ideally, it should inherit all of them. Having made these decisions, we then create a new subclass under the new abstract class, paste in the appropriate set of attributes, and remove the original subclass.

On first sight, it may seem that multiple inheritance could help us with some of this reorganization. For example, to move a class to a different superclass we could simply add a new inheritance link to that superclass. However, if a class is misclassified, then it would be wrong to leave it connected to the original superclass and, therefore, we still need to remove the original inheritance link—that is the problem we were trying to avoid in the first place. In fact, multiple inheritance may be counterproductive in such situations, since it offers what appears to be a quick and easy solution but which, in the long run, leaves us with a corrupted class hierarchy.

9.1.9   Maintenance Issues

By "maintenance" we generally mean small-scale modifications that are done in order to remove relatively minor defects. Modifications performed on a concrete class will impact only that class. Modifying an abstract class will affect not just its immediate subclasses, but also all their descendants. The ramifications of a change to a class that is high in the class hierarchy can be quite extensive. For example, it has been demonstrated ([Perry90]) that, when a change is made to an abstract class, the following regression tests may have to be performed:

- The changed class may have to be completely retested.
- All descendants of the class may have to be retested.
- All classes using either the modified class or any of its descendants have to be retested.

Because of this, it is good practice to make sure that a change to an abstract class is propagated only to that subset of subclasses that needs it. If a change applies to only a subset of subclasses, then it may be worth inserting a new abstract class especially for that subset (as shown in Figure 9.2). The change is then placed in this new abstract class and will have no effect on the remaining subclasses. As noted previously, all efforts should be made to ensure that this abstract class is meaningful and not just the result of a mechanical intersection of sets.

---

[3] In some cases, there may not be a common ancestor.

It is sometimes claimed that inheritance exacerbates the maintenance problem since a small change can have far-reaching consequences. However, if we always adhere to the minimal subset rule described previously, then the change will affect only those classes that need to be changed and no others. In fact, inheritance aids the maintenance process in several important ways. First, it provides a systematic framework of abstractions that helps us determine the appropriate abstraction level at which to introduce a change. Second, it allows the change to be made in only one place and thereby avoids expensive and error-prone copying. Finally, if supported by tools (such as compilers) it automatically propagates the change to all the right places.

9.1.10 Management Issues

The complex mechanics of class hierarchy rearrangement remind us that design and maintenance of class hierarchies require substantial effort and ingenuity. Furthermore, because rationalization of the class hierarchy normally happens in the latter phases of a project (after the prerequisite experience has been accumulated), it is not unusual to find this activity still going on even after full functionality has been achieved in the product. This makes it difficult to justify in enterprises where funds are allocated to projects rather than to products. Refining the class hierarchy ostensibly increases the cost of the project and delays its completion. The benefits of this extra effort, on the other hand, are only reaped by subsequent projects and often in ways difficult to quantify precisely. In such circumstances an impatient investor may only perceive needless delay. The desired system is fully functional, yet the development group is still withholding delivery.

Investing resources for future gain is certainly nothing new in software development but, in the past, it tended to be diffused and was often discretionary. In the case of inheritance hierarchies, the cost of this investment is much more visible and, hence, much more open and susceptible to critical scrutiny and "penny-wise pound foolish" attitudes. In organizations where such attitudes are prevalent, in order to obtain full benefits of inheritance, a fundamental cultural change may be required at all levels and not just among technical groups.

9.2   Inheritance in ROOM

In ROOM, all objects, at the Detail Level and the Schematic Level, are specified through classes. Even the highest-level system is defined by an actor class. A running system is, therefore, simply an instance of some high-level class. This is a departure from the majority of current object-oriented languages and methods, in which a "system" is specified as an aggregate structure of objects, but which itself is not a class.

There are two major advantages to the ROOM approach. First, by defining the system as a class, it becomes possible to define variations of the system for different situations by using standard inheritance mechanisms. Second, it makes it easier to incorporate a complete system as a component of some greater system. This is particularly useful when we consider the current trend of integrating previously isolated systems through networking.

In discussing the structural concepts of ROOM in Chapter 6, we encountered two different types of class specifications: *actor classes* and *protocol classes*. A third type of class is the data class, which is discussed in Chapter 10. Since these class specifications describe very different types of objects, each has its own class inheritance hierarchy independent of the others. Moreover, the inheritance rules across the different hierarchies are not uniform, but are customized to the specific needs of the different object types. This, too, is different from what is found in current object-oriented languages, all of which are based on the notion of a single comprehensive class hierarchy. This not only leads to large unwieldy class hierarchies, but also forces common rules and representation for all object types.

In the remainder of this chapter, we examine how inheritance works for actor and protocol classes. In the case of actor classes, we discuss separately how inheritance works in the structural dimension and how it works in the behavioral dimension.

9.2.1 Structural Inheritance

We first look at how ROOM applies inheritance in the structural dimension.

9.2.1.1 Structural Attributes

Structure at the Schematic level is captured through actors and their decompositions. When we refer to structural inheritance, we mean the structural attributes of actor classes. The main structural attributes are

- Ports
- SAPs
- SPPs
- Component actors
- Bindings
- Layer connections
- Equivalences

In addition, some of these have further ("nested") attributes of their own. For instance, component actors have attributes that specify their replication factor, class, dynamic properties, and so forth. In principle, the same inheritance rules apply uniformly to all structural attributes.

9.2.1.2 Actor Class Inheritance Rules

The inheritance rules for actor classes are

- An actor class can have at most one parent class.
- A class automatically inherits all of the attributes of its parent class.

- Any inherited attribute can be excluded.
- Any inherited attribute can be overridden.

The first rule means that only single inheritance is supported for actor classes. While this may seem restrictive at first, as we shall see later in this section, there are ways to achieve the same effect as multiple inheritance without incurring its drawbacks. Both exclusion and overriding of structural attributes (including nested attributes) are allowed as a pragmatic measure for dealing with large and complex class hierarchies. (Note that this means that an actor class may not necessarily be a subtype of its superclasses.) The general guidelines described previously on how to use these capabilities should be applied in this case. Exclusion should be avoided except in situations where that would result in a major overhaul of the inheritance hierarchy, and overriding should be used only for refinement purposes.

Attributes not inherited from a superclass are called *local* attributes. All overridden attributes are considered local attributes.

9.2.1.3   Notational Conventions

When examining an actor class specification in its graphical form, it is most useful to see the complete specification, including all inherited attributes, in a single diagram. In order to distinguish inherited attributes from local ones, we will use a convention in which inherited attributes are drawn using a lighter line style (grey), whereas local attributes are drawn with black lines. This is illustrated in Figure 9.5, which shows an example of a parent class and two of its subclasses. Both subclasses inherit all of the attributes of their parent (component actors A and B, bindings b1 and b2, and relay ports p1 and p2). To these they add their individual local attributes.

Clearly, this notational convention works best if it is supported by a computer-based graphical editing tool, since it is difficult to achieve variations in line shading by using conventional pencils or markers. This fits in with one of the basic principles of ROOM, that is oriented toward taking maximum advantage of the power nascent in computer-based tools. Nevertheless, if suitable tools are not available, some other notational convention may be used (for instance, inherited attributes may be drawn using dashed lines or lines of a different color).

9.2.1.4   Abstract Structures

What does it mean for a structure to be abstract? The most obvious way is for it to contain component actors or interface components that are themselves abstractions of their corresponding full-fledged counterparts. For example, a port may be defined in terms of an abstract protocol class that omits low-level detail (such as acknowledgment messages), or a component actor may be specified by an instance of an abstract class that only provides a high-level simulation of a concrete class. In this case, the structural specification is *com-*

Figure 9.5 Notation for Inherited and Local Attributes

(a) Parent class

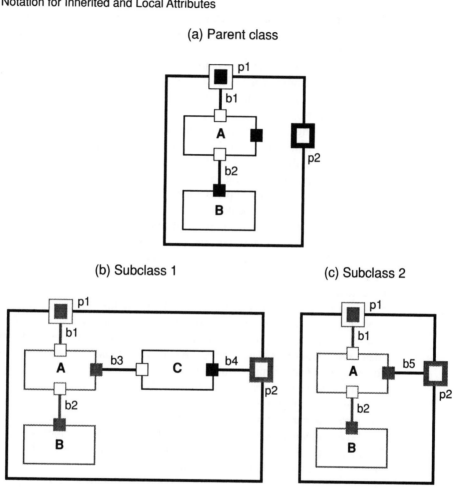

(b) Subclass 1   (c) Subclass 2

plete in the sense that all the major functional components and relationships are present in the specification, even though some detail pertaining to this functionality is omitted.[4]

A second type of abstract structure is one in which major functional components, relationships, or interface components are missing. This is usually done because the missing

---

[4] The distinction between major functionality and detail is a relative one, and depends on the level of abstraction being considered.

functionality may be implemented differently in different subclasses. An example of this type of abstract structure can be seen in the parent class in Figure 9.5a. This class does not show the relationship between relay port p2 and the rest of the structure. The missing relationship is defined, in two different ways, by each of the two subclasses (Figure 9.5b and Figure 9.5c).

Previously in this chapter we noted that we should strive to make all classes in the class hierarchy meaningful. The difficulty with *incomplete* abstract classes is that this is not always possible. For the abstract class in Figure 9.5a, we can only guess at the possible relationship between the interface port p2 and the rest of the structure. As it stands, any messages arriving on that interface component will be discarded, making one wonder why it was defined in the first place. To put this problem in perspective, imagine the difficulty of trying to describe how a jet airplane works while avoiding any mention of the engines.

One technique for avoiding incomplete specifications is to insert an abstract "placeholder" component actor to represent the missing functionality. The various realizations of this functionality then can be defined as subclasses of the abstract placeholder class.

Another problem with incomplete abstract classes is that, with major functionality absent, they either are not executable, or, if they are, then their behavior is not representative of the behavior of their corresponding concrete class. This means that they cannot be used as high-level lightweight simulators of their corresponding system. The ability to execute an abstract architecture and thus obtain early feedback on its potential is one of the underpinnings of the ROOM methodology. For this reason, it is recommended to provide abstract classes that are both complete and executable. We will refer to such abstract classes as *simulation classes*, since they can be used in architectural simulations. In the ideal case, all abstract classes should be simulation classes. However, if pragmatic issues force us to rely on incomplete abstract classes, then we should consider specifying at least one subclass that can serve as a simulation class.

In addition to their role in architectural evaluation, simulation classes, being executable specifications, can also be used as a basis for discussing system requirements with customers and for conveying design intent to members of the development team who need a high-level understanding of the class. It is possible to have multiple simulation classes of a concrete class, each at a different level of abstraction. These successions of simulation classes are often the normal by-products of top-down development, and it is usually beneficial to retain them in the class hierarchy even after the abstract class has been refined.

Finally, the third way in which structures can be abstract is if some of the component actors are defined as generic or substitutable. In this case, refinement takes place by mechanisms other than inheritance (either at the time the system is configured in preparation for execution or, dynamically, as the system is executing). This topic was discussed in detail in Section 6.4.3.

9.2.1.5   Subclassing

We now turn our attention to techniques for subclassing abstract structures. If we adhere to the guidelines described in Section 9.1, this involves either adding more attributes or replacing (overriding) existing ones with more refined versions. In certain special and infrequent cases, we may also need to delete an attribute.

To better understand all the issues, we use the example of a simple abstract client-server system depicted in Figure 9.6.

Figure 9.6   A Simple Client-Server Structure

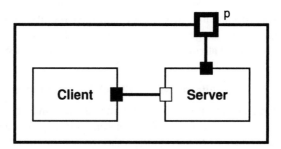

The most common and simplest refinement involves substituting the class of either component by a more refined subclass. For instance, the server component in the initial abstract class may be just a simulation class and we may want to replace it with the actual concrete class. The first dilemma facing the designer in this situation is whether to modify the existing abstract class or to create a new subclass. To determine the right course of action, it is necessary to ask the following questions:

- Does the abstract class already have subclasses?
- If the class has subclasses, are there subclasses to which the modification should not apply?
- Is the abstract class a simulation class that may be useful in the future?

If we answer "yes" to any of these questions, then it is better to leave the abstract class unchanged and create a new subclass to which the modification can be made.

Another common type of refinement during subclassing involves replacing an abstract protocol (such as the one between the client and server actors) with a more detailed one. Since the protocol is a part of the type specification of the component actors, this means that they, too, must be replaced by more detailed classes that are capable of handling the more refined protocol.

Changing the inherited interface components in a subclass means that we are changing the type of a class. We must be aware that, unless the new interface components are compatible with the old ones, we cannot place instances of the new subclass in positions previously occupied by its abstract class, and may be forced into a cascade of similar refinements in other classes that incorporate this one.

Another common refinement of abstract structures is changing an attribute (such as a component or an interface) from being nonreplicated to replicated. This type of change usually entails changes in other structural parameters. For example, if we make the client actor in Figure 9.6 replicated, then we must change the interface of the server class to include a replicated port.

In most cases, we would prefer to refine an abstract class into a subclass without changing its semantics, perhaps by some formal means. That would ensure that any properties established for the abstract class are propagated automatically to the subclasses. Unfortunately, the current state of the art is far from this ideal, so the responsibility of preserving the desired semantics across subclassing operations is mostly dependent on the skill of the designers. The danger of corruption is greatest with overriding, since we can never be sure that an abstract attribute and its refined version are indeed compatible.

9.2.1.6   Alternatives to Structural Inheritance

We have already noted that, in some cases, it may be possible to avoid subclassing by directly modifying a class. Another common way of avoiding inappropriate subclassing is to use inclusion. For example, although one might be misled into defining a telephone handset class as a subclass of microphone, it is much more appropriate to include a microphone as a component of the handset actor structure (see Figure 9.7). The concept of relay ports, as defined in ROOM, makes this technique quite appealing since the only overhead associated with inclusion is to add a binding from a relay port to the corresponding interface component of the included component. In most implementations, any run-time overhead caused by the presence of relay ports can be optimized out.

Inclusion, in combination with relay ports and bindings, also practically eliminates the need for multiple inheritance for actor classes. In our telephone handset example, in order to make a handset behave like combination of a microphone and a speaker, all that must be done is to incorporate the necessary components into a new composite class.

Figure 9.7   Inclusion as an Alternative to Inheritance

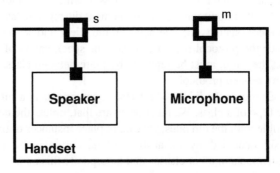

Naturally, not all situations will be as clear-cut as this "caricature" example. The decision to use a "part-of" (inclusion) relationship or a "kind-of" (inheritance) relationship requires experience not only with inheritance and the object paradigm, but more importantly, with the application at hand.

9.2.2 Behavioral Inheritance

We now examine how inheritance is used in the behavioral dimension of the Schematic Level.

9.2.2.1 Behavioral Attributes

Behavior is just one of the attributes of an actor class specification. Consequently, the same inheritance rules, and most of the same general guidelines, apply. The principal attributes of an actor class that define actor behavior are

- Functions
- Extended state variables
- States
- Transition segments
- State decompositions
- Entry and exit actions
- Transition triggers
- Transition actions
- Choicepoint branch conditions

As with structural attributes, any of these attributes and their subattributes can be added, deleted, or overridden in a subclass.

9.2.2.2 Abstract Behavior

The hierarchical ROOMcharts formalism describes abstract behaviors well. The most abstract behavior is captured in the top-level state machine, while detail is added by successively decomposing high-level states into sub-machines. In Section 8.3.2.11, we noted that in many real-time systems the top-level state machine captures the "control" behavior of an actor. This is the behavior required to bring a system into an operational state and to maintain it in the face of various disruptions (such as failures, operator intervention, and so on). An illustration of this is included with the example in Section 9.3.

There is a great deal of symmetry in how abstraction is performed between structure and behavior, and most of the techniques described for structure apply equally to behavior. For example, a natural point for introducing behavioral abstractions occurs when there are variations in the way that the underlying detailed behavior is performed, just as in the case of abstract structure. Since behavior is encapsulated in an actor, an actor class may be sub-classed whenever there are variations either in structure or behavior.

An abstract finite-state machine specification is one that contains abstract states, abstract transitions, or both.

Abstract states represent high-level views in which some detailed behavior is intentionally ignored. In ROOM, abstract states are modeled as leaf (nonhierarchical) states that are to be refined at some later time. This refinement is typically done in subclasses. For example, a physical device that is part of some embedded system may be in a "maintenance busy" state. While in this state, we may run a series of diagnostic tests on the device. At a higher level of abstraction, however, we may not be concerned with the details of how these diagnostics are performed, or that they are even taking place.

Transitions can be abstract in any of the following ways:

- They may have abstract trigger specifications.
- They may not have a trigger specified.
- The action code associated with the transition may be completely omitted, or may contain a very high-level form of the actual behavior.

An abstract trigger specification is one that will be refined in a more concrete specification. For example, the trigger may not have a guard condition defined, whereas in the final version a complex guard condition may be used. Another possibility is that the triggering signal is just an abstract version of the concrete signal that will ultimately trigger that transition. The second case is just a special case of the first. If a transition is specified with no trigger, it is usually because the appropriate event is dependent on lower-level detail captured in the subclasses. Nevertheless, it is useful to include the transition at the higher level of abstraction in order to provide a complete view of the abstract behavior.

Once again, we should strive to make abstract behaviors complete and executable. For a given abstraction level, the set of events that should be handled by the behavior is defined by the set of incoming signals of all behavioral interfaces. The level of detail specified for event handling of events in an abstract class should be such that it captures the detailed behavior common to all subclasses. This also determines the type and number of extended state variables.

These and other practical techniques are illustrated in the example in Section 9.3.

9.2.2.3   Subclassing

As already noted, subclassing primarily involves the further refinement of abstract states into encapsulated sub-machines. In this regard, behavior has an advantage over structure in that it is usually not necessary to override the definition of a state (although it may be necessary to exclude its entry and exit actions). Also, it typically involves adding more detail to the actions associated with transitions, which requires overriding any abstract versions of this detailed code. In cases of abstract triggers, these, too, may have to be overridden in the subclass.

9.2.3   Protocol Inheritance

Finally, we look at the application of inheritance to protocol classes. Protocols are different from other types of objects in that they do not have implementations. This is because they are used to specify interface components. Despite this unique quality, inheritance plays much the same role as in the case of other object types. It serves as an abstraction and reuse facility. Also, many of the standard techniques described previously apply equally well here.

9.2.3.1   Protocol Attributes

The principal attributes of protocol classes are the incoming and outgoing message type sets.[5] A message type is defined as a combination of a signal and an optional data class.

9.2.3.2   Protocol Class Inheritance Rules

The rules for protocol inheritance are similar to those for actor classes.

- A protocol class can have at most one parent class.
- A class automatically inherits all of the attributes of its parent class.
- Any inherited attribute can be excluded.
- Any inherited attribute can be overridden.

As with actor classes, attribute exclusions are allowed as a pragmatic measure, although they should be avoided if possible. Keep in mind that rearranging the protocol hierarchy not only affects the hierarchy, but also all the actor classes incorporating the protocols that are being rearranged. This can be much more extensive than a change in the actor hierarchy.

It is interesting to note that strict inheritance would not be particularly useful for protocol hierarchies even if it were enforced. The idea behind strict inheritance is that, by not allowing the removal of existing attributes during subclassing while permitting the addition of new ones, the properties of the superclass still will be retained in the subclass. Consequently, the reasoning goes, a subclass can be used wherever the superclass is used. This rationale does not work for protocol classes: if, in a subclass, we add just one new message type to the set of inherited *outgoing* signals, then the new class no longer will be compatible with the same set of protocols as its superclass. This is because the protocols at the other end of a contract will not be able to recognize the new signal if it is not part of their set of incoming message types.[6]

---

[5] As discussed in Chapter 6, at the present time we disregard the other two attributes of protocol classes (the specification of valid message-exchange sequences and the quality of service) until the relevant theoretical work has been done.

[6] This perhaps unexpected phenomenon is known as *contravariance* and is the source of difficulty in some object-oriented programming languages that make no distinction between subtypes and subclasses [Cook89].

9.2.3.3   Abstract Classes

An abstract protocol class is intended to provide a high-level view of a protocol. This may mean one of several things.

- Some detailed message types (for example, acknowledgment messages) may be omitted.

- One or more message types may represent abstraction of complete message-exchange sequences in the concrete protocol. For example, a disk write operation may involve a complete two-phase commit protocol, but, in the abstract version of the protocol, this may be all abbreviated to a single message type.

- The concrete data class associated with a particular message signal may be omitted or replaced by a more abstract data class.

9.2.3.4   Subclassing

The most common form of subclassing involves the addition of both incoming and outgoing message types to the appropriate inherited message type sets. (Note that this means in almost all cases a protocol subclass is not a subtype of its superclass.)

Examples of the use of inheritance with protocol classes can be found in the following section.

9.3   Inheritance Example

We illustrate the various inheritance rules and heuristics through an example of a simple Device Management Subsystem (DMS). This is a software system responsible for initializing and controlling a disk and a tape attached to a computing system.

9.3.1   Specification

We would like to be able to control the complete system from a single point by instructing it to start and stop as needed. When we ask the system to start, we would like both devices to become operational simultaneously and, similarly, we want both devices to cease operation when we instruct the DMS to stop. In addition, the entire system must respond to a "soft" reset signal that restores all devices to a known state. On occasion, we may need to force the system to run through a set of device-specific maintenance diagnostics. For simplicity, we will assume that maintenance is performed on both devices simultaneously instead of individually. Finally, we want to have the ability to query the entire system at any time regarding its current operational state.

The informal structure diagram of this system is shown in Figure 9.8. This specification does not mention any device users. The relationship between devices and users is assumed to be specified in some other subsystem not related directly to the DMS.

Figure 9.8   The Device Management Subsystem

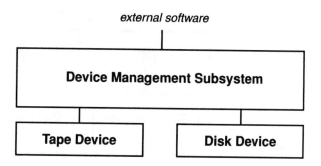

9.3.2   Analysis and Design

For pedagogical reasons, the following discussion attempts to re-create a "typical" evolutionary analysis and design process. The study is not meant to be prescriptive in the sense that all similar design problems must be tackled using the process described here. Different designers would likely proceed in different ways, depending on experience and personal inclinations.

We begin by formalizing the specification of the protocol between the DMS and the software that controls it. If we take the perspective of the DMS, then there are five input signals and one output signal,

```
protocol class ControlProtocol:
    in:    {{start, null}, {stop, null},
           {diagnose, null}, {reset, null},
           {query, null}
           }
    out: {{status, null}}
```

where null implies an unspecified and possibly empty data class.

The requirements specification for the DMS states that there should be a single access point for the system. On the other hand, we can expect tapes and disks to be sufficiently different to require specific forms of management. For example, tapes can be rewound, but not disks. Moreover, since the peripheral devices are implemented in hardware and are truly concurrent, it makes sense to control them through separate actors. The results of this short analysis suggest that a "star" configuration would be appropriate, consisting of a central coordinator actor and two device manager actors, one per device. The corresponding actor class structure is shown in Figure 9.9.

The container actor *is* the DMS. It encapsulates both device managers. The actual physical devices and their matching software drivers are not part of the diagram (or the DMS) since they are part of a lower layer and are accessed through service access points attached to the device managers.

Figure 9.9   The Structure of the Device Management System Class

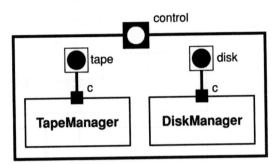

In this first cut at the system, we have three actor classes (one per component of the DMS) and three protocol classes. Since we have not yet looked at the protocols between the DMS container and the individual device drivers, the protocol classes associated with the internal end ports of the DMS are simply empty classes.

9.3.2.1   The Abstract Controlled Component

One of the main functions of the container actor is to synchronize the states of devices and their managers with its own state. When the DMS is instructed to stop, then both managers and their respective devices also should stop. Similarly, a start command to the DMS requires that both managers (and devices) also start, and so on. This leads us to the realization that the device managers are driven in almost the same manner as the DMS itself.

We can take advantage of this similarity and factor it out through inheritance. Since none of the objects is a "kind of" any of the other objects (for example, a tape manager is not a kind of DMS, or vice versa), the solution is to specify a common abstract class for all three actors. This class represents an *abstract controlled component*. It has almost the simplest possible structure with no component actors and a single end port whose type is defined by the control protocol class above (see Figure 9.10).

Figure 9.10   The Structure of an Abstract Controlled Component

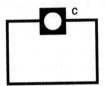

If we take advantage of this commonality and make the three actor classes subclasses of the new abstract class, then the new inheritance hierarchy will have the structure shown in Figure 9.11. This rearrangement will involve some redefinition of the actor classes already defined. However, since we have not yet put much effort into them, the cost is not too high. If suitable tools are available, then the cost will be even less.

Figure 9.11   The Actor Class Hierarchy of the DMS (Second Version)

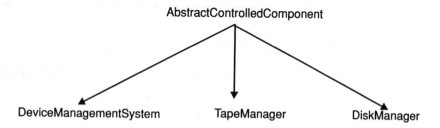

The structure of the device managers will only require a redefinition of the types associated with their interface ports. The DMS class will need to redefine its internal end ports and remove its own definition of its interface port (control), since that port is now inherited from the abstract class. The new structure with indications of local and inherited attributes shown is provided in Figure 9.12.

Figure 9.12   The New DMS Structure

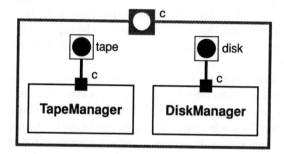

9.3.2.2   The Abstract Behavior

The behavior of this new abstract class is also abstract. It is directly derived from the control protocol specification, since the abstract class has only one interface component. The ROOMchart of this finite-state machine is shown in Figure 9.13.

Figure 9.13   The State Machine of an Abstract Controlled Component

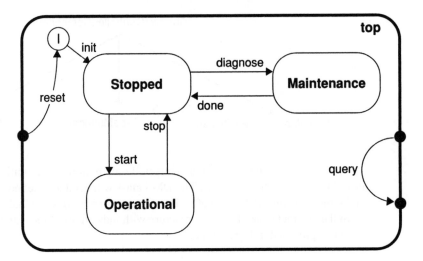

With the possible exception of the query transition, all the transitions in this diagram are abstract in the sense that they have no action code associated with them. The details of what is to be done for each transition depends on the functionality of each individual subclass. This means that the action code will be supplied by the subclasses. All the states are also abstract in that there is no refinement provided for them. This, too, is left to be defined in the subclasses.

An interesting special case is the done transition that originates from the Maintenance state. While all the other transitions in this state machine are triggered by the corresponding message types of the control protocol, there is no message type in the protocol for this transition. This is because the completion of the maintenance activity is not determined by the external system, but rather by factors internal to the actor. As a result, the done transition is left with an undefined trigger in the abstract class. The trigger must be supplied by the subclasses.

9.3.2.3　　　The Abstract Device Manager

A closer examination of the class hierarchy in Figure 9.11 reveals that the two device manager classes are conceptually much closer to each other than to the class representing the DMS. This might encourage us to look for commonality between the device managers that is not shared with the DMS class. For instance, since hardware devices can fail completely if they lose power, it may be useful to introduce another state in the abstract state machine for the device managers. This state would correspond to the "not responding" situation. In order to introduce this commonality, we need another abstract class between the abstract controlled component class and the device managers. The resulting class hierarchy is shown in Figure 9.14.

Figure 9.14　　The Actor Class Hierarchy of the DMS (Third Version)

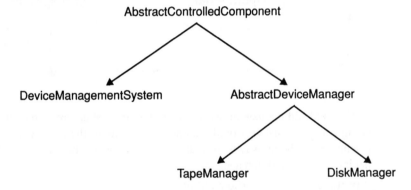

The behavior of this new abstract class is a variant of the behavior of the abstract controlled component class and includes a new NotResponding state[7] as illustrated in Figure 9.15. Since a device can fail at any time, the transition that takes us into this new state is defined as a group transition from the top-level state.

9.3.2.4　　　The Device Control Protocol

When a device fails to respond, we may want to inform the DMS coordinator by sending it a "device failed" message. Since this is a new message type, the protocol between the DMS and the devices needs to change.

---

[7] In order to keep the example simple, we ignore the issue of how this situation is detected.

Figure 9.15   The State Machine of the Abstract Device Manager Class

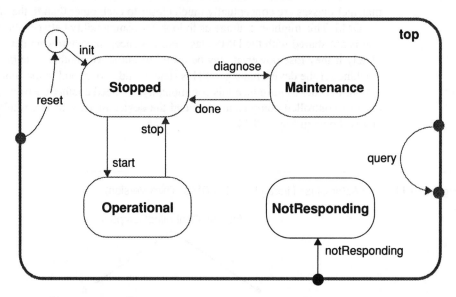

We could add the new message type to the original control protocol, but this would be wrong since the change would then also propagate to the DMS class where it would be meaningless. A better way is to create a new subclass of the original control protocol class that includes the additional signal.

> **protocol class** DeviceControlProtocol:
>   **inherits** ControlProtocol
>   **adding**
>   **out**: {{deviceFailed, null}}

This new class would have to replace the type specification of the interface port on the abstract device manager. This, in turn, means that the DMS class must change its internal end ports as well. Finally, it also means that the DMS behavior must be modified to handle the deviceFailed message type. This will likely be a new transition and possibly a new state added to the state machine inherited from the abstract controlled component class.

9.3.2.5   Other Behavior Refinements

Two other types of inheritance-based refinements also are common. The first, abstract state refinement, involves adding a sub-machine within an abstract state. The second is the addition of action code to abstract transitions in order to specialize them for a subclass.

As an example of abstract state refinement, consider the Maintenance state of the tape manager class shown in Figure 9.15. Assume that the diagnostic procedure for this device requires that the tape is rewound back to the beginning, followed by the execution of two separate tests. The actual tests are not performed by the device manager but by the device itself, following a command from the device manager. When a test is complete, the device reports the results back to the device manager. The maintenance activity is considered complete either when a test fails or when all the tests have been completed successfully. Figure 9.16 shows the detailed sub-machine within the Maintenance state corresponding to this specification.

The same Maintenance state for the disk manager subclass would have a different sub-machine matched to the diagnostic sequence appropriate for disk devices.

To demonstrate how action code can be used to specialize an abstract transition, we examine the case of the start transition, which takes us from the Stopped state and into the Operational state. In the abstract class, this transition is abstract with no action code attached. In the DMS subclass, which acts as a coordinator of the device managers, the action in response to the start event is to start up the tape and disk managers. If we are using C++ as our Detail Level language, the action code corresponding to this might be

```
transition start:
    triggered by: {{start, c, true}}
    action:      {
        disk.send (start);
        tape.send (start);}
```

where disk and tape are the names of the end ports connected to the disk and tape managers, respectively.

For the tape manager subclass, this same transition only requires that a rewind signal be sent to the drive.

Figure 9.16   The Sub-Machine in the "Maintenance" State of the Tape Manager

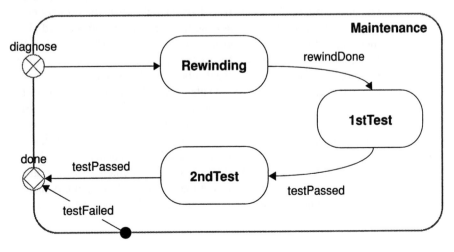

> **transition** start:
>> **triggered by**: {{start, c, true}}
>> **action**:   {device.send (rewind);}

We can see from these examples how objects with very different detailed behavior can still share a common abstract behavior.

As we add details to the action code, we may find that we need to add additional extended state variables and functions to the class specification. Some of these may lead to the definition of new detailed object classes.

9.4   Summary

The use of inheritance in software design is still in the early stages and much of its practical and even theoretical foundations have yet to be firmly established. Inheritance has been proposed and used for a variety of purposes, including reuse, abstraction, and version management. These different uses can have different objectives and may clash with each other. In order to reduce entropy, it is important to define a dominant purpose for the class hierarchy to which all others are subjugated. In ROOM, inheritance is primarily viewed as an *abstraction* mechanism that helps us deal with complexity by allowing detail to be introduced gradually. The alternative would be to base inheritance on reuse. The problem with this approach is that it often leads to confusing class hierarchies that are optimized around implementation issues and, thus, more susceptible to change ([Cook92]). In practical terms, the two approaches are not substantially different and can lead to class hierarchies that have the same global structure, but differ in detail. This means that significant reuse is possible even in case of abstraction-based inheritance. Another common way of achieving reuse in abstraction-based inheritance is to use inclusion as an alternative to subclassing.

With the abstraction-based approach, abstract classes play a pivotal role. The definition and preservation of the integrity of abstract classes is the primary concern in dealing with inheritance. Each abstract class should symbolize a well-defined abstraction with a clear meaning. Abstract classes usually occur where variations of a common pattern are required with the abstract class capturing the common aspects, while the differences are partitioned among the specialized subclasses. If the variations are relatively small, parameterization can be used in lieu of subclassing. In keeping with the abstraction bias of inheritance, abstract classes may sometimes occur independently of variants. In these cases, they capture some convenient level of abstraction, mainly as a documentational aid. To avoid unnecessary coupling, concrete classes should not be subclassed.

Exclusion of inherited attributes in a subclass is generally not desirable since it reverses the general-to-specific flow of inheritance hierarchies. However, in practical applications involving large class hierarchies, it may be difficult to avoid. A sure sign of the misuse of attribute exclusion is inverted inheritance in which the abstract class contains the superset of all the attributes of its subclasses. Overriding attributes, on the other hand, is used much more but should only be undertaken to refine an attribute and not to change its meaning.

Designing an inheritance hierarchy, like any other form of design, requires time and experience. This entails complicated manipulations of the class hierarchy and the classes themselves. Attributes may have to be promoted and demoted between classes, classes may have to be moved to different superclasses, and so on. Such operations are best done if automated tool support is provided.

Class hierarchies do require a substantial amount of maintenance, but this effort is usually worthwhile and pays for itself easily by reducing the cost of subsequent development. To minimize the effect of changes, in principle, a change to a class should be propagated only to those classes to which it is relevant. This may sometimes require the creation of a new abstract class.

Investing resources in such nontraditional activities as class hierarchy maintenance requires a culture change not only within the development team, but also in management. To ensure that long-term objectives are not jeopardized by short-term concerns, software development funds should be allocated to products rather than to projects.

In ROOM, inheritance plays a fundamental role, since all designs are specified as classes. Three different class hierarchies are supported: the actor hierarchy, the protocol hierarchy, and the data object hierarchy. The inheritance rules of data objects are determined by the Detail Level language used in modeling. Actor classes allow both high-level structure and high-level behavior to be subclassed, providing for a much higher form of reuse than is available in traditional object-oriented programming languages. Only single inheritance is supported for actor classes, and exclusion and overriding of attributes is allowed.

Abstract structures contain abstract versions of interface components and components that can be refined by subclasses. The designer should strive to make all abstract classes meaningful by ensuring that they are complete and executable. An executable abstract class is called a simulation class, since it can serve as a lightweight substitute for a concrete class while evaluating larger designs. Subclassing involves the substitution of abstract attributes by more refined ones.

Abstract behavior is captured by abstract ROOMchart diagrams. These diagrams may have abstract states and abstract transitions. These are refined by subclasses by adding sub-machine decompositions to abstract states and action code to abstract transitions.

Protocol classes have the same inheritance rules as actor classes with single inheritance and exclusions. Protocols are normally refined by adding new message types or refining the data classes associated with message types.

CHAPTER 10

The Detail Level

When we look at any industrial product, we rarely appreciate the amount of effort that is put into what we might consider as "detail." The very mention of the word brings to mind soporific images of crossing "t's" and dotting "i's" and, in general, things that are petty and uninteresting. Yet, as any engineer or software designer can corroborate, by far the greatest amount of effort invested in a technical design consists of detail.

Another reason to appreciate detail is that it sometimes plays a critical role, particularly in software systems. A modern urban legend has it that, in the early days of the American space program when there were many costly launch failures leading to multimillion dollar losses, the culprit was found to be a punctuation error in a FORTRAN program! Such extreme sensitivity is still present in the software systems of today. A single unfortunately placed instruction, for instance, can cause the collapse of a continent-wide telephone network.

In ROOM, "detail" is used primarily to specify what an actor does in the course of a transition from one state to the next. Even the most abstract of ROOM models still require detail in order to be executable. At the very least, Detail Level code is required in order to send messages between actors. Moreover, if ROOM is used for the full development cycle (including implementation), the amount of Detail Level work that must be invested can overshadow (by sheer volume if not by significance) any effort put into higher-level aspects. In the early phases of development, a relatively small amount of detail must be specified. As development progresses, more and more detail is added. If the design is done properly and our luck holds, the latter phases of development should consist almost exclusively of filling in the details.

Detail Level specifications occur in the following two primary forms:

- As action code in finite-state machine specifications for transition segments, state entry and exit actions, and so on
- As fine-grained passive objects that are used for extended state variables, or as holders of information to be transferred between actors

This level of detail is handled quite adequately by existing programming languages. The passive objects at the Detail Level include traditional programming items such as numbers, characters, and data structures of various degrees of complexity (for example, queues, arrays, record structures), and the action code manipulates these objects with the usual complement of imperative and conditional statements. The approach taken in ROOM, therefore, is to use an existing language for this purpose, rather than to devise yet another one.

This chapter examines the issues and techniques used to specify the Detail Level aspects of a ROOM model and how these fit in with the concepts introduced in the previous chapters (see Figure 10.1). Issues pertaining to all three modeling dimensions are explored. In addition, near the end of the chapter we include a general description of how a ROOM model (comprising a combination of high-level graphical attributes and textual Detail Level code) can be turned into an executable program.

Figure 10.1   The ROOM Conceptual Framework: The Detail Level

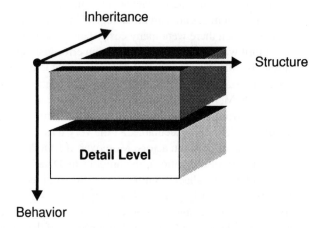

Note that the detailed code specifications for system services provided in this chapter are just examples and should not be considered definitive. The intent is to convey the genral semantics and format of the various service primitives rather than the precise syntax. The syntax is likely to vary with a particular implementation of the ROOM virtual machine, the implementation language used, and the needs and preferences of the development organization.

10.1   The Linkage Between the Detail Level and the Higher ROOM Levels

In principle, almost any programming language can be used as the Detail Level language. However, object-oriented languages are the most appropriate if we want to maintain consistency with the overall ROOM orientation toward the object paradigm. This ensures that there is no sudden paradigm shift when Detail Level issues are addressed. (Recall that during modeling, it is usually necessary to work at all three levels simultaneously.) In the remainder of this chapter and throughout most of this book, we use C++ as a representative of languages that are suitable for use at the Detail Level. There is nothing special about this choice. Other object-oriented languages, such as Eiffel or Smalltalk, can also be used.

The high-level ROOM concepts (actors, hierarchical state machines, ports, and protocols) are defined independently of any specific Detail Level language. On the other hand, the concepts supported by a standard programming language are, of course, independent of ROOM. One possible technique for linking the two would be to add extensions to the programming language. This approach is used often in research projects, but is not practical for pragmatic industrial application since it would be difficult to guarantee adequate support for the language in terms of compiler availability and quality. Instead, the coupling between the two worlds is done through a special library of objects that can be referenced when compiling Detail Level code. These are objects whose semantics are defined by ROOM, but whose concrete representation is expressed in the syntax of the chosen Detail Level programming language. They include objects that are accessible in both environments such as behavior interfaces (that is, end ports, service access points, and service provision points) and inter-actor messages. We call these objects *Detail Level linkage objects*.

Since their syntactical form is based on the Detail Level language, these objects look like any other passive objects, although their functionality is specific to ROOM. An end port, for example, might be defined as a data class that includes in its interface specification an operation that sends an asynchronous message through a binding.

During the execution of a ROOM model, the linkage between the two worlds occurs through an actor's behavior interfaces. Although they appear like any other detailed objects, behavior interfaces are connected to the underlying ROOM virtual machine. This machine is responsible for implementing the ROOM execution semantics. For example, when an end port is asked to send a message, it relays the relevant data to the virtual machine, which then delivers the message to the proper destination port and schedules its state machine for execution. The functionality of the virtual machine is packaged as a set of system services, accessed through their appropriate service access points. This includes communication services for inter-actor communications.

10.2   State Machine Action Code

Detail Level code is required to specify the following aspects of state machine behavior:

- The action code of transition segments
- The guard conditions of trigger specifications
- State entry and exit action code
- Internal functions associated with state machines
- Choicepoint branch conditions

The following is an example, based on C++, of a typical transition specification that includes action code and a complex guard condition:

```
transition midnightChimes:
    triggered by: {
        {chimeSignal, auralPort,
        {// guard condition:
         int t = timeServiceSAP.currentTime ()
         return (t == midnight);
        }
    }
    action: {
        // destroy the component whose id is stored in the extended
        // state variable 'carriageId' and create a new component in
        // its place:

        frameSAP.destroy (carriageId);
        carriageId = frameSAP.incarnate (vehicle, NULL, Pumpkin);

        // send a message through the 'locomotionPort':

        locomotionPort.send (Run);
    };
```

The effect of the complex guard condition is to ensure that the transition is triggered upon the arrival of the chimeSignal only if the current time is equal to the value of the symbolic constant midnight. The current time value is obtained through a service access point on the Timing Service. The form of the guard condition corresponds to the body of a function that returns a Boolean value.

The action code of the transition removes one component actor from the decomposition frame and then incarnates another one using the Frame Service of the ROOM virtual machine. The new component, which is specified to be an instance of the Pumpkin class, is created in the reference slot named vehicle. In the final step, a message with a signal value of Run is sent through one of the end ports.

Most state machine action code follows the pattern exemplified by the previous transition. Action code typically involves communicating with other actors through behavior interfaces and accessing standard ROOM services, such as the Timing Service and the Frame Service. The remainder of this section focuses on the capabilities of these services and how they are used in practice.

10.2.1 Inter-Actor Communications

In principle, communication between ROOM actors is achieved exclusively by exchanging messages. This communication can be either *synchronous* or *asynchronous*. Asynchronous communication allows the sender to continue execution as soon as the message has been handed over to the underlying communication service. Its principal advantage is that the interval during which the behavior is unresponsive is short and the communication mechanisms required to support it are relatively simple. This makes it suitable in situations where a rapid response is critical. Synchronous communication, on the other hand, combines synchronization with the exchange of information. The sending actor is blocked until it receives a reply. During this interval, it cannot respond to any other inputs. The advantage of this form of communication is that it provides some degree of control over the ordering of activities.

The issue of which is the "right" form of communication for distributed systems has been the subject of much debate over the years. If we neglect the various emotional issues and take a pragmatic approach, we may conclude that both forms have a place. For example, the initial version of the Ada[1] language supported only a synchronous form of communication known as the "rendezvous." More recent proposals for upgrading the language include asynchronous communication, in recognition of the limitations imposed by the original approach [Ada90].

10.2.1.1 Behavior Interface Objects

Messages are both sent and received through specialized *behavior interfaces*. A component of a behavior interface can be any of the following:

- An end port
- A service access point (SAP)
- A service provision point (SPP)

These objects represent the linkage between behavior and structure. In the behavioral dimension, they appear in the form of passive Detail Level data objects similar to extended state objects. Communication is initiated by invoking a suitable primitive operation on a behavior interface component. For instance, if C++ is used to specify the Detail Level behavior, initiating a communication has the general form

---

[1] Ada is a trademark of the U. S. Department of Defense (Ada Joint Project Office).

result = interfaceObject.comOperation (par$_1$, par$_2$, ...);

where comOperation is the name of the desired communication operation, result is an object that can be queried subsequently to determine the outcome of the operation, and par$_i$ represents the parameters to the operation.

10.2.1.2   Communication Services

The exact semantics of the communication primitives are determined by the qualities of the underlying communication service. This is specified by way of the quality of service parameter associated with the protocol attribute of the interface component. The quality of service defines characteristics (such as the probabilities of losing, reordering, or duplicating messages, transmission delay characteristics, and so on). Unless stated otherwise, the examples in this book are all based on a reference communications service called the *Basic Communication Service*, which is provided by the ROOM virtual machine. This service has a low, but finite, probability of losing, reordering, or duplicating messages.

10.2.1.3   Asynchronous Communication

In asynchronous communication, the sender passes a message to an interface component and immediately resumes execution with the following instruction. For example, if aPort is the name of an end port, then, using C++, an asynchronous message is sent using the primitive

aPort.send (signal, priority, dataObject);

where signal is a symbolic name for a message signal, priority is an object that specifies the desired priority level of the message, and dataObject is a reference to a data object that is to be sent to the far end. The send operation makes an exact copy of the data object so that the original remains unchanged. In our examples, we also use the following form for data-less messages (that is, messages that consist of only a signal) that are sent at the "default" priority:

aPort.send (signal);

No objects are returned as a result of an asynchronous send operation.

The dispatched message is conveyed by a communication service by way of the route specified by the structure and eventually placed on the queue of the destination interface component. When its turn comes around, the message is scheduled for processing and handed over to the destination behavior where it *may* trigger a transition. If the current state of the destination does not have a trigger that is satisfied by this message, the message is simply discarded and no error indication is given to the sender. This simple model is suitable for efficient high-performance implementation.

10.2.1.4 Synchronous Communication

Synchronous communication in ROOM consists of a controlled exchange of messages between a sender and a receiver (see Figure 10.2). The sender dispatches a message by using a special "invoke" primitive. This message is conveyed by the underlying communication service to the destination actor in the same way as in the case of the asynchronous communication. The message is then queued at the destination where, when it is eventually scheduled, it triggers a transition in the destination behavior.[2] The action associated with this transition *must* perform a special *reply* operation, which returns a message back to the sender through the same interface component on which the invocation message was received.

Figure 10.2 Synchronous Communication Model

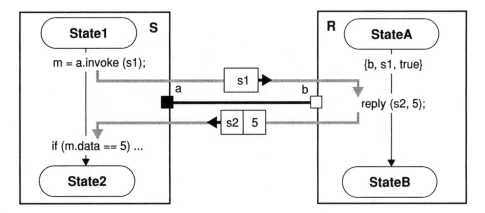

The reply message *always* takes precedence over any messages that may have been queued at the sender, regardless of priority. This ensures procedure-call type semantics for synchronous communication. In effect, the reply message is a message of a greater priority than any other message. When the reply message is received and dispatched, the sender is unblocked and continues with the next instruction following the synchronous invoke.

The basic form of synchronous communication primitive is illustrated by the C++ instruction

retMessagePtr = aPort.invoke (signal, dataObject);

or, if there are no input parameters in the invoke,

---

[2] If a suitable transition exists in the current state.

retMessagePtr = a.Port.invoke (signal);

where dataObject is the object that specifies the parameters of the invoke and retMessagePtr is either a pointer to the object that contains the reply message (sent by the receiving actor) or a NULL pointer. The latter is an indication that the synchronous communication operation was not successful. A communication failure can occur, for instance, if the interface component is not connected, or if the actor at the receiving end does not reply to the invocation. Note that synchronous invokes do not provide for a priority parameter, since they take place at the highest possible system priority.

As noted, the receiver of a synchronous communication *must* reply to the invoker. Furthermore, the reply must occur within the same transition that was triggered by the invoke. The reply primitive used for this purpose has the forms

msg -> reply (signal, replyObject);

or

msg -> reply (signal);

where replyObject is the optional object containing the results of the reply. A copy of this object is embedded in the result of the invoke operation (retMessage).

Synchronous communication comes at a price that may be particularly expensive for fault-tolerant real-time applications. One of its major drawbacks is *deadlock*. The most obvious form of deadlock occurs when two behaviors simultaneously invoke each other synchronously. In that case, since both behaviors are blocked, neither is capable of replying to the other. Unless the actors are restarted by some external means, they will remain suspended forever. A more insidious form of deadlock occurs when there is a circular chain of invokes (for example, actor A invokes actor B, which in turn invokes actor C, which, finally, invokes actor A). Such circularities can be difficult to detect.

A second problem with synchronous communications is that it reduces the responsiveness of the sending behavior. Since it cannot respond to other inputs while blocked in a synchronous communication, the time spent in this mode should not exceed its maximum allowed latency. Unfortunately, in distributed systems, these delays can be quite long for a variety of reasons. First of all, there is a potential for long and highly variable transmission delays through the distributed communication network, as described in Section 2.1.6. On top of this, there may be variable queueing delays at the server because of load surges in the network. Last but not least, the receiver itself may take an inordinate amount of time to respond to a request since it may be have been designed independently of its clients. This effectively leaves the sender at the mercy of the receiver. When the total of all these delays is calculated, it may exceed the maximum latency of the sender.

One common way to get around both of these problems is to "abort" a pending synchronous communication if it has exceeded some predefined delay value. This can be achieved through a special *timed invoke*. A timed invoke specifies a maximum time interval during which the reply must be received by the sender. If the reply is not received within this interval, the synchronous communication is aborted and an exception is raised. The C++ primitive for this has the form

retMessage = aPort.invoke (signal, dataObject, timeoutValue);

where timeoutValue specifies the maximum time permitted to wait for a reply starting from the instant the invoke was initiated.

10.2.1.5 Receiving Messages

In a state machine formalism, there is no need for an explicit "receive" operation, since a receive is automatically asserted whenever the behavior enters a leaf state. Also, for synchronous communication, there is a special implicit receive within the invoke operation. An important feature of this model is that both synchronous and asynchronous communications are received in exactly the same way.

To take advantage of this, the reply primitive described previously is defined in a generic way. It can be used to respond to the most recently received message, regardless of whether that message was sent as a synchronous or asynchronous communication. This allows the receiver be designed independently of the communication mode used by the sender. Such an arrangement is well suited for implementing client-server type applications, since it reduces the coupling between the server and its clients. The same server can be used to support either synchronous or asynchronous clients, and even different combinations of clients.

The behavior of an actor often needs to access the information embedded within the message it just received. We will assume that all incoming messages are instances of a special Detail Level class called ROOMMessage.[3] To access the data embedded in the message, the following primitive is used:

aMessage.data

In C++, this returns a pointer to a data object. In principle, this can be an instance of any user-defined data class, so it is necessary to coerce the result of this operation to be a pointer of the desired type. For example, if the receiver knows that the data in a message is an instance of the class MyClass, it can extract that object using the following statement:

MyClass* dataPtr = (MyClass*) aMessage.data;

To determine the behavior interface component on which a message arrived, we use the primitive

aMessage.interface ()

which returns a pointer to an instance of a special class called ROOMInterface. All end ports, SAPs, and SPPs are subclasses of this class. Finally, to access the signal associated with a message, the primitive used is

---

[3] We examine this and other "system" Detail Level classes in more detail later in the chapter.

aMessage.signal

which returns an instance of the special system-defined class called ROOMSignal.

Throughout this text, we will use the convention that the message most recently received by the behavior is indicated by a special system-defined extended state variable called msg. Since this variable contains a *pointer* to an instance of the ROOMMessage class, it is most often used in conjunction with the C++ pointer dereference operator "->". For example, to access the signal value of the current message we would use the following expression:

msg -> signal

10.2.1.6   Event Deferral

Because of the highly asynchronous nature of reactive systems, it often happens that an unwanted message arrives in the midst of some complex event sequence. If this message requires immediate processing, then we have no choice. However, in many cases, the nature of the event may be such that we can postpone (within limits) the processing of such messages until we are finished with the current sequence.

Consider, for instance, the case of a print controller responsible for handling requests to output user-supplied files to a printer device. Service requests are processed in the following way. If the printer is idle, the request is printed by printing a header sheet first, followed by the printing of the actual file. When the printer completes the printing of a request, it informs the controller with a printDone message. This sequence is illustrated by the state transition diagram in Figure 10.3.

Unfortunately, service requests arrive at random intervals, so it is quite possible to get a request while the system is busy printing. Since the printer can print only one file at a time, we must enqueue subsequent requests until the current file is printed. When printing is

Figure 10.3   Print Service Request Processing

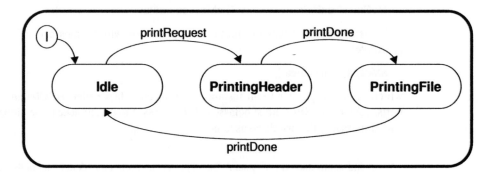

complete, if the queue is empty, we return to the Idle state. Otherwise we return to the PrintingHeader state. There are two drawbacks to this approach. First, the application code within the print server must perform the queueing and queue management functions. While these usually are not overly complex, they add overhead to action code. Second, the handling of requests is not uniform. Request handling can be initiated either in the transition from the Idle state to the PrintingHeader state, or in the transition from the PrintingFile state back to the PrintingHeader state (for queued requests). This forces duplication of code across the two transitions, and increases the probability of design or coding errors.

To simplify the handling of this relatively common situation, ROOM provides applications with the ability to "defer" incoming events. Event deferral is simply a means to allow applications to control the sequence of events. A deferred event is queued on its incoming interface component and held until explicitly released by the application code. In other words, by deferring an event, an application can behave as if that event has not yet occurred. When a deferred event is eventually resubmitted, it is received in exactly the same way as if it had just arrived.

To defer an event, the action code of the transition triggered by that event must issue the following primitive:

```
msg -> defer ();
```

This will enqueue the current message in first-in-first-out order at the interface component on which it was received.

To recall the *first* deferred event for a particular interface component, the transition code performs the operation

```
anInterface.recall (frontFlag);
```

where frontFlag is a Boolean that, if set to true, will ensure that the recalled event will be put at the front of its priority queue. This allows the preservation of temporal ordering and ensures that the deferred event is handled before any similar events that arrived between its deferral and its recall. If the frontFlag is set to false, then the deferred event is placed at the end of its priority queue.

To recall *all* deferred messages on an interface component, the following is used:

```
anInterface.recallAll (frontFlag);
```

If there are no messages in the defer queue of an interface component when the recall operations are performed, the operations will have no effect.

Use of event deferral in the print server example is illustrated in Figure 10.4. Here, the top-level group transition printRequest is used to trap any service requests received in either of the "printing" states. Its action consists of a single defer statement that will force all service requests to be queued. That group transition is overridden by the printRequest transition when the system is in the Idle state. Finally, to ensure that deferred events are handled properly, the outgoing printDone transition from the PrintingFile state will include the statement

```
servicePort.recall (true);
```

Figure 10.4 Use of Event Deferral

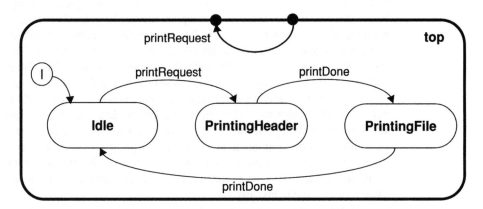

where servicePort is the name of the port on which service requests arrive. This will force the first deferred event to the front of the queue on the servicePort interface component.

Another common use of the defer mechanism is to allow handling of complex synchronous requests. Normally, the reply to a synchronous request must be sent within the same transition that was triggered by the request. This limitation can be overcome by deferring the synchronous request, performing all the activity required to generate the information required for the response, and then recalling the request and replying to it. During the time that the request is deferred, *the sender remains blocked.*[4] We illustrate this with another example.

A database query server acts as a front end to a database (see Figure 10.5) and keeps a local memory cache of the most frequently requested data so that it can respond quickly. Occasionally, a request comes in for data that is not in the cache, so the server must retrieve it from the database and update the cache. This requires the server to wait for the database to respond. We will assume that the real-time requirements are such that the server must use asynchronous communication when communicating with the database.

The portion of the behavior of the query server that deals with handling requests is shown in Figure 10.6. While waiting for requests, the server is in the Idle state. A query request is triggered by a dataReq message on the server's client port (port c). Choicepoint inCache evaluates a Boolean predicate to determine if the required data is in the cache. If it is, the true transition segment is taken and a reply is returned immediately using the data in the cache. If not, then the false branch is taken. In this transition segment, the request is deferred, a query is sent to the database, and the system is forced into the Busy state. Any service requests arriving while the system is in this state are also deferred to ensure that

---

[4] We must be careful if the request is a timed invoke, since a timeout may force the invoke to abort.

Figure 10.5 The Database Query System

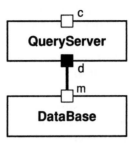

queries are handled in first-come-first-serve (FCFS) order. Finally, when the database responds, the data from the database is added to the cache and *all* deferred requests are recalled to the *front* of the queue (because of the FCFS requirement). When the request is received the second time, the right data will be in the cache and it will be handled by the action in the true segment.

Figure 10.6 Synchronous Request Handling

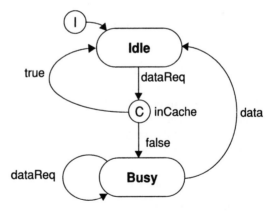

10.2.2 Dealing with Time

For obvious reasons, time plays a major role in real-time systems. Two general situations pertaining to time are of interest.

- The expiration of some time interval and

- The occurrence of a set moment in time

For example, after sending a message off to a remote object, we need to know whether we get a response within some predefined time period. If the time interval expires before a reply is received, we may conclude that the far end is defective in some way and act accordingly. The second situation deals with absolute time. For instance, it may be required in some system to generate a daily status report at a particular time of day.

In order to adapt them to the ROOM behavioral model, these types of events must be converted into messages. This, in turn, requires a source for sending the messages and an interface component through which to receive them. Since timing facilities are typically required by many actors in a real-time system, it is natural to provide this as a shared service of the ROOM virtual machine. This service provides the fundamental timing capabilities which can be used, if necessary, to construct more sophisticated or application-specific timing services.

The basic usage model is as follows. A service request is submitted through a SAP on the Timing Service. The request may specify a time interval or an absolute time of day. This results in the creation of a dedicated "timer" within the service. Each request has a different timer so that multiple parallel requests can be made. When the service detects that the appropriate moment has arrived, it sends a special timeout message to the SAP through which the request was made. This message can then trigger a transition just like any other message. The timeout message is queued and scheduled like any other event and, depending on its priority and the current processing load, there may be an additional delay before it is actually received.

The basic primitive for interval timing has the following general form in C++

```
timerId = timingSAP.informIn (interval, applicId, priority);
```

where timingSAP is a SAP on the basic timing service, interval identifies the duration of the time interval relative to the current moment, applicId is an optional application-specific data object that will be returned with the timeout message, priority is the priority at which the timeout message will be delivered, and timerId is an instance of a special system-defined class ROOMTimer that uniquely identifies the timer created for this request. Since multiple timers can be outstanding, the application-specific applicId can be used to differentiate them.

To cancel an outstanding timer, the following operation is invoked

```
timingSAP.cancelTimer (timerId);
```

where timerId is the identifier returned by a previous service request operation. The timer will be cancelled even if it has expired but the timeout message has not yet been received because of queueing delays. Canceling timers that are no longer needed (but that are still pending) is important, but is frequently forgotten in practice. This results in spurious timeout messages and can lead to subtle errors in which a timeout message from a previous timer can be misinterpreted as belonging to a more recent timer.

To get a timeout message at a particular time of day, the primitive has the form

timerId = timingSAP.informAt (time, applicId, priority);

where time is a specification of the absolute time when the timeout message is to be dispatched.

The ability to specify priorities for timeout messages can be used to realize hard real-time periodic tasks. This is achieved by asking for a timeout message to be delivered at the highest available priority, with the interval set to the period of the task. When the timeout occurs, the timing request is repeated, followed by the actions that must be performed periodically. This cycle is then repeated *ad infinitum*. If the scheduling discipline is customized for the priority level of the timeout signal, the interference of other tasks of lesser priorities can be minimized.

10.2.3   Interaction with Dynamic Structure

Section 6.8 discussed the concept of dynamic structures and the related concepts of dynamic actors and imported actor references. However, that section only dealt with the representational aspects. We now complete the picture and examine the procedures by which behavior can control dynamic reconfiguration.

10.2.3.1   The Frame Service

In traditional operating systems, applications create and destroy tasks or processes issuing service requests to the underlying operating system. This is also the case in ROOM, where the mechanics of creation and destruction of actors is the responsibility of a system service provided by the ROOM virtual machine. This service is called the *Frame Service*.[5] Service access points on the Frame Service provide a set of operations that can be invoked within transition actions to control dynamic structures.

10.2.3.2   Identifying Actors

To manipulate dynamic components, it must be possible to identify them in some way. The Frame Service recognizes two types of actor identifiers. The first of these is the *reference name*. A reference name is the symbolic name given to a component actor within a decomposition frame. This identifier is static. The reference name is unique and meaningful only within the scope of a decomposition frame. The second type of actor identifier is called the *dynamic incarnation identifier*. It uniquely identifies each actor incarnation in the system and, hence, has a global scope. The dynamic identifier is unique not only in space but in

---

[5] The service derives its unusual name from an analogy with a motion picture film strip in which moving pictures are described by a series of static frames. A composite actor that includes dynamic components (dynamic and imported actors) can be viewed as a specification for a *set* of different internal configurations, or "frames."

time. That is, if a component actor in a given decomposition frame is created and destroyed multiple times, it will have a different dynamic identifier each time it is created. This allows different incarnations of the same object to be distinguished, if necessary.

An actor can obtain its dynamic identifier by making a call to a special primitive available from a Frame Service SAP,

    actorId = aFrameSAP.me ();

where actorId is an instance of the class ROOMActorId, and aFrameSAP is a SAP on the Frame Service.

The strong encapsulation of actors implies that they cannot reference other actors in their own environment or within their component actors. This leaves only the behavior component with the ability to manipulate other actors within its scope. This scope is defined by the decomposition frame of a composite actor.

10.2.3.3   Dynamic Actors

Dynamic actors are actors that are dynamically created and destroyed, as the need arises, by the behavior component of an actor. The basic service primitive for creating a dynamic actor has the following form in C++,

    actorId = aFrameSAP.incarnate (actorRefName, initData);

where actorRefName is the reference name of the actor component to be created, initData is an optional data object that is passed in a message to the initial transition, and actorId is the dynamic incarnation identifier of the newly created actor. The class of actorId is ROOMActorId.

If the dynamic actor is specified as substitutable, then the primitive has the form

    actorId = aFrameSAP.incarnate (actorRefName, initData, actorClass);

where actorClass is the class of the actor that will actually be incarnated. This class must be of a compatible type with the class specified for the actor.

If the actor being incarnated is a composite actor, then all its fixed components are created as well. The order of creation is such that all components are created before the behavior component. Thus, when the behavior component runs its initial transition, all the other components will have been created.

If the actor reference being incarnated is a replicated actor, then just *one* additional actor incarnation is created, unless the upper replication limit has been reached. In the latter case, an exception is raised.

The "destroy" operation is used to destroy a dynamic actor,

    aFrameSAP.destroy (actorId);

where actorId is the dynamic incarnation identifier of the actor to be destroyed.

10.2.3.4 Imported Actors

Imported actor references are used to denote "slots" into which existing actor incarnations can be inserted in order to involve them in dynamically established relationships with other actors. Recall from Section 6.7 that only actors having explicit equivalence relationships can be inserted into an imported actor reference.

The basic "import" primitive has the following format in C++,

result = aFrameSAP.import (actorId, actorRefName);

where actorId is the dynamic incarnation identifier of the actor to be imported, actor-RefName is the reference name of the imported actor reference "slot," and result is a Boolean result object that specifies whether the operation was successful (result = true) or not (result = false). The operation can fail if any of the following is true:

- The actor being imported is of a class not compatible with the class of the imported actor reference.

- The actor being imported cannot satisfy all the contracts specified for the imported actor reference (for example, some ports required by the reference may already be bound in other containing actors).

- The imported actor reference is replicated and the number of previously imported actors is already equal to the upper limit of replication (that is, all the slots are filled).

An actor is removed from a slot with the following Frame Service SAP primitive operation,

aFrameSAP.deport (actorId, actorRefName);

where actorId is the dynamic identifier of the actor being removed and actorRefName is the reference name of the imported actor reference from which it is being removed.

10.2.4 Behavior and Replicated Structures

At higher levels, replication is a simplifying concept. It allows us to deal with a plurality of instances in a uniform manner. At the Detail Level, however, it is sometimes important to distinguish the individual instances from the group. In that case, replication adds complexity. This section examines how replication is handled at the Detail Level.

All replicated ROOM interface components, regardless of type, can be viewed either as integral "multipoint" interface components or as collections of individual interface components. In the former case, the replicated interface component is treated as a single complex object, whereas in the latter it is reminiscent of a traditional array of homogeneous objects. We will refer to these two views as the *group* and *individual* "views" of an interface component.

10.2.4.1   The Group View

The essential feature of the group view is that it allows us to induce the same effect in all replicated instances. For example, if aReplicatedPort is a replicated end port, then the following primitive will *broadcast* the same asynchronous message through all the instances:

    aReplicatedPort.send (someSignal);

A more complex situation occurs when a replicated interface component is used for a synchronous communication, as shown in the following:

    replies = aReplicatedPort.invoke (someSignal, someData);

While it may be intuitively obvious that this will send the same synchronous invoke to all the individual instances, it may not be obvious as to what happens to the replies. In ROOM, a synchronous invoke on a replicated interface component results in a set of concurrent individual invokes. The sender is blocked until *all* the invokes have completed (successfully or unsuccessfully). On the receiving side, each receiver is only blocked until its portion of the invoke is completed, after which, in principle, it can continue independently of whether the whole communication is complete. Thus, the replicated invoke only ensures synchronization between the sender and individual receivers but not between receivers. For example, the first receiver to reply may have responded to further events (from other sources) before the last receiver has had an opportunity to send its reply.

In C++, the result of a synchronous communication on a replicated port is a collection (array) of pointers to reply messages, one from each receiver. Formally, the type of the variable replies is ROOMMessage**. If one or more receivers fail to respond, the appropriate entry will contain a NULL pointer.

10.2.4.2   The Individual View

Replication generally implies that the replicated components are to be dealt with in some homogeneous manner. Nevertheless, even in these cases it is sometimes necessary to distinguish the individual interface components. The simplest way is to use indexing. For example, if i is an integer, the command

    aPort [i].send (someSignal);

will send a message through the i-th instance of a replicated port.

Using indices to distinguish individual instances is not always satisfactory since the distinction is based on a practically meaningless integer. While an index value of "5" may have meaning for the original designer of a system, its significance may be completely lost to someone trying to understand the design at a later time. In most situations, it is preferred to differentiate replicated instances based on some application-specific and more meaningful symbolic name. This requires maintaining a mapping between symbolic names and indices. Such a mapping might be provided by a general-purpose "dictionary" object.

Consider the example of the Lines Subsystem in the simple intercom switch introduced in Section 6.8.3 (see Figure 10.7). This subsystem incorporates a set of lines modeled by a replicated component actor Lines. In some situations it is more convenient for the behavior component of the Lines Subsystem to identify the individual lines not by their index, but by their calling number. We will assume that there exists a library class called Dictionary that stores a set of associations of the type <calling number, pointer to port instance>. We further assume this class has a member function at () that retrieves the port pointer corresponding to a given calling number. In that case, sending a message to a particular line actor can be accomplished with

CNDictionary.at (callingNumber) ->send (aSignal);

where CNDictionary is an instance of the C++ class Dictionary that keeps the mapping between calling numbers and port instances, and callingNumber is the calling number of the line to which we want to send the message.

Figure 10.7 The Lines Subsystem of an Intercom System

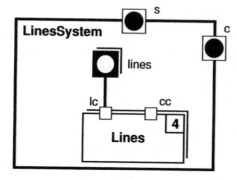

If the member function add () is used to add associations to instances of the Dictionary class, then the calling number dictionary may be initialized with statements of the form

CNDictionary.add (callingNumber, lines [i]);

where i is the index of the port corresponding to the calling number specified by the parameter callingNumber, and lines is the reference name of the replicated end port.

10.2.5 Interaction with External Entities

The ultimate role of any real-time system is to control some external entities. These entities could be either hardware devices (such as actuators for the control surfaces of an aircraft) or software entities (such as file systems or databases). The most natural way to access such entities in ROOM is through specialized service access points connected to the appropriate external entities. A service request is made through such a SAP by invoking a specialized member function, and the results of handling the request are returned in the form of inter-actor messages. This is similar to the way the Timing Service operates. (The Timing Service can be viewed as an interface to an external real-time clock device.)

For example, assume that we need to access a disk drive directly from a ROOM actor. If diskSAP is an instance of a SAP specialized for this purpose, then to have it perform a "read" operation, we might use a statement of the general form

diskSAP.readSector (diskId, sectorNumber);

where readSector is a special member function that initiates a disk read operation, diskId is a device identifier, and sectorNumber is the address of the disk sector that we want to access. The device will eventually respond with the data we requested. This data is packaged by custom code within the virtual machine into a normal ROOM message, which is then delivered through the diskSAP interface component on which the request was initiated.

All necessary translations between the ROOM environment and the external environment are performed by the specialized SAP and its underlying mechanisms, all of which are embedded in the ROOM virtual machine.

10.2.6   Exception Handling[6]

In the description of some of the primitive service operations, we noted that in some cases of invalid usage, run-time exceptions can be raised. Exceptions may also occur because of other invalid specifications in application code (such as arithmetic or array boundary overflows). In order to support the realization of fault-tolerant applications, ROOM provides for an application-specific exception handling policy that is adapted to its event-driven model.

There are two possible levels of exception handling in ROOM. The first level is *language specific* and depends on the exception handling facilities of the underlying language. The second level is ROOM specific and is based on generating a special exception event that can be handled by a transition. In the ROOM exception handling model, language-specific handling (if it is defined) always takes precedence over the more general ROOM exception mechanism.

10.2.6.1   Language-Specific Handling

The handling of exceptions varies widely across different programming languages [Liskov79]. In most cases, it consists of explicitly identifying statements that are "protected" against failure and specifying application-specific recovery actions in case failures

---

[6] This section contains advanced material that can be omitted on first reading.

occur while executing those statements. For example, the following is an example of exception handling in C++ [Ellis90],

try {a = c / d;} catch (Zerodivide&) {a = maxInt;};

which protects the arithmetic statement a = c / d from a division by zero. In this case the recovery is accomplished by assigning a very large integer value (maxInt) to the result of the failed computation.

In most languages, exception handling is nested so that, if the lexical level at which the exception was detected cannot handle it, the exception is passed to the next higher level for handling, and so on.

10.2.6.2   ROOM Exception Handling

ROOM exception handling occurs only if the language-specific handlers were not successful in dealing with the exception. Unhandled exceptions are trapped by a primitive service of the ROOM virtual machine called the *Exception Service*. This service packages the exception information in a special *exception message*, that is then sent to the behavior that experienced the exception. In order to receive this message, the behavior must have a service access point to the Exception Service of the ROOM virtual machine. It also must provide the appropriate transitions with the action code to handle exceptions. The exception SAP can also be used to induce exceptions when necessary (for example, during testing).

A typical example of ROOM exception handling is shown in Figure 10.8. Two exception handlers are defined: handler h0 which is defined at the topmost level and handler h2 (defined within state S2). We assume that both of these are triggered by the same event:

{error, exceptionSAP, true}

Figure 10.8   ROOM Exception Handlers

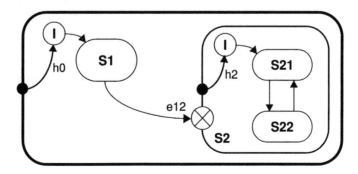

where error is the default signal for all exception events and exceptionSAP is a SAP to the Exception Service.

The usual scoping rules apply to these transitions. If the exception occurred while the behavior was in state S2, then handler h2 will be executed. Otherwise, handler h0 will be executed. In this example, both handlers perform some type of "reset" by forcing the behavior through an initial transition at the appropriate level. This is standard procedure for many types of exceptions, but is not mandatory. For example, a handler might perform a simple self-transition to history.

If an exception is not handled by a ROOM handler, the behavior is automatically forced into an *exception mode* by the ROOM run-time system. In this mode, the behavior no longer responds to incoming events. When this happens, a special *component exception* message is sent to the behavior component of all[7] of its immediate containing actors that have an Exception Service SAP. If a containing actor does not handle the exception, then it, too, is placed into exception mode and the process is repeated at the next level. If the top level actor is reached, it, too, is placed in an exception mode, in which case recovery must be undertaken by some external agent that interacts with the ROOM run-virtual machine.

In order to prevent infinite recursion, if a second exception occurs while executing the action code of an exception handler, the behavior is automatically forced into the exception mode.

When a component fails and enters the exception mode, the containing actor can restart it with a special Frame Service primitive,

aFrameSAP. restart (actorId, dataObject);

where actorId is the dynamic identifier of the actor that failed and dataObject is an optional data object that can be embedded in the message for the initial transition. For the behavior component of a restarted actor, a restart is functionally equivalent to a re-creation. A new dynamic identifier is allocated to the actor, and its behavior is restarted with the topmost initial transition. Furthermore, restarting an actor also will restart any of its component actors that are in exception mode or in reset mode (described later). On the other hand, actors in normal operational mode are unaffected by a restart of their containing actor.

A more drastic recovery action is a "reset" that transitively resets all the component actors:

aFrameSAP.reset (actorId);

This will restore the actor to its status prior to start of execution. All its dynamic components will be destroyed and all importations annulled. All remaining components also will be reset (as will their components, and so on). An actor in reset mode is practically nonexistent as far as other actors in the system are concerned. To restore a reset actor into normal operational mode, a restart command must be issued.

---

[7] Recall that an actor can be contained in multiple composite actors.

The three operational modes of an actor described previously (reset, operational, exception) can be considered as the *metastates* of an actor and should not be confused with the application-specific states. The simple state transition diagram in Figure 10.9 describes the relationship between the various metastates of an actor. The top-level state machine of the behavior of an actor can be viewed as a sub-machine of the operational metastate.

Figure 10.9   The Metastates of an Actor

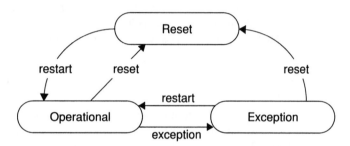

The handling of a component exception must be done with care. If a component fails while it is contained in multiple actors, then multiple actors will be notified of the component exception. In that case, it is critical that the recovery action undertaken by the various containing actors is coordinated. The best policy to ensure against conflicting recovery actions is to designate one of the containing actors as the "controller" of the component, whereas other containing actors are just "users" of its services. In that case, the recovery of the failed component is performed exclusively by the controller and the recovery action of the remaining actors is limited to recovering from the effects of the failure.

The application can also raise an exception to itself,

exceptionSAP.raise (exceptionType);

where exceptionType is a passive object that specifies the type of exception generated. This will result in an exception event being generated and received through exceptionSAP. This can be used in situations where the application code detects some type of inconsistency in its operation. Perhaps the most useful application of this is to allow an actor to place itself in the exception metastate in order to take advantage of standard high-level exception recovery mechanisms. This is achieved by raising an exception *for which the behavior does not have a handler*. When the exception message is delivered, it forces the behavior into the exception state, which propagates the exception to the next structural level and thus activates the appropriate recovery procedures.

10.2.7   Inheritance and Action Code

In some cases, it is necessary to access a segment of action code that is defined in a super-class. Consider the common situation in which the initial transition of an actor performs some initialization of local extended state variables. For example, if a and b are extended state variables in some actor class, the initial transition segment might include the following action code:

```
a = 5;
b = "uungh";
```

Assume that we now must define a new subclass of this class, and that this new subclass has an additional variable, c, that also must be set up in the initial transition.

To do this, we must override the entire initial code segment of the parent class,[8] copy over its initialization code, and include the additional statement to initialize the new variable. The code in the subclass would then be as follows:

```
a = 5;
b = "uungh";
c = 3.14;
```

Unfortunately, this requires "cloning" of the appropriate code of the parent class (the first two assignment statements in this example), which leads to potential maintenance problems. What happens if, at a later time, we must add another variable to the parent class that also must be primed in the initial transition? If we fix it in the superclass, the change will not automatically propagate to the subclasses, since the entire code segment has been replaced. Instead, we would have to "manually" transcribe the new code into all the subclasses in which the original code was overridden, a potentially error-prone process (for example, we may forget to do it or make a transcription error).

In order to overcome this limitation, ROOM defines the concept of a *callsuper* action for action code as follows:

```
CALLSUPER;
c = 3.14;
```

The effect of a callsuper action is to invoke the corresponding action code segment of the superclass. This eliminates the need for code cloning. A callsuper action can only be invoked for an attribute (transition segment, guard condition, entry or exit action, choice-point condition) that has been overridden.

A special form of this capability is defined for internal functions that have been overridden in subclasses. For instance, assume that the function sum2 (int a, int b), originally

---

[8] In ROOM, individual action code segments (on transition segments, guard conditions, and so on) are treated as indivisible attributes from an inheritance point of view. This means that it is *not* possible to selectively inherit portions of a code segment (such as individual statements), but only the entire segment. This allows Schematic Level concepts to be decoupled from the idiosyncrasies of particular Detail Level programming languages.

defined in the actor class Master, has been redefined in a subclass SpecialMaster. In that case, explicit calls to sum2 made within the SpecialMaster class will default to the locally defined version of this function and not the inherited one. However, in some situations, it may be useful to access the parent's version of a function. ROOM provides an explicit *superclass reference* facility for this purpose. In C++, this facility has the following format:

    SUPER::sum2 (5, 6);

This will result in the inherited version of the internal function being invoked instead of the locally defined version.

10.3   Detail Level Objects

The second major aspect of the Detail Level, in addition to action code, is the passive objects that capture fine-grained detail. These objects are passive in the sense that they do not have their own threads of control. Instead, their functionality is executed only in the context of the thread of an actor's behavior. These objects are used in the following situations:

- As extended state variables in the state machine of an actor

- As temporary stack variables in action code segments

- As parameter values in action code segments

- As data objects that can be included in ROOM messages and passed between actors

- As interface components to the ROOM virtual machine (only if they are behavior interface objects)

If the Detail Level language is an object-oriented programming language that supports inheritance, then these objects will be defined by classes that are organized in a class hierarchy. The inheritance rules are dependent on the chosen programming language and may be quite different from those used in other ROOM inheritance hierarchies (see Chapter 9). For example, if C++ is used, the class hierarchy may exhibit multiple inheritance, whereas actor and protocol classes only support single inheritance.

Detail Level objects used in modeling can be classified into two groups: ROOM linkage objects and user-defined objects.

10.3.1   ROOM Linkage Objects

Linkage objects connect the Detail Level to the higher conceptual levels of ROOM. They are objects that can be referenced in all scopes. For example, the name of an actor reference is defined as part of the structural decomposition of an actor, but can also be referenced when the reference is being incarnated. The following objects belong in this group:

- Behavior interfaces (end ports, SAPs, and SPPs)

- Dynamic actor identifiers
- Actor reference names
- Actor class names
- Inter-actor messages
- Signal names
- Message priorities

We have already discussed the semantics and usage of these objects in the previous section. In this section we will focus mainly on the formal interface specifications of the most important of linkage objects. However, the specifications provided in this section are meant only to illustrate the essential aspects and are incomplete. They should not be taken as reference specifications.

10.3.1.1   ROOM Messages

Messages are the sole means of communication between actors. In Section 6.3, we saw that a message had the following three essential components:

- A signal
- A priority
- An optional data object

Clearly, instances of ROOM messages should have member functions that allow these components to be accessed. In addition, as a practical measure, it is often convenient to be able to ask a message on which interface component it arrived. This leads us to the following definition of the interface to the ROOM message class in C++:

```
class ROOMMessage {
public:
        ROOMSignal      signal;          // message signal
        ROOMPriority    priority;        // message priority
        void            *data;           // pointer to optional data
        ROOMInterface   *interface ();   // interface component on which message
                                         // arrived
        void            defer ()         // used to defer a message
};
```

Note the use of the generic void* pointer type for the data member since a ROOM message may carry objects of different types. According to the rules of C++, a generic pointer must be explicitly cast to the pointer of the desired type whenever it is referenced. For example, assume that the variable msg contains a pointer to the message that triggered the current transition. Also assume that, if the message has a signal equal to stringMsg, then it contains an instance of a user-defined class String, but that otherwise it contains an instance of the Character class. The following code could then be used to extract the information from the message:

```
Character    *chPtr;
String       *strPtr;

if (msg->signal == stringMsg)
     strPtr = (String*) msg->data ();
else
     chPtr = (Character*) msg->data ();
```

10.3.1.2   ROOM Communication Interface Components

Behavior interface components are used to send and receive messages. They include end ports as well as SAPs and SPPs. The different communication models supported by ROOM and the semantics of the corresponding primitives are described in Section 10.2.1 and in Section 10.2.4. In this place we just summarize the generic definition of a ROOM communication interface component:

```
class ROOMInterface {
public:
     // asynchronous communication primitives:
     void            send (ROOMSignal signal);
     void            send (ROOMSignal signal, ROOMPriority priority,
                          void *dataObjectPtr);

     // synchronous communication primitives:
     ROOMMessage    *invoke (ROOMSignal signal);
     ROOMMessage    *invoke (ROOMSignal signal, void *dataObjectPtr);
     ROOMMessage    *invoke (ROOMSignal signal, void *dataObjectPtr,
                          int timeOutValue);

     // replying to (synchronous or asynchronous) messages:
     void            reply (ROOMSignal signal);
     void            reply (ROOMSignal signal, void *dataObjectPtr);

     // recalling and purging deferred messages:
     void            recall (Boolean frontFlag);
     void            recallAll (Boolean frontFlag);
     void            purge ();

     // identity test functions:
     int             operator == (ROOMInterface &interface);
     int             operator != (ROOMInterface &interface);
};
```

The member functions are independent of the protocol associated with the interface component. Note that the constructor and destructor functions are not included in the public interface, since interface objects are created only by the ROOM virtual machine. There are no primitives to receive messages, since that is handled by the ROOM virtual machine.

For example, the following code segment can be used to relay the most recently received message through some port destPort:

```
destPort.send (msg -> signal, msg -> priority, msg -> data);
```

A replicated ROOM interface component is a subclass of a simple interface component with some member functions overridden and others added to access individual instances:

```
class ROOMReplicatedInterface : public ROOMInterface {
public:

        // synchronous communication primitives (return arrays of replies):
        ROOMMessage   **invoke (ROOMSignal signal);
        ROOMMessage   **invoke (ROOMSignal signal, void *dataObjectPtr);
        ROOMMessage   **invoke (ROOMSignal signal, void *dataObjectPtr,
                                int timeOutValue);

        // locating the instance connected to a particular actor:
        ROOMInterface   *interfaceTo (ROOMActorId &actorId);

        // utilities:
        ROOMInterface   *operator [] (int i);
        int             size;
};
```

Although the asynchronous send primitives still have the same interface definitions, their implementation is redefined to reflect broadcast semantics. That is, a send function on a replicated port resolves to as many individual sends as there are interface component instances.

10.3.1.3   ROOM Service Interface Components

These are SAP interface components that are used to access predefined system services. These are either services that are generally useful in real-time programming (such as timing services), or services that support some basic ROOM functionality (such as dynamic structure). In either case, they are provided as an integral part of the ROOM virtual machine.

The Timing Service is used to perform both absolute and relative timing functions. Its SAP is defined as follows (refer to Section 10.2.2 for details):

```
class ROOMTimingSAP {
public:
```

```
// absolute time functions:
Time              &currentTime ();
ROOMTimer         informAt (Time timeValue);
ROOMTimer         informAt (Time timeValue, void *data,
                      ROOMPriority priority);

// relative timing functions:
ROOMTimer         informIn (int timeoutValue);
ROOMTimer         informIn (int timeoutValue, void *data,
                      ROOMPriority priority);

// canceling outstanding timers:
void              cancelTimer (ROOMTimer timerId);
};
```

The Frame Service is used to create and destroy dynamic actors as well as to create dynamic relationships. The details of how this service is used are provided in Section 10.2.3. The interface of a Frame Service SAP is defined by

```
class ROOMFrameSAP {
public:

    // creating and destroying component actors:
    ROOMActorId     incarnate (ROOMActorReference &actorName,
                        void *data);
    ROOMActorId     incarnate (ROOMActorReference &actorName,
                        void *data, ROOMActorClass &classId);
    void            destroy (ROOMActorId &actorId);

    // accessing own actor id:
    ROOMActorId     me ();

    // importing and deporting actors:
    int             import (ROOMActorId & actorId,
                        ROOMActorReference &actorName);
    void            deport (ROOMActorId & actorId,
                        ROOMActorReference &actorName);

    // component actor control:
    ROOMActorId     restart (ROOMActorId &actorId, void *data);
    void            reset (ROOMActorId &actorId);
};
```

The Exception Service is used to pass exceptions not handled by the internal language-specific handler (see Section 10.2.6). Its SAPs have the following interface definition:

```
class ROOMExceptionSAP {
public:
```

```
        void            raise (ROOMSignal signal);
};
```

10.3.2   User-Defined Classes and Libraries

Classes in this group can be of two kinds. The first kind are generally useful classes such as collection classes or classes that support graphs, linked lists, and other common paraphernalia familiar to most programmers. These classes are not specific to any application. There are numerous class libraries that provide these capabilities. They are either available in the public domain or can be purchased. In choosing a library for use with ROOM, we may have to pay special attention to its real-time characteristics, particularly if we want to generate implementations from ROOM models. Unfortunately, many of the most popular libraries were not designed with real-time applications in mind.

The second kind of user-defined classes are those created specifically for the application at hand. For instance, if our application involves simulation, we might have in our class library classes that specify random-number generators corresponding to different probability distributions.

10.3.2.1   Restrictions

In most cases, external class hierarchies can be used directly with ROOM designs without any modification. However, care must be taken to avoid classes that are semantically incompatible with higher-level ROOM concepts. A typical example is classes that support concurrency, since they would likely clash with the ROOM concurrency model. Another group of classes that should be avoided is those requiring the presence of shared data. In the ROOM context, the term "shared data" applies to data simultaneously accessible by Detail Level code or objects in more than one actor (for example, the static class members in C++).

Shared data is undesirable for several reasons. First, it allows two or more actors to communicate independently of the contract and message-passing mechanisms of ROOM. This communication could be violating architectural intent, but may remain undetected since it would not be visible in structure diagrams. Second, it introduces concurrency back into the Detail Level. For safety reasons, any actors accessing global data would have to ensure mutually exclusive access by using the primitive synchronization constructs of the Detail Level (such as semaphores or critical regions). One of the central tenets of ROOM is that concurrency is better and more reliably handled at higher levels of abstraction. Finally, global data imposes limitations on the distributability of models. Clearly, all users of a common global data item must share the same address space.

10.3.2.2   Portable Objects

In principle, every actor state machine represents a separate address space. This means that to send data from one actor to another, a *copy* of that data must be created and sent across. This seems simple enough. We first obtain a communications buffer of the right size, copy the data bitwise from the original, and pass it on to some communications software. A similar process takes place at the receiving end, where the data is copied from the receiving communication buffer into its final destination.

While this simple scenario holds for basic data types and structures, in the world of Detail Level objects, matters are much more complicated. To see why this is so, consider a complex object such as a linked list. The first thing that might strike us about this is that *the object is not contiguous*. This means that we cannot do a simple bitwise copy on it. The second thing that we may notice is that the linkages between the elements in the list are implemented by using pointers. The original values stored in these pointers will clearly not be meaningful when we move to a new address space.

To move a noncontiguous complex object requires that its internal structure first be encoded into some context-independent intermediate and contiguous form suitable for transfer, and then re-created at the receiving end.

The traditional way of dealing with the problem of moving noncontiguous data structures was to write custom code that did all the necessary disassembly and assembly. In the object paradigm, this must be performed by the object itself since, by definition, its implementation is private. If an object cannot do this, then *it cannot be moved from one address space to another*. People who are new to the object paradigm are sometimes surprised upon first encountering this restriction and may feel that it is, somehow, a side effect of the paradigm itself. After all, our intuition tells us that such a nicely encapsulated unit as an object should be possible to move about with ease. However, the problem is inherent in the complexity of the data structures. The object paradigm neither exacerbates nor solves it.

In this text, we refer to those classes that can be moved across address spaces as *portable* classes. For a class to be portable, the following is required:

- An operation on the object that returns its "packed" form

- An entity at the receiving end that will re-create the object by "unpacking" the packed form

While this could be done for each class separately, it is more convenient to define a polymorphic packing function for user-defined classes that can be invoked by the underlying virtual machine software in a generic way. Of course, each user-defined class has to provide its own implementation of this function.

If a common packing format is supported for all portable classes, then it might also be possible for the virtual machine to automatically reconstitute the moved object by creating an instance of the class and invoking its polymorphic unpack operation using the intermediate form as the input parameter. In order to determine which class must be created, the intermediate form could include a special "tag" field that identifies the class.

Knowing which classes are portable (or need to be) is an important consideration when dealing with user-defined classes and libraries.

10.4   Code Generation[9]

For the curious, as well as for those who are interested in implementing their own ROOM toolset, we summarize one approach by which a ROOM model can be turned into executable code.

We start with a ROOM design that, in its original form, is defined by a combination of graphical and textual specifications. This includes embedded segments of detailed code written in the chosen Detail Level programming language, with references to class specifications and other snippets of code[10] imported from elsewhere, all written in the same programming language. For convenience, we shall refer to the chosen programming language as "L."

The first step in the code-generation process is to transform the graphical-textual hybrid into a purely textual form that can be parsed more easily. We refer to this as the *ROOM linear form*. The portion of the linear form that describes the high-level attributes of a model is independent of the Detail Level programming language. However, the linear form will contain within it segments of Detail Level action code.

In order to allow the whole specification to be compiled in a consistent manner, the next step involves translating the linear form representation into an equivalent program in language L. This new representation can now be passed to a compiler for language L.

At this point, we can include other source code, such as the definitions of the external classes used in the model, as well as the ROOM Interface Object specifications (written in L, of course). When all the necessary files have been collected, the result can be compiled to produce an object module.

As the last step in the process, the compiled code is linked with the ROOM virtual machine code and other necessary run-time library modules to produce an executable program.

The compete set of steps involved is depicted in Figure 10.10.

10.5   Summary

The Detail Level deals with fine-grained actions and fine-grained objects. All elements of concurrency and high-level architectural issues are filtered out and dealt with at higher abstraction levels. As a result, the complexity of the specifications at this level is greatly reduced. Detail Level actions capture the behavior that occurs during transitions of a state machine from one state to another. Fine-grained objects are used either to capture the extended state of a state machine, or as information units that can be transferred between actors.

---

[9] This section contains advanced material and may be omitted on first reading.

[10] For example, in addition to class libraries, we may want to take advantage of some useful definitions and library routines.

Figure 10.10 Generating an Executable Program

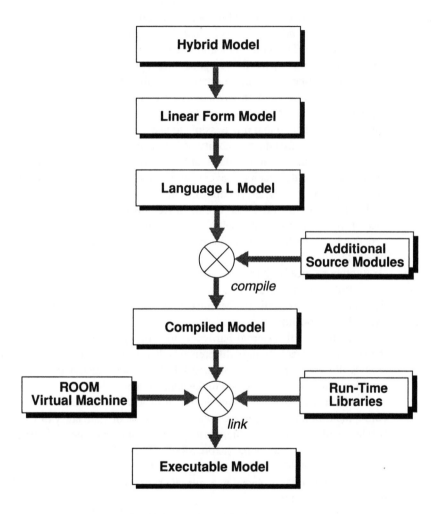

The nature and relative simplicity of the specifications at this level are easily handled by most standard programming languages. The Detail Level is open to a variety of standard programming languages, although object-oriented languages have the advantage of conveniently blending in with the object orientation of the other ROOM levels. The linkage between the higher-level ROOM concepts (such as structure and hierarchical state machines) is achieved through special objects that support ROOM semantics, but whose interfaces are expressed using the syntax of the chosen programming language. These linkage objects are a means by which Detail Level code can access the capabilities of the ROOM virtual machine. The role of the virtual machine is to support the semantics of the higher-level concepts during model execution.

One of the most important functions of Detail Level action code is to initiate communication with other actors. This is achieved through a special communication service of the virtual machine. This communication service is connected to all the interface component objects of an actor's behavior component (end ports, SAPs, and SPPs). To send a message, a behavior invokes a primitive operation on the appropriate interface component object. For greater flexibility, both asynchronous and synchronous communication models are supported. The receiver of a message is generally unaware of the communication model used by the sender so that it is possible to use the same server for both forms of communication. This increases the reusability of behavior specifications.

Event deferral is a facility that can be invoked on any interface component object. It is used to postpone the receipt of events until some later, more convenient time. The recall of deferred events is fully under control of the receiver.

The handling of time-based events in ROOM is done through another specialized service of the ROOM virtual machine: the Timing Service. This service allows events to be generated at a particular absolute moment in time, or at the expiration of some relative time interval.

Another service built into the virtual machine is the Frame Service. This service is used to control dynamic structures. In particular, it allows the creation and destruction of dynamic actors as well as the importing and deporting of individual actors in valid dynamic relationships.

Interactions with external hardware and software entities follow the paradigm set by the system services. The only difference is that, instead of using predefined SAPs, customized SAPs are required. These special SAPs are integrated into the ROOM virtual machine, but also are connected to the appropriate devices or device software handlers.

The Exception Service allows handling of low-level exceptions that occur while executing the action code associated with a transition, or state entry or exit actions. There are two levels of exception handling. Language-specific handling takes precedence and can be used to "protect" individual expressions. If the language-specific handling fails, the higher-level ROOM handling takes over. If no exception handler is successful, then the behavior component is placed in a special exception mode from which it can be recovered by a containing actor.

The other major element of the Detail Level is data classes. These objects do not have their own thread of control. This means that they cannot initiate their own activity, but only perform in the context of the control thread of the actor that encapsulates them. Detail Level data classes are categorized in two groups: ROOM linkage object classes and user-defined classes. The first category includes inter-actor messages, various communication interface components, and special service SAPs. The second category includes classes developed especially for the application at hand as well as standard libraries of generally useful classes. In choosing a standard library, we must be aware of its real-time characteristics and we must ensure that it does not clash with fundamental ROOM assumptions. In particular, we must ensure that the classes do not imply their own model of concurrency and that they do not assume the presence of global data objects.

If objects that are instances of user-defined classes need to be communicated between actors, they must be capable of being converted into a portable form (that is, a form that can be transferred as a unit from one address space to another). This can be optimized if all portable user-defined objects provide their own implementations of appropriate "pack" and "unpack" capabilities.

CHAPTER 11

Implementing ROOM Models

The ultimate product of many high-level analysis and design methodologies is a system specification formulated in terms of the relatively sophisticated concepts supported by the methodology. For example, a specification might include state machine descriptions, data flow diagrams, and structure charts of various kinds. A serious drawback in the application of such methodologies stems from the difficulty in transforming these specifications into full-fledged implementations. These difficulties can be traced to two primary causes. In some cases the modeling concepts provided by a methodology are defined informally, resulting in an ambiguity regarding the precise meaning of a specification. This lack of formality may also mean that the design is inconsistent or incomplete in some nonobvious, yet crucial, way. A second source of difficulties arises when there is a significant semantic gap between the implementation language and environment and the modeling concepts. For example, some formal modeling techniques are based on idealized communications facilities that may not be achievable, even approximately, in an actual implementation environment.

The ROOM methodology was conceived in part with the objective of minimizing or even completely eliminating these implementation difficulties. The modeling concepts are not only formal, but also designed to match the mechanisms encountered in most standard implementation environments intended for concurrent and distributed systems. The majority of current real-time operating system kernels have standardized on concepts such as tasks (processes), messages, sockets, and timers, all of which have their ROOM counterparts.

A ROOM model specification can be converted into an implementation in one of two ways:

- By combining it with a suitable implementation of the ROOM virtual machine, in which case the model *is* the implementation

- By mapping the elements of the model into their functional equivalents in the target environment

The first of these is clearly preferable since it not only eliminates a potential source of errors, but also reduces the development effort required. However, even the second approach is not as problematic as it might be in the general case (because of the domain-specific nature of the ROOM concepts) and it may even be possible to automate much of the mapping process.

In this chapter, we discuss both alternatives. We first look at the high-level architecture of the ROOM virtual machine. This description is not intended to serve as a reference model. A complete and fully formal specification of the virtual machine is well beyond the scope of this book. Our purpose is to provide a broad outline of how such a system can be constructed for those interested in doing so or, for the curious, who want to know how it all works.

The second part of the chapter describes the alternative approach to implementation: mapping a ROOM model in the context of a traditional real-time implementation language and development environment. This includes techniques for realizing hierarchical state machines and the mapping of ROOM structure diagrams into equivalent structures involving tasks and interprocess communication channels.

Since the specification of the ROOM virtual machine given in the first part is formulated as a ROOM model, it is possible to apply some of the techniques described in the second part to that specification in order to implement the virtual machine.

Readers should note that the material in this chapter is highly specialized, and is intended primarily for implementors rather than users of the ROOM modeling language.

11.1   The Architecture of the ROOM Virtual Machine

The ROOM virtual machine is a hypothetical hardware device capable of directly executing ROOM model specifications. This means that it must directly support the high-level ROOM concepts such as actors, contracts, or ROOMcharts. While it is certainly conceivable to construct such a device in hardware, it is usually more practical to implement it in software so that it can be easily ported to a variety of processing platforms and environments. This also allows us to take advantage of the latest technological advances in hardware.

11.1.1   Format and Scope

The ROOM virtual machine is precisely the type of complex, highly concurrent system for which the ROOM methodology is intended. This makes it quite natural to specify the virtual machine as a ROOM model. In order to simplify the specifications, we examine only the case of a *nondistributed* realization. However, given the inherently distributed nature of ROOM specifications, most of the same architectural description also applies to the nondistributed case. Finally, we only describe the minimal machine that contains just the essential system services. An actual implementation is likely to include additional services, such as application-specific device interfaces.

11.1.2   Structures

The ROOM virtual machine is situated as a single layer between the target environment and the executing application, as shown in Figure 11.1. The application consists of an incarnation of the top-level actor class that typically includes other component actors within. Most applications use at least the elementary system services provided by the virtual machine that include the Frame Service (accessed via the frame SPP), the Basic Communications Service (comm), the Timing Service (time), and the Exception Service (excpt). The "target environment" underneath could be as complex as a full-fledged real-time operating system on top of which the ROOM virtual machine is executing as one or more concurrent processes, or it may be something as rudimentary as raw hardware with, perhaps, a minimal layer of firmware and software on top.

Figure 11.1   The Locus of the ROOM Virtual Machine

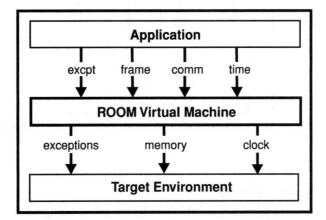

In its minimal form, the ROOM virtual machine requires basic services of this environment including, in particular, a real-time clock and timing facility (clock), a dynamic memory management service (memory), and the underlying exception handling mechanisms (exceptions). If the ROOM application communicates with other external applications, then the target system's communication services also might be used by the virtual machine. Similarly, if the virtual machine is implemented as a set of processes, then the target system "tasking" service also might be used. Naturally, none of the target system services are implemented as ROOM services, nor do they provide ROOM-like SAP interface components. However, they are represented this way in the diagram for clarity.

The top-level structure of the virtual machine itself is shown in Figure 11.2. It has just two components. The *Services System* implements the functionality of at least the elementary services. These services are exported, by way of layer connections, to the application.

The application has SAPs that may be attached to the corresponding SPPs of the virtual machine. The second major component of the virtual machine is the *Control System*, which takes care of controlling and coordinating the operation of the services and, indirectly, of the application itself. To allow external control of the entire system, the Control System has a port (port c) through which it can communicate with an external higher-level control system. The precise linkage of this port to an external control system is specific to each target environment. For example, it could be implemented by using a common "socket"-based mechanism.

Figure 11.2   The Top Level Structure of the ROOM Virtual Machine

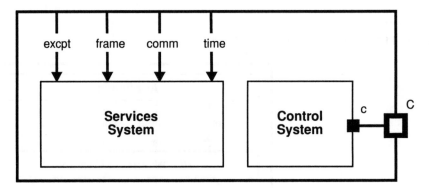

11.1.3   The Services System

The Services System of a minimal virtual machine consists of four essential services (see Figure 11.3). The Frame Service is responsible for realizing the structural aspects of a ROOM specification. This includes the creation and destruction of actors, importing and deporting, and the imposition and removal of contracts (bindings and layer connections). The Communications Service is responsible for the dynamic construction and destruction of communication channels, as well as the actual transport and delivery of messages. The Processing Service handles the scheduling, dispatching, and execution of behaviors, including the detection and handling of run-time exceptions. The Timing Service provides absolute and interval timing. The functionality and interfaces for each of these services are described in more detail in Chapter 10.

The services are mutually dependent. The Frame Service asks the Communications Service to establish or remove the appropriate communication links between interface components. When a new actor is created, the Frame Service informs the Processing Service that a new concurrent thread needs to be instantiated and initiated. All of these ser-

Figure 11.3   The Services System

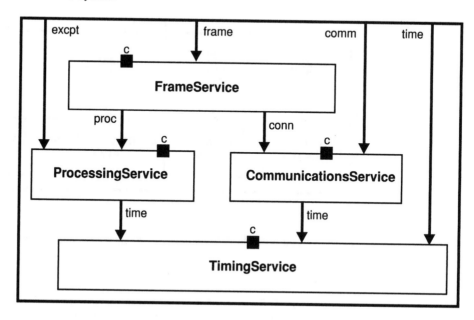

vices can also make use of the Timing Service. For example, the Processing Service needs to be informed about the passage of time in order to provide time-equitable scheduling. The Communications Service needs access to the Timing Service in order to perform the timing required to detect lost messages. We examine the details of these interactions more closely later in this section.

Note that each service has a port labeled as c. This port is used for control purposes and is bound within the Control System view (described next).

11.1.4   The Control System

The Control System is responsible for coordinating the activities of the individual services and also ensuring that those are synchronized with the activities of an external control system. The internal structure of this system is shown in Figure 11.4. The service components shown in this diagram are the same ones shown in the Services System diagram (multiply contained actors).

From the perspective of the Control System, the simplest approach is to have each of the services controlled in the same way. This leads to the notion of a common control protocol and a uniform model of a controlled component regardless of its functionality. This idea can be captured by defining an abstract actor class that embodies such a component. The simplest version of this class has just one port through which it receives control sig-

Figure 11.4 The Control System

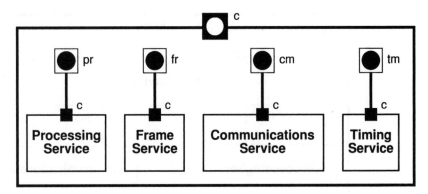

nals. A basic variant of the high-level behavior of such an abstract component is shown in Figure 11.5.[1]

Figure 11.5 The High-Level Behavior of the Common Controlled Component

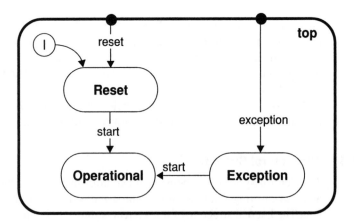

The Reset state is the initial, pristine state in which the controlled object is still not capable of performing its primary purpose. For example, it may be missing key opera-

---

[1] The state machine described here is simplified for pedagogical reasons. A fully detailed implementation would likely have a more sophisticated behavior.

tional data. It is moved out of this state and into the Operational state by the arrival of a start message from the controller. This message may carry the operational data required by the object. The Operational state is the state in which the actor performs its primary function. Typically, this requires further state machines within the Operational state.

The actor usually enters the Exception state as a result of some disruption. This signal comes from within (for example, it may be generated by the Processing Service) rather than the controller of the object. In the general case, the actor can be restored to full functionality by another start signal from the controller.

Finally, the component can always be reset by the arrival of a reset signal from the controller. This allows a system, no matter how complex and regardless of its current state, to be forced into a known initial state from which it can then be placed in the desired operational state. This reset capability is analogous to the much-used reset button found on most computers. The abstract control protocol corresponding to this state machine is represented by

> **protocol class** AbstractControlProtocol:
>   **in**:   {{start, OperationalData}, {reset, null}}
>   **out**: {{started, null}, {resetDone, null}}

Clearly, all services are candidates to be subclasses of the abstract controlled component class. Furthermore, since we have said that the virtual machine itself is a controlled element, then it makes sense to make the Control System a subclass of the same abstract class. The Control System then acts to relay commands to its minions. For example, when told to reset itself, the Control System will not only reset itself, but will also reset all the services.

The services should be initialized in order, based on the dependency relationships between them. Thus, it is helpful if the Timing Service is initialized first, since other services may need its capabilities during their own initializations. This should be followed by the initialization of the Processing Service, followed by the remaining two services. Upon reset, the order should be reversed to allow an orderly shutdown if possible.

11.1.5 The Timing Service

This service responds to the protocol derived from the Timing Service interface specification (see Section 10.3.1),

> **protocol class** TimingServiceProtocol:
>   **in**: {{currentTime, null}, {informIn, TimingData},
>   {informAt, TimingData}, {cancelTimer, TimerId}
>   }
>   **out**: {{timeout, TimingData}, {timeNow, Time}}

where TimingData is a system-defined data class that contains the specification of the timing interval required, TimerId is a timer identifier, and Time is a system-defined data class that includes an instance of a timestamp.

For each independent request, the Timing Service incarnates a separate timer. When the timer expires, or when it is cancelled, the Timing Service destroys the timer. These considerations lead to the relatively simple internal structure of the Timing Service shown in Figure 11.6.

Figure 11.6   The Structure of the Timing Service

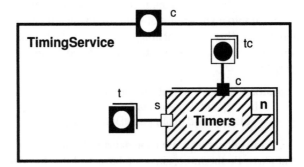

The Timing Service actor accepts service requests through its SAP, and creates and destroys individual timers as necessary. A currentTime request is replied to immediately by obtaining the current time from the underlying real-time clock facility of the target environment. An informIn or informAt request results in the creation of a timer and the passing of the request information to it. A cancelTimer request results in the destruction of the appropriate timer actor. If a timer expires (signaled by the arrival of a timeout message on port t), the Timing Service behavior destroys the corresponding timer actor and relays the timeout message to the client that made the request.

Individual timers also are controlled in the same way as other actors and their top-level behavior should conform to the general control protocol. Hence, they, too, can be made subclasses of the same abstract superclass. In addition to its inherited control port (port c), which uses the standard control protocol, each timer has another port (port s) for service-related communication. This port uses a conjugated version of the timing service protocol defined previously. The high-level state machine of a timer actor is defined by the abstract superclass, but within its Operational state, the behavior is specified by the sub-machine shown in Figure 11.7.

The startTimer transition is initiated by the arrival of either the informIn or the informAt signals on the service port and the stopTimer is triggered by a cancelTimer request or a timeout signal from the underlying target environment.

Figure 11.7   The "Operational" State of a Timer Actor

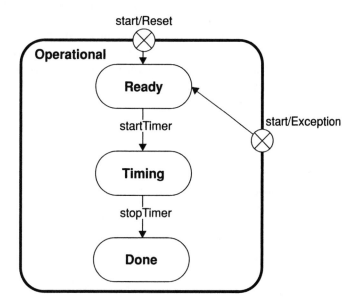

11.1.6   The Processing Service

The Processing Service is primarily responsible for allocating processor resources. For simplicity, it only understands the concept of a "work order," which represents a prioritized request for processor time. The Processing Service allocates processing time based on these requests and its scheduling policies. The service protocol for using the Processing Service is quite simple:

```
protocol class ProcessingServiceProtocol:
    in:   {{run, WorkOrder}, {yield, null}}
    out: {{schedule, WorkOrder}, {workDone, null}}
```

Clients of the service make requests by invoking a schedule request with the priority specified in the work order data item associated with the request. When the Processing Service allocates the processor to the requestor, it sends a run message. When the transition processing is completed, the client responds with a workDone message. The Processing Service then schedules the next work order.

In most real-time schedulers, it may be necessary to suspend a process that is taking too long to complete. For this reason, the Processing Service times the current user of the processor. If the timer expires before the workDone signal is received, the Processing Service will suspend the current actor by issuing it a yield message. The currently running client must yield the processor at this point and the Processing Service will schedule the next work order. The original work order will be retained by the Processing Service and enqueued, to allow the suspended client to be resumed eventually without having to issue another work order.

In order to track outstanding work orders, the Processing Service keeps a simple set of queues, one queue per priority. Scheduling takes place when a work order request is received and the Processing Service is idle, or when a client completes processing and there are still outstanding work orders, and, finally, when a timeout is received from the Timing Service. The behavior of the Processing Service in the Operational state is shown in Figure 11.8.

Figure 11.8   The "Operational" State of the Processing Service

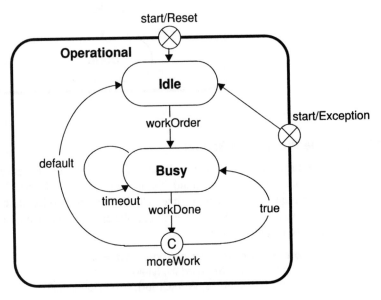

The Processing Service also handles low-level exceptions detected by the underlying target hardware or software. This service is offered as the Exception Service through a specialized SAP. The protocol associated with this SAP is:

protocol class ExceptionServiceProtocol:
    in: {{raise, ROOMSignal}}
    out: {{exception, ROOMException}}

11.1.7   The Frame Service

The Frame Service is, perhaps, the most complex of the system services. It is responsible for creating and destroying actor incarnations and maintaining the dynamic structural relationships between them. A simplified version of the service protocol for the Frame Service on its SAP is

protocol class FrameServiceProtocol:
    in: {{incarnate, ActorSpec}, {destroy, ROOMActorId},
            {me, null}, {import, ImportSpec}, {deport, ImportSpec},
            {restartActor, RestartSpec}, {resetActor, ROOMActorId}
            }
    out: {{actorCreated, ROOMActorId}, {actorId, ROOMActorId}}

All of the incoming service requests are handled only if the service is in the Operational state.

Each application actor is represented by a corresponding *meta-actor* within the Frame Service. A meta-actor is incarnated whenever its matching application actor is incarnated, and it is destroyed whenever its application peer is destroyed. This leads us to the relatively simple structural model of the Frame Service shown in Figure11.9.

Figure 11.9   The Structure of the Frame Service

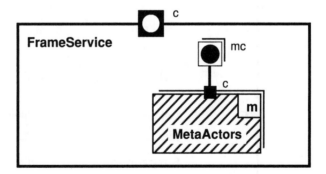

This meta-actor is yet another controlled component and, therefore, has the usual high-level behavior description. The Frame Service controls the individual meta-actors through a replicated control port (port mc).

To understand how the Frame Service works, we first examine the simple case of incarnating a leaf (noncomposite) actor. This is triggered by the arrival of an incarnate message on the SAP. The information in the message indicates the class of the actor to be created, as well as where it is to be created in the overall structural framework. The Frame Service creates the appropriate meta-actor and, if the actor class has a behavior associated with it, it must arrange to have its initial transition scheduled. Consequently, the Frame Service brings the meta-actor into the Operational state. This results in the meta-actor issuing a service request to the Processing Service (by sending a schedule request). When the Processing Service eventually schedules the request, it informs the meta-actor (a run signal). The meta-actor executes the application code either until it completes, or until the Processing Service demands that it to yield the processor.

The behavior in the Operational state of a meta-actor is shown in Figure 11.10. When first created, the meta-actor immediately goes into the Ready state in which it is ready to run and is waiting for a signal from the Processing Service. When that signal is received, it enters the Running state. (Note that the complete application-level state machine corresponding to the actor is, conceptually at least, contained as a sub-machine within the Running state.)

Figure 11.10 The "Operational" State of a Meta-Actor

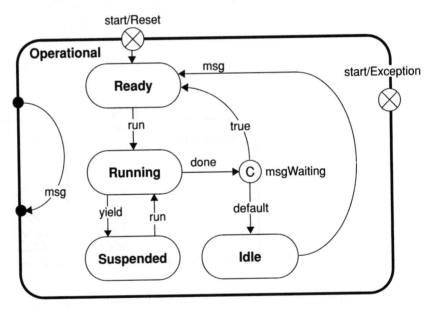

While running, it may be asked to yield the processor, in which case it goes into the Suspended state until given processor time again.[2] When it completes the transition (the

---

[2] This requires that the yield signal have high priority that can interrupt the active process and that the meta-actor have control over the application actor's process thread.

done event), the meta-actor normally will go into the Idle state (since it has no work left to do), unless a message was received previously on one of the behavior interfaces of its corresponding actor (signified by the arrival of the msg signal from the Communications Service). If this message arrives while the actor is busy with a previous transition, it is simply queued at the appropriate interface component. When the run is completed, the meta-actor will make a request to the Processing Service and go back into the Ready state instead of the Idle state. If the meta-actor is in the Idle state and a message arrives for its actor, then it will ask the Processing Service for processor time and enter the Ready state.

When incarnating a complex actor with internal components and bindings, the entire internal structure must be established before the actor's meta-actor is placed in the Operational state. Whenever an actor with interface components is incarnated, it registers its interface components with the "connection SAP" of the Communications Service. Once all its interface components are registered (as well as the interface components of all its container and contained actors), the meta-actor will also ask the connection SAP of the Communications Service to establish any valid contracts (bindings and layer connections) within that actor's decomposition frame. This allows the Communications Service to keep track of all the connections between actors. Naturally, when an actor incarnation is destroyed, this process is reversed with bindings being torn down followed by the deregistering of interface components.

For the Frame Service to keep track of containment relationships, it must keep a dynamic data structure that represents these relationships. From this complex object, it can deduce which actors need to be removed when a composite actor is destroyed. This structure is also used to validate and track dynamic relationships that are established through importing of actors.

Finally, the Frame Service must have information about the structure (component actors and valid contracts) for each actor class, to establish them dynamically upon the creation of actor incarnations. This information is loaded by way of the Control System as part of the initialization of the Frame Service actor.

11.1.8 The Communications Service

This service provides two types of services. It is responsible for establishing, maintaining, and removing connections between all actor interface components. This is the "connection service" facility (the conn SPP). The protocol for this service is described by

```
protocol class ConnectionServiceProtocol:
    in:   {{registerInterface, InterfaceSpec}, {deregisterInterface, InterfaceSpec},
           {connect, ConnectionSpec}, {disconnect, ConnectionId}
          }
    out:  {{connectionEstablished, ConnectionId}, {msg, ROOMMessage}}
```

The application must register interface components before establishing connections.

The second type of service is the transporting of messages between interface components (the comm SPP). All application-actor interface components are attached to this SPP, so that when they ask for a message to be delivered, the Communications Service relays it through the established connections and delivers it to the final destination. If the destination is a behavior interface, then the corresponding meta-actor is notified (the msg event—see Figure 11.10)). The simplest version of the protocol associated with this type of service is:

```
protocol class TransportServiceProtocol:
        in:   {{sendMessage, ROOMMessage}}
        out: {}
```

11.1.9   Other Services

Other services (including application-specific services) can be implemented in much the same way as the elementary services. A central service master, reporting to the Control System, provides a service provision point through which service requests are received and handled. When an actor that accesses this service is created, its service access points are bound to the service provision point.

11.2   Mapping ROOM Specifications into Real-Time Environments

Although the approach based on implementing the ROOM virtual machine has numerous advantages, it may not always be the most practical approach. For example, we may be required to tightly integrate our ROOM model into an existing run-time environment. In such situations, we may have to resort to the second implementation alternative: transforming a ROOM model specification into an implementation based on concepts supported by more traditional real-time implementation environments. Fortunately, since many of the ROOM concepts were based on generalizations of existing real-time concepts, this mapping is straightforward in most cases.

In this section we examine the general techniques for mapping ROOM models. This is supplemented by a detailed code example in Appendix B, which illustrates, in a concrete way, some of the most important aspects of the mapping process. To encompass as many different cases as possible, the description given here is based on minimal assumptions about the properties of the actual target environment. This leaves plenty of opportunity to customize the techniques described here and to take advantage of the specifics of a particular environment. In almost all cases, this should lead to more efficient realizations than the general approach described here. Furthermore, it is straightforward to automate much of the mapping through custom post-processors that would generate a specification suited to the target system based on the output of a toolset that directly supports the ROOM concepts.

We first examine the basic assumptions about the target environment and the implementation programming language. Next, we look at what is usually the most complex aspect of the implementation: the realization of hierarchical finite-state machine specifications. This is followed by a description of how to map the structural attributes of a ROOM model specification. Finally, we discuss the issues of realizing the system services.

11.2.1 Environment Assumptions

An implementation environment consists of two parts: a programming environment (including a programming language) and a platform run-time environment (usually an operating system kernel). The primary assumption about this environment is that it supports some type of *concurrent programming paradigm*. This paradigm may be supported directly in the language (as in Ada) or it may be supported through a suitable run-time library. For example, the C language does not support concurrency, but it is still possible to write concurrent applications in C, provided that a multitasking run-time library is included with the application. Although there is a wide variety of real-time operating systems, most of them share some standard features. The mapping approach described here is based on the most common of these features.

11.2.1.1 Programming Language

We assume that a conventional third-generation block-structured imperative language will be used for implementation. A significant simplification of the mapping process can result if the language supports procedure variables (so-called "function pointers" in C), but this is not crucial. For generality, the detailed algorithms and structures involved in the mapping process that are described in this chapter are given in pseudo-code as opposed to a particular programming language. However, for readers interested in a more concrete view, a fully worked-out example (implemented in C++) is provided in Appendix B.

11.2.1.2 Multitasking

It is assumed that the underlying kernel supports some form of lightweight concurrency unit or *thread*. Each thread must have its own context in which state information is stored during the times when the thread is not executing. If the design has a dynamic structure, then it must be possible to dynamically create and destroy threads through the action of other threads.

11.2.1.3 Thread Synchronization

In the general case, the interleaving of multiple threads on a single processor can lead to undesirable interference between them. This is usually avoided by using complex and error-prone mutual exclusion facilities. In the pure ROOM model, there is no need for thread synchronization, since there is no shared memory and because the basic processing paradigm is "run-to-completion" (described in Section 8.1).

However, if the underlying Detail Level language supports shared memory, it is still possible for threads to communicate by way of shared memory. We may decide to do this for performance reasons. In such situations, it will be necessary to use classical synchronization mechanisms (for example, semaphores, critical regions, monitors) in situations when threads access shared data.

11.2.1.4   Interprocess Communication

The basic communications paradigm in ROOM is message passing. A discrete data unit is generated in the context of one thread and transferred to the context of another. Ideally, once a message has been sent, it should no longer be accessible to the sender thread. Most real-time kernels directly support the concept of messages.

The simplest form of communication is an asynchronous message send. Since multiple messages for the same destination can arrive concurrently, some form of message queueing is required in the underlying kernel. This is usually provided through a mailbox, socket, or pipe concept.

If the design calls for synchronous communication between concurrent units, then the kernel should support either a rendezvous or a remote procedure call facility.

11.2.1.5   Scheduling

As a rule, ROOM makes very weak assumptions about the semantics of event priorities. Hence, for most designs, the underlying scheduling facilities of the underlying run-time environment are usually adequate. However, problems can occur if a design makes an assumption that messages are processed strictly in message priority order since most kernel priority schemes are based on thread priorities. In such cases it may be necessary to augment or even replace the host kernel scheduling facility with one that schedules threads on the basis of message priorities. If the target kernel allows it, the priority of a thread could be dynamically adjusted to match the priority of the next highest-priority incoming message.

11.2.1.6   Memory Model

In ROOM, all memory references are local to an actor. This obviates the need for individual protected address spaces for individual actors. However, if the implementation language supports shared memory, then a memory protection scheme (ideally with a granularity corresponding to individual threads) would significantly increase the reliability of the implementation.

11.2.2   Implementing High-Level Behavior

The relatively complex semantics of hierarchical state machines make Schematic Level behavior the most difficult aspect of the mapping problem. In this section, we describe one method for implementing hierarchical state machines by using standard imperative language control constructs. The techniques described in this section are illustrated by a detailed example provided in Appendix B.

11.2.2.1   The Approach

At first glance it may appear that the most straightforward approach is based on converting a hierarchical state machine into an equivalent nonhierarchical one. A *flat equivalent* of a hierarchical state machine is a state machine that has no hierarchical states, but which, for a given sequence of input events, generates the same outputs as the original hierarchical state machine.

A flat state machine can be represented by a two-dimensional state-transition matrix, as shown in Figure 11.11.

Figure 11.11 A Flat State Machine Represented by a Two-Dimensional Matrix

	'event1'	**'event2'**	**...**	**'eventM'**
'state1'	transition11	transition12	...	transition1M
'state2'	transition21	transition22	...	transition2M
...	...	...	...	...
'stateN'	transitionN1	transitionN2	...	transitionNM

A two-dimensional matrix structure can be easily implemented in a traditional programming language by using a set of nested "case" statements.

case (currentState) **of**:

```
'state1' : case (currentEvent) of:
        'event1' : transition11;
        'event2' : transition12;
           etc...
        'eventM' : transition1M;
   endcase;

'state2' : case (currentEvent) of:
        'event1' : transition21;
        'event2' : transition22;
           etc...
        'eventM' : transition2M;
   endcase;

   etc...
```

endcase;

In this example, the primary case differentiation is based on state, while the secondary differentiation is based on events. However, it is equally possible to differentiate first on the basis of events, and then on the basis of state. In general, there is no special advantage of one approach over the other since the structure of a matrix is invariant under rotation. Nevertheless, in special cases, it may be advantageous to favor one approach over the other. For example, if an event is always handled in the same way, regardless of state, it may be better to differentiate first on the basis of events.

The simplicity of this approach can be deceiving. A closer examination of the process of flattening out hierarchical state machines reveals a surprising combinatorial explosion effect. Consider, for example, the simple hierarchical state machine shown in Figure 11.12, which includes the use of history and group transitions. In its hierarchical form, this state machine has just six states and six transitions.

Figure 11.12 A Simple Hierarchical State Machine

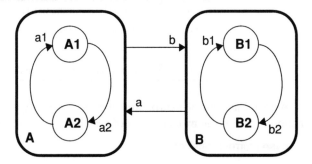

The flat equivalent for this state machine has a noticeably more complex structure with eight states and 16 transitions, as shown in Figure 11.13.

This complexity increase is nonlinear, so that for even a slightly more complex state machine such as the one in Figure 11.14, the flat state machine equivalent has 24 states and 72 transitions. A graphical representation of such a complex state machine would be practically unreadable, yet such a state machine is not unreasonable in practice as we have seen from some of the examples covered previously.

This increase in apparent complexity is caused by the history and group transition features of hierarchical state machines. These are, of course, precisely the features that give hierarchical state machines their expressive power (that is, the ability to graphically capture much more complex systems than conventional flat state machines).

From this it is obvious that, unless some kind of automated tool support is provided, the approach based on flattening out hierarchical state machines is impractical. However, even if such a tool were available, it is highly likely that the resulting code output would be incomprehensible to the human reader, making it very difficult to maintain.

This leaves only the following two alternatives:

- Provide a generic interpreter that would directly execute hierarchical state machine specifications.

- Individually program the functionality of the interpreter into each hierarchical state machine.

Figure 11.13 A Flat Equivalent to the State Machine in Figure 11.12

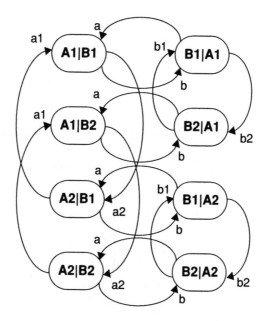

These two approaches are quite similar in that they both require more or less the same algorithms to implement the semantics of hierarchical state machines. The main difference is that, in the first alternative, this code is centralized, whereas in the second one, it is replicated for each different state machine. Because of this commonality, we only describe the second approach in detail. However, at the end of this section, we briefly describe how to implement the generic interpreter solution.

The selection of an approach in a given situation depends on the requirements. If performance is a primary concern, then the second approach is more appropriate, since it provides plenty of opportunities for customization. For example, where a general version of an algorithm requires a procedure call, we might eliminate that overhead in a particular case by including code directly in line. The drawback, of course, is that this approach usually involves more work and is potentially less reliable because of possible transcription errors.

11.2.2.2   Example

In order to illustrate the mapping techniques, we use the relatively simple state machine example shown in Figure 11.15.

Figure 11.14 A More Complex Hierarchical State Machine

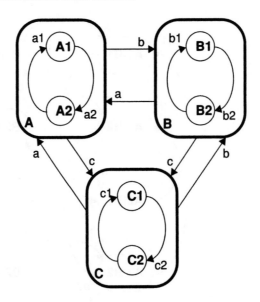

Figure 11.15 A Simple Hierarchical State Machine

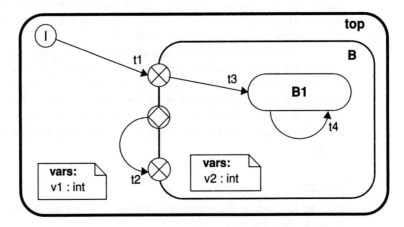

State B1 is a leaf state and has no internal variables, but has both an entry action (defined by the procedure entryB1 ()) and an exit action (defined by procedure exitB1 ()). We can represent that by using the following semiformal textual specification:

state B1:
    entry action: {entryB1 ();}
    exit action: {exitB1 ();}

State B is a composite state with one internal variable (v2 of type int), its own entry and exit actions, as well as internal substates and transitions. Using the same notation, the specification for this state is

state B:
    vars: {{v2 : int}}
    entry action: {entryB ();}
    exit action: {exitB ();}
    substates: {{B1}}
    transitions: {
        {**transition** t4:
          triggered by: {s2, p1, (v2 == 0)}
          action: {transitiont4 ();}
        }
        {**transition** t3:
          action: {transitiont3 ();}
        }
    }

This specification tells us that transition t4 has an action code specified by the procedure transitiont4 () and is triggered by the arrival of a message whose signal value is s2 on the interface component p2 provided that the guard condition (v2 == 0) is true. Similarly, transition t3 has an associated code action defined by procedure transitiont3 (). Finally, the top-level state specification is given by

state top:
    vars: {{v1 : int}}
    substates: {{B}}
    transitions: {
        {**transition** t1:
          action: {transitiont1 ();}
        }
        {**transition** t2:
          triggered by: {s1, p1, true}
          action: {transitiont2 ();}
        }
    }

11.2.2.3   Representation

The specification of a state machine is represented by a set of functions and data declarations specific to that class. Instances of a state machine, on the other hand, are represented by instances of class-specific data structures that capture the current status of that machine.

11.2.2.4   State Indices

For convenience, the following encoding scheme can be used. Each state is allocated a unique non-negative index. This allows us to use array indexing as a means of quickly locating the context of a state. The top state is allocated the value 0,[3] while subsequent states take on successive integer values using a breadth-first traversal of the state hierarchy. Such a numbering scheme ensures that a substate always has an index that is higher than the index of its parent state. This property is exploited in the implementation for greater efficiency.

Applying this encoding to our example yields the following state index values:

```
top      = 0;
B        = 1;
B1       = 2;
```

11.2.2.5   Control Blocks

Each state machine instance is represented by a two-level tree of linked control blocks. At the root of the tree is the control block that maintains the context for the entire state machine. The second level consists of a set of control blocks for the individual states.

The root control block has the general format

```
structure fsmCB
        integer      currentStateIndex;
        pointer      stateCB_ptrs[*];
        ...local state machine variable declarations...
endstructure;
```

where

- currentState is the state index of the current state. This is usually a leaf state.

- stateCB_ptrs[*] is a table of pointers that allows direct access to individual state control blocks. The relative position of a pointer in this array is determined by the index of a state. The size of this array depends on the number of states in the state machine.

---

[3] The value of the top state should be equivalent to the lowest valid index value supported by the implementation language.

- *...local state machine variable declarations...*is a list of all the local variables of all the states. They are all collected in a common block instead of being dispersed across the corresponding state control blocks. This simplifies the implementation.

The last two items depend on the particular state machine being modeled so that, in general, each state machine needs to specify its own version of this control block.

Each state has its own control block structure that has the universal form

```
structure stateCB
     integer      parent;
     integer      history;
endstructure;
```

where

- parent is the state index of the superstate of this state. The top state has no super-state so its index should be set to a value that is lesser than the state index of the top state (for example, -1). It is through this field that the state control blocks are connected into a secondary tree structure matching the topology of their containment relationships.

- history is the state index of the substate of this state that was current at the time when the most recent event (which forced the state machine out of this state) occurred. If the state had not been visited before, or if it is a leaf state (which means that it has no history), then this field contains an invalid index value (for example, a negative value).

For our example state machine, the resulting data structure would look as shown in Figure 11.16.

11.2.2.6   FSM Control

The three types of control actions that we invoke on a state machine are

- CreateFSM is used to create a new instance of a state machine. This allocates memory for the various control blocks and initializes the values that are constant throughout the lifetime of the machine (for example, the control block linkage data). It is invoked only once for each instance desired.

- StartFSM is used to execute the initial transition of the state machine. It first resets all variable control block data to appropriate initial values, and then starts the initial transition. An initial message is also provided as an input parameter. This control action is invoked at least once, after the state machine has been created. It may also be invoked subsequently in cases when the state machine is restarted (as long as it has not been terminated).

- TerminateFSM is used to destroy the state machine and return any resources appropriated for it back to the system. Like the CreateFSM action, it is invoked only once for each instance of a state machine.

Figure 11.16 The Data Structures for the State Machine in Figure 11.15

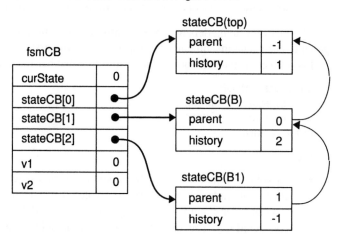

The life cycle of any state machine can be described by the state machine diagram in Figure 11.17.

11.2.2.7   Message Processing

Message processing is performed after the state machine has been started. The state machine receives a message and performs one processing step, depending on its current (application) state. Because of the presence of group transitions, history, entry and exit actions, and guard conditions, the algorithm for this is not trivial.

Perhaps the biggest complication stems from the interaction of the group transition and the exit action features. When a message is received that is not expected by the current leaf state, we have to search up the state hierarchy of the current state to determine if any of the containing states responds to that event. The search proceeds until either

- The top of the hierarchy is reached (that is, the message does not trigger any transitions, not even in the top state).

- A state in the search path actually responds to this event.

If the latter occurs, we must execute the exit actions (and record history), starting with the current state and ending with the exit action of the state that reacted to the event. Conversely, if the event did not trigger a transition, then we must return to the current state without having executed any of the exit actions.

A second complication is caused by the history feature. Since states can contain other states, we must enter history recursively until a leaf state is encountered.

Figure 11.17 The Life Cycle of a Hierarchical State Machine

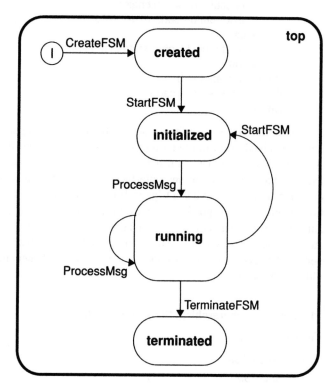

The summary result of a transition in a hierarchical state machine is the execution of a chain of code segments corresponding to the transition segments, entry and exit actions, and choice points encountered along the path from the source leaf state to the destination leaf state. Such a chain of code segments is called a *transition chain*. For example, the transition chain for the initial transition in our example is

```
code for transition t1;
entry code for state B;
code for transition t3;
entry code for state B1;
```

The algorithm for processing a newly arrived message has the following general form:

procedure ProcessMsg (event);

    start from current state;
    repeat

```
        if this state responds then
            execute exit actions;
            execute transition chain;
            exit from procedure; //-------->
        else
            try the next higher state in the state context;
        endif;
    until (top state tried);
    flag unexpected message;
    return;
```

This algorithm is, in effect, a search for the first trigger that can be satisfied by the newly received event in the current state context. We start the search with the innermost state in that context. This is usually a leaf state. For a particular state in the context, we evaluate the trigger conditions (interface component, signal, and guard condition) of each outgoing transition that has a trigger. If one evaluates to true, we must execute the transition chain that corresponds to this event. However, before doing that, we must first execute any nested exit actions up to this point, since we will be leaving the current state. We cannot execute these actions earlier, since we have no guarantee that the search for a trigger will be successful. An example of a concrete implementation of this algorithm is provided in Appendix B.

11.2.2.8   Hierarchical State Machine Interface

The basic functions

- CreateFSM
- StartFSM
- TerminateFSM
- ProcessMsg

represent the *interface* of a hierarchical state machine. The first three are used to control its operational status, while the last one is used for scheduling. While ProcessMsg is likely to be the same in all cases, the control interface functions are specific to each different actor class.

Most of the technique described previously can be automated by post-processing the output of a ROOM toolset that generates ROOM models. Even many of the standard optimization techniques (such as inlining) can be handled automatically.

11.2.2.9   Implementing a Hierarchical State Machine Interpreter

We now look at the alternative to individual mapping of each state machine–that is, constructing a generic interpreter of hierarchical state machine specifications.

For this implementation we will assume that the language supports procedure variables. These are variables that can be assigned the name of a procedure and subsequently invoked to have the associated procedure executed. This allows the specification of a hierarchical state machine to be defined as a set of data structures used to control the execution of a set of generic algorithms. The procedure variables would bind in the different versions of the state machine interface functions createFSM, startFSM, terminateFSM, and ProcessMsg.

11.2.2.10 Data Structures

Since the specification of each state machine is captured in data blocks, the structure of these blocks is important. The general arrangement of data structures is retained. A single control block for the entire state machine is the root of a hierarchy of state control blocks. As before, in addition to being directly accessible from the root, the state control blocks are mutually interconnected in a way that reflects their containment hierarchy.

The *root* control block should have the general format

```
structure fsmCB
        integer      currentStateIndex;
        pointer      stateCB_array;
        pointer      vars_array;
        pointer      ports_array;
endstructure;
```

where

- currentState is the index of the current state.

- stateCB_array is a pointer to an array of pointers to individual state control blocks. Note that, in contrast to the previous approach, this array itself is not part of the root control block. This enables the control block to be uniform for all state machines, regardless of the size and topology of the state machine, which simplifies its handling by a generic algorithm.

- vars_array is a pointer to the memory block containing the individual local variables of the state machine. (It is convenient to use this block to store the current message as well.) This data has also been removed from the root control block for the same reason explained previously. Another advantage of separating this array from the rest of the data is that this is, in normal circumstances, the only data area that is accessed directly by user code. For those systems that have a memory access hierarchy, this data would be part of the user space, whereas the rest would be part of the supervisor or system space.

- ports_array is a pointer to a memory block containing an array of port data blocks. These are described later in this section.

The *state* control blocks could have the form

```
structure stateCB
        integer      parent;
```

```
        integer      history;
        boolean      isLeafState;
        pointer      interfaceTrigsArray;
        pointer      entryProc;
        pointer      exitProc;
        pointer      initialTransChainProc;
    endstructure;
```

where

- parent is the state index of the superstate of this state.

- history is the state index of the history substate.

- isLeafState is a Boolean function indicating that this state has no decomposition (this is handy to quickly determine if we need to enter history).

- interfaceTrigsArray is a pointer to an array of pointers to individual event triggers. The array itself serves to cut down on the search time required to determine if the current event triggers a transition in the associated state (recall that an event is a combination of an interface component, a signal, and an optional guard condition). Each entry in the array is either a pointer to an array of triggers (described later) or it is NULL, indicating that, for this state, no events are triggered by the arrival of a message on the respective port. There is a separate instance of this array for each state (since each state has its own set of events to which it responds).

- entryProc is a pointer to a procedure that contains the entry code for the state (or NULL if there is no entry code).

- exitProc is a pointer to the exit code procedure or NULL.

- initialTransChainProc is a pointer to the procedure that contains the transition chain of the initial transition of this state (or NULL).

The individual transition chains are specified in the form of procedures. Each such procedure contains a sequence of procedure calls (for invoking the action code of individual transition segments in the chain) and conditional statements (for implementing choice-points).

Finally, the following structure is used to specify an individual trigger,

```
structure triggerSpec
    ROOMsignal   signalId;
    pointer      guardProc;
    pointer      transitionChainProc;
endstructure;
```

where

- signalID is the identifier of the signal that triggers the event.

- guardProc is a pointer to the Boolean function that contains the code for the guard condition (or NULL).

- transitionChainProc is a pointer to the procedure that contains the transition chain corresponding to this event (or NULL).

The interface component of an event is not present, since the trigger specification is already defined in the context of a particular interface. The resulting data organization has the form shown in Figure 11.18.

Figure 11.18 The Data Structures for a Generic State Machine Interpreter

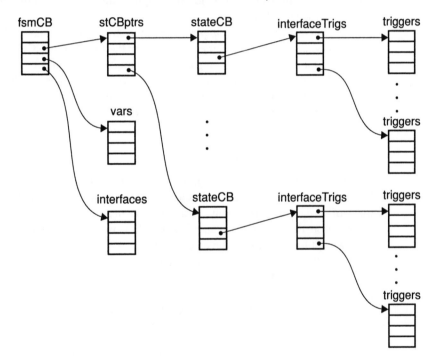

11.2.2.11   Algorithms

The general form of the algorithms for dealing with this type of specification is, with one exception, quite similar to the algorithms described previously. The only difference is that, instead of the calls to individual functions being imbedded directly in the code, they are invoked indirectly by through procedure variables encountered in the various control blocks.

The one exception is the createFSM algorithm, which is responsible not only for creating and linking up all the control blocks, but also for initializing each with the values of the appropriate procedures. It is possible to construct tools that automatically generate this procedure for each state machine based on the output of a ROOM toolset.

11.2.3   Implementing Structure

The various structure-related concepts of ROOM (such as interface components, contracts, containment, dynamic structure, and so on) serve to specify either *actor dynamics* (that is the creation and destruction of design components over time) or the *connectivity* between structural elements.

The principal difficulty of implementing the structural aspects of a ROOM model in a non-ROOM execution environment stems from the fact that, in ROOM, it is assumed that many design-time assertions regarding dynamics and connectivity are *automatically enforced by the underlying execution environment*. For example, when we incarnate an aggregate actor, all of its fixed component actors are incarnated as well. Unfortunately, traditional operating system kernels simply do not have such sophisticated built-in facilities.

11.2.3.1   The Approach

When faced with the task of mapping the structural aspects of a ROOM model to a non-ROOM target environment, the fundamental issue is whether we want automatic enforcement of design-time assertions. This decision must be made early in the development cycle, before design starts, because it affects how we use ROOM in design.

If we opt for run-time enforcement, then there is little choice but to put a layer of software over the target run-time environment that would implement the enforcement capabilities of the ROOM virtual machine. The realization of this alternative was described previously in this chapter.

On the other hand, if we choose *not* to go with automatic enforcement, then we have two alternatives:

- We can restrict our ROOM models to use only those concepts that have appropriate support in the target environment. For instance, we may decide not to use actor containment since our operating system may not support task hierarchies.

- We can realize the desired structural relationships by explicitly coding them into the behavior of individual actors. For example, when an aggregate actor is created dynamically, we would include, in the initial transition of that actor, code to explicitly create each of its component actors. Note that this approach still limits us in the use of the ROOM concepts, but much less so than the previous one.

In this text we will describe the latter alternative, since it is more general.

11.2.3.2 Implementing Actors

The basic unit of scheduling in ROOM is an actor with an associated state machine. The most straightforward way of implementing an actor is to match it to the basic scheduling unit of the host environment. We will refer to this unit as a *thread*.

Some operating system kernels support the concept of thread aggregates and it may seem convenient to map actors to such units instead of threads. However, in most cases, only one level of aggregation is supported (for example, multiple threads per task), whereas ROOM aggregation is open-ended and, in most cases, is at least two levels deep.

The thread that is associated with an actor should be created in such a way that the appropriate CreateFSM procedure is called to set up the control structures. Naturally, the address space in which these control structures are built must be in the domain accessible by the thread. If the system supports it, it is useful to separate out the data block containing local variables and assign it to so-called "user" space while protecting the rest of the structures in system space. Each such thread should provide access to the three basic functions that comprise the state machine interface (ProcessMsg, StartFSM, and TerminateFSM).

An alternative to mapping actors to threads is to encapsulate the entire complex of ROOM actors comprising the design into a single scheduling unit and then provide an internal customized multitasking environment within that unit. This kernel-within-a-kernel approach usually requires more work, but provides an opportunity for much greater throughput. For example, during a single timeslice of the encapsulating thread, the internal scheduling system could perform many internal schedules (message-exchanges) between actors. Recall that ROOM supports a run-to-completion programming paradigm, which makes the implementation of such a package much simpler and more lightweight than most kernels can provide.

11.2.3.3 Scheduling

We have already noted that ROOM scheduling is done on the basis of message priorities rather than task or thread priorities. However, most real-time kernels are based on the latter. This apparent dilemma can be overcome in any of several ways:

- The design may avoid using priorities altogether.
- The system scheduler might be changed to account for message-priority scheduling.
- For those systems where thread priorities can be dynamically assigned, the priority of a thread can be dynamically changed to match the priority of the highest-priority message waiting on that thread.

11.2.3.4 Behavior Interfaces

The message-passing paradigm of actor interaction is best modeled by kernel-supported message queues. The most convenient arrangement is to have a separate message queue dedicated to each state machine thread, regardless of the number of interface components associated with the actor. This conforms to the ROOM run-to-completion processing model, which serializes message handling. It also simplifies the implementation, since an actor thread only needs to look at one queue instead of many.

Behavioral interfaces (end ports, SAPs, and SPPs) are best represented by data structures of the form

```
structure interface
        integer       interfaceIndex;
        pointer       peerMsgQ;
        pointer       deferQ;
endstructure;
```

where

- interfaceIndex is the integer value that identifies this interface component in the scope of the actor. (We recommend a numbering scheme in which interface components are identified by indices. This can be used for quick reference.)

- peerMsgQ is a pointer to the message queue of the peer actor at the far end of the binding. (In case of a remote destination in a distributed system, this would be a distributed "network pointer."). If the interface component is not bound in a contract, then this field is set to NULL.

- deferQ is a pointer to a message queue used to hold any messages that may have been deferred on this interface component.

All the interface component data blocks associated with an actor are collected in a single array attached to the state machine.

11.2.3.5   Contracts

When a contract is created in ROOM, a communications connection between two interface components is established automatically by the run-time system. That is, actors do not have to explicitly include code that constructs the communication channel. This is a fairly complex capability that requires the kernel to establish and maintain a complex dynamic connectivity graph. In this text, we will take the simple approach in which the concepts of contracts and relay interface components are *not* supported in the target environment.

Note that these concepts should still be used in the design because they are useful for automated design validation, as well as for documentation. However, in such designs, we do not take advantage of the automatic connection establishment provided by bindings. Instead, the behaviors of actors are adjusted to explicitly connect the two ends whenever a contract is created[4] and to disconnect them when the binding is destroyed. In many cases this may require additional states and transitions, as well as additional bindings.

---

[4] A contract is created either when an actor is incarnated or when an actor is imported.

In this approach it is good practice to provide an actor with the message queue addresses of all of its peers (if available) in its initial creation message. This gives it instant access to all the actors with which it has contracts.

If the underlying kernel provides a name service facility, it can be used to establish connections without requiring that the address information be relayed in a message from some other actor. Also, if the kernel supports compile-time static names, this feature also can be used to simplify the setting up of connections.

11.2.3.6   Messages

Messages are data structures with the general format

```
structure message
       integer      interfaceIndex;
       signal       signalId;
       integer      priority;
       ...message data (optional)...
endstructure;
```

where

- interfaceIndex is the index of the interface component on which the message arrived.

- signalId is the message signal identifier.

- priority is the priority of the message.

Ideally, messages should be true transient objects that, once dispatched by an actor, are no longer accessible to it. This prevents accidental coupling between actors. One way to ensure this is to always make a copy of the message and send the copy, instead of the original, to the destination queue.

11.2.3.7   Actor Containment and Dynamic Structure

When a composite actor is created, any fixed component actors in its decomposition frame are automatically created along with it. This feature applies equally to the component actors and their components, so that the incarnation of an actor can be a very complex operation. As noted previously, most operating systems do not support atomic creation of process hierarchies. Although it is not too difficult to add a facility to provide this feature, a much simpler alternative is to make all component actors dynamic in a ROOM specification. This matches the capabilities of most standard operating systems in which it is assumed that tasks are created explicitly, one at a time.

11.2.3.8   Multiple Containment

The main effect of importing or deporting an actor is to create or destroy bindings. Thus, it is handled by the same techniques already described.

11.2.3.9   Replication

Replication of actors can be handled simply by dynamically creating the appropriate number of threads. Replicated interface components can be represented by a slightly modified version of the interface component data structure,

```
structure replicatedinterface
    integer     interfaceIndex;
    pointer     peerMsgQArray;
    pointer     deferQ;
endstructure;
```

where peerMsgQArray is a pointer to an array of pointers to the different message queues located at the opposite end of a contract.

11.2.3.10   Summary

The implementation approach described here hinges on restricted use of the structuring capabilities of ROOM during design. Adhering to these restrictions, although not crucial, can significantly simplify the implementation in a traditional kernel environment. The following summarizes the proposed restrictions:

- If the target kernel does not support message priorities or dynamic task priority assignment, do not use message priorities in the design (that is, use the same priority for all messages).

- Use bindings and relay interface components to specify the communication relationships in a design, but also include code that explicitly creates and destroys them.

- Make all component actors dynamic (optional or imported).

- If synchronous communication is used, assume that the bindings are unidirectional. This may mean that, in some cases, we would interconnect two actors with two bindings, one for each direction. The rationale for this constraint is explained in the next section.

11.2.4   Implementing Services

The principal virtual machine services provided in ROOM (such as Communications or Timing) are common to the majority of real-time kernels. The main issue, then, is how to map a specific ROOM service interaction model to the model supported by the services of the underlying kernel.

11.2.4.1 The Approach

The ROOM service interaction model is characterized by the following:

- Service requests are made by a synchronous "procedure call" in the action code of an actor. This is the common form for most operating system kernels. The mapping of these is straightforward and consists of determining the proper form of the kernel primitive and encapsulating it in a ROOM-specific procedure that makes it ROOM-like (for example, it refers to a SAP).

- In the opposite direction, a service generates an asynchronous indication to an actor in the form of an incoming message. This is much less common.

Since most kernel services do not generate messages, the most convenient way of dealing with this is to have a service agent thread that mediates between the two models. On one end, this agent communicates using the ROOM message-passing model, while on the other it uses the host environment model. There should be at least one such agent for each service.

11.2.4.2 Communications Service

In the case of the Communications Service, asynchronous communication is handled easily through the message queueing mechanism described previously. A message is sent using a synchronous procedure call that references the outgoing behavioral interface component. Based on the peer addressing information in the interface component, the message is enqueued on the appropriate message queue. When the receiving thread/actor is scheduled to handle the message, the thread's ProcessMsg procedure is invoked.

For synchronous communication, the situation is more complex. This is because, in the ROOM processing paradigm, the receiver of a message is generally unaware of whether it was invoked synchronously or asynchronously. Unfortunately, in the majority of real-time kernels, this is not the case. The mechanisms for receiving an asynchronous message are quite different from those for accepting a synchronous invocation from another thread.

One way of dealing with this issue is to insert a specialized "communications agent" thread between the invoker and the receiver, as shown in Figure 11.19. This thread transforms the synchronous invocation into a message send. The client remains blocked until the server has replied. The agent then relays the reply message back to the client as it completes the synchronous call.

This approach ensures that the synchronous and asynchronous invocations are processed using the same scheduling mechanisms (that is, no priority given to one or the other form of communication).

The communications agent can be associated with either the client or the server, but, for the sake of retaining ROOM semantics, it is recommended to associate it with the client. The lowest overhead occurs if the agent thread is created along with the client thread. A single agent thread is sufficient for each actor making a synchronous call (only one synchronous call can be outstanding at a time). Note that, in this case, the agent should have

Figure 11.19 The Use of Agents to Implement Asynchronous Communication

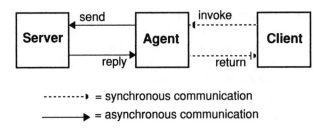

--------▸ = synchronous communication

——————▸ = asynchronous communication

its own message queue that is separate from the client's queue. This ensures that other messages directed at the client do not interfere with the synchronous call. It is the responsibility of the client to ensure that the proper queue address is given to the server's interface component when the connection is established.

The above synchronous mechanism, unfortunately, works only in one direction. If the design calls for the server to invoke the client independently, then this should be modeled with another set of interface components and a separate binding.

11.3   Summary

There are two ways in which a ROOM model specification can be converted into an implementation. In the first case, the design is simply bound together with a software implementation of the ROOM virtual machine and executed so that no further transformations of the design are necessary. The second alternative is more traditional. A series of mappings is applied to the specification, transforming it eventually into an implementation that is based on the functional capabilities of the target platform. The first approach has the advantage that it is more reliable and also reduces development effort. However, if a suitable ROOM virtual machine is not available, or if the design must be very tightly integrated within an existing legacy system, the second approach might have to be taken.

For those interested in constructing their own version of the virtual machine, this chapter provided a description of the architecture of the ROOM virtual machine. This includes a definition of the high-level structures, the high-level behavior of the main components, and the principal intercomponent protocol specifications. This virtual machine specification is decomposed into two main subsystems: the Control System and the Services System. This organization reflects the separation of control and functional concerns.

The Control System acts as the coordinator of the services within the Services System, and also acts as the intermediary between the virtual machine and a higher-level external control system. The Services System contains the essential and other services that are used by the actors in the design. The essential services include the Communications Service, the Frame Service, the Timing Service, and the Processing Service.

Each of these services provides one or more SPPs through which application actors can access the respective services. In order to simplify the control of the system, all services and many of their components (as well as the Control System itself) are required to respond to a common control protocol. This leads to a common superclass with a common high-level state machine description that describes the behavior of a generic controlled component. All the main architectural components of the virtual machine are defined as subclasses of this abstract class.

In the second part of the chapter, we described techniques for mapping a ROOM model into an implementation targeted at a standard real-time kernel and a traditional block-structured imperative programming language. The approach taken can be summarized as follows:

- In mapping hierarchical state machines, we ensured an exact mapping of the model to an implementation. This means that the full expressive power of ROOM state machines can be used in the model, regardless of the underlying target environment.

- In mapping the structural aspects of a model, the approach was more constrained. Namely, depending on the host environment and our objectives, we recommended certain restrictions on the modeling concepts and techniques used so that the resulting specification becomes easier to transform into an implementation. These restrictions depend on the capabilities of the target implementation environment but are, in most cases, relatively minor and do not detract significantly from the modeling power of ROOM.

As noted previously, the techniques described here are quite general and can be optimized (or even completely altered) in any particular environment. Furthermore, much of the design-to-implementation transformation process can be automated.

PART FOUR

Process Issues

In this part, we ascend beyond the ROOM modeling language and examine the higher methodological levels pertaining to its application: the modeling heuristics and work organization. As we move up this methodological scale, things become increasingly less formal because of the diversity of potential applications and specific organizational requirements. In the face of this diversity, it is unwise to be overly prescriptive. The material in this part should be viewed as guidelines and suggestions rather than gospel.

The three chapters in this part are as follows:

- Chapter 12, "Model Development Heuristics," describes an iterative approach to model construction and validation based on ROOM. These heuristics are useful in any phase of the development cycle that involves building models.

- Chapter 13, "Architectural Heuristics," examines modeling heuristics that pertain to creating the architecture of a real-time system.

- Chapter 14, "Work Organization," discusses various project management aspects of system development and introduces the key elements of a product-oriented organizational framework that exploits the benefits of an operational approach to system development.

CHAPTER 12

Model Development Heuristics

Previous chapters have described the ROOM modeling language, which provides the foundation for a real-time methodology. In this and the following chapter, we discuss methods of applying that language (see Figure 12.1). A *heuristic* is defined as a "process that may solve a particular kind of problem but offers no guarantee of success" [Flew79]. Heuristics, like folk proverbs, capture common wisdom and provide sound guidelines on what to do in given situations. However, like proverbs, they should be applied judiciously rather than rigidly. A large part of what we commonly call "experience" consists of knowing the set of relevant heuristics, as well as understanding when and how they can be used.

Figure 12.1　The Role of Modeling Heuristics in a Methodology

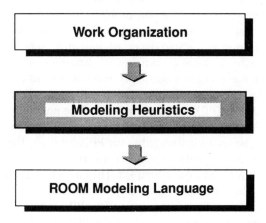

This chapter describes an iterative approach to model construction and validation—a model development process. It also discusses associated fundamental heuristics, such as

how to pick actor classes. Model development is part of the larger process of product development covered in Chapter 14. Product development involves teams of people with activities spanning multiple models, with an emphasis on project management techniques. In contrast, model development and its activities focus on a repeatable approach that a single developer or small team uses to build the individual models that make up products.

Readers should initially approach this chapter as an overview of the heuristics. However, it also can be used subsequently as a reference during modeling. In the first part of the chapter, we work our way through a simple example in order to provide readers with an intuitive feel for the essence of the heuristics. The second part generalizes and details these heuristics. An iterative process, by its nature, offers a variety of possible paths, so that no linear description of it can be complete or definitive. Therefore, readers are encouraged to adapt the suggestions described here to fit their specific situations.

12.1   Example: Introduction

In order to convey more directly the true nature of iterative development, we proceed through this example in much the same way as a hypothetical team of modelers[1] would. We postulate that some specifier has given a small development team (two people) a written specification for a system. The members of the team (experienced modelers) want to understand and validate the requirements by constructing an operational model. This narrative describes the modelers' actions, and includes iterating to address requirements omissions and afterthoughts. It also includes the model refinement that naturally occurs as insights are gained into the problem and its solution. We assume that this is a new model and that there is no existing class library on which to build.

This example introduces an important subset of the basic modeling heuristics. It describes building an initial model based on written requirements from a specifier. However, the techniques also apply to enhancements to existing models.

In this case, the specification given to the modelers describes a Private Branch Exchange (*PBX*) used to provide telecommunication service for a small business. The PBX's basic function is to allow users to talk with other users, as shown in Figure 12.2. Telephones are connected to the PBX by *lines*. The PBX can connect these lines to each other, or to a public telephone network.

PBXs can be quite complex. They usually support a rich set of capabilities beyond simple telephone calls (for example, forwarding calls from one telephone to another). The maintenance and management of the PBX is performed by trained *administrators* who can change the "configuration" of the PBX. Configuration changes include assigning telephone numbers to new users, or telling the PBX when users have moved to new offices.

---

[1] We prefer to use the term "modelers" over the more conventional "developers" since models may be built for a variety of reasons, not just for design or implementation purposes. For instance, a standards organization might produce models of standards specifications.

Figure 12.2 The PBX Example

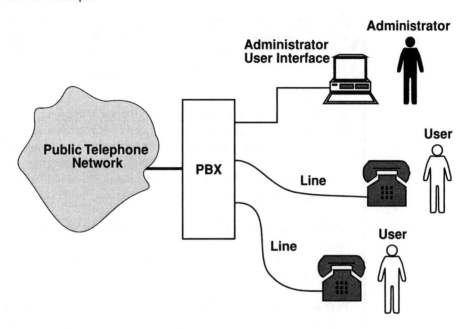

12.2   Example: Model Requirements

One of the most frequent and convenient ways of describing the functional requirements of a model is through scenarios. A *scenario* relates, by an action or sequence of actions, how something is used or what it must do. Scenarios describe not only external requirements of products, but also the requirements of internal design components. Most scenarios can be translated into a series of messages exchanged between objects in a model.

In this example, the specifier has provided the modelers with the scenarios shown in Figure 12.3. The modelers use the scenarios to guide the construction and testing of the model.

12.3   Example: Modeling the System and Its Environment

The modelers have never modeled this type of problem, and do not have an existing class library upon which to draw. They have been given some requirements, but they need to discover whether the requirements are complete and consistent. We call this modeling

Figure 12.3   Model Requirements as Scenarios

Model Requirements

Telephone Call: A user (Ray) wants to call another user (Corinne) on the same PBX. Ray lifts his handset ("goes off hook"), and hears dial tone. After dialing Corinne's complete telephone number, Ray hears a tone ("ring-back"), telling him that Corinne's telephone is ringing. Corinne answers the call by lifting her handset. The ringing and ringback tone stop, and a voice connection is made between the two telephones. Ray and Corinne talk for a while. Either Ray or Corinne can hang up ("go on hook") to end the call.

Last Number Redial: Having made a call, Ray decides to call the same person again. As in "Telephone Call," Ray goes off hook, and presses a Last Number Redial button on his telephone. This automatically redials the last number he dialed.

Putting a Telephone Into Service: The PBX administrator is told that a new user needs phone service. The administrator, through an administrator user interface, selects a new number for the user and tells the PBX to put it into service. Users can now make calls to that number.

Taking a Telephone Out of Service: The PBX administrator is told that a user no longer needs phone service. The administrator, through an administrator user interface, tells the PBX to take the user's phone number out of service. Users can no longer call that number.

activity *discovery*,[2] since its goal is to establish an understanding of what the system has to do. Discovery involves supplementing the specifications that have been given to the modelers with whatever else they can uncover.

To start the model, they discriminate between the system that must be built and its relevant environment. We call this the *system boundary*. A model captures both the system and the objects outside the boundary that participate in the scenarios and thus directly influ-

---

[2] To the best of our knowledge, use of the term "discovery" as opposed to "analysis" was originated by Grady Booch.

ence the system. To construct the model, the modelers must understand the objects both inside and outside the boundary.

The modelers read the scenarios to help identify the boundary. The PBX itself obviously is inside the system. They include the telephones in the system because the users interact with them, and telephones may have some functions that are not completely specified. For example, it is not clear from the scenarios whether the telephones or the PBX generates the various tones used in a call. The public telephone network does not participate in the scenarios, so it is not included in the model. Figure 12.4 shows the chosen system boundary.

Figure 12.4   System Boundary

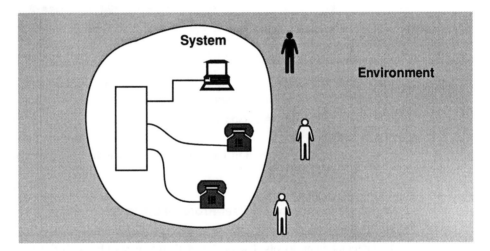

12.3.1   Capturing the Initial Model

The modelers first capture an initial ROOM model that represents the system and its environment. As shown in Figure 12.5, the users and the administrator are modeled as actors, as they are obvious concurrent physical objects identified by the model requirements. For simplicity, the modelers choose only two users and one administrator. These environment objects will form the basis for testing the system. A separate actor represents the system to be developed.

To keep track of the primary purpose or responsibility of each actor class, the modelers annotate each class with a description of its purpose (enclosed in quotes):

Figure 12.5   Initial Model: System Boundary

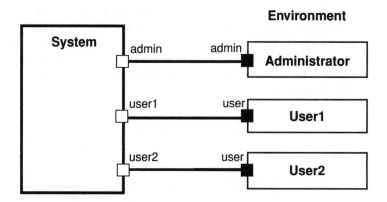

- *User*: "A person using the PBX." User functions include making or answering calls and using the Last Number Redial capability.

- *Administrator*: "A person who configures the PBX to put telephones in or out of service."

- *System*: "A collection of hardware and software that provides telecommunication services for users."

12.3.2   Deriving the Admin and User Protocol Classes

The previous step outlined only the high-level classes of the model, but did not address their interaction protocols. The modelers, therefore, start by analyzing the scenarios. In the scenario for the administrator (used by the admin port), they discover that a phone number, although required as a message type for this interface, is not fully defined. However, from experience they know what phone numbers look like, and proceed to define the following data class:

data class PhoneNumber: String
      "The complete number that identifies a user. It may include
      digits, dashes, and parentheses."

With that data class defined, the modelers can complete the protocol definition. The scenario implies which signals are involved in the protocol. The modelers choose to define the direction of the protocol from the viewpoint of the administrator.

protocol class AdminInteraction:
    in: {}
    out: {{PutInService, PhoneNumber}, {PutOutService, PhoneNumber}}

Figure 12.6 A Telephone Call (User's View)

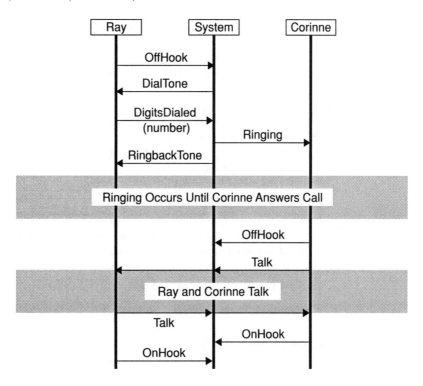

"This protocol changes the configuration of the PBX"

The telephone call scenario is moderately complex. At first, the two modelers are unsure of the completeness of the scenario description, and, thus, of the protocol between the user and the system (captured in the ports marked user). For this reason, the modelers transform the textual scenario into a message sequence chart, so that the protocol can be better understood. A message sequence chart shows the sequence of messages exchanged among entities in the scenario. Many actions in the scenario involve audible information such as tones and speech. For the purposes of this high-level model, such information, although not inherently message based, still can be modeled by "abstract" messages. For example, the modelers use a DialTone message to denote that a dial tone is being generated. Similarly, the PBX relays abstract Talk messages between the two users to simulate a connection. Figure 12.6 shows the resultant message sequence chart.[3]

---

[3] This chart contains some minor simplifications, such as not showing the removal of DialTone as soon as the number has been dialed, and RingbackTone after the call has been answered.

The modelers use the message sequence chart to see all the messages flowing into and out from the user. They construct the UserInteraction protocol class referenced by the two user ports in Figure 12.5. The modelers decide to define the direction of this protocol from the viewpoint of the user. For example, DialTone is a message being sent to (and thus heard by) a user, while OffHook is sent out from the user. Since the Last Number Redial scenario also involves the user and the system, the modelers examine that scenario, and add a LastNumberRedial message to the definition of the UserInteraction protocol. The resultant definition of this class is

> **protocol class** UserInteraction:
>   **in**:   {{DialTone, null}, {RingbackTone, null},
>   {Ringing, null}, {Talk, null}}
>   **out**: {(OffHook, null}, {DigitsDialed, Number},
>   {Talk, null}, {OnHook, null},
>   {LastNumberRedial, null}}
>   "This protocol represents the user's interaction with the telephone"

The modelers define a new data class associated with the protocol class. They know from experience that users do not always dial complete numbers, so that knowledge is captured in the description of the Number data class.

> **data class** Number: String
>   "one or more digits, may not be a complete phone number"

The modelers have not specified any behavior, so the model is not yet executable.

12.3.3 Capturing the User Behavior

Protocols are closely associated with behavior. The modelers capture a preliminary version of the User actor's behavior in order to understand the user's participation in the scenarios. This is shown in Figure 12.7. The telephone call scenario implies what the user's states are. For the time being, the modelers do not bother with defining transitions, as they just want a quick impression of the states. It appears that a single User class can be modeled to represent either a user calling someone or a user being called. Later, when the modelers employ the User actor to validate the system, they will take a more formal approach to define its behavior.

12.4   Example: Modeling the System

After modeling the environment, the next step is to model the components of the system.

12.4.1 Deriving the Top-Level System Actors

The modelers first identify the obvious components of the system, the physical objects from the requirements specification. These are modeled as actors contained by the System actor.

Figure 12.7   User Behavior

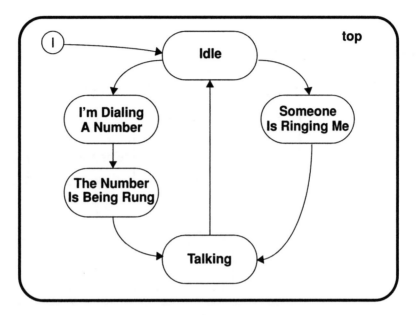

- *Telephone*: "The device that a user operates to make or receive telephone calls, and to operate the Last Number Redial function." This contains a handset, buttons, and so on. A quick analysis indicates that an important attribute (property) of a telephone is whether it is ringing. The modelers can portray attributes as states or as extended state variables.

- *AdministrationUserInterface* "The device that the administrator operates to make configuration changes to the PBX."

- *PBX*: "This actor provides interfaces to telephones and makes connections between them."

The modelers include these actors in the model, as shown in Figure 12.8. This model of the System makes the simplifying assumption that there are only two telephones, to correspond to the assumption of two users.[4] The Telephone class has two interface components: a user interface that is a reference to the UserInteraction protocol class, and the tel interface that is based on a new TelephoneInteraction protocol class, which is yet to be defined. The modelers need the TelephoneInteraction protocol to assert that there is some connec-

---

[4] The modelers elect not to use replication. They first want to confirm their understanding of what the system needs to do, before considering the effects of many users.

tion between the telephone and the PBX, but they do not yet know what the details are. Initially that protocol class is generic and has no message types specified.

Figure 12.8   System Structure

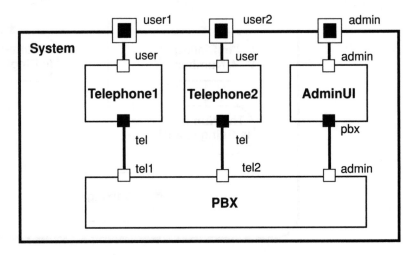

The modelers represent the lines between the telephones and the PBX as bindings, since they appear to be straightforward communication links. These are connected to the tel interfaces on the PBX, which are based on the conjugated TelephoneInteraction protocol.

The AdminUI actor (of class AdministrationUserInterface) simply relays information between the administrator and the PBX by using the AdminInteraction protocol. The modelers put it in, although they could have replaced its function with a binding. They want to represent the structural information that the user interacts with a physical terminal, rather than directly with the PBX. In the future, the AdminUI actor may have its own behavior.

12.4.2   Examining the Telephone Call Scenario

As described, the written model requirements did not give sufficient detail to define the interface between the telephone and the PBX (the TelephoneInteraction protocol class). In those circumstances, the modelers must ask the specifier for information on that protocol.

They capture what they discover in the message sequence chart[5] shown in Figure 12.9. Note that the user's involvement in the call[6] (as first described in Figure 12.6) is included

---

[5] For the purposes of the example, this protocol has been vastly simplified compared to the actual one used in telephony.

[6] The UserInteraction protocol class captured the interface between the Telephone and the User.

to show the relationship between the two protocols. The modelers realize the protocol implies that some functions are in the telephone rather than the PBX. For example, the PBX does not send the telephone a message to turn off ringing when a user answers a call. Therefore, the telephone must do this automatically when the user goes off hook. The PBX controls other aspects of the call, such as deciding which telephone should be rung when the user has dialed a number.

Figure 12.9 A Telephone Call (Including the Telephone)

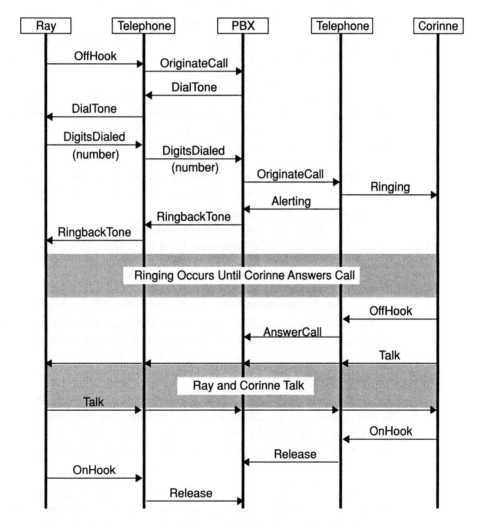

The signal definitions are

- OriginateCall: "A request to initiate a call." The receipt of this signal requests the telephone to ring. Sending this message is a request to originate a call.
- DialTone: "An indication that dial tone is being transmitted to the user."
- DigitsDialed: "A signal indicating some number has been dialed by the user." This includes the data class Number, which may be a single digit or series of digits.
- Alerting: "An indication that alerting (ringing of the telephone) has begun."
- RingbackTone: "An indication that ringback tone is being transmitted to the user originating the call."
- AnswerCall: "A request to answer a call."
- Talk: "An indication of voice information sent or received by a user once a user is connected to another user."
- Release: "A request to end a call."

All the messages between the telephone and the PBX are on the same physical interface. They also appear (not surprisingly) to be closely related in function. They all are associated with making telephone calls rather than other functions (such as making configuration changes). Therefore, the modelers group all the signals into a single TelephoneInteraction protocol class. They elect to define this asymmetric protocol from the viewpoint of the Telephone. This is consistent with the approach taken for the UserInteraction and AdminInteraction protocols, which were both defined from the client side of a client-server relationship.

protocol class TelephoneInteraction:
    in: {{DialTone, null}, {RingbackTone, null},
         {Talk, null}, {OriginateCall, null}}
    out: {{Talk, null}, {OriginateCall, null},
         {DigitsDialed, Number}, {Alerting, null},
         {AnswerCall, null}, {Release, null}}
    "This protocol represents the users interaction with the telephone"

The modelers now have several protocol classes defined. They may, at this point, consider whether any commonality exists that could be captured through inheritance.[7]

12.4.3   Modeling the PBX Actor

At this point, the modelers have a basic understanding of what the PBX must do. In order to further assess the viability of these requirements, they must understand whether a system that meets these requirements is feasible. For this purpose, they must sketch out a preliminary solution to the problem posed by the requirements. This is a creative activity so

---

[7] To simplify the example, the results of the modelers' examination of inheritance are not described. There is a strong resemblance between the TelephoneInteraction and UserInteraction protocol classes. The common audible signals, such as Talk, could be grouped in a new superclass called AudibleInformation.

that we refer to this aspect of modeling as *invention*.[8] Invention includes the creation of new classes in addition to those that result from the discovery activity.

It is important to note that the solution devised at this early stage is for the purpose of gaining deeper insight into the requirements and does not represent a commitment to any particular design alternative. It is quite possible that this and other early solutions will be discarded when the modelers switch their focus from analysis to design. (However, the experience gained even with a naive early design certainly will be useful later when more serious design takes place.)

In our example, the PBX actor is the focus of this invention activity. The total functionality could be modeled solely by the behavior of the single PBX actor. This could result in a complex state machine that would be difficult to evolve if other scenarios were introduced. Therefore, the modelers decide that it is better to partition the PBX's functionality among component actors. The PBX actor forms an abstraction container for these components.

It is often useful to formalize the coordination relationships between objects. In the telephone call scenario, coordination is required between the two telephones in the call. Some entity must decide when it is appropriate to start ringing one telephone while giving ringback tone to the other. When a telephone has answered the call, both telephones must be connected to each other to allow them to talk. Either telephone can hang up. The connection must be undone and the other telephone informed that the call is over. The modelers resolve this by defining a "call" actor that is an abstract coordinator actor encapsulating this functionality.

- *Call*: "The relationship between two users, including originating a call to a user, connecting the users, and eventually disconnecting the users."

The modelers now look at the Last Number Redial and administrator scenarios. There are attributes that refer to a single user, rather than a pair of users involved in the call. For example, a telephone has an attribute of being in service or not being in service. Something must keep track of the last number that a user dials for the Last Number Redial scenario. The modelers examine the protocol between the telephone and the PBX, and realize that the telephone just informs the PBX that the Last Number Redial button has been pressed. It does not tell the PBX what that number is. The number must therefore be stored inside the PBX.

Given the trends toward more sophisticated hardware, the modelers may realize that the interface between the PBX and the telephone may change if new types of telephones are introduced in the future. In order to shield the Call actor from such details, they insert a TelephoneHandler actor inside the PBX to act as an intermediary. This actor has the same interface to the Call actor, regardless of the type of telephone that is attached to it.

---

[8] The use of the term "invention" rather than "design" also seems to have originated with Grady Booch.

- *TelephoneHandler*: "This class abstractly represents whatever telephone is attached to the line." Its attributes include a phone number and the last number dialed.

12.4.4   Completing the PBX Structure Capture

The modelers refine the model to include the two new classes they have invented for use in the PBX. They place two references of the TelephoneHandler actor class and one reference of the Call actor class inside the PBX's structure, as shown in Figure 12.10.

Figure 12.10 Initial PBX Structure

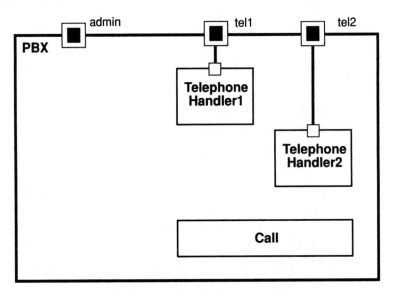

Often omissions become obvious when models are depicted. Here, the modelers realize that they must make more structural decisions. They have only partially addressed the administration scenarios. There is no interface between the TelephoneHandler and the admin port of the PBX. For this purpose, they invent a new actor class, AdminHandler, to route messages from the admin port to the TelephoneHandler actors. As each telephone is placed or taken out of service, the AdminHandler must communicate with the appropriate TelephoneHandler actor. For example, when putting the TelephoneHandler in service, it passes the phone number of the telephone represented by the TelephoneHandler. Since it just routes messages without changing their contents, the previously defined AdminInteraction protocol is used to communicate with the TelephoneHandler.

- *AdminHandler*: "This actor acts as an agent inside the PBX actor on behalf of the external administrator actor." It routes messages to the appropriate entities representing the telephones affected by the administration commands.

The TelephoneHandler actor is involved in multiple communication relationships. Each TelephoneHandler reference interacts with the associated line in the System, thus ultimately communicating with the telephone. The TelephoneHandler also must communicate with the Call actor for the call scenario, as it represents each telephone in the call. The modelers reuse the TelephoneInteraction protocol[9] between the TelephoneHandlers and the Call actor. Figure 12.11 shows the result of the model capture.

Figure 12.11 Final PBX Structure

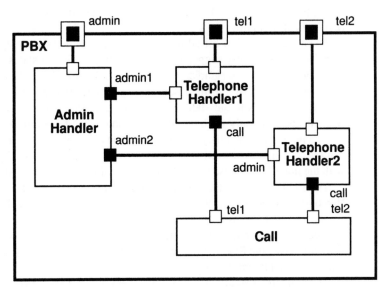

At this point, the PBX actor has been decomposed into components that appear simple enough that their functionality can be captured directly without further decomposition. In order to check the validity of this system (and through it, the system requirements) by executing the model, it is necessary for the modelers to specify the actors' behaviors.

---

[9] This is a simplification. When the modelers review the protocol classes, they realize they need a new CallInteraction protocol class. This would be a subclass of TelephoneInteraction but does not require the LastNumberRedial signal. The TelephoneHandler supports the function of translating LastNumberRedial into the appropriate number; the LastNumberRedial signal is therefore not relevant to the Call actor.

12.4.5   Capturing Behavior

The capture and subsequent execution of behavior often uncover deficiencies in model requirements or designs. In Figure 12.7, the modelers took a very loose approach to behavior in order to get a general idea of the User actor's behavior. The modelers now decide to specify sufficient PBX behavior for an early executable model. They derive the behavior of each actor by examining the scenarios it is in and considering the attributes or properties that it has. Actor class attributes are modeled either as states or as extended state variables.

The modelers start with the PBX actor itself. It does not require an explicit state machine, since all its external interactions are handled by its components. Its behavior is the result of the various actors that it contains. The modelers decide to specify the TelephoneHandler behavior first, because it is crucial to the function of the PBX, and because it may be complex (since it is involved in multiple scenarios and relationships). Generally, it is appropriate to face the difficult issues first, since that is where potential fundamental requirement flaws often lurk.

The modelers review the administrative scenarios that take telephones in and out of service. This immediately suggests the two obvious top-level states (InService or OutOfService) for the TelephoneHandler actor, shown in Figure 12.12. As the modelers capture the state transitions between these states, they realize that the requirements omitted saying what a telephone's initial state is. The modelers assume that it should start in the OutOfService state, and only go to the InService state when the administrator requests this. They make a note that, when they test this actor, the order of the scenarios that drive it is significant.[10] The modelers next define triggers for the transitions. Each transition is labeled with the underlying cause of the transition (in this case, the sole signal that triggers it).

The modelers next define extended state machine variables (UserNumber and LastNumberDialed) to represent those actor attributes that may be required in any state or transition. The state transition code they capture in this early model is very simple and includes the bare minimum to enable model execution. For example, the PutInService transition takes the PhoneNumber in the PutInService message that triggered it, and stores it in the UserNumber variable.

The modeling team now reviews the telephone call scenario. That scenario implies that some messages must be relayed between the Telephone actor and the Call actor (for example, the OriginateCall message). Consequently, they define a self-transition on the InService state triggered by all messages coming from the telephone. This involves multiple triggers, so the modelers select TelephoneInput as the label, because the underlying cause of the transition is any input from that port.[11] The code in this transition simply relays any messages it receives to the port that the TelephoneHandler uses to talk to the Call actor.

---

[10] They should test the call scenario both prior to and after putting the telephone in service.

[11] The trigger signals are all the outgoing signals for the TelephoneInteraction protocol (Talk, OriginateCall, DigitsDialed, Alerting, AnswerCall, and Release).

Figure 12.12 Telephone Handler Behavior

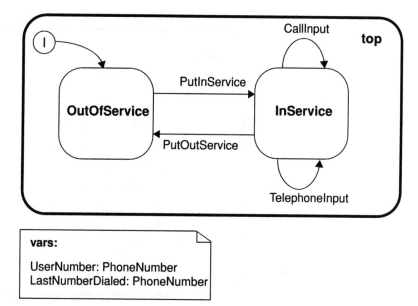

The CallInput transition does the same operation in the opposite direction, from the Call to the telephone.[12]

Upon rereading the Last Number Redial scenario, which involves the TelephoneHandler, they realize that to support the scenario properly, they must know when the TelephoneHandler is participating in a call. This is because the LastNumberDialed state variable only should be updated if the digits are dialed while making a call. It is undesirable to remember digits pressed by the user when the telephone is not being used (perhaps the user is absentmindedly playing with the buttons on the telephone). The required basic call state information only makes sense in the InService state. The modelers therefore enhance the behavior by converting the InService state into a hierarchical state that includes Idle and Active substates to differentiate whether the telephone is in a call (see Figure 12.13).

Continuing the depiction of the Last Number Redial scenario, the DigitsDialed message from the telephone triggers the DigitsDialed transition. With this arrangement, the transition will be triggered only when the telephone is in service and in a call. The code on that transition relays digits to the Call actor, and stores the digits in the LastNumberDialed variable.

---

[12] The trigger signals are all the incoming signals for the TelephoneInteraction protocol (DialTone, RingbackTone, Talk, and OriginateCall).

Figure 12.13 Substates of the TelephoneHandler InService State

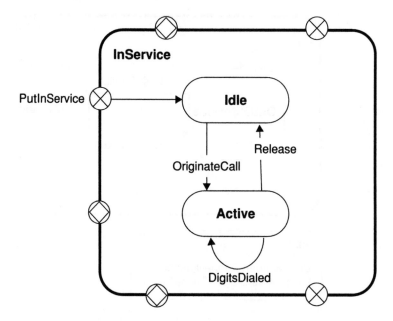

     To complete the behavior, Release messages from the telephone or the call actor trigger the Release transition.[13] The OriginateCall transition is also triggered from both ports, by the OriginateCall message.[14]

12.4.6   Validating the TelephoneHandler: Executing the Model

The TelephoneHandler's behavior is now complete. It can be compiled and executed. The modelers decide that, before capturing the behavior of any of the other actors, they will unit test the TelephoneHandler. We refer to this activity as *validation*, since its objective is to validate that the requirements for that single actor are complete and that the solution to these requirements is feasible.

---

[13] If the Release transition is triggered from the tel port (that is, the telephone), the code relays the Release signal to the Call actor. The Call actor will then tell the other TelephoneHandler associated in the call to release. If the Release message comes from the Call actor, the TelephoneHandler just changes state to Idle with no other actions required.

[14] The DigitsDialed and OriginateCall signals in the CallInput transition's trigger are redundant and can be removed since this is now handled by the substate.

The modelers take a simple approach to validation. They compile and load just the TelephoneHandler actor into a model execution environment. They validate the administration scenarios by injecting PutInService and PutOutService messages into the TelephoneHandler's admin port. This approach simulates that part of the system relevant to the TelephoneHandler for this scenario. As discussed in Section 4.1.9, the modelers animate the state machine diagrams to see the results and verify that the TelephoneHandler is indeed switching between the two states as expected. The modelers then test the Last Number Redial scenario by injecting the proper sequence of messages into the tel and call ports. The modelers view the messages sent out from the TelephoneHandler on its call port in response to the messages they have injected and determine that the design properly stores and replays digits.

They also could manually simulate the complete telephone call scenario. However, the two modelers decide that scenario is too dependent on the Call actor. It is better to first capture its behavior and also to capture the rest of the system, and then to test the entire model.

12.4.7   Capturing the Remaining Behavior

To validate the entire system, each component must be operational. However, the modelers know from experience that they do not have to depict excessive detail to meet this objective. Instead it is more important to achieve a consistent level of completeness among the components that interact with each other. Initially, the actors must be complete enough to support their interfaces to each other, but no more. Often this requires a state machine of manageable complexity but sometimes a state machine is not even needed. In this example, only the Call actor has a sophisticated state machine. The behaviors for the AdministrationUserInterface, AdminHandler, and Telephone actors are much simpler, as shown in Figure 12.14.

The AdministrationUserInterface actor class is very simple. It relays messages (with no routing or manipulation) between two interfaces. It does not need a state machine. The modelers use a binding internal to the actor between its two interfaces to simulate its relay-like function.

The AdminHandler class simply routes messages from the AdministrationUserInterface to the TelephoneHandlers. Its behavior consists of a single state with self transitions to handle this simple logic. A review of the message sequence chart in Figure 12.9 shows that the Telephone actor is also quite simple. It requires two states: Idle and Ringing. The Ringing state is needed to decide when an OffHook message should be translated into an OriginateCall message or an AnswerCall message.

The Call actor's behavior is more complicated. The modelers review the telephone call scenario, and capture the state diagram shown in Figure 12.15. The only problem they encounter is in the logic for deciding when to ring a telephone. A complete phone number must be dialed by a user before the Call actor can know who is to be rung. Since phone numbers usually require multiple digits, they put in a choicepoint named NumTrans. This choicepoint determines whether the user has dialed a complete phone number. The logic for

Figure 12.14 AdministrationUserInterface, AdminHandler, and Telephone Behavior

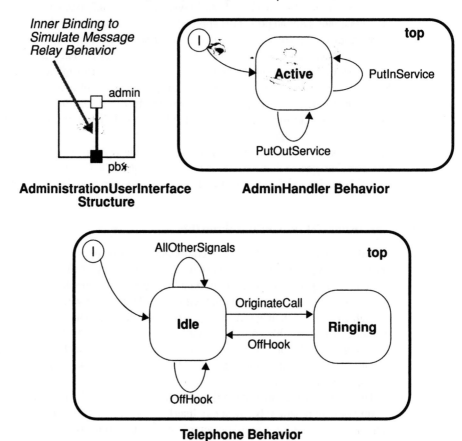

AdministrationUserInterface
Structure

AdminHandler Behavior

Telephone Behavior

translating numbers is initially trivial[15] and could be put in-line. However, it will likely become more complicated in future models, so it is represented in a function called by the choicepoint. A connection between users is simulated by the Connected state's Talk transition. Its code relays Talk signals from one telephone to the other.

In this early model of the Call actor, the code on the transitions is simple. For example, on the Release transition, if it is triggered by a message on the tel1 interface, the Release

---

[15] The modelers assume that two digits are required, with "11" representing one phone and "22" representing the other.

Figure 12.15 Call Actor Behavior

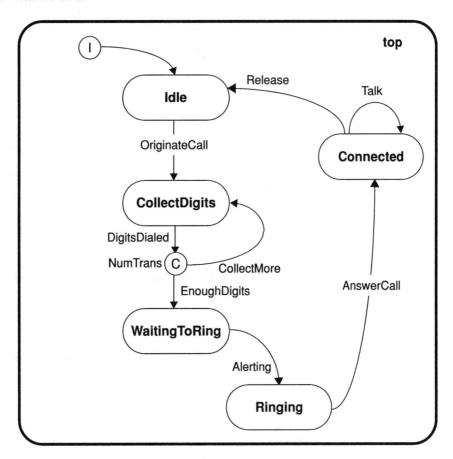

message is relayed to the tel2 interface, and vice-versa. This ensures that both Telephone-Handler actors go back to idle at the end of a call.

The modelers have completed the behavior capture for all PBX components. They could validate the model by manually injecting messages, but decide to take a more automated and repeatable approach. For this purpose, they create the validation components described in the next section.

12.4.8 Constructing the Validation Components

The modelers' first approach to validation in Section 12.4.6 was simple. For the TelephoneHandler actor, they manually injected messages into the actor and monitored the results. To validate complex scenarios affecting several components, it is preferable to create explicit validation components. These components support an automated and repeatable validation technique. Validation components are like any other part of the model—they are constructed using the ROOM modeling language.

The modelers decide that the system's environment forms a basis for validation. Figure 12.16 shows the validation components they add to the model.

Figure 12.16 System and Validation Components

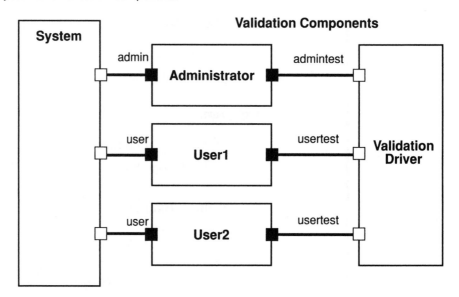

There is often a requirement to coordinate the various scenarios being validated, so the modelers provide a new ValidationDriver actor. This actor will initiate the scenario for putting the telephones in service before attempting the call scenario. They define a test control protocol between the ValidationDriver and the User actors. This protocol includes commands for the User to originate or answer a call, or to initiate a Last Number Redial request. The modelers enhance their early simplistic behavior for the User actor to use it for validation. The User actor's behavior now can represent the user in its various functions for validation purposes. The modelers capture the Administrator actor behavior for the same purpose.

12.4.9   Validation Results

During the early construction iterations of the model, the modeling team identified various deficiencies in the requirements. Executable models, especially those enhanced by validation components, can uncover further problems. These problems may not be found by a static inspection of the model. Even if the specification is complete and the modeling correct, execution can provide early confidence in the soundness of the model.

The modelers decide to validate all the scenarios. The execution traces for the telephone call and Last Number Redial scenarios indicate the proper message flow. This proves that the proposed user and telephone protocols appear to be properly specified and modeled. The administrator scenarios also pass.

Now that the individual scenarios are validated, the modelers decide to run the scenarios concurrently. They know that sometimes such tests can uncover subtle flaws. Their intuition is correct, as they find the following problem:

- For the simple case of no calls currently in progress, there are no side effects from the administrator putting telephones in and out of service. However, the specifier forgot that such service requests can happen concurrently with the telephone being involved in a call. As presently defined, a call in progress is taken out of service, with no warning to the users involved in the call. This is not desirable, so the scenario should be redefined to allow telephones to be taken out of service only if they are completely idle. If they are not idle, the TelephoneHandler state machine should defer the request to take them out of service until the telephone is idle. The modelers must rework the model to fix this problem.

The modelers are now wary of their early confidence in the correctness of the telephone call scenario. They rerun the model, and simulate the situation where the originator of a call ("Ray") hangs up while ringing the destination ("Corinne"). This case was not considered in the original specification. It only covered the optimistic case of users hanging up after they have been connected. The model, since it directly reflects the specification, does not handle this case properly. The Call actor remains permanently stuck in the Ringing state and thus does not bring the call back to idle.

The modelers refine the model's Call actor behavior to address this flaw, as shown in Figure 12.17. They add a group transition, triggered by Release, to take the state machine back to Idle.[16] Thus, the user can hang up any time and the call is undone properly. The modelers ask the specifier to update the specification.

12.5   Example: Synopsis of the Modeling Process

Before continuing with the last part of the example, we will step back and summarize the process that the two modelers took.

The modelers had clear objectives for creating a model. They wanted to understand and validate the requirements for the system. As one of the first steps, a boundary was defined to distinguish between the system and its environment. Scenarios, obtained from the

---

[16] The modelers later realize that they should add a Busy state to cover the case where it is detected that the person being called is already in another call.

Figure 12.17 Call Actor Behavior (Refined)

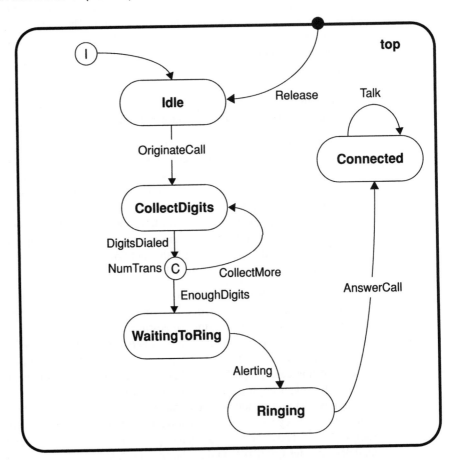

requirements, helped them derive the key protocols that cross this system boundary. Next, they captured an early view of the system structure. The initial set of actors was implied by the concurrent physical components described in the scenarios. As they defined the actor, protocol, and data classes, they documented the purpose of each class.

Throughout the process, the modelers balanced their effort between structure capture, behavior capture, and model execution. They did not have to fully define a particular aspect of the model before commencing other parts. At a very early point, they captured some preliminary behavior to better understand the purpose of the user in the problem. Abstract actors were defined for coordination and interface decoupling purposes. By incrementally capturing more structural details, they uncovered the need for further protocol definition. At various stages, they made assumptions to simplify the modeling, and uncovered specification deficiencies.

The modelers validated the model at the earliest possible time. Rather than defining the behavior for all actors in one step, they selected and validated a key actor first. The behavior for this actor was derived by studying the scenarios that it supported. They completed the system behavior capture and created validation components to validate the entire system. The concurrent execution of scenarios uncovered subtle problems that drove further iteration of the model.

The next section describes the final iteration of this example model.

12.6   Example: Distributed System Impacts

Assume that our team of modelers is not familiar with telephone system design, but that they have had experience with distributed systems. They know that in distributed systems, individual components can fail, as well as the communication paths between them. These problems are frequently overlooked in specifications given to development teams, since they are (somewhat idealistically) considered as "implementation" concerns. It is often left to the developers to apply their domain knowledge to address these issues. A quick review of potential distribution effects uncovers the following scenario:

- **Transmission Link Failure:** During a telephone call, the communication link between the telephone and the system breaks.

To model this problem, the modelers enhance their validation approach. They review the simple binding they used to model communication between the PBX and the telephone. They replace it with an actor that mimics the characteristics of real lines. This new Line actor is inserted in the system structure, as shown in Figure 12.18.

- *Line*: "The communication link between the PBX and the telephone." An attribute of a line is whether it is operational or broken.

Note that this is a validation component inside the system. Previous validation components only existed in the environment.

The two Line actors relay the protocol between a telephone and the PBX. The Line actors have a linetest control interface component, based on a new LineTestControl protocol. The linetest interface is used to instruct the Line actors to simulate communication link failures. The Line actor's behavior either relays or ignores the messages on the tel and pbx interfaces, depending on the state of the link failure.

Often it is useful for abstraction purposes to encapsulate all components that are strongly related to each other. For this reason, the modelers create a new ValidationSystem actor, as shown in Figure 12.19. The ValidationSystem contains all the components

Figure 12.18 Iteration of System Structure

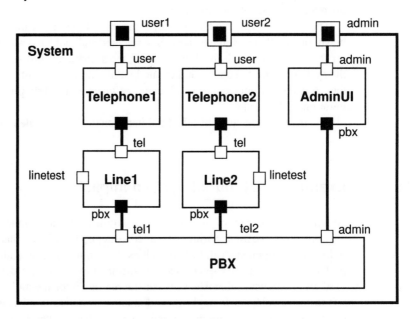

strongly related to validating the system, but may not be considered to be directly interacting with the system. This includes the Line actors, which are contained in both the System
and the ValidationSystem. The modelers use multiple containment because the Line actors
are logically part of two systems simultaneously.

Without changing the design of the PBX and its contained components, the modelers
run the new scenario with the following results:

- It appears that distribution has an unforeseen effect on the telephone protocol specification. The modelers execute the telephone call scenario simultaneously with the
  transmission link failure scenario. After an OriginateCall message is sent from the
  PBX, and the transmission link breaks, the PBX never receives the corresponding
  Alerting message. This causes the Call state machine to get stuck in the WaitingToRing
  state shown in Figure 12.17. The telephone protocol should be made more robust. A
  timeout on the message could be considered.

- The PBX does not know whether other messages ever get to the telephone. For
  example, the telephone may never receive the OriginateCall message commanding
  it to ring. This suggests that an acknowledgment message should be added to the
  protocol to help the PBX detect transmission link failures.

Figure 12.19 Iteration of the Validation System Structure

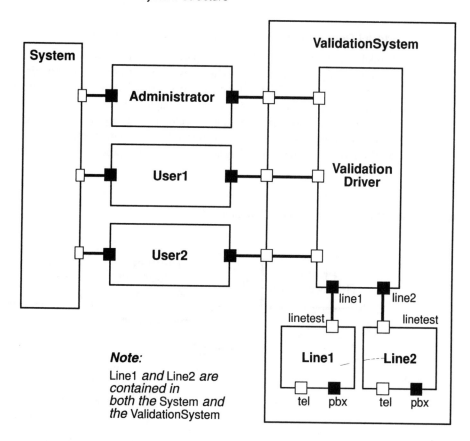

Note:
Line1 *and* Line2 *are contained in both the* System *and the* ValidationSystem

Based on the validation results, further iteration of the model is required. However, rather than continue with our hypothetical case of following the actions of two experienced modelers, we will now step back from the example and complete the chapter by providing a general treatment of model construction.

12.7   An Introduction to Model Development

The preceding example provided a flavor of model development. The rest of this chapter generalizes and details the heuristics. Readers not completely familiar with the ROOM modeling language should initially scan through these sections, and revisit them as required.

12.7.1   Model Development versus Product Development

Model construction and validation is part of a greater *product development process*. This section briefly discusses the product development process to provide a context for the description of the model development process that follows. More information on the product development process can be found in Chapter 14.

Figure 12.20[17] describes product development as a process by which product requirements are transformed into products through development activities (analysis, design, validation). (For simplicity, the diagram does not show product evolution and maintenance.)

Figure 12.20 Simple View of Product Development

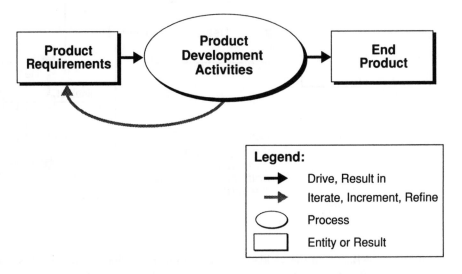

A product is a *system* as indicated in Figure 12.21. Systems may be hierarchically decomposed into smaller systems, each of which is composed of yet smaller systems, and so on. The lowest-level systems are of a size and complexity that match the cognitive abilities of a single developer or a small team. In product development, the higher-level systems, although broad in scope, also may be matched to small team sizes during their early

---

[17] The legend in this figure also applies to subsequent figures in this chapter.

development (as in the PBX example). However, such high-level systems are very soon decomposed into systems of smaller scope to help manage complexity.

Figure 12.21 Products, Systems, and Models

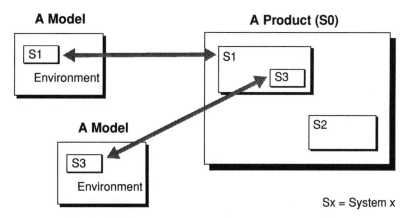

The broad scope of the ROOM modeling language permits the construction of operational models for any system in this hierarchy, regardless of its size. Each model is composed of a set of actor, protocol, and data classes that describe the system proper, as well as its pertinent environment. Traditional development results (such as user interface prototypes, requirement specifications, design documents, and technical notes) supplement the models.

In summary, product development involves a team of people, with activities spanning multiple models that are continually evolving. In contrast, model development involves an individual or a small team, with activities oriented to constructing a particular instance of a model. The two development processes are closely related–the progression of a product toward completion relies on the cumulative effect of multiple model developments.

12.7.2 Model Development Objectives

The value of executable models comes at the cost of creating sufficient detail to run the model. It is important to focus a modeler's activities by clearly stating the objectives of the model, to ensure that the effort is well placed. Modeling objectives help the modeler decide which aspects of the model must be detailed and complete, and which aspects can be left more abstract. Sometimes, as in the PBX example, developers make models to obtain a better understanding of high-level product functionality. Usually, a single modeler (or small team of modelers) is concerned with the design of a particular low-level system. Whatever the modeling objectives, the model must be consistent and detailed enough to be validated through execution.

The PBX example captured several stages of such a model, and included specific validation components. Some modeling objectives may require the interfacing of the model with external components. If the user interface to a system is a prime concern, the executable model may be tied in with external interface mock-ups, or even with the actual devices. In the PBX example, if there was apprehension about users understanding the features, real telephones could be used to interact with the model.

12.7.3 Model Development Overview

This section is an overview of model development. The remaining sections of this chapter expand on these subjects.

An overview of model development is shown in Figure 12.22. Development starts from a set of model requirements. Scenarios describe some of those model requirements as an action or series of actions to realize a function. Text represents simple scenarios, while scenarios depicted as message sequence charts help the modeler understand complex scenarios. If the requirements are not already in scenario form, the modeler should transform them.

A modeler focuses the modeling activities of discovery, invention, and validation on the creation of a single model, rather than the series of models that span the entire product. The discovery activity clarifies the model requirements. It includes the modeler demarcating the system to be developed from the relevant external components that form its environment. Often this boundary is obvious or predetermined. For example, in Figure 12.21 the boundary for S3 was already identified during the earlier model that focused on S1. Invention produces the classes that meet the requirements. Existing models often form the basis for constructing these new classes and the environment (for example, the S1 model forms a basis for the S3 model). Validation confirms that the requirements and the solution to them are correct.

Model development is an incremental and iterative process. Models are constructed incrementally as new components are added to meet small sets of additional requirements. This contrasts with attempting to meet large sets of requirements in any one increment of the model. In the PBX example, classes are initially identified to represent the system boundary. Additional classes are created for the initial set of scenarios. The continuation of the PBX model would involve adding more classes to address additional scenarios.

The PBX example has many situations where the model required iteration and refinement. This cycling through model construction and validation provides the experience necessary to understand requirements and pick optimal solutions. Temporarily taking false paths is part of the learning process (often we learn more from our failures than from our successes). As modeling occurs, there may be enhancement to the requirements as more is learned about them. In the PBX example, various deficiencies in the requirements were uncovered.

Figure 12.22 Model Requirements and Development Activities

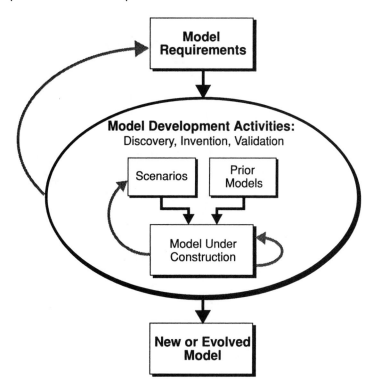

12.8   Modeling Activities

Modeling activities are small versions of the higher-level product development activities of analysis, design, and validation. They address the development of a version of a model rather than the whole product. They should not be confused with model construction steps or phases, as modeling activities are continuous over time and do not have a strict ordering.

Each activity has a different objective, but there are relationships among them, as shown in Figure 12.23. Regardless of the type of component being created for a model, the modeler cycles between discovering what the model needs to do and inventing how the requirements can be solved. The validation activity continuously validates both the requirements and the solution. As more is discovered, more is invented. Invention may spur the need for further discovery if the model requirements appear inadequate or inconsistent when the modeler attempts a solution to them.

The following sections provide more detail on the activities.

Figure 12.23 Modeling Activities

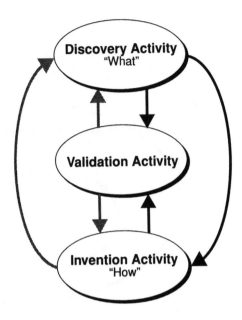

12.8.1   Discovery

A modeler *discovers model requirements* and *understands those requirements*, with the minimal possible dependence on potential solutions.[18] Discovery typically complements the obvious requirements already *given* to the modeler. It uncovers model requirements deficiencies and inconsistencies. It considers not only the stated requirements, but also unstated inherent aspects of the problem domain. In the PBX example, the modelers discover the effects of distribution (communication link failures) on the protocol between the telephone and the PBX. Often, discovery includes determining the demarcation of the system from its environment.

---

[18] We have argued elsewhere in this book that it is not appropriate to completely ignore potential solutions during discovery, since feasibility issues may reflect back on the requirements. For example, a specification may require a microsecond response across a wide-area network, which is beyond the current state of the art (and, likely, beyond the laws of physics). In such situations, the requirements must be changed.

12.8.2   Invention

Invention is the creative activity of *devising a solution to the model requirements*. It typically requires devising new classes to supplement or replace the discovered classes. In the PBX example, invention occurs in the creation of classes inside the system, such as the decision to create a call actor. It also occurs in the development of validation components, such as the validation driver actor. Often there are several promising solutions to problems, so invention includes prototyping alternatives. Creating *architectures* that form a basis for a variety of designs also is an important aspect of invention. (The topic of devising architectures is discussed in the Chapter 13.)

12.8.3   Validation

Validation confirms whether the *model meets the requirements*. It also validates the hypothesis that the modeler is *solving the right requirements*. By executing a model, the modeler finds nonobvious problems that inspection (during specification or design) might not have discovered. In the PBX example, it was not immediately obvious that there is an interaction between the telephone call and taking telephones out of service. Validation also helps confirm user requirements, as operational models are good mechanisms for eliciting user reaction. The same scenarios that drive the discovery and invention activities also drive validation. Validation is based on specific validation components (created using the ROOM modeling language) that are both in the environment and in the system. Design components of the system itself also assist in validation. The Call actor in the PBX example is, in effect, validated by the external components (such as User), and the internal design components with which it interacts (such as the TelephoneHandler actor).

12.9   Scenarios

Scenarios play an important role in the above modeling activities. Scenarios express functional requirements for products, models, and components inside models. Traditional quantitative requirements (such as performance and cost) complement scenarios. For example, a complete description of a PBX includes not only the usage scenarios described in the example, but also requirements for its real-time capacity (for instance, how many telephone calls it should support simultaneously). We now describe in more detail what scenarios are, and how they can help in the design of components.

12.9.1   Definition and Scope

Requirements often describe what systems do (or how they are used) as individual low-level component functions. However, most users typically do not conceive of invoking a single function, but instead prefer to think of causally chained sequences of events or functions that represent some useful higher-level capability they desire. For example, a user does not think of holding a telephone handset or dialing digits as single significant functions, but rather as part of the complete act of making a telephone call. We address this by using scenarios to describe how a component will be used. A scenario may be a single action, but usually it is a predicted sequence of actions (for example, withdrawing money from a banking machine involves many steps). Often scenarios translate into a sequence of events between objects in a model.

Our use of the term "scenario" is similar to a "use case" as described in [Jacobson92] or a "scenario" as described in [Rumbaugh91]. However, we subsume not only descriptions of how a system is *used*, but also event sequences that occur inside the system (such as component failures). Initial scenarios may focus on objects that interact with the system. To these are added new scenarios created as a result of discovery. A model's intrinsic domain often is a source of scenarios. For example, a distributed environment, with its relativistic effects and partial failure modes, leads to a variety of additional scenarios that might not have been in the original requirements specification.

We suggest that modelers use scenarios as the primary means of expressing functional requirements, since a good way to specify and understand a system is to describe the various ways it is used. Neither developers nor customers can be certain that a system is correct until they try to use it for its intended purposes. This encourages developers to think about a problem from a wider perspective. For example, in automobile design, the location of the sparkplugs as viewed solely from the engine's functional perspective is insufficient. When one starts to detail a typical maintenance scenario (such as "changing the sparkplugs") the physical placement of the engine in the engine compartment also is significant. Any mechanic who has had to change sparkplugs in the crowded engine compartment of a modern car can attest that these scenarios are not always considered by the automobile designer.

There are many examples of systems that are best described by the scenarios that drive them. From consumer electronics, the most complex (and least understood) scenario is programming a VCR to record a television show. The PBX example focuses on the everyday scenario of making a telephone call. The initialization of a complex software system may require a strict sequencing of events best described by scenarios.

Some predicted circumstances for a product or model involve modifying its construction. These are constructive *scripts* and are a type of requirement closely related to scenarios. Scripts describe a real-life construction situation that will occur during model evolution. They are executed not by models, but by the modelers themselves. An example is a script requesting a new designer to examine the system and describe how a current function works. A manager may ask a designer to outline how a new function could be added to the system. A constructive script for the PBX example is requesting a designer to add a feature to record details about the duration of and the people involved in calls. Constructive scripts played early in product or model development give an early assessment of the degree to which a system can be easily evolved.

12.9.2 Describing Requirements as Scenarios

Sometimes requirements are directly expressed as scenarios. Simple scenarios are usually expressed in text, such as the description of Last Number Redial in the PBX example. Message sequence charts graphically portray complex scenarios as time-sequenced, pairwise exchanges of messages describing the scenario events. For example, the modelers of the PBX example use the message sequence chart in Figure 12.9 to understand the telephone call scenario. Expressing scenarios as message sequence charts has several advantages. A chart is complete and understandable. It describes the temporal behavior in the system, rather than focusing on the data in the system.

Modelers should consider not only the scenarios for normal operations, but also special cases (such as alternative paths or error situations). The latter are of particular concern, as they may have the most complex logic, and thus are often difficult to design properly.

Large or high-level scenarios can be defined in terms of other component scenarios. For example, a grocery shopping scenario may include other scenarios (such as drawing up a shopping list, getting money for the purchases from a banking machine, and so on). Returning to the PBX example, in a comprehensive design, the telephone call scenario would consist of detailed scenarios such as the complete set of messages between the call actor and the hardware system to make and break voice connections between users.

12.9.3 Scenarios for Design and Concurrency Resolution

Often modelers drive the initial discovery activity by studying the scenario participants external to the system (for example, scenarios initiated by a user, or by the environment, such as money jamming in a banking machine). Scenarios can also be initiated by scenario participants inside the system (for example, the internal components of the system), and thus can be used to drive the detailed internal design activities, as shown in Figure 12.24. An example of a scenario initiated by a design component is a self-test or audit sequence initiated by a maintenance component in the system.

Figure 12.24 Scenarios and Initiators

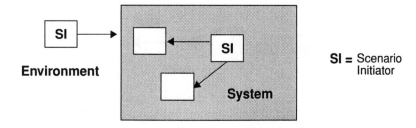

By focusing on sequencing, scenarios provide a good start for concurrent object selection. Furthermore, modelers derive an actor's interface type and behavior by examining the scenarios (including the alternate error or variant flows) in which the actor is involved.

Scenario initiators often are independent and thus may be concurrent. This implies that components of the system must handle the effects of such concurrency. One can visualize a series of objects involved in the scenario when it executes—a stream of execution. Figure 12.25 shows the effects of concurrency on the PBX example.

Figure 12.25 Scenario Concurrency

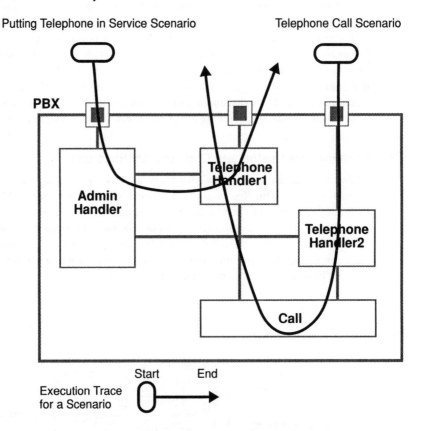

There are objects that must resolve the nondeterministic interaction among the concurrent streams of execution (scenario conflicts). In the PBX example, the TelephoneHandler is involved in multiple communication relationships associated with multiple scenarios (telephone calls and taking telephones in and out of service). A major challenge in real-time system development is to identify such objects, and design them to properly handle concurrent scenarios. State machine-based behavior, in particular, helps in their construction because it reminds the designer of the various state and event combinations.

12.9.4 Scenario Packages

Modelers may guide model construction by considering one scenario at a time. This has the advantage of supporting the earliest possible model execution, but sometimes means revision as the examination of the subsequent scenarios invalidates previous modeling. Modelers also may elect to study all or a large portion of the scenarios at once, delaying model execution but often reducing model revisions. Both techniques are valid. However, it is often more convenient and effective to choose the intermediate position of a *scenario package*.

A scenario package groups together several scenarios for modeling. For every major model construction cycle, the end goal is to satisfy all the scenarios in the package. The PBX example was small enough that all of the scenarios could be considered a single package. The modeling effort was initiated by considering scenarios that included the basic function of the PBX (making calls), a simple administrative action (taking telephones in and out of service), and a simple feature (Last Number Redial). This provided the modelers with an overview of the system. The modelers captured detailed telephone handler behavior by considering the scenarios one at time.

By starting with a representative portion of the scenarios, the breadth of the system is better understood, and that helps in the discovery of the system boundary. During model construction, this breadth can help to create a general-purpose, high-level design for the system. It is also valid to incrementally capture the model. A modeler may construct a model for just a few scenarios at a time, until the complete package is addressed.

There are several approaches to partitioning scenarios into a package. One approach is to package a broad set of scenarios that represent most of the major requirements of the system. This was the approach taken in the PBX example. Alternatively, one can pick a set of scenarios that are strongly related to each other and thus narrow in scope (for example, all scenarios related to making various types of telephone calls). The complete package should be small enough that the modeler achieves the goal of early validation.

There are also several techniques for defining a series of packages. The user of a system may already know what key capabilities to validate first. Development costs, time to market, and staffing issues also drive the selection of packages. Sometimes project risk may be a prime criterion for prioritization, as discussed in [Boehm88]. By this criterion, some scenarios should be in early packages to help the developers learn whether the model or product is even possible. At the outset of development, the risk can be very high, since neither the true requirements nor the necessary solution may be fully understood. As understanding increases over time, the total risk drops. Contenders for early scenario packages include key product features, least-understood features, and the most difficult parts of the implementation.

12.9.5   Summary of Scenarios

Scenarios are a primary method for describing the requirements of real-time systems. A scenario identifies the sequence of actions for some overall use of a system, or a component inside it. They can be depicted in either textual or message sequence chart form. Scenarios are used to express both normal and unusual (for example, alternate path or error situation) operations. Complex scenarios may be recursively defined in terms of other simpler scenarios. A constructive script is a concept closely related to scenarios. The major difference is that scripts predict future model construction situations that will be performed by the modeler, not the model.

Because scenarios focus on objects and the sequence of messages among objects, they are particularly useful for deriving components and their requirements. Scenarios that can be independently initiated suggest to the modeler the inherent concurrency that must be addressed by the components. Often this requires components to resolve the interaction between intersecting scenarios.

Not all scenarios must be addressed in one modeling cycle. It is often convenient to assemble in a scenario package a subset of scenarios to be modeled. Such packages may contain a broad set of scenarios, or a set of closely related scenarios.

12.10   System Scope: Environment and Validation Components

Figure 12.21 showed that a model's scope includes the system and its environment. Scope also includes the up-front consideration of validation components.

12.10.1   Definition of System Boundary

A system usually is conceived with the intention of understanding its function and ultimately building it as part of a product. A modeler must, therefore, clearly discriminate the extent of the system. To help in this activity, it is useful to consider the environment that surrounds, and thus influences, the system. The demarcation between the system and its environment is called the *system boundary*. The environment contains those objects outside the boundary. Environment objects participate in the scenarios driving the system and are therefore important for validation. Both the system and its environment are important to the modeler and must be understood to create the system. For example, environment objects often are modeled to understand their influences on the system, even if they are not the responsibility of the modeler. In the PBX example, the users are important objects in the environment because they initiate and participate in the primary scenarios driving the system.

What is relevant to the modeler (and thus what the system is) may change over time, so the system boundary may shift, as shown in Figure 12.26. Software developers initially may include hardware (for example, telephones, fluid control valves) as part of the system. When more system requirements are known and the hardware is developed, the system boundary may shrink to contain just the software with which the developers are concerned.

Figure 12.26 Boundary Creation and Evolution

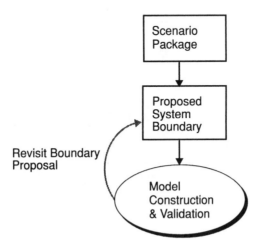

12.10.2 Modeling the Boundary

Often the system boundary is predetermined by prior system development. For example, a system inside a larger, previously modeled system already has its boundary defined. For new systems, the boundary is frequently obvious, because the requirements will state what needs to be built. Clearly, there are some objects that modelers know they may have to understand, but do not have to design, such as the people using a system.

If the boundary is not apparent, it must be discovered. Demarcation starts with a broad examination of the scenarios. People participating in the scenarios are obviously external to the system, and can form the basis for a speculative boundary. This boundary may shrink as detailed scenarios are inspected. For example, the scenarios (and thus interfaces) between the hardware with which the user interacts and an inner system may be known. In the PBX example (Figure 12.27), this is the interface between the telephone and the PBX. If the interface and the telephone's function are fully understood and valid, one may not need to model them in detail. The telephone could be proposed to be part of the environment as well. The PBX is now the system to be modeled. Telephones, rather than the users themselves, are the external objects of most relevance to the system. The telephones drive the scenarios influencing the system model.

Figure 12.27 The Complete Structure of the PBX Example

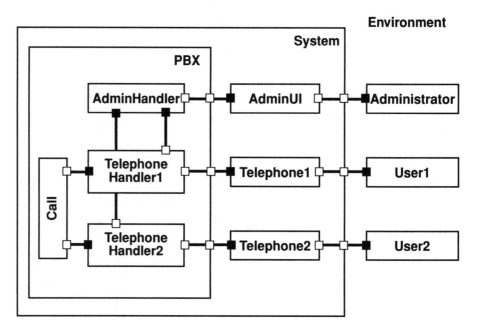

Having settled on a proposed system boundary, the modeler captures the interface between the system and environment objects directly connected to the system, as shown in Figure 12.28. As in the first instance of the PBX model, the outcome of this is an initial set of protocol classes and actor classes for the environment objects that participate with the system. Their behavior represents the externally observable event sequences as seen by the system. In the PBX example, the modelers capture a simple view of the user's behavior to better comprehend the protocol. Boundary creation also may initiate a revision of the message sequence charts to include more detail.

12.10.3 Validation Components

The environment objects participating in the scenarios form the basis for black box system validation. However, validation components can be inside the system as well. Internal validation components may be the design components (or variants of them) that already surround the design component to be validated. Sometimes there is a need to have special components inside the system purely for validation purposes. In the PBX example (Figure 12.19), actors that simulate communication link failures to the telephone serve that purpose. Modelers usually need to design new components to coordinate the various valida-

Figure 12.28 Modeling the Environment

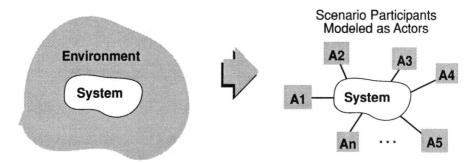

tion components. Sets of validation components may be large enough to be considered as autonomous systems themselves. Section 12.14 provides more detail on approaches to validation.

12.11 Model Development Strategy

We have provided an overview of model development and the key concepts on which it is based (activities, scenarios, and system boundaries). We now expand on the subject of incremental and iterative development. The specific model construction activities, model commencement criteria, inheritance, and requirements traceability are discussed.

12.11.1 Incrementing and Iterating Models

The strategy for developing ROOM models is guided by a single principle—the modeling approach must reflect the natural process that developers undertake in industrial product development. That principle translates into an emphasis on incremental and iterative development methods shown in Figure 12.29.

Incremental development matches the human cognitive process. It is very difficult for most developers to understand (and therefore solve) very large and complex problems in a single step. It is easier to start from a reduced set of requirements, initially laying aside some details, and gradually extend the model until it addresses the complete requirements. An incremental approach aligns with the goal of early model validation. The fewer requirements a model must support, the earlier it can be constructed, executed, and validated. In Figure 12.29, from a scenario package the modeler selects a subset of the scenarios for each modeling cycle, evolving the model until it meets all the scenario package requirements. In the PBX example, the number of scenarios was small enough that they

Figure 12.29 Incrementing and Iterating a Model

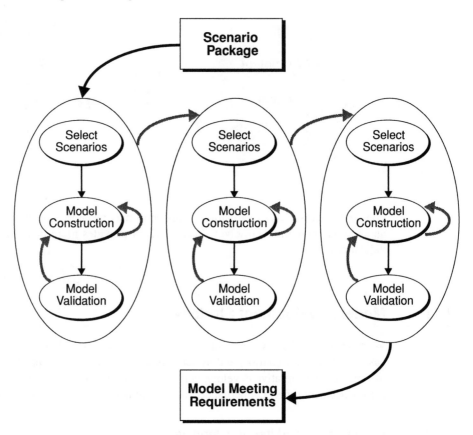

were all considered together (Figure 12.3). The diagram in Figure 12.29 is simplified in that it does not show the iteration (redefinition) of the scenarios as various requirement deficiencies are uncovered.

During model construction, there is a continuous blend of discovery and invention activities, complementing the validation that interplays with construction. Model construction, as shown in Figure 12.30, consists of element identification, consolidation, and behavior capture.

Initially, the modeler identifies *elements* that are the fundamental building blocks for models. They include actor classes, actor attributes (properties of actors such as candidate states or state variables), data classes, and protocol classes or individual signals. This exercise results in several *candidate* (or hypothetical) elements being tabled. This can be

Figure 12.30 Model Construction

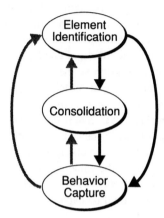

sketched out on paper or with tools. The modeler examines the reuse of existing classes or the creation of variants through inheritance.

Associated with element identification is the necessary process of consolidation. Consolidation unites the elements into classes, and involves the elimination of some candidates and the creation of new ones. There are also various relationships between objects (such as containment and communication) that can help consolidate.

Actor classes have an additional aspect of construction, namely behavior. High-level behavior capture (states and transitions) and detail-level coding must take place. However, we suggest that modelers strive for a balance among behavior capture and other aspects of model capture (such as containment and communication). For example, behavior capture should not be left until the end of construction, as behavior often enhances the modeler's understanding of communication relationships (perhaps affecting the definition of protocol classes). Conversely, an overly deep focus on behavior may be premature when the structure of the model is not well known.

Concurrent with the previously described incrementing of the model, modelers iterate or return to review previously captured parts of a model. This is shown in Figure 12.29 and Figure 12.30. Iteration is important, as modelers seldom pick optimum solutions to modeling requirements the first time. The best solutions come about from direct feedback and experience. If developers do not already have the specific experience required, they must get it quickly. A good way to gain that familiarity is to construct and validate a particular approach as early as possible. The modeler uses insights from each modeling pass to iterate the model. As new requirements and the approaches to solving previous ones are reviewed, the model is steadily refined or improved upon. The incremental and iterative approach to model construction ultimately attains the goal of having a model that meets the complete model requirements.

12.11.2 Model Commencement versus Completion

The considerations of incremental requirements and the associated model construction cycles are not as linear as Figure 12.29 and Figure 12.30 might suggest. Not all of the model construction for the scenarios needs to take place before model validation can start. Not all of the element identification or consolidation is required before behavior can be addressed. Model execution and validation may initiate further model construction or element identification to improve the model.

Throughout this, the modeler takes advantage of the *substantial and important difference between the criteria for when a model can be considered complete (meets all requirements), versus when model construction and validation can commence.* Model construction can commence at a very early stage, as noted in Figure 12.31. For each model increment there is an optimum point, balancing efficiency of model capture (looking at a large number of components at a time) with the value of the earliest possible insight to be gained from modeling a small subset of components. An example is deciding how many actors to define before protocols or behavior should be captured. A single actor may be of insufficient breadth, while tens of actors may be too many.

Figure 12.31 Model Commencement versus Completion Criteria

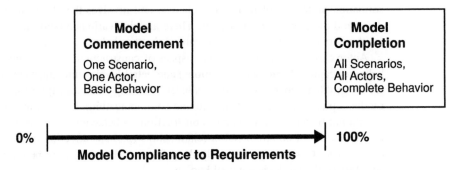

Consistency also comes into play when deciding how to model. For validation, all the elements of a model that interact with each other must be consistent enough to execute. For example, two actors that communicate with each other need compatible protocol classes and behavior.[19] Finally, the modeler can make various simplifying assumptions in order to commence modeling early. For example, protocol signal names are needed for early execution, but the data classes for message bodies may be initially ignored.

---

[19] Consistent behavior does not mean that both actors must go to the same level of detail. All that is required is that the interface is supported, by whatever means. In the PBX example, the AdminUI actor only required an internal binding to satisfy the model execution requirements.

12.11.3 Inheritance and Iteration

An important aspect to consider during model construction is inheritance, which is often based on iteration. Inheritance is sometimes overlooked as modelers initially focus on creating and validating a model's function. However, it is important during the cycle to continually revisit the class inheritance hierarchy. Taking actor classes as an example, it is valuable to check the class library when starting a modeling cycle. An actor may have already been defined that has a similar purpose, or one can be easily created from appropriate component actors already in the class hierarchy. Problem domain expertise may suggest an initial class hierarchy. The modeler, based on further insight, may reorganize the class hierarchy. For example, the modeler generates new abstract classes by combining the attributes of several subclasses. This often occurs because inheritance usage is based on a threshold of understanding that may not be achieved until the modeler has created several concrete classes.

More heuristics pertaining to inheritance are described in Chapter 9.

12.11.4 Requirements Traceability

Throughout model construction, for many systems it is important to create and maintain requirements traceability. This refers to the ability to track the relationship between system requirements and the classes that address them. This helps developers decide if all requirements have been considered, and provides a mechanism for assessing the impact of changes to requirements. A simple traceability technique is to assign a requirement number to each root or elemental requirement. These requirement numbers are allocated originally to the candidate model elements that each requirement implies. As consolidation and further refinement of the classes takes place, it is important to revisit the allocations so accurate allocation is preserved. Similarly, as the requirements change, it is important to evaluate the classes that are affected.

12.11.5 Summary of Model Development Strategy

The human cognitive process drives the model development strategy, resulting in an incremental and iterative approach to modeling. Each modeling cycle addresses a small increment of model requirements. Iteration occurs as the modeler revisits the classes created in previous cycles.

Throughout these cycles, there is a continuous interplay of the discovery, invention, and validation modeling activities. Discovery clarifies and completes the specification of the model or component requirements. Invention devises solutions to these requirements. Validation confirms that the requirements and the solution are correct.

Model construction also involves the exercises of identifying the basic elements that will make up the model. Consolidation refines or unifies these elements. For actor classes, a behavior capture exercise also is required.

Throughout model development, the modeler balances the end goal of a model that completely meets the requirements, versus the earlier opportunities to start modeling a smaller portion of the problem. The latter approach is favored as it allows the modeler to gain the earliest possible experience with the problem or its solution. Inheritance and requirements traceability also are considered throughout the model development cycle.

12.12   Techniques for Element Identification and Consolidation

The previous section gave a general description of the strategy of model development. This section discusses in detail how requirements are translated to ROOM classes by focusing on element identification and consolidation. Subsequent sections provide details for particular types of classes (for example, actor class identification and consolidation).

12.12.1   Element Identification

As previously stated, models are built from intrinsic building blocks called elements. The input to candidate element identification consists of model requirements (either directly given to, or discovered by, the modeler), previous models, and the modeler's domain experience. From that input, there are various general methods for identifying elements. Initially modelers should take a brainstorm approach where elements are quickly proposed without excessive review. Elements are often obvious from the problem domain. Scanning the requirements descriptions for nouns (potential actors) and verbs (potential signals) gives the modeler an initial set of candidate elements.[20]

Each candidate should have a purpose, a single sentence that explains its essential nature and thus why the element exists. In the PBX example, the purpose of the Administrator class was defined as "a person who commands the PBX to put telephones in or out of service." Each candidate can be tagged with a requirement number for traceability.

While identifying candidates, it is important to realize that the elements should be defined autonomously (standalone purpose and functions) to enable their use as reusable components. Particular relationships with other elements are captured in separate classes (for example, composite actors). This focus on environment-independent definitions is analogous to hardware design, where the objects (integrated circuits) are described in terms of what they do (for example, Boolean "NAND" functions). They are seldom described by the circuit configurations they are in.

---

[20] As will be described later, there are many more techniques than noun and verb scans, especially for identifying actor classes.

12.12.2 Element Consolidation

The raw list of candidates proposed during the element identification exercise usually needs to be consolidated. This involves regrouping according to relationships and throwing away redundant or poorly defined candidates.

Redundant classes have semantically identical purpose descriptions. One class should be retained and the rest discarded.

Poorly defined candidates are ones where the description looks weak. The purpose could be subsumed by another class. Such weak classes may have too limited a scope of responsibility, or the scope may be too broad. As an example of limited scope, in the PBX example, the modelers could have proposed actors that only handled small portions of the call (for example, originating the call, releasing the call). Instead they realized that those are all just parts of the total responsibility of a call, and thus should be subsumed by a Call actor. As an example of overly broad scope, an actor could have been defined that included both the TelephoneHandler and Call actors' responsibilities. That would be an incorrect mix of responsibilities. Sometimes it would be concerned about purely local telephone capabilities, while at other times it would be responsible for the relationship of multiple telephones in calls.

Relationships create new classes. Relationships include structural relationships between actors (layering, containment, communication) and inheritance relationships, as shown in Figure 12.32. In distributed real-time systems, most concrete relationships involve containment and communication, so attention to those is especially fruitful when inventing new classes. The detailed communication relationships drive the identification of further candidate protocol classes and further data classes. Raw signal elements may be grouped into protocol classes. This candidate list of classes is additionally consolidated or refined by removing any redundant or inadequately defined classes. The resulting actor, protocol, and data classes form the basis for completing the behavior definition. However, as stated previously, behavior modeling can commence at a very early stage. It does not have to wait for all classes to be defined.

Lastly, consolidation often implies further refinement. As Figure 12.33 shows, the refinement of protocol classes can influence the interface types of actor classes. Refinement of data classes affects both the attributes of actor classes and the message bodies of protocol classes. As the classes are being consolidated and refined, it is important to keep the requirement number tags current for each class.

In summary, element consolidation unifies the initial raw elements into the set of actor, protocol, and data classes to be modeled. It does this by examining elements for vagueness or redundancy, and by considering layering, containment, communication, and inheritance relationships. A further process of refinement involving relationships among the classes completes consolidation.

12.12.3 Actor Class Identification and Consolidation

The previous section discussed element identification and consolidation in general. This section expands on the issue of identifying and consolidating actors. Actor classes usually are the most important target in any class creation exercise.

Figure 12.32 Elements and Relationships

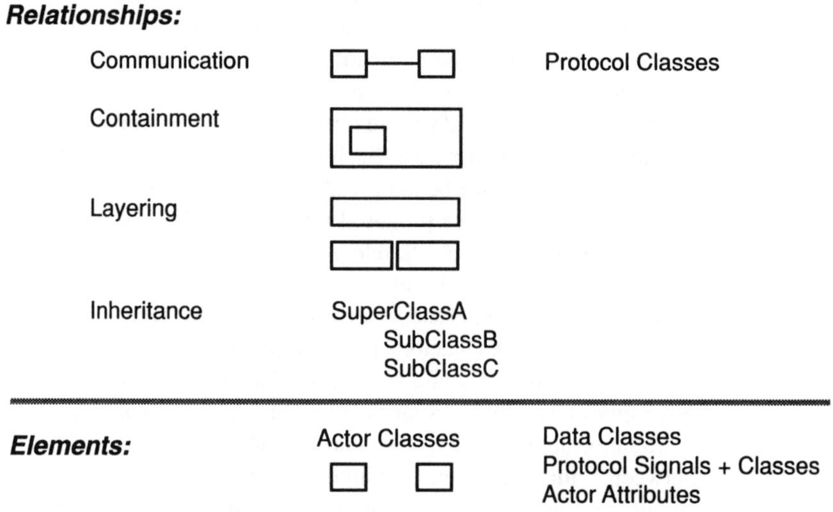

Relationships:

Communication	▭—▭	Protocol Classes
Containment	▭	
Layering	▭	
Inheritance	SuperClassA SubClassB SubClassC	

Elements:

Actor Classes   □   □   Data Classes
                        Protocol Signals + Classes
                        Actor Attributes

When identifying an actor, it is important to recall its definition. An actor is an active, event-driven object that has a behavior[21] whose its state must be retained over time. Actors encapsulate major data attributes, which are represented either as states or extended state variables. Although each actor has a single purpose, it may play various roles or provide various functions in a system. Actors should be defined by what they do (not by what they are connected to) to increase reuse.

12.12.3.1   Candidates

There are several techniques for actor identification. The following criteria can—and usually do—overlap. A simple method described previously is to scan the requirements and message sequence charts for nouns. Every noun could be a potential actor. We caution that the noun approach should not be the only technique. This is because nouns from a specification have a very wide mix from high level (problem domain) to low level (implied design decompositions). Scenarios depicted as message sequence charts provide stronger candidates, because they focus on objects that exchange messages with other objects.

When considering concurrency, candidate actors often are hardware entities (or the software in charge of them) and abstractions of other physical entities. Examples include

---

[21] Composite actors are somewhat different, in that they may be created for abstraction purposes and may not necessarily have their own behavior. The complete behavior of a composite actor is the sum of the behaviors of the contained actors, plus its own direct behavior.

Figure 12.33 Element Identification and Consolidation

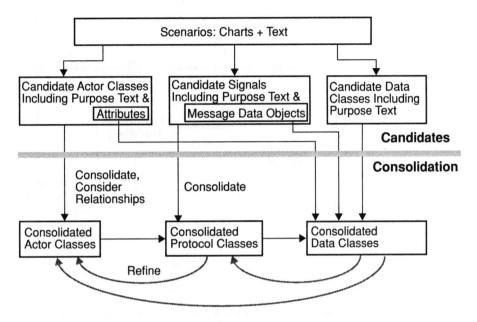

the user and telephone actors in the PBX model. Concurrency also may be logical in cases where the actors are interacting with real-world components that are concurrent themselves. For example, the Call actor in the PBX example (shown in Figure 12.34) could be considered concurrent, as people can initiate calls any time. Wherever there is a need to focus on a single control element to resolve concurrent scenarios of interaction, an actor may also be needed. Such actors often have multiple distinct interfaces.

Actors often are created to hold containment relationships. Such composite actors allow modelers to express abstractions or encapsulate lower-level concerns in a very concrete and formal fashion. The ValidationSystem and PBX actors in the PBX example are such actors. Containment can represent very complex relationships, such as multiple containment and dynamic structure. The containers themselves also may have their own behavior that adds to the relationship of the contained actors by coordinating them.

Sometimes actors are more conceptual than physical. Such abstractions are made concrete when they are represented as *coordinator actors*. These actors may be created when there is a need to have a mediator between various actors to encapsulate a process. The call actor in the PBX example serves a coordination function (see Figure 12.34). Coordinator actors are examples of abstract actors, invented by the modeler, to which the requirements may not directly refer. A coordinator actor is likely to be less persistent than classes directly identified from the problem domain. It may only exist for the time the scenario

Figure 12.34 Composite, Coordinator, and Interface Actors

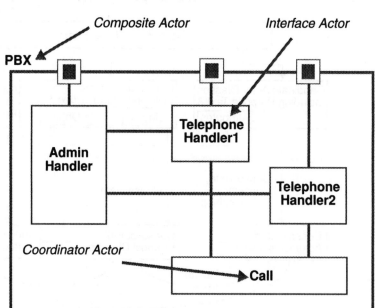

executes. Returning to the PBX example, the call actor did not need to be statically incarnated. It could have been dynamically incarnated only when calls were required.

A final type of actor is an *interface actor* as proposed in [Jacobson92]. An interface actor decouples the system from its interface, on the premise that the interface is likely to change. An interface actor reduces the dependence of the system on external interfaces. The TelephoneHandler actor in the PBX example is an interface actor (see Figure 12.34).

12.12.3.2   Consolidation

Candidate actors must be consolidated. The general heuristic of merging redundant classes and purging weak classes applies. In addition, it is often discovered that a candidate actor is really an attribute, a data class to be contained in another actor.

Often, the most consolidation results from further considering relationships. This may merge some actors, and spawn the creation of new ones. If the purpose of an actor is too broad, or sounds like multiple purposes, it may be a composite actor. A keyword to look for in the purpose is "and." The multiple purposes can be divided into contained actors, while retaining the container (composite class) for its abstraction value. This was the case for the PBX actor in our example. Although wide in scope, it served as a convenient abstract container for several actors with very specific purposes. Communication relationships also are important to consolidation. Those candidate actors with no communication relationships are suspect. Many times the most important consolidation relationship is inheritance, where the class library is searched to find existing actors with similar purposes to the newly required ones.

12.12.4 Protocol Class Identification and Consolidation

When identifying protocols, a modeler should recall that a protocol class is a set of incoming or outgoing message types consisting of high-level signals. It optionally includes message data objects, and a prescribed set of message exchange sequences. A signal is a high-level indication of the intent of the message (for example, "PutInService"). The message data object holds the specific parameters (for instance, what should be put into service). A protocol class sometimes is a derived class, in that it captures and, therefore, follows the communication relationships defined among actors or layers.

12.12.4.1   Candidates

The specification may already be prepartitioned into protocol classes, or a protocol class may be intuitive. In the PBX example, the protocol classes were easy to identify. When the protocol classes are not obvious, a modeler should create a set of candidate signals. Each signal would have a one line purpose description (for example, Release: "A request to terminate a call"). The events described in message sequence charts form a basis for raw candidate signals. The verbs in textual requirements sometimes suggest candidate signals.

Each signal's name should describe the high-level purpose of the message, not how to achieve the purpose. In the PBX example, the signal PutInService does not concern itself with how the system will achieve this request. A signal name also should not have any destination dependency in its name (for example, "RequestInformationOfLeftTerminal") that would minimize its reuse potential.

12.12.4.2   Consolidation

The modeler should eliminate redundant signals from the set of raw signals. Vague signals are removed or made concrete. The resultant set of signals should be partitioned into candidate protocol classes. Examining the message sequence charts, all messages from one actor to another may fully define a protocol class.

Sometimes when examining such a protocol class, it may be evident that the protocol class is a mixture of concerns. In such cases the protocol class should be divided into subset protocol classes based on those concerns. In the PBX example, the protocol that the TelephoneHandler uses to talk to telephones is quite different from its interaction with the administration aspect of the system.

The inverse of this may also occur. Various protocols between actors may be aggregated into a superset protocol class. For example, even if a particular scenario only uses a few signals, a general control protocol may be defined. This control protocol would include many more signals when other similar communication relationships are considered. In other words, an individual actor reference may not necessarily use all the signals in a protocol class.

Most protocols are asymmetrical and use different signal names for in versus out. When in doubt the signal direction should be defined from the client (user) rather than server perspective.[22]

The modeler should check for redundant or weak protocol classes, and consider inheritance relationships. Some protocol classes may be described in abstract terms, and inheritance can be used to specify detailed variants (such as the addition of signals for handling error situations). Signals common to several protocol classes can be migrated up in the hierarchy. In the PBX example, the UserInteraction and TelephoneInteraction protocol classes both contain signals representing audible information (for example, "Talk"). A new superclass called AudibleInformation would contain those common signals. If protocol classes already exist, inheritance should be used to define the new protocol classes as refinements of existing ones.

12.12.5 Data Class Identification and Consolidation

Modelers should recall that finite-state machine extended state variables and message bodies use data classes. Contrasting with actor classes, a data class is not concurrent in that it does not have its own thread of control.

The specification, especially any protocol definitions that include message bodies, can suggest candidate data classes. Actor attributes also are a good source of candidates. Data classes sometimes can be discovered by examining all nouns in a requirement description that are associated with a possessive phrase. For example, "the temperature of the tank" suggests that temperature may be an attribute. During redundancy removal, some attributes do not disappear but become states rather than extended state variables (in the PBX example, the ringing attribute for a Telephone results in a Ringing state being defined). Data classes are consolidated by examining inheritance relationships. As the modeler defines behavior, often new data classes are created.

12.12.6 Layer Identification

Very high-level relationships between actors are often represented by layers. Because layers are an abstraction, problem descriptions seldom directly identify them. Although it would be ideal to define layers first, and then put actors in them, often it is the other way around. Modelers sometimes cannot recognize layers until they have a large set of actors. Modelers are seldom faced with the problem of eliminating redundant layers or consolidating layers into metalayers.

---

[22] Since each service usually has multiple clients, defining protocols in such a manner reduces the need to conjugate interface components.

There are several criteria for identifying a layer. The most obvious use of layering is where there are ubiquitous or shared services used by many objects. Time-of-day services are an example. Such services should be grouped into a layer, which can be thought of as a virtual machine providing low-level services to higher layers. Modeling the services as actors with bindings would result in visual overload. The bindings to such a service actor would obscure more important communication paths. Layers can also be used for very high-level conceptual boundaries, where a modeler may want to hide irrelevant detail (for example, virtual machines). For further layering heuristics, see Section 7.4.

12.13   Behavior Capture and Consolidation

Previous sections have described element identification and consolidation, which apply to all ROOM classes. Actor classes have an additional activity to consider, as they are not complete until their behavior has been captured by ROOMcharts.

When capturing behavior, it is important to distinguish between actor attributes expressed as states, and those represented by the values of extended state variables. A state is a quiescent point where the actor is waiting for an event to trigger it back into action.[23] The value of an extended state variable may not be a quiescent point. For example, a counter or a fluid level is a finite-state machine variable, whereas "waiting for keyboard input" is a state. State variables are captured using traditional programming languages and are not discussed here. This section instead focuses on the more challenging problem of state capture.

As discussed previously in Section 12.11.2, a major difference exists between when state machine capture can commence versus when it is complete. Modelers can start proposing states and attributes as soon as they have identified an actor, even if the actor has no interface ports. Modelers can elect to examine all scenarios the actor is in before commencing behavior work, or they can capture and validate behavior on a per scenario basis. Most heuristics in this section refer to completeness rather than commencement criteria.

Associated with the heuristics described here is a process of higher-level consolidation. The modeler visits the actor class inheritance hierarchy to see which common behavior patterns are evident as the state machine is being developed. For actors with similar behavioral requirements, it is much simpler to create them as subclasses of an existing actor than to create completely new behavior.

12.13.1 Scenarios

The scenarios the actor is in and the actor's attributes help identify the states for that actor. As shown in Figure 12.35, all scenarios for an actor must be reviewed before the behavior is complete. Message sequence charts are particularly useful. The resting points between

---

[23] More formally, the deepest nested substates are the actor's resting spots.

the events are states. If modelers do not want to identify all the states in the first pass, they can rough in only the basic operational states. The error or unusual states can be added in a later pass. However, this approach sometimes ignores key control behavior and may mean that the behavior design must be restructured.

Figure 12.35 Complete State Definition

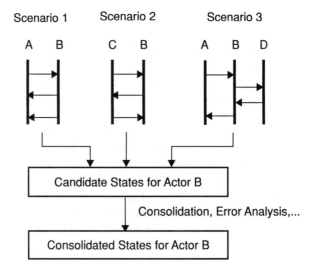

A modeler may first look at the scenarios individually. This was the approach to constructing the telephone handler in the PBX example. After the states implied by the individual scenarios have been identified, it is important to assess the effects of multiple scenarios on that actor. Looking at multiple scenarios forces the modeler, for each state, to assess what inputs could occur. The modeler must confirm that each input is handled properly (either in that state, or in a group transition higher up in the state hierarchy). The modeler may do this during the initial state representation, or as a consolidation phase once the basic operational state machine has been defined. In either case, the modeler decides what changes are required for the state machine if it is in a particular scenario and a new one impacts it. This usually creates new states and transitions, which might not be apparent if the modeler just looks at the scenarios individually. In the PBX example, the Telephone-Handler actor supports both telephone call and administrative scenarios. However, the modeler did not initially assess the impact of the concurrent execution of the scenarios, with the result that validation uncovered an error.

12.13.2 Scenario Conflict Resolution

There are various ROOM capabilities that help resolve the effects of intersecting concurrent scenarios (scenario conflicts). A primary method is message deferral (described in Section 10.2.1.6). Instead of having unduly complex state machines to handle every message any time, a message is deferred when it comes in at an inappropriate or awkward time. The message is recalled when the state machine is better able to handle it. For example, a command request message may spawn a complex interaction with other actors. This may involve a whole set of states to completely process that request. In the middle of processing a current command request, a new command request can come in. The state machine should defer the request and recall it once the previous request has been processed. This is simpler than immediately starting a response to that command interleaved with the previous command.

Group transitions and history also are very effective in scenario resolution. At any time, an actor might have to respond to a maintenance query about the value of an internal state variable such as a counter. A transition that handles that maintenance request is compactly modeled as a group transition to history, against the topmost state in the behavior. This contrasts with handling this event on each individual state.

12.13.3 Capturing States and Transitions

Having learned what the behavior requirements are, the modeler has several approaches to capturing them. The modeler can initially focus on capturing the states and their names, and ignore transitions. If possible, the state capture begins with state hierarchy. The top-level states are defined first. Sometimes major top-level states may not be evident until all the states have been portrayed in a flat nonhierarchical form. At that point, logical groupings of states may be more obvious.

After states have been captured, the transitions can be specified. An efficient, but not exclusive, order for defining transitions is to identify the start points, end points, and transition labels first. The triggering events and action are defined later, once the modeler is confident that the right transitions are in place.

Transition labels should reflect the underlying cause of the transition. Where there is only a single trigger, the label should be the triggering signal name. If there are multiple triggers, a common abstraction of the signals may be used as a label. If no common feature exists, the most significant trigger or a label suggesting the action taken on the transition can be selected.[24] In the early stages of modeling, the complexity of transition guard conditions often can be avoided.

---

[24] Lack of a common feature or abstraction triggering the transition may be a sign of a poorly designed state machine.

12.13.4 Coding

Code is an important aspect of capturing operational behavior. ROOM supports code on state transitions (including guard conditions), state entry, state exit, and choicepoints. The type of code required for initial versions of an executable model depends on the nature of the problem. Sometimes, concurrency issues are the most important ones to understand early. In that case, the modeler focuses on simple message send commands, with minimal emphasis on algorithms or message data objects. In contrast, an earlier focus on algorithms is required for those scenarios where getting the detailed function correct is a concern. Eventually both aspects must be complete.

Calls to functions, rather than in-line code, improve future flexibility. This not only makes the transitions easier to understand, but also helps future transformation of the state machine. For example, if there is a massive change in the states or the transitions, the modeler can reuse the functions.

The modeler can follow conventional coding practices. However, code reviews do not have to be to the same level of detail, as the code on transitions should be simple. The more difficult code normally reviewed would be associated with the infrastructure of the state machine. With ROOM models, this does not have to be reviewed at the code level, as it is asserted and reviewed graphically.

12.13.5 Summary of Behavior Capture and Consolidation

Scenarios, especially message sequence charts, are the prime input to behavior capture. Modelers have a variety of commencement points for behavior capture. The points range from picking a single scenario and deriving the states from that, to attacking the complete requirements of all scenarios in which the actor is involved. Whatever the starting point, for those actors involved in multiple scenarios, there is often the added challenge of resolving the interactions among scenarios. Such interactions can be addressed through message deferral and group transitions to history.

At a lower level, the primary heuristic to employ is a consistent naming convention for transition labels. We suggest that the underlying cause of the transition be used for the labels. Regarding coding, conventional heuristics apply. However, the modeler in the early stages may take a simple approach to coding to get the model running as early as possible. For example, if concurrency is the primary aspect to model, the modeler may focus on simple message sends, rather than prematurely attacking the detailed algorithms involved in the transitions.

12.14 Validation

Previous sections have described how to construct models, but not how to validate them. As early validation is a major benefit of operational models, it is important to use effective approaches to validation. This section is not intended to be a general discussion on validation, but instead highlights some unique aspects of validation based on ROOM models.

12.14.1 General Approach

The ROOM modeling language is precise enough to support formal analytical approaches to validation. However, currently such approaches are only mature enough to deal with the most abstract levels of modeling. For that pragmatic reason, validation of ROOM models is primarily by execution of scenarios. As Dijkstra points out [Dijkstra72], this technique is imperfect. It can never prove the total absence of defects, only their presence.

Modelers will recognize that executable scenario validation is similar to the familiar practices of test case drivers and stubs. Specific validation components such as drivers or stubs can be part of either the model environment or the system. Validation components are created using the same ROOM concepts employed for general modeling. Validation components, together with the other components naturally associated with a design component, form the basis for validation. Traditional top-down or bottom-up approaches to validation are appropriate.

One major difference from current practice is that with a suitable model execution environment, modelers can observe and debug the model using the same high-level graphical abstractions that they used during construction. Contrasting with traditional techniques, ROOM models are executable from the very early stages so that modelers can start validation early. However, modelers must balance validating with each microstep in the model construction cycle, versus not validating until the completion of the model.

12.14.2 Detailed Techniques

We now examine how this general approach is resolved in more practical terms.

12.14.2.1 Validation Actors

The primary validation technique is to create actors that drive and validate the various scenarios used during model construction. Capturing the validation drivers as actors helps in regression validation, as tests can easily be repeated. These validation actors can be organized on a per concurrent scenario basis. This approach allows scenarios to be examined individually, or concurrently to help expose scenario interaction problems. The PBX example illustrates this, where the components representing the users of the system could be instructed to make calls or invoke the Last Number Redial features. These can be validated concurrently with requests to the Administrator actor to take telephones in and out of service.

12.14.2.2 Interface Simulation and Integration with External Components

Actors send and receive messages through an end interface, rather than communicating with a particular destination. Since the actor under validation does not know the difference, it is easy to use validation actors to simulate or stub out another actor in a relationship. It is also easy to place a validation actor in the middle of a binding representing a communication link, as shown in the PBX example (Figure 12.18). This provides several validation capabilities, including monitoring message flow and perturbing message flow (for example, dropping of messages, misordering, total communication link, or processor failure). By simulating such occurrences, the modeler can assess the robustness of the design to these problems.

This characteristic of actors also allows executable models to tie into other parts of a system that support message-based interfaces (for example, as previously stated, user interfaces, the real hardware, or the external environment).

12.14.2.3   Inheritance

Inheritance can be used to limit the amount of intrusion by validation components. A design with additional embedded validation instrumentation can be constructed as a subclass of the model to be validated. This cleanly discriminates the model for product implementation from the model for validation. The modeler also can use validation actors in the model that take advantage of generic substitution. Depending on what validation must be run, a different concrete class of actor would be incarnated for the generic validation actor.

12.14.2.4   Multiple Containment

The multiple containment feature of ROOM allows the validation model to have validation actors embedded inside the system. This reduces the perturbation to the system under examination, because there is no need for explicit communication links that would cut through the system structure to communicate with the other validation components in the environment. The second iteration of the validation components for the PBX example (Section 12.6) took this approach. Figure 12.36 expands on the ideas of multiple containment and generic substitution.

12.14.2.5   Structure Debugging

In model construction, the completion of behavior is contingent on capturing the structural framework (containment and communication) within which behavior operates. This holds true for validation. If the structure of a model is incorrect, the behavior cannot meet its intended purpose. Therefore, although variations are both valid and encouraged, it often is most effective to debug structure first. Behavior debugging at the state and detailed code level can proceed when the modeler is comfortable that the structure is valid.

Correct message sequencing is an important part of structure validation, as it was during model construction using scenarios. The quickest approach to validation is for the modeler to use validation actors to drive various scenarios, while the model execution environment records the actual message sequences the model produces. The modeler also

Figure 12.36 Exploiting ROOM Concepts for Validation

(a) Original Design

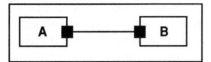

(b) Subclass of Design, in a Validation Situation

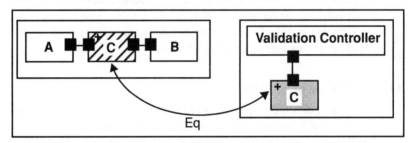

Actor **C** = Validation actor, generically substitutable and contained in both the design and the validation subsystem

can manually inject and trace messages on the actor interfaces of interest. To validate, the modeler can compare the real scenarios with the intended ones.

There are a variety of lower-level techniques. A modeler can animate the high-level structure during execution. This allows the modeler to see rough message flow without tracing the individual messages. This provides a quick view as to whether the model is functioning correctly, although it is certainly not as precise as comparing scenarios. For a more controlled view of message flow, the model should be "stepped" at the level of ROOM abstractions (namely, state transitions being triggered).

When an individual message fails to flow properly through the desired components, it is important to see exactly where the flow was first in error. Borrowing a technique from electronics signal tracing, modelers should look first at messages at the originating and terminating points of the flow. If the messages are incorrect, they should monitor a message point halfway through the logical message trace, often inside a composite actor. Based on whether the messages at that point are faulty, it is possible to narrow down the source of the problem to one half of the overall flow. Further subdivision in this manner eventually will identify the place at which a fault first occurs. Associated with this technique, it is also valuable to set breakpoints on certain messages being sent or received.

12.14.2.6   Behavior Debugging

A variety of approaches exist to validate behavior. Depending on the size of the model, the modeler should view the states for the key actors simultaneously. Important state diagrams should be animated during execution. With appropriate model execution environments, a modeler can simulate processor halts or communication link failures by turning off the behavior of an individual actor or all contained actors in a container actor. This allows the modeler to validate the resilience of other parts of the system to those faults. The modeler can put breakpoints on individual states or transitions, especially to capture "should not happen" situations. Related to this, a valuable feature of a model execution environment is the ability to automatically produce a message log for *unexpected events*. An unexpected event is an event that comes into a finite-state machine, but at a point in its state machine logic where a transition has not been designed to handle it.

Lastly, validation often leads the modeler to examine extended state machine variables and transition code. For validating and debugging this lower-level detail, modelers can use traditional language-oriented approaches.

12.14.3 Summary of Validation

The basis of validation is the execution of scenarios, driven by validation actors. Such actors ideally are created on a per-scenario basis, so that scenarios can be run either individually or concurrently to uncover scenario interaction problems. Specific validation components outside or inside the system can be used. The design components that surround the component to be validated also help in validation.

Validation takes advantage of interface simulation to stub out actors or to emulate various component failures. Inheritance allows variants of models with validation components to be cleanly separated from pure design models. Multiple containment allows validation components to be simultaneously part of a validation system and the system under examination.

At a more detailed level, it is often fruitful to validate the structure of the model before going too deep into the behavior. Structure debugging involves comparing intended message sequences with the ones resulting from model execution. Message flow tracing can be used to detect at which point in a scenario trace a fault has occurred. Behavior debugging relies primarily on animating state diagrams and setting breakpoints. Detail-level code is examined using traditional methods.

12.15   Summary

This chapter discusses the subject of modeling heuristics. Heuristics are informal guidelines, based on experience, about how to construct and validate models using the ROOM modeling language. Model development heuristics focus on the techniques that an individual modeler or small team of modelers applies to building a single model. This contrasts with product development heuristics (described in Chapter 14) pertaining to larger teams working on a product (which normally involves the building of multiple models).

Most modelers are responsible for a particular system that must be understood and subsequently built. These small systems usually are parts of a larger system that may be part of a larger system, and so on. With that in mind, the model to be developed is always wider in scope than the particular system for which the modeler is responsible. The modeler must consider the objects in the system's environment that influence the system. A system boundary separates the system from its environment, and guides the modeler's efforts by clearly defining the extent of the system. Often the boundary is obvious, particularly when the system to be developed is inside a previously defined system. However, sometimes the boundary is not so obvious, so it must be discovered. The environment objects, together with components inside the system and other specific validation components, help to validate the system.

Model development is an incremental and iterative process that considers the modeler's capabilities to handle complexity and detail. Rather than attempting to satisfy large portions of the model requirements at a time, a modeler takes an incremental approach where a manageable set of new requirements is considered in each modeling cycle. Iteration reflects the phenomenon that it is often very difficult to create optimum solutions the first time a requirement is addressed. Experience gained by attempting a solution provides insights into better solutions. As a result, the modeler iterates or returns to previously captured classes to enhance them.

Model construction and model validation alternate during model development. They are based on general continuous activities, rather than discrete modeling steps. The modeling activities are discovery, invention, and validation. Discovery occurs as modelers add to the initial specifications given to them by uncovering further requirements, or inconsistencies in the requirements. Discovery helps the modeler to learn what the system or a component inside the system must do. How the requirements are solved is addressed by the invention activity. Invention is a creative activity where classes supplement or replace classes suggested through discovery. Validation is tightly associated with both activities and involves continually confirming that the problem is well understood and the solution is sound.

Model requirements drive and coordinate the modeling activities. Although there are a variety of ways to express requirements, a particularly effective approach for complex real-time systems is to describe requirements as scenarios. Scenarios describe a high-level product capability as a sequence of causally related actions to achieve it (for example, all of the actions that contribute to making a telephone call). Scenarios are expressed by text or by message sequence charts. They are especially applicable to object-oriented modeling, as they suggest the objects and the communication among them for a particular requirement. Scenarios often are concurrent, and modelers must allow for that, particularly in the behavior of those actors at the intersection points of various scenarios. When there are many scenarios, it is recommended that modeler partition them into packages to facilitate incremental development.

Returning to the subject of model construction, interleaved with the modeling activities are the specific exercises of model element identification, element consolidation, and actor behavior capture. Element identification recognizes that models are built up not only of basic building blocks (including the various types of classes), but also more fundamental entities (such as individual message signals). Initially a broad-brush or nonconsolidated list of elements comes about from examining the model requirements. These elements must be unified or consolidated into a set of actor, protocol, and data classes to be modeled. Consolidation considers how strong or unique the primary purpose is of each proposed or candidate element. Often modelers use the object relationships of layering, containment, and communication to consolidate classes and coin new ones. Inheritance, a class relationship, also is very important to consider, not just during consolidation, but also during any modeling cycle. Actor behavior also must be considered. Scenarios help in the derivation of behavior. Scenario conflicts or intersections may be solved by message deferral or group transitions.

Model validation is strongly associated with model construction. Both are driven from the same model requirements. In the incremental and iterative approach that we recommend, validation through operational models occurs as early as possible. A modeler does not have to analyze all the requirements or construct all of the model before validation can occur. Validation itself comes about from the capture of validation components using the ROOM modeling language. It exploits a variety of modeling language capabilities (including interface simulation, inheritance, and multiple containment). Validation components should be organized around the various scenarios being considered, so that the scenarios can be executed individually or concurrently to uncover undesirable interactions.

It is important to note that a common theme in model development heuristics is balance. This is expressed in the frequent alternation between model construction and model validation. It also applies to the specific approaches to the construction (for example, not modeling the structure too deeply to the neglect of the associated behavior, or vice versa). A final balance involves the heuristics themselves. Although they point the modeler in the right general direction, they will not be optimum for every particular situation. The modeler must consider this, and regard the heuristics as a general guideline, but not a prescription to be followed inflexibly.

CHAPTER 13

Architectural Heuristics

Chapter 12 described general modeling heuristics for model construction and validation. In this chapter, we examine modeling heuristics that pertain to the architecture of a system, which forms the basis for the system's long-term evolution. These heuristics are based on the authors' experiences with large real-time systems, and offer suggestions for creating architectures of such systems.[1] In particular, we discuss an architectural design principle that ensures the proper handling of a critical, but often overlooked, aspect of system design.

13.1   The Definition of Architecture

Architecture is the quintessential part of a system's composition on which all other parts of the system depend. The architecture of a software system typically consists of its high-level structure and high-level behavior. These are the software equivalents of load-bearing frames in buildings.

Since an architecture is the supporting framework for all other components, a change in the architecture can have extensive, and, usually costly, consequences. On the other hand, a change in the nonarchitectural components will have little or no impact on the architecture. Because of its foundational role, an architecture imposes fundamental limitations on

- The possible ways in which a system can be customized to meet different particular requirements (product variants, for example).
- The ability of the system to evolve to meet new requirements.

For systems where these issues are important, a well-designed architecture is critical. In addition, a systematic and elegant architecture has the advantage of being easy to understand, which can simplify its construction.

---

[1] For an excellent treatment on architectural concerns, especially for telecommunications systems, the reader should refer to [Lemay87].

As a rule, architectures apply to more than individual systems. The architectures of large systems are recursively defined by the architectures of the smaller systems of which they are composed, and so on. Product architectures are the cumulative result of a set of system architectures. Even the validation components in a ROOM model may have an architecture (such as the basic infrastructure for initiating various validation cases and recording the results).

The architecture of a system can be abstract in that it need not be concerned with too low a level of detail. It also can be generic, and thus form the basis for a variety of concrete designs. However, this does not imply that architectures are at a uniform abstraction level. In addition to encompassing basic structural and behavioral forms, they also may include the fundamental detailed algorithms influencing the system. By including key detail-level operations (such as the sending of high-level messages), architectures also can be executable in spite of being abstract.

13.1.1   Properties of Good Architectures

Although every system has an architecture, its influence on the evolution of the system is not always positive. Inadequate architectures can be a significant limitation to system understandability and evolution. Good architectures attempt to foresee the evolution of a system by taking both a wide view and long-term view of system requirements. As a result, good architectures are long-lived and should not need to change significantly during the life of the system. (For example, architecture A in Figure 13.1 is better than architecture B for the evolution path shown.) This contrasts with more detailed designs, which usually focus on current requirements and, thus, are more likely to change.

Figure 13.1   Two Architectures and the Evolution of a System

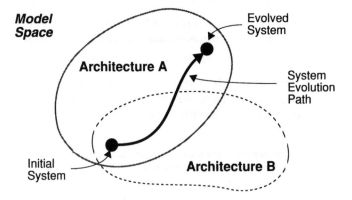

For instance, consider the architecture of a process control system for a factory assembly line. This involves an approach to synchronizing and coordinating the various parts of the line (for example, if one part slows down or breaks, the operation of the other parts must be adjusted). In this case, a good architecture is one that remains unchanged over the lifetime of the control system, despite massive technological and other changes in the various components of the line.

A personal computer is another example. Major changes may occur in the user interface (for example, evolution from a command-line interface to a window-based one), but the underlying basic operating system may not change. In the automobile industry, architecture often is manifested in product line platforms. These generic frame, engine, and transmission structures provide a base for a whole range of vehicles from compact cars to minivans.

13.1.2 Architecture of the PBX Example

The final version of the PBX model described in Chapter 12 is shown again in Figure 13.2. That structure diagram, along with the basic state machines, defines an initial version of the PBX architecture with the following desirable attributes:

- The impact of future changes to the types of telephones the PBX must support has been isolated to a single actor (TelephoneHandler). For example, the capabilities of the Call actor should not have to change if calls are made between two telephones of different types, since the interface between the Call and TelephoneHandler actors can be generic.

- Similarly, the addition of new capabilities that relate purely to calls is isolated in the Call actor, with minimum effect on the TelephoneHandler. For example, if the system now must support a three-person conference call capability, the details of that are isolated to the Call actor.

Both the Call and TelephoneHandler actors are key high-level components that influence the most fundamental operation of the PBX (namely, making calls). Only one item detracts from its architectural capability—it cannot handle multiple calls. Replicated rather than fixed actors are required for the TelephoneHandler and the Call actors to handle multiple calls. This limitation is easily overcome, as shown in an evolved model of the PBX in Figure 13.3.

As requirements change over time, certain architectures may not form a stable envelope for the required evolution. We could hypothesize that the PBX evolves from a simple voice communication system to one that provides multimedia capabilities. For example, video or data connections between sophisticated telephones are required. As a result, the PBX architecture evolves to handle this situation, as shown in Figure 13.3.

The new version of the architecture captures an important decision about how connections are made. This is a fundamental part of the PBX's operation. Connections include controlling the often complex hardware required for setting up and breaking down communication paths for various media (voice, video, data). This connection responsibility is

Figure 13.2   The Initial Architecture of the PBX

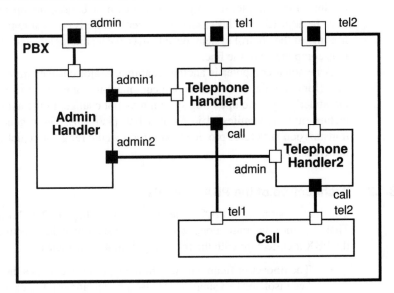

Figure 13.3   The Evolved PBX Architecture

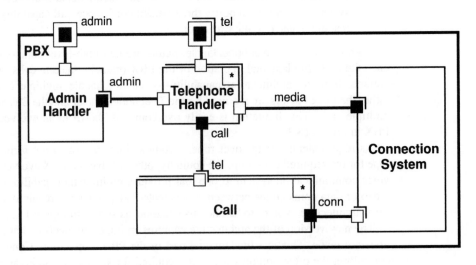

moved from the Call actor to a new ConnectionSystem actor. The ConnectionSystem knows how to talk to the hardware to make various connections, perhaps involving different hardware for different media. A Call actor now is purely responsible for the coordination function involving multiple telephones, regardless of the media. The Call actor decides when to make requests of the ConnectionSystem, but no longer is concerned with the details of making the connections. A benefit of this is that many basic call capabilities originally developed for voice calls can be made generic and easily can apply to multimedia calls. Evolution of connection types is now isolated to the connection system.

In summary, architectures may have to evolve to meet unforeseen requirements. It is rare that the initial architecture is so good that all system evolution falls within it.

13.2   Approaches to Architecture

There are likely as many approaches to developing good architectures as there are opinions on what is a good architecture. This section discusses some broadly applicable approaches.

Architectures reduce mental clutter without ignoring important lower-level design issues. This often is accomplished by creating abstractions of the lower-level concerns. As shown in Figure 13.4, the modeler depicts the structure of all the major components of the system, even if the design for such components is not yet known. During the refinement of architecture, a continuous merge of more refined parts replaces earlier stubs. The high-level components may be simple in the first version of the architecture. When the modeler refines them, they are subsequently reintegrated by replacing the abstract or high-level classes with more refined versions. With such a process, a mixture of abstraction levels is both necessary and highly encouraged.

Figure 13.4   The Evolution of a Component in an Architecture

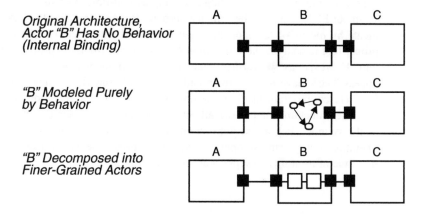

Original Architecture,
Actor "B" Has No Behavior
(Internal Binding)

"B" Modeled Purely
by Behavior

"B" Decomposed into
Finer-Grained Actors

A modeler can create an architecture with a top-down approach, bottom-up approach, or both. Starting top-down can divide the problem into portions of manageable complexity. From this stable architectural base, two alternatives are possible. If reuse is a key concern, the creation of bottom-up reusable components is suggested. ROOM makes it very simple to create intermediate levels of detail through container classes. Therefore, it is also possible to continue rapidly through a top-down process to provide a context or justification for the lower-level components. At the higher levels, the entire architecture may be a subclass of a previously defined abstract or concrete class. A top-down approach may take a single actor with its behavior and partition its total functionality (and, therefore, states and transitions) into several component actors.

Modelers also may refine state machines in a top-down approach. In early versions, the behavior may represent only the most important states with minimal detail. With refinement, more detailed substates are added in the previously defined states. Note that with the addition of more detail, the early state diagrams may not remain completely high-level or abstract. Various transitions may be associated with lower-level detail placed in the top state diagram. For example, a group transition may be at the top state to handle a detailed audit request.

A final architectural approach involves protocol classes. Protocol classes initially may be defined very abstractly to assert high-level interactions among architectural components. A very high-level binding (perhaps a single one between actors representing many protocols) may be asserted until more detail is known. Refinement, as in structure, includes partitioning that original high-level protocol class into several protocol classes based on different concerns. At the structural level, this implies that the architecture may migrate from a single binding to several bindings.

13.3   Internal Control: The Neglected Essential

The previously discussed architectural approaches are very generic, and apply to most systems. We now turn to a specific high-level modeling heuristic that can be used to derive a generic architecture for many large or complex real-time systems.

In our PBX example, the primary purpose of the system was to allow users to communicate by means of telephones. When first faced with such a problem, it is natural and proper first to analyze these *functional* aspects concerning the primary reason for the system. However, as we further analyze the requirements, other aspects of the problem appear. These have to do with so-called "support" functions (such as putting a telephone into service, program loading, system initialization, fault detection and recovery, and so on). Such functions, metaphorically speaking, can be considered as the "care and feeding" of the system. They are seldom an end to themselves, but are essential to the successful operation of a system. An operating system, for example, is not useful by itself, but rather by virtue of its ability to support application programs.

13.3.1   Internal Control

We refer to such essential support functions as the *internal control* aspects of a system. The term "control" is borrowed from classical control theory—where it refers to the set of activities required to define a desired operational state for the system and to maintain it in that state in the face of various disruptions (such as component failures, restarts, operator interventions, and so on) ([Gupta70]). Responsibility for control typically is associated with a component called the "controller" that is distinct from the remaining "functional" part of the system, as shown in Figure 13.5.

Figure 13.5   Classical Control System Model

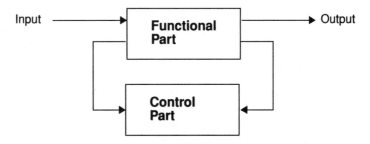

Internal control includes the following categories of activities:

- On-line installation (loading) of new hardware and software
- System activation and deactivation
- Failure detection and recovery
- Preventive maintenance
- Performance monitoring and statistics gathering
- Synchronization with external control systems

On-line installation typically is required for systems with high availability requirements that cannot be taken out of service during the time that installation is being done. A particularly difficult problem is the installation of new software while the old software is still running.

System activation is the process of bringing a software system to its operational state. It includes activities such as obtaining operational (configuration) data and synchronization with other components before commencing full operation. For example, after adding a new node into a computer communication network, the node first may have to synchronize with other nodes to obtain its routing data.

Failure detection and recovery involve pinpointing the exact source of a problem to isolate it or undertake remedial action. This can be particularly difficult in a concurrent system, since a single failure quickly can lead to multiple other failures. The fault isolation and recovery mechanism must then decide which of the many reported failures is the original source of the problem.

Preventive maintenance sometimes includes very complex diagnostic procedures and background audits intended to detect problems before they become critical. A diagnostic procedure typically is invoked in response to an apparent problem. An audit runs periodically to ensure that the system is in a consistent state.

Performance monitoring and statistics gathering are a form of status feedback to some higher-level control systems (these could even be human operators). This data is used to detect if a system is in some type of load imbalance (such as overload or underload).

Finally, *synchronization with external control systems* is required if the system is part of a greater complex. This higher-level system might be a human or an automatic control system. Like any control interaction, this often is characterized by asynchronous interactions.

13.3.2   The Disregard for Internal Control Issues

Since their purpose is to support the mainline functional activities, internal control concerns often are underestimated or even overlooked during analysis and high-level design. The natural inclination is to focus on the functional part at the expense of the "housekeeping" aspect. Yet, in most large real-time systems (and particularly in those concerned with high availability), the internal control aspects are the bigger and often more complex portion of the system. For instance, most developers would agree that a multitasking operating system (a support component) is more complicated than most of the applications it supports.

The danger stemming from this situation is twofold. First, by neglecting the internal control aspects until late in the development, we are in danger of postponing what may turn out to be the tougher part of the design problem. The second problem is that internal control issues may not receive the attention and systematic treatment that they deserve, given their complexity. This yields systems that are very difficult to observe and control during operation.

13.4   Approaches to Internal Control

We now turn to an architectural approach that ensures proper treatment of internal control issues.

13.4.1   Separating Internal Control from Function

A marked difference usually exists between issues relating to function and issues concerning internal control. For example, setting up voice connections between two PBX users is quite different from the loading and linking of software, or from handling administrator commands. The two aspects are clearly related, since they involve the same entities. However, by keeping them as separate as possible, we can reduce the relative complexity of each of the two parts, and it becomes easier to modify one without affecting the other. This is useful, since we may want to change the internal control policies of a system without changing its functionality, and vice versa.

Once again, operating systems are a good example of a clean separation of these two aspects. Imagine how complicated applications would become if the functionality of complex services (such as interprocess communications or task creation) was imbedded directly within the application code. The important thing then is to create a clean partitioning of responsibilities between internal control and function, and to specify explicit interfaces between them. Examples of this approach were provided in Section 8.3.2.11.

13.4.2   Control Policies and Control Mechanisms

Control strategies in many systems are prone to change. For example, a PBX that may have started as a standalone system might later be integrated into a greater corporate communications network. This means that its internal control system would have to evolve from being an autonomous unit into an executive agent for a higher authority. For this purpose, it is useful to separate *control policies* from *control mechanisms*. Control policies are realized by software that makes decisions based on state feedback and that issues commands to secure those decisions. Control mechanisms, on the other hand, are the components that provide feedback and that respond to commands.

For example, in a PBX system, a component that detects the failure of a transmission link is part of the control mechanisms. However, a component that performs the fault-recovery procedure would be part of the control policies. By cleanly separating the two, it becomes possible to change the recovery procedure without affecting the failure-detection software.

13.4.3   The Canonical Real-Time System Model

The principle of separating internal control from function yields the *canonical real-time system model*, represented in Figure 13.6 by an abstract ROOM actor structure.[2] The purpose of this system is to provide the functionality realized by a collection of one or more *functional components* to external clients. This is accessed through the *functional interface* of the system. The state of the functional components is controlled by the *internal control* component of the system that realizes a consistent set of control policies. The control policy either may be integrated into the system, or it may come from an external higher-level control system through the *control interface* of the system.

---

[2] In cases where the internal control functions are simple enough not to require decomposition into component actors, the role of the internal controller can be taken over by the behavior of the containing actor.

Figure 13.6   The Canonical Real-Time System Model

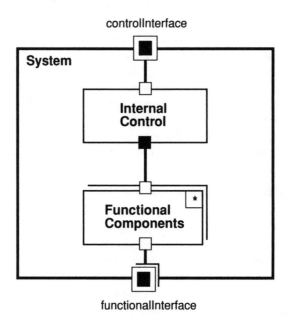

In this model, each functional component has two interfaces: a control interface to the internal control system and a functional interface to the clients. (Note that, from the viewpoint of a functional component, the internal control component is an external controller.) The same approach was taken in the PBX example. The telephone handler had interfaces for talking to call actors and to the administration system. This structural approach also can be used to model each of the functional components in a generic system, and so on, as shown in Figure 13.7. This recursive feature of the canonical model means that it is applicable to systems of arbitrarily large scope.

Practical examples of the application of this model can also be found in Section 8.3.2.11.

13.4.4   Modeling the Behavior of Controlled Components

In the structural dimension, the principle of separating control and function implies segregating components that are part of the internal control system from those that are a part of the function. Ultimately, however, a functional component (as well as any other controlled component) must interact with its direct controller through its control interface. From the perspective of separating control from function, this interaction should not depend on the functionality of the controlled component. This suggests a generic (function-independent) model of behavior as observed by the controller.

Figure 13.7 Recursive Application of the Canonical Model

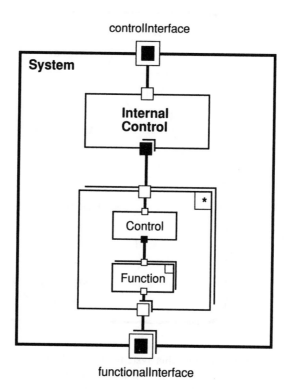

controlInterface

functionalInterface

For a controlled component to perform its function, it must first be in the appropriate operational state. Most active components do not instantaneously come up in an operational state, but instead require some dynamic initialization. For example, an actor may first have to synchronize with other actors that provide the services it needs. This means that, in terms of modeling behavior, *control predicates function*. We can see this in the PBX example. The telephone handler in Figure 13.2 must be in the InService state before it can provide its primary services.

It is normally the responsibility of the controller to bring the controlled component to the necessary operational state. For hierarchical state machines, this means that the functional behavior is embedded within the control behavior. That is, *the top-level state machine of actors is usually the control machine*. This emphasizes that architecture often has a generic behavioral form. A typical control behavior description is illustrated in Figure 13.8. This behavior is controlled by signals coming through the control interface generated by the controller of the component.

Figure 13.8   A Typical Control State Machine

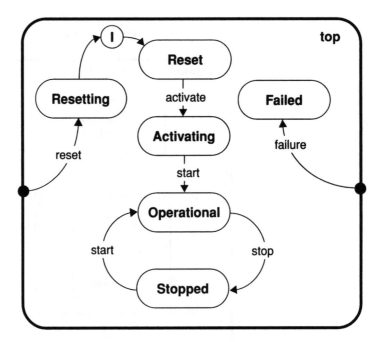

Following creation, this system starts in the Reset state. This is a virgin state in which the system is out of touch with its surroundings, since it has not yet communicated with any external entity. For example, it may be lacking the necessary operational data that provide its context for the particular environment in which it is located. A state such as this is often useful, since it provides a clean and unbiased starting point for restarting an actor. It is common practice, for example, to restore actors to this state as part of a failure-recovery sequence.

The preparation of the actor for operation begins with the receipt of an activate signal from the controller. This message, which may also contain some initial operational data, forces the system into the Activating state. Typical activities in this state involve obtaining further operational data from the controller (such as obtaining the telephone number of a particular TelephoneHandler) and synchronizing with other actors with which it has contracts.

Once the activation sequence is complete (and assuming that it was successful), the actor is finally ready to perform its primary function. The transition to the operational state may follow automatically upon completion of the activation sequence, but often it is preferable if this transition occurs through an explicit start command from the controller. This gives the controller the opportunity to coordinate the startup of several components in a desired order.

The Operational state is the main functional state of the system. It encapsulates the function-specific state machines, such as the algorithm that controls the origin and receipt of telephone calls in a PBX. This function-specific state machine will be devoid of most control concerns, since these are all handled by the upper-level state machine. In this way, we achieve the objective of decoupling internal control and function in the behavior domain. For instance, we can change the functional state machine without disturbing the control state machine, and vice versa.

In some cases it may be necessary to temporarily suspend the operation of a system. For example, a failure in some auxiliary component may require the controller to undertake a recovery action. In such circumstances, it might be convenient to halt all but the recovery activities to minimize external interference. This is the function of the Stopped state. In this state, the actor is fully primed to run and is only awaiting the start signal to resume where it had left off. (By returning to the history of the Operational state, it could even resume at the exact point where it had been suspended.)

If a failure is significant enough, it will force the behavior into the Failed state. Recovery out of this state will depend on the needs of the application. Sometimes it may be possible to restore the system into the Activating state or even to the Operational state. Alternatively, we may decide to reset the system, as indicated in the diagram.

A reset signal from the controller will drive the system into the Resetting state. In this state, the system is gradually and systematically shut down in a reversal of the activation process. Once the reset is complete, the system reverts to the Reset state.

13.5   Summary

Every system has, at its core, an architecture. This is the essential framework of the structure and behavior of a system on which all other aspects of the system depend. An architecture, therefore, has a fundamental impact on the evolution of a system, as well on the set of possible product variations that can be derived from it. Architectures can be defined recursively in that high-level system architectures are the result of the combination of architectures of the contained systems. A good architecture usually is easy to understand and supports graceful evolution of the system.

There are a variety of general approaches to designing architectures. Architectures normally include components that abstract lower-level detail. As a particular system is developed from an architecture, the abstract placeholders are replaced by more concrete components. From a solid architectural base, a modeler either can create bottom-up reusable components or continue with a top-down approach by using container classes. The same top-down technique can be used for abstract state machines and protocol classes.

A particularly useful approach to designing the architecture of many large or complex systems is to explicitly segregate the functional aspects of a system from the internal control aspects. Internal control aspects (which include such support functions as online software installation or failure detection and recovery) are essential, but often overlooked, during system design. Yet, they are often the larger and more difficult part of the system design.

Fortunately, there are several approaches to internal control. The control and functional aspects of a system should be clearly delineated, to enable evolution of one without detriment to the other. It is also possible to separate control policies (strategies) from the control mechanisms that carry them out. From these two approaches, we derive a canonical approach to architectural modeling that has a standard structural form separating control from functional components. Furthermore, it has a standard behavioral form. The top-level state machine has generic states supporting the control function, with a specific operational state encapsulating the functional states.

CHAPTER 14

Work Organization

The preceding chapters focused on high-level and low-level modeling heuristics based on the ROOM modeling language. We now move up one level on the methodological scale (see Figure 14.1) and address the top-level process issues involved with creating products and managing projects. These aspects are collectively called *work organization*.

Figure 14.1 The Role of Work Organization in a Methodology

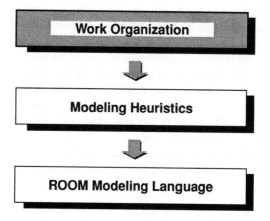

Work organization refers to management-level concerns such as who is selected to do the work, how the work is allocated among the developers, how the progress of the work is tracked and controlled, what the intermediate deliverables are, what the criteria for evaluating deliverables are, and so on. A useful summary of these issues will be found in [Constantine93].

We believe that, in many cases, the ROOM modeling language and heuristics can be adopted by a system development organization without substantial changes to the existing development process. However, it is unlikely that simply switching to using the ROOM language and heuristics will take full advantage of the capabilities of ROOM. We therefore explore various ways in which the features of ROOM interact with the development process, and offer a number of suggestions for possible process changes. This chapter advocates, in outline form, a *product-oriented* development methodology centered on ROOM. While we are actively working to develop this methodology further, we feel that the key elements have a solid empirical base and will remain stable.

In particular, we examine

- The distinction between a project-oriented and a product-oriented approach to the development process
- The identification, organization, and prioritization of product requirements
- The activities and deliverables involved in product development
- The creation and maintenance of sequences of models
- The organization of project teams
- Project management and tracking

We emphasize that these are suggestions, not prescriptions. The ideas discussed here are based primarily on actual industrial experience with large complex projects. However, some aspects are not fully proven in practice. Given the relative newness of object-oriented development in general, and executable models in particular, we emphasize that the reader should view the suggestions as possible approaches, but certainly not the only ones. There is a wide assortment of valid approaches to higher-level process management for various project situations, and no single prescription for a development process can be a panacea. In particular, on individual projects, the process should be continually tuned and adapted as more real-world experience is gained.

Although the ideas presented here have developed in the context of building large, complex systems, we believe that they are applicable to smaller projects as well.

14.1   Product-Oriented versus Project-Oriented Development

Except for the small minority of projects with an explicit focus on research, systems development projects aim to create products, or systems that will be incorporated into products. Very few of these products will persist in their initial form throughout their lifetimes. Products *evolve*. They are enhanced to add features, they are diversified into product families, or, at a minimum, they are modified to correct shortcomings discovered by the user. The span of time over which a product actively evolves is typically much longer than the span of time over which it was initially created. Therefore, an overall evaluation of the success of a product must take into account the ease with which its evolution can proceed.

A typical evolution scenario for a large software product is shown in Figure 14.2. The initial product P_0 is evolved into product P_1 in response to new requirements. At this point, it may be decided to split off a related product Q_0, that is based on P_1, while simultaneously evolving the original product into version P_2, and so on. The result is a *family* of products, all evolved from a common root through a sequence of distinct *projects*.

Figure 14.2   The Lifetime and Evolution of Products

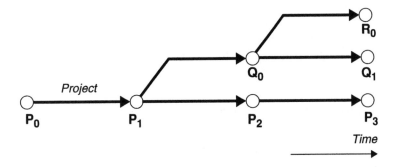

Unfortunately, development projects all too commonly end up focusing on the short-term goal of producing an adequate initial product, rather than the longer-term goal of producing a product that can evolve effectively. There are a variety of reasons for this. Often, project-oriented budgeting and accountability practices punish, rather than reward, product-oriented thinking. Even within a product-oriented development context, the developers sometimes are overwhelmed by the complexities of the development process and are forced to direct their efforts to more limited, project-oriented goals. In either case, the development process, as actually carried out, is suboptimal from the perspective of product development.

A crucial element contributing to the success or failure of a product is its architecture. As noted in Chapter 13, the architecture defines the envelope within which a system can vary (either for evolutionary reasons or for product diversification). For products that are anticipated to evolve, it is necessary to invest substantial up-front effort in a sustainable architecture.

The ROOM modeling language (with its ability to model architectures) and the associated heuristics can help developers cope more effectively with the complexities of real-time product development. As discussed in Chapter 3, ROOM was devised to create effective models of real-time systems and to support common model-building strategies by incorporating three key features: executable modeling, a single notation used throughout the development process, and the object paradigm. ROOM can thus greatly increase productivity over traditional modeling approaches. From the management point of view, this increased productivity is a dividend, and the appropriate use of this dividend deserves some thought. While the dividend can be reinvested in the faster, cheaper creation of adequate products, it also can be reinvested in the creation of properly "architected" (that is, evolvable) products. Thus, the productivity improvements made possible through ROOM can be used to redirect the systems development process from a project-oriented style of development to a product-oriented style.

Product orientation does not mean extending the duration of an individual project to cover enhancements to a product or to cover development of a family of products. It means conducting an individual project, to deliver a preliminary or enhanced individual version of a product, with evolution in mind. For the remainder of this chapter, we will use the term "product development" to refer to systems development that leads to the creation or enhancement of an incarnation of an evolvable product. This product-oriented style has ramifications for the identification of requirements, for the activities and intermediate deliverables involved in development, for the selection of team members, and for the tracking of progress. The following sections will explore these ramifications.

14.2   Product Requirements

Experienced developers understand that an original statement of requirements often is incomplete, and that fixing this problem can involve extensive analysis, interviewing of the specifiers, creation of prototypes, and so on. It is less commonly understood that even a set of requirements that is complete by conventional criteria may be inadequate as a guide to product development. The missing requirements tend to fall into the following categories (see Figure 14.3):

- *Nonobvious functionality.* Certain requirements may not be identified by traditional requirements analysis methods. For example, a product that has a large number of features is subject to "scenario conflict," meaning that the interaction of scenarios may lead to unanticipated requirements (such as the necessity to restrict the concurrent use of certain product features).

- *Implementation constraints.* The viability of a product may depend on requirements because of implementation constraints. For example, a distributed implementation may introduce requirements for operating in the presence of, or for recovering from, communication errors. In general, requirements based on the characteristics specific to real-time systems discussed in Chapter 2—timeliness, dynamic internal structure, reactiveness, concurrency, distribution—often are missed in requirements definition.

- *Anticipated future needs.* The product must often evolve to meet needs that are different from the needs that shaped the initial requirements. This may require specific product features to accommodate specific anticipated change, and also more general features (such as ease of upgrading).

Figure 14.3 Factors Driving Product Requirements Identification

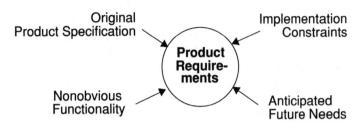

In general, *product-oriented* requirements definition means taking into account more requirements and different requirements than *project-oriented* requirements definition. The use of ROOM can impact the requirements definition phase of the product development process in two ways, one general and one specific. In general, the increased ability to handle complexity provided by ROOM can make it feasible to carry out a more intensive, broader-scope requirements definition process with a given set of resources. More specifically, the ability of ROOM to capture high-level, architectural abstractions (such as complex actors and layers) makes it possible to identify and preserve features that must remain intact if a product is to evolve successfully. Also, the ability to use executable models provides an objective basis for requirements elicitation and negotiation involving customers and developers, often leading to the early uncovering of missing requirements.

The handling of a larger set of requirements means that more thought and care must go into the organization, packaging, and prioritization of the individual requirements. This is especially true of an approach that uses executable modeling. The verification of a requirement using an executable model means the investment of a significant amount of time in low-level, detailed modeling. An uncritical *prioritization* of requirements could mean that significant time is wasted on executable verification of relatively unimportant requirements. An uncritical *packaging* of requirements could mean that potentially conflicting requirements may not be verified in combination until late in the development process.

As discussed in the chapter on modeling heuristics (Chapter 12), scenario packages are a useful approach to requirements organization and prioritization. A well-chosen scenario package can group requirements that are critical to some aspect of product verification, or that are potentially in conflict, and can guide the construction of executable models that focus on these issues.

14.3   Product Development Activities

Chapter 12 introduced the activities involved in the building of an individual model—discovery, invention, and validation. At a higher level, one can also identify *product develop-*

ment activities that span the entire development process. These activities are conventionally identified as analysis, design, and testing. However, the product development activities are very similar in character to the product modeling activities. In particular, analysis (that is, identifying what the system under development should do) is largely characterized by discovery. Design (that is, identifying how implementation technology should be employed to realize the system) is largely characterized by invention. Testing is, of course, a specific form of validation.

Even in development projects that use traditional modeling technologies, the activities of analysis, design, and testing tend to be interleaved, as suggested by Figure 14.4. This tendency is enhanced by the use of ROOM. The availability of a single modeling notation encourages cycling back and forth between analysis and design activities, and the existence of executable models tends to spread testing more evenly throughout the development process. (In fact, when executable modeling is used, "validation" is a more appropriate term than "testing" to describe the determination of correctness of a deliverable. Since "testing" has the connotation of applying only to the final code, we will henceforth use "validation" rather than "testing.")

Figure 14.4 Distribution of Activities in Conventional Development

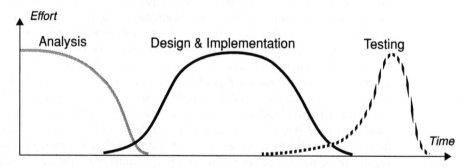

Figure 14.5 suggests the nature of the interleaving of the product development activities of analysis, design, and validation using ROOM, as contrasted with the conventional distribution of activities in Figure 14.4. The key difference is the ability to gain early practical experience resulting from working on design and validation from the earliest stages of the project. That is, the use of early design and validation enhances analysis and later enhances further design and validation. Note also that analysis typically will continue late into the development cycle. The distribution of activities also has a recursive character. As lower-level components of a model are produced (for example, as objects are introduced as lower-level components of objects), the distribution of activities for the model component will tend to follow the distribution for the project as a whole.

Figure 14.5 Interleaving of Product Development Activities in ROOM

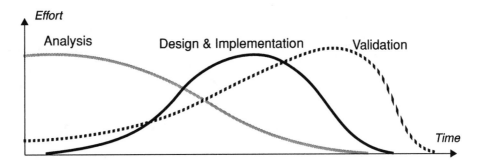

The character of the analysis and design activities also tends to change when ROOM is used. In particular, the ability of ROOM to capture high-level architectural abstractions means that attention can be focused on requirements and design structures that are likely to persist over multiple versions of a product or multiple products in a family.

Figure 14.5 is not meant to suggest that the activity of project management has the same character as the various activities that comprise product development. In fact, project management is largely linear in nature, since it must track and control progress toward a final goal by way of a sequence of intermediate milestones, as suggested by Figure 14.6. A methodology that incorporates ROOM must provide for reconciliation of the linear management process with the concurrent, interleaved development process, as suggested by Figure 14.7.

Figure 14.6 The Project Management Process

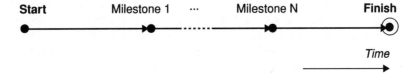

One possible strategy for reconciliation involves using the extra productivity provided by ROOM to allow time for interleaving of activities in the periods between project milestones. For example, a percentage of the time period preceding the delivery of a requirements model could be reserved explicitly for the exploration of design alternatives and for the feedback of the results into the requirements model. Of course, this strategy requires

Figure 14.7   Product Development versus Project Management

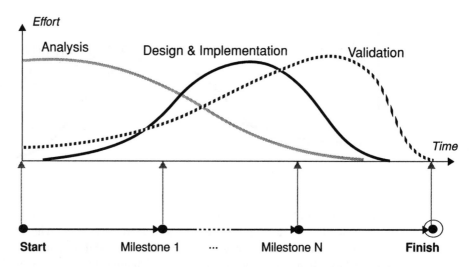

that the exploratory activities be tracked and controlled, so that the exploration remains goal-oriented and does not become an end in itself.

14.4   Deliverables

The executable nature of ROOM means that the executable models produced during development can have a much larger impact than traditional nonexecutable models. In particular, it is possible that the large narrative documents often defined as intermediate deliverables of a product development project can be replaced by much shorter documents accompanied by executable models. A narrative document, at best, can *describe* the features of a system under development to an interested party. An executable model, when provided with a suitable graphic interface, can be used to *demonstrate* the features of a system under development to a customer or end-user. Executable models also are useful as unambiguous specifications that can be produced by high-level design teams to be passed to detailed design teams. An executable model also has an important internal use as a project management milestone, in additional to its external uses as a deliverable.

14.5   Universal Model Relationships

Independent of the significance of particular models created within a development process, product development always involves a progression of models, increasing in completeness until the final model (the source code, in the case of a software project) is created. Much of the variation among development processes is caused by different decisions about which of the intermediate models are to be *preserved* and which are to be *maintained*. The possible approaches span a spectrum, from no preservation or maintenance of any but the final model, to preservation and maintenance of a number of intermediate models.

The most effective approach, in terms of resources devoted to model building, is to create a partially complete model, check and correct the model, and then to incorporate further enhancements back into the same model (see Figure 14.8). The progression of models thus consists of the various partially complete stages, and the end result is that only a single model is preserved. However, the dilemma posed by this approach is that the early stages of the model (since they focus largely on requirements) are useful for purposes such as assessing the impact of subsequent requirements changes. As the model is evolved to include more design and implementation detail, this type of evaluation becomes less practical because of the increased complexity.

Figure 14.8   Development via Stages of a Single Model

The value of the intermediate models can be preserved by maintaining them periodically to reflect the relevant changes introduced into the later models. This strategy is suggested by Figure 14.9. Using this approach, one or more up-to-date intermediate models may persist until a system is implemented, or even beyond implementation into post-implementation enhancement. The preserved-and-maintained intermediate models can be useful (for example, in assessing the impact of a post-implementation change in requirements).

Clearly, ongoing maintenance of intermediate models can be costly. However, it is no different, in principle, than trying to keep documentation up to date with evolving software. In fact, the purpose in both cases is much the same. We can consider the maintained intermediate models as a form of executable documentation.

The potential impact of ROOM on the generic modeling strategies just described is to change the cost-benefit ratio. In general, the increased productivity caused by the use of ROOM can be "reinvested" in preserving and maintaining intermediate models. More specifically, two features of ROOM aid in the preservation and maintenance of intermediate models. First, as mentioned previously, the use of a single notation means that models can be preserved simply by evolving the original (for example, by adding detail to a subclass). Second, the fact that a ROOM model consists of a library of class definitions means that

Figure 14.9   Development via Preservation and Maintenance of Intermediate Models

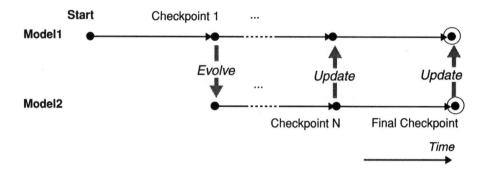

some of the class definitions can be part of two or more models. Thus, revision of these class definitions in the later models will, in some cases, automatically cause the earlier models to be updated.

14.6   Specific Model Types

Model types in conventional methodologies typically are correlated with differences in the notations used for model building. ROOM uses a single notation for all models, and thus the basis for distinguishing model types is significantly different.

Before discussing differences among ROOM model types, it is important to recall a characteristic that all model types in a ROOM-based methodology should have in common, and that was discussed in detail in Chapter 12 (modeling heuristics). Because of the executable character of ROOM, all models should be broader in scope than the system under development. The models each should consist of a system component, and also validation components used for simulating the system's environment when the model is executed.

We will discuss specific types of ROOM models by introducing two dimensions along which such models can vary, as suggested by Figure 14.10. The horizontal dimension, implementation dependence, refers to the incorporation of more and more implementation details as a project progresses from requirements through design. Implementation dependence is almost universally recognized as a dimension of development methodologies. Whether development proceeds by elaboration of a single model or by building of different models, the successive model stages are characterized by increasing implementation dependence. The vertical dimension, genericity, is much less common. More generic models are characterized by architectural details (that is, details that should remain invariant over revisions to a single system, or over variations among a family of related systems).

Figure 14.10 Dimensions of Variation of ROOM Model Types

Figure 14.10 Dimensions of Variation of ROOM Model Types

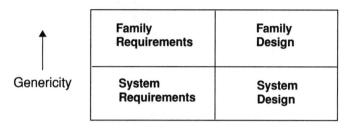

Genericity is related to reuse. For example, in the case of a family of related systems, a generic model might capture details that are common to all members of the family. However, reuse often is used to mean only the incorporation of low-level code modules developed for one system into other systems. Generic models, in contrast, capture high-level, architectural details rather than low-level details. This form of reuse has a much more substantial impact on productivity, since the scope of what is being reused is much greater. With ROOM, for example, it is possible to relatively easily combine very high-level generic components (including models of entire products) to explore significant new product opportunities.

Figure 14.10 also illustrates the simplest set of ROOM models that takes into account variations along these dimensions, namely the following:

- *Family requirements*, a generic, implementation-independent model
- *System requirements*, a specific, implementation-independent model
- *Family design*, a generic, implementation-dependent model
- *System design*, a specific, implementation-dependent model

Note that the generic models in Figure 14.10 explicitly refer to a family of products. It is certainly possible to build a generic model that captures architectural-level details for a single product, However, although a model always should embody architectural *thinking*, a separately preserved architectural *model* may be justified only if a family of products is to be developed.

In a large project, it is likely that more than one intermediate deliverable will be based on each model type. In other words, preliminary versions of the various models will be produced and reviewed as the project proceeds. The contents of such preliminary models are driven by the packaging of requirements. In other words, a given preliminary model will be produced so that its execution will test a particular scenario package.

14.7   Project Team Organization

According to Boehm [Boehm81], the skills of the members of the development team are as much as four times more important than the methods and tools used on a project. This suggests that it is important to examine how incorporating ROOM into the development process affects project teams.

As mentioned previously, a general effect of using ROOM is increased productivity. One way of making use of this productivity is to decrease the size of the development team for a given project. A smaller number of developers can mean simpler communication channels among developers and fewer levels of project management. Given a fixed pool of developers from which team members are drawn, a smaller team also means that, with judicious selection of team members, the average skill level of the team can be higher.

The shift in project activities caused by ROOM also suggests that the specific mix of skills required on a team may be different. For example, the increased importance of architectural thinking suggests that developers with relevant experience should be explicitly incorporated into the team as *architects* from early in the project, so that they can "live with" the architecture as it evolves, continually steering it based on continuous feedback from the rest of the team. Furthermore, the extensive prototyping capability afforded by executable models suggests a larger role for team members with the skills needed to interact with customers in evaluating prototypes.

Finally, a transitory (but extremely important) project team issue is the management of the culture change introduced by the paradigm shift from traditional functional development to the use of object-oriented executable models. Providing for education of team members and managing anxiety about, or resistance to, the new approaches is an important aspect of project management.

14.8   Project Management and Tracking

As just mentioned, the adoption of ROOM is a major paradigm shift that may have a significant impact on the development team. For instance, the emphasis in ROOM on detailed validation of requirements may mean, in some cases, that more time must be allotted for requirements analysis and validation. Also, the interleaving of analysis and design requires that time be allotted early in the project for prototyping of design alternatives. This means that the manager must encourage (but also carefully track and control) these early life-cycle activities.

The effect of redistributing the time allotted to project activities is not limited to the team itself. Deliverables explicitly tagged as finished code may not emerge until late in the process, raising fears that the project is "wasting time on modeling." Therefore, an important role for the project manager in the early stages of ROOM adoption is managing the expectations of higher-level managers. Convincing skeptics that intensive requirements analysis and early prototyping of alternative designs will save coding time and improve quality is an important task.

Paradoxically, another problem caused by ROOM has almost the opposite symptoms. The executable character of ROOM, and the ability to port ROOM models to the implementation hardware, means that realistic prototypes can be produced early in the development process. This raises the danger that market pressures will induce a development team to release a prototype prematurely as a product. Discouraging the conversion of inadequate prototypes into products is another important task of the development manager.

Another consideration is that the ability of ROOM to capture high-level, architectural abstractions gives the project manager the opportunity (and the corresponding responsibility) to encourage, track, and control the capture of architectural details as the project proceeds.

Finally, a consideration for an initial project that employs ROOM is the learning curve as developers become familiar with the language. A useful heuristic is that the productivity increase caused by ROOM may be approximately offset by the learning curve on the initial project. Thus, while the first project using ROOM may not take less time than a traditional one, it should not take much more time. Furthermore, the product quality should be higher.

With respect to project tracking, a special caveat is in order. The tracking of projects using object-oriented technology is relatively new, and the tracking of projects that combine object orientation and executable modeling is even newer. The following suggestions are based on relatively limited real-world experience.

In general, executable modeling permits intermediate models to be used as project milestones. An obvious possibility for project tracking is to validate satisfaction of particular scenarios by particular executable models. The progress of a project ought to be closely related to the number of scenarios that can be demonstrated to be satisfied by the existing models.

Two figures of merit, particularly pertinent to ROOM, may be useful for more fine-grained tracking of project convergence. The first of these is the *rate of flux of high-level, architectural actor and protocol classes*. Since these easily identified classes are used to capture architectural abstractions, a reduced rate of change in them should indicate that the system architecture is stabilizing.

We can get similar information about the progress of a project from the *depth of its class hierarchies*, particularly when monitoring the key architectural classes. Namely, deep class hierarchies may be indicators of mature, well-understood abstractions, and, hence, of a stable designs.

14.9   Summary

ROOM provides an increased capability for handling complexity. This increased capability can be used to introduce features into the development process that may not be feasible or cost-effective with more traditional modeling approaches. In particular, a larger set of requirements may be taken into account, and more attention can be given to capturing architectural abstractions, allowing for a product-oriented rather than a project-oriented approach to development. This product-oriented style has ramifications for the identification of requirements, for the activities and intermediate deliverables involved in development, for the selection of team members, and for the tracking of progress.

APPENDICES

APPENDIX A

The ObjecTime Toolset

The ROOM methodology, with its orientation toward formal and executable models and the potential for automatic code generation, reaches its full potential with the availability of computer-based tools. In this appendix, we briefly describe the ObjecTime toolset, which was specifically designed to support the ROOM methodology and its concepts.

A.1   History and Objectives

The purpose of the ObjecTime toolset is to support the creation, validation, and management of ROOM models and their transformation into executable programs.

ObjecTime was originally developed by the Telos Group at Bell-Northern Research. The Telos Group was founded in 1985 by Jim McGee to investigate advanced systems architectures for integrated voice and data telecommunications applications. Later, this role was expanded to include research into software technologies to support large-scale systems architecture capture and computer-aided software development. This research led to the development of ObjecTime.

Much of the early research focused on development of concepts and technologies for modeling complex layered and distributed control system architectures. A key goal was that an architectural model should persist and evolve throughout the development life cycle, providing both guidance and constraints to more detailed development. In other words, all software development would take place within a constraint framework defined by high-level architectural models.

The importance of this goal is based on the common observation that, after even a few months of detailed development, the *actual* form of a system can stray a long way from its intended architecture. Whether or not the change from the original architecture is intentional, we often end up in a situation where the detailed software code is *de facto* the design, implementation, and documentation of the system. The lack of a clear and accurate model of the actual system architecture has a severe impact on system understandability, and is a prime contributor to system evolution and maintenance costs.

A second goal was that models could be formal and executable even when still abstract and incomplete, allowing for the earliest possible exploration of alternatives and detection of errors and omissions.

A third goal was that the chosen modeling abstractions would support the automated transformation of suitably detailed models to high-performance implementations on real-time operating systems. This would help eliminate the error-prone semantic gap between design and implementation.

After five years in research and development, ObjecTime was brought into production use in Bell-Northern Research in January, 1990. On October 1, 1992, ObjecTime Limited, a fully independent spin-off from Bell-Northern Research, was formed to continue research and development, and bring ObjecTime to the open market.

ObjecTime is only one component in an overall system development environment. System development environments for embedded applications often contain capabilities for software, hardware, and firmware development. Here we will limit our scope to the typical software development. This appendix outlines the role of ObjecTime in a software development environment and contains a brief high-level description of the components of the ObjecTime toolset.

A.2   Software Development Environments

A typical software development environment containing ObjecTime is shown in Figure A.1. In general, tools produce and consume data, often in different formats. The toolset framework supports communication between tools, communication between users and tools, and access to data objects (for example, a design model, a requirements document) by way of the shared repository. The repository also is responsible for the persistent storage of relationships between data objects and the version management of objects and relationships.

In addition to the ObjecTime modeling environment, a typical software development environment might include components for

- Project and process management
- Documentation creation and management
- Requirements specification and management
- Programming language (for example, C++) development
- Graphical user interface development
- Other modeling environments

A.3   ObjecTime Model Development Environment

The individual components of a specific modeling environment often require more finely grained integration than that available from the main toolset framework. This is often

Figure A.1   A Software Development Environment

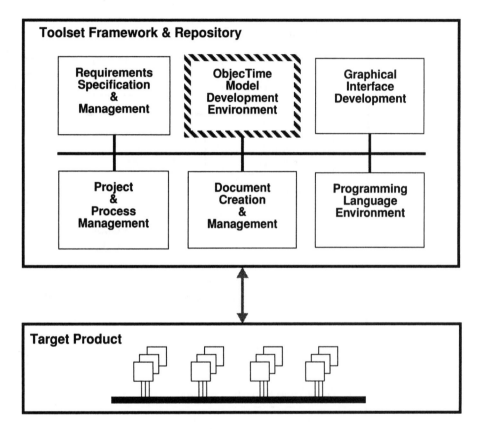

achieved by using a sub-framework encapsulated in the main toolset framework. As shown in Figure A.2, all ObjecTime tools are integrated into the ObjecTime toolset framework.

A.3.1   Model Management

The multiuser development environment supports the cooperative development of models by teams of ObjecTime users. Actor, protocol, and data classes may be stored in a library, or as individual files in a directory. The library system provides for formal storage of classes, including check-in, check-out, and version control. (Versioning and storage are provided by the configuration management system of the main development environment.) Special capabilities include load building and intelligent merging of classes from multiple users.

Figure A.2   The Structure of the ObjecTime Toolset

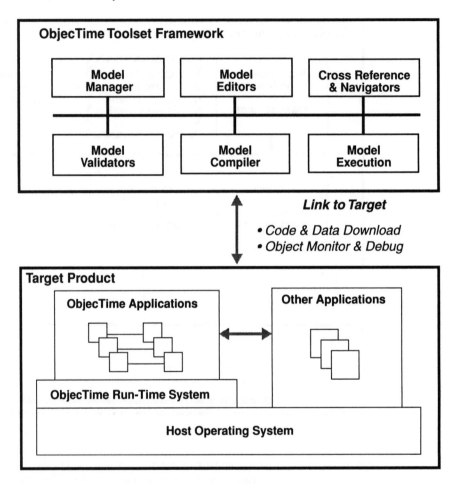

A.3.2   Model Editors

Various editors provide for the creation, modification, and viewing of the elements of ROOM models (including actor class structure, state-machine behavior and functions, protocol classes, and data classes). Documentation objects can be associated with the various elements of a model. The graphical and textual representation of a model (including associated documentation objects) can be output to standard documentation systems for incorporation into project documents.

A.3.3 Model Cross Reference and Navigators

ObjecTime provides an online cross-reference (for example, show all usages of a given component) and a set of navigators to speed the traversal from one element of a model to another.

A.3.4 Model Compiler

The formal semantics of ROOM concepts are defined in terms of their operation on the ROOM virtual machine. ObjecTime includes an incremental model compiler to translate models into high-level source code (for example, C++) programs that are then compiled to run on a ROOM virtual machine.

A.3.5 ObjecTime Run-Time Systems

Implementations of the ROOM virtual machine are called run-time systems in ObjecTime. The ObjecTime development environment has an integrated run-time system. This run-time system runs on one or more workstations and provides capabilities for model execution and debugging. Special capabilities include model animation and optional discrete event simulation.

The services of the virtual machine (such as "send message" or "create actor") have been carefully selected to support high-performance execution on available real-time operating systems. A product environment run-time system enables the direct execution of ROOM models on production real-time platforms. In this way, the final detailed design model for an application also becomes the implementation.

A.3.6 Model Validation

ObjecTime can check for various errors during model construction, compilation, and execution. Static checks include invalid binding of actor ports, invalid replication factors, and invalid actor containment relationships. Dynamic checks include invalid message reception, and invalid creation, destruction or importation of actors in addition to run-time exceptions such as message send time-outs.

The run-time system also includes the following set of capabilities to assist in the testing of models:

- Individual actors can be stopped and stepped.
- Delays can be associated with event processing and message transmission.
- Messages can be injected or traced at any actor port.
- Trace and break points can be placed at various points on an actor's structure and behavior.

This test instrumentation can be persistently stored with models in the library. Executing models can also interwork in real-time with other software applications (for example, a graphical model of a user interface) or physical devices. This results in a far more realistic test-bed environment during the early stages of the model development life cycle.

Finally, formal ObjecTime model descriptions can be output to other tools for more specialized analytic or simulation-based analysis.

APPENDIX B

An Annotated Implementation Example

In situations where a convenient implementation of the ROOM virtual machine is inappropriate or unavailable, it becomes necessary to transform a ROOM design specification into an implementation by recasting the specification in terms of the concepts supported by the target programming language and environment. Perhaps the most complex part of this process is the mapping of hierarchical state machine specifications. This is because of the intricacies and interdependencies of the various advanced modeling features (such as history, entry and exit actions, or group transitions). In this appendix, we provide an almost complete example, written in C++, of how such a mapping can be done. The techniques illustrated are based on the ones described in Chapter 11.

Even though the programming language of the example is C++, the coding style is effectively language-neutral. Namely, the coding constructs used were restricted to only those that can be found in most standard block-structured imperative languages. For example, no attempt was made to exploit some of the object-oriented features of C++, even though that would have been beneficial. This allows a relatively straightforward mapping of the demonstrated techniques to other similar languages such as Pascal or Ada. It also means that any particular concrete implementation would likely improve on the efficiency of the general solution described here.

B.1   Introduction

The example chosen is based on the simple state machine described in Section 11.2.2.2 of Chapter 11 (see Figure B.1). It was selected because it contains almost all of the complex features of ROOMcharts while still being simple enough that it, and the resulting implementation, can be followed relatively painlessly.

The code is broken up into five major parts that are presented in the following order:

Figure B.1   The State Machine Used in the Example

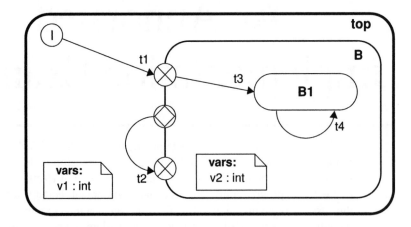

- *Generic Definitions.* This part contains common data type specifications and declarations. It is generic in the sense that this code is independent of the particular state machine being modeled.
- *FSM[1]-Specific Definitions.* This part contains data type specifications and declarations that are specific to the state machine being modeled. Thus, while the format of these declarations would be the same for all state machines, the contents would be different.
- *Generic Utility Routines.* These typically are small utility routines that are used by all the other functional units. The code in these functions is independent of the state machine being modeled.
- *FSM-Specific Routines.* These are routines that are specific for each state machine. Typically, they bear generic names, but their implementations are very specific to the topology of the state machine.
- *Generic Routines.* These are key procedures that implement the essentials of the hierarchical state machine paradigm. They are generic and their form is independent of the state machine being modeled. They invoke state machine-specific functions and, therefore, cannot be made global.

The order of presentation of these parts reflects the single-pass paradigm of C++ in which an entity typically must be declared before it is referenced. In languages where

---

[1] The abbreviation FSM is used throughout the example as a shortened form of the phrase "finite state machine."

there is no need for such strict ordering of declarations, it may be worthwhile combining all the generic parts into a single module and all the state machine-specific parts into a single state machine-specific module. The packaging of parts into modules depends on the language. In the example, all the code is assumed to be in a single compilation unit in order to simplify the description. However, in a practical situation, it certainly would be more convenient to separate the generic parts. These modules then could be imbedded (by way of compiler directives) into the compilation units for each individual state machine. Thus, such common code would be implemented only once and re-used as many times as necessary.

B.1.1   Elements of C++ Syntax

For those unfamiliar with C++ syntax, the following are some specific points to assist in following the code:

- The "case" construct in C or C++ is implemented by the **switch** statement. In contrast to most other languages, execution begins at the case that matches, but then continues sequentially through following cases until the end of the switch statement. If this is not desired, a **break** statement will perform an early exit out of the switch statement.

- By default, each procedure (function) in C++ is assumed to return a value. Hence, each procedure is typed. If no value is returned, the type of the procedure is declared as **void**.

- Pointer variables are indicated by an asterisk (*) following the type declaration (for example, **int* intPtr;** is a pointer to an integer). If pointer **p** points to some structure and we want to extract component **c** from that structure, the notation used is **p->c**.

- Statements of the form **cout << "some text"** are used to output a string literal to some output device.

More information on the C++ language can be found in [Ellis90].

B.1.2   Generic Definitions

```
1.     #include <stream.h>
2.
3.     /*******************************************************************************/
4.     /******* (1) GENERIC DEFINITIONS:                              ***********/
5.     /******* These are type and data definitions that             ***********/
6.     /******* are common to all FSMs                                ***********/
7.     /*******************************************************************************/
8.
9.     const int noHistory = -1;        // indicates this state has no history
10.    const int noParent = -1;         // indicates this state has no parent (top)
```

```
11.
12.     /* type definitions for readability                           */
13.
14.     typedef int state;              // states are mapped to integer indices
```

> *Lines 15-16*: The following two declarations are included here for completeness, but normally would be included in some other header file, since their scope extends beyond the behavior domain.

```
15.     typedef int msgPort;            // ports are mapped to integer indices
16.     typedef int msgSignal;          // signals are mapped to integers
17.
18.     /* the structure of a control block for a state:               */
19.
20.     struct stateCB
21.         {
22.         state parent;               // index of parent state's CB
23.          state history;             // index of the history of this state
24.         };
```

> *Lines 26-33*: Note that only the header portion of the message is provided here. This specification is shared by other units and likely would be declared in some other commonly used header file. It is included here for completeness.

```
25.     /* the structure of a message header                          */
26.     /* (included for completeness)                                */
27.
28.     struct msgHeader
29.         {
30.         msgSignal signal;           // the signal of the message
31.         msgPort port;               // the port on which the message arrived
32.         };
```

> *Lines 35-38*: These two pointers are primarily for efficiency. Instead of passing the current state machine and message block to each separate routine, these are set up at the start of message processing (procedure **processMsg**) and are then used for quick reference by other procedures.

```
33.     /* common data pointers shared by many utilities              */
34.
35.     struct fsmCB* fsm;              // CB pointer for current FSM
36.     struct msgHeader* msg;          // holder of the current message
37.
```

B.1.3   FSM-Specific Definitions

```
38.     /****************************************************************************/
39.     /******* (2) FSM-SPECIFIC DEFINITIONS:                              *******/
40.     /******* These are type and data definitions that are              *******/
41.     /******* specific to each FSM                                       *******/
42.     /****************************************************************************/
43.
44.     /* state indices: used to quickly locate a state CB.                */
45.     /* NB: the relative numbering of states is signifi-                 */
46.     /* cant; the top state must have an index of 0 and                  */
47.     /* a child state must have an index value that is                   */
48.     /* higher than the value of its parent state (i.e.,                 */
49.     /* breadth-first numbering scheme)                                  */
```

Lines 50-51: The following declaration takes advantage of the fact that, in C, enumerated types are mapped into integer values and the individual elements are assigned successive integer values starting from zero (that is, "top" = 0). Several algorithms take advantage of the fact that a substate has a higher state index than its parent. (Note also the declaration of the value **noHistory** in Line 10.) Another advantage of this declaration is that it gives us symbolic names for states for improved readability of the code. Naturally, the value of variable **numStates** should match the number of states declared.

```
50.     enum {top, B, B1};              // symbolic names for states (1/state)
51.     const int numStates = 3;        // total number of states in this fsm
52.
```

Lines 53-63: These lines are included here for completeness, but normally would be included in some other imbeddable header file, since they are usually shared by more than one state machine.

```
53.     /* input signal values                                             */
54.     /* (included for completeness: these actually belong               */
55.     /* in a protocol class spec)                                        */
56.
57.     enum {init, sig1, sig2};        // symbolic names for signals
58.
59.     /* port values                                                     */
60.     /* (included for completeness: these actually belong               */
61.     /* in the structure part of an actor spec)                         */
62.
63.     enum fsmPorts {sysPort, port1};
64.
65.     /* transition chain values                                         */
66.     /* one value per transition chain (NB: the value                   */
67.     /* noTrigger must be = 0)                                          */
```

```
68.    /* This list must be coordinated with the procedure              */
69.    /* "transitionChains" as well as the individual                  */
70.    /* state trigger procedures                                      */
71.
72.    enum {noTrigger, t1chain, t2chain, t4chain};
73.
74.    /* a control block for an FSM: represents the data               */
75.    /* for one instance of an FSM. Note that the first               */
76.    /* three data fields (curState, numSt, states[]) are             */
77.    /* common to all FSMs. However, each FSM will have               */
78.    /* its own list of local variables appended to the               */
79.    /* end of the control block.                                     */
80.
81.    struct fsmCB
82.        {
83.        state curState;                          // current state index
84.        int numSt;                               // indicates number of states
85.        struct stateCB* states[numStates];       // array of ptrs. to state CB
86.        int v1;                                  // local var "v1"
87.        int v2;                                  // local var "v2"
88.        };
89.
```

B.1.4   Generic Utility Procedures

```
90.    /***********************************************************************/
91.    /******* (3) GENERIC UTILITY PROCEDURES:                    ********/
92.    /******* These are utility functions that are common        ********/
93.    /******* to all FSMs. (NB: they all assume that the         ********/
94.    /******* shared pointer "fsm" has been initialized          ********/
95.    /******* to point to the current FSM.)                      ********/
96.    /***********************************************************************/
97.
98.    /* utility to change the current state                            */
99.
100.   void nextState (state st)
101.       {fsm->curState = st;};
102.
103.   /* utility to get the current state                               */
104.
105.   state currentState ()
106.       {return fsm->curState;};
107.
108.   /* utility to return the index of the parent of a state           */
109.
110.   state parentOf (state st)
111.       {return (fsm->states[st])->parent;};
```

```
112.
113.    /* utility to return the history of a state                          */
114.
115.    state historyOf (state st)
116.        {return (fsm->states[st])->history;};
117.
118.    /* utility to set the history of a state                             */
119.
120.    void setHistory (state st, state histSt)
121.        {(fsm->states[st])->history = histSt;};
122.
123.    /* utility for reporting that a message was not handled              */
124.    /* (this is just a prototype version; the actual code               */
125.    /* would depend on the application).                                */
126.
127.    void unhandledMsg ()
128.        {cout << "Unhandled Message" << '\n';};
129.
```

B.1.5   FSM-Specific Routines

```
130.    /*******************************************************************************/
131.    /******* (4) FSM-SPECIFIC ROUTINES:                              *******/
132.    /******* These procedures are specific to each FSM               *******/
133.    /******* and typically depend on the FSM graph                   *******/
134.    /*******************************************************************************/
135.
136.
137.    /******************************************************************/
138.    /*                    createFSM                        */
139.    /*                                                     */
140.    /* This procedure is used to create the control        */
141.    /* block tree for one incarnation of this FSM.         */
142.    /******************************************************************/
143.
144.    fsmCB* createFSM ()
145.
146.        {
147.        fsmCB* cbptr = malloc (sizeof (fsmCB));
148.        cbptr->numSt = numStates;
149.
150.        // allocate state CBs:
151.
152.        for (int i = 0; i < numStates; ++i)
153.            cbptr->states[i] = malloc (sizeof (stateCB));
154.
155.        // link each state to its parent state:
```

```
156.
157.        (cbptr->states[top])->parent = noParent;
158.        (cbptr->states[B])->parent = top;
159.        (cbptr->states[B1])->parent = B;
160.
161.        return cbptr;
162.        };
163.
164.    /****************************************************************/
165.    /*                    releaseVars                            */
166.    /*                                                           */
167.    /* Release the memory held by any variables                 */
168.    /* that were dynamically created by a previous              */
169.    /* call to the "initVars" procedure.                        */
170.    /* NB: this example does not have such vars so              */
171.    /* this is just a dummy procedure.                          */
172.    /****************************************************************/
173.
174.    void releaseVars (fsmCB* fsmPtr)
175.        {};
176.
177.    /****************************************************************/
178.    /*                    initVars                               */
179.    /*                                                           */
180.    /* Initialize the values of all local variables             */
181.    /* to defaults appropriate to the type                      */
182.    /* NB: since this procedure can be invoked many             */
183.    /* times, care should be taken to release any               */
184.    /* memory that might have been allocated on                 */
185.    /* previous invocations.                                    */
186.    /****************************************************************/
187.
188.    void initVars (fsmCB* fsmPtr)
189.
190.        {
191.        releaseVars (fsmPtr);
192.        fsmPtr->v1 = 0;
193.        fsmPtr->v2 = 0;
194.        };
195.
196.    /****************************************************************/
197.    /***** State-specific procedures:                      *****/
198.    /***** These are procedures that are unique            *****/
199.    /***** to each state (entry, exit actions,             *****/
200.    /***** transitions, and triggers).                     *****/
201.    /*****                                                 *****/
202.    /***** NB: This example contains "dummy"               *****/
```

```
203.    /***** code. For real implementations, the              *****/
204.    /***** actual code would be used. Also,                 *****/
205.    /***** all local var references would have              *****/
206.    /***** to be modified to use a pointer                  *****/
207.    /***** dereference to "fsm"; e.g.:                       *****/
208.    /*****                                                   *****/
209.    /*****            v1 = 5;                                *****/
210.    /*****                                                   *****/
211.    /***** would change to:                                 *****/
212.    /*****                                                   *****/
213.    /*****            fsm->v1 = 5;                           *****/
214.    /****************************************************************/
215.
216.    /****************************************************************/
217.    /*                      state B1                              */
218.    /****************************************************************/
219.
220.    void enterB1 ()             // entry procedure for B1
221.        {cout << "entered <B1>" << '\n';};
222.
223.    void exitB1 ()              // exit procedure for B1
224.        {cout << "exited <B1>" << '\n';};
225.
226.    /****************************************************************/
227.    /* B1 trigger routine: detect if the current                  */
228.    /* message is one that triggers a transition                  */
229.    /* that initiates from state B1. If it does,                  */
230.    /* then return the transition chain index that                */
231.    /* corresponds to the transition that will be                 */
232.    /* executed. Trigger detection is performed                   */
233.    /* through a series of nested "if" statements.                */
234.    /****************************************************************/
235.
236.    int B1trigs ()
237.        {
238.        if (msg->port == port1)             // check port first
239.            if (msg->signal == sig2)        // check if signal matches
240.                if (fsm->v2 == 0)           // check guard condition
241.                    return t4chain;         // -- trigger t4 activated ---->
242.        return noTrigger;                   // default return if no trigger activated
243.        };
244.
245.    /****************************************************************/
246.    /*                      state B                               */
247.    /****************************************************************/
248.
249.    void enterB ()
```

```
250.        {cout << "entered <B>" << '\n';};
251.
252.    void exitB ()
253.        {cout << "exited <B>" << '\n';};
254.
255.    void t4 () // transition t4 procedure
256.        {cout << "transition <t4:B> executed" << '\n';};
257.
258.    int Btrigs ()
259.        {
260.        if (msg->port == port1)
261.            if (msg->signal == sig1)
262.                return t2chain;
263.        return noTrigger;
264.        };
265.
266.    /*****************************************************************/
267.    /*                        top state                            */
268.    /*****************************************************************/
269.
270.    void t1 ()
271.        {cout << "transition <t1:top> executed" << '\n';};
272.
273.    void t2 ()
274.        {cout << "transition <t2:top> executed" << '\n';};
275.
276.    void t3 ()
277.        {cout << "transition <t3:top> executed" << '\n';};
278.
279.    int toptrigs ()
280.        {
281.        if (msg->port == sysPort)
282.            if (msg->signal == init)
283.                return t1chain;
284.        return noTrigger;
285.        };
286.
287.    /*****************************************************************/
288.    /*                    doInitTransFor                           */
289.    /*                                                             */
290.    /* This procedure invokes the initial transi-                  */
291.    /* tion for the state specified by <st>                        */
292.    /*****************************************************************/
293.
294.    extern void transitionChains (int t);          // forward declaration
295.    extern void enterHistory (state st);           // forward declaration
296.
```

```
297.    void doInitTransFor (state st)
298.
299.        {
300.        // since this FSM has only one initial transition
301.        // we use an "if" statement; for more complex
302.        // machines, a "case" (switch) construct would
303.        // be more appropriate
304.
305.        if (st == top)
306.            transitionChains (t1chain);
307.        };
308.
309.
310.    /*****************************************************************/
311.    /*                    doHistoryFor                         */
312.    /*                                                         */
313.    /* This procedure is invoked to enter the his-            */
314.    /* tory of the state <st>. This is normally               */
315.    /* realized as a series of nested "case" state-           */
316.    /* ments with the outer case based on <st> and            */
317.    /* the inner case based on historyOf(st). For             */
318.    /* our simple example, the inner case state-              */
319.    /* ments have been simplified to an "if" state-           */
320.    /* ment.                                                  */
321.    /*                                                         */
322.    /* Note that entering history involves execut-            */
323.    /* ing the entry action of the history state.             */
324.    /* If the history state is also a hierarchical            */
325.    /* state, then the procedure "enterHistory" is            */
326.    /* invoked (this is done recursively until a              */
327.    /* leaf history state is reached).                        */
328.    /*****************************************************************/
329.
330.    void doHistoryFor (state st)
331.
332.        {
333.        state hist = historyOf (st);
334.        switch (st)
335.            {
336.            case top: if (hist == B)              // only 1 possible history
337.                {
338.                enterB ();                        // perform the entry action
339.                enterHistory (B);                 // since B is a non-leaf state
340.                return;
341.                };
342.            case B: if (hist == B1)
343.                {
```

```
344.            enterB1 ();
345.            return;                      // NB: B1 is a leaf state
346.            };
347.        };
348.      };
349.
350.   /******************************************************************/
351.   /*                    doExitFrom                              */
352.   /*                                                            */
353.   /* This procedure invokes the exit action of                 */
354.   /* the state specified by <st>                                */
355.   /******************************************************************/
356.
357.   void doExitFrom (state st)
358.
359.      {
360.      switch (st)
361.         {
362.         case top:      return;          // top does not have exits
363.         case B:        exitB ();
364.                        return;          //------->
365.         case B1:       exitB1 ();
366.                        return;          //------->
367.         };
368.      };
369.
370.   /******************************************************************/
371.   /*                    transitionChains                        */
372.   /*                                                            */
373.   /* This procedure invokes the appropriate tran-              */
374.   /* sition chain specified by <triggerIndex>.                 */
375.   /* The chain index is determined by a state                  */
376.   /* trigger procedure. Each chain is a sequence               */
377.   /* of procedure invocations of entry and tran-               */
378.   /* sition actions along the chain. Any choice-               */
379.   /* points would be implemented using simple                  */
380.   /* "if" statements.                                          */
381.   /******************************************************************/
382.
383.   void transitionChains (int triggerIndex)
384.
385.      {
386.      switch (triggerIndex)
387.         {
388.         case t1chain:    t1 ();          // transition t1 segment
389.                          enterB ();      // enter state B
390.                          t3 ();          // transition t3 segment
```

```
391.                          enterB1 ();              // enter state B1
392.                          nextState (B1);          // set current state = B1
393.                          break;
394.          case t2chain:   t2 ();
395.                          enterB ();
396.                          enterHistory (B);
397.                          break;
398.          case t4chain:   t4 ();
399.                          enterB1 ();
400.                          nextState (B1);
401.                          break;
402.          };
403.      };
404.
405.  /*****************************************************************/
406.  /*                     getTriggers                            */
407.  /*                                                            */
408.  /* This utility is used to invoke the trigger                 */
409.  /* procedure for the state specified by <st>.                 */
410.  /* The value returned is either the index of a                */
411.  /* transition chain, if the state reacts to the               */
412.  /* current event, or the value "noTrigger" if                 */
413.  /* it does not.                                               */
414.  /*****************************************************************/
415.
416.  int getTriggers (state st)
417.
418.      {
419.      switch (st)
420.          {
421.          case top: return toptrigs ();           //---------->
422.          case B: return Btrigs ();               //---------->
423.          case B1: return B1trigs ();             //---------->
424.          };
425.      return noTrigger;
426.      };
427.
```

B.1.6   Generic Routines

```
428.  /**********************************************************************************/
429.  /******** (5) GENERIC ROUTINES:                                        ********/
430.  /******** These functions are common to all FSMs;                     ********/
431.  /******** however, they cannot be global since for                    ********/
432.  /******** each FSM, different versions of specific                     ********/
```

```
433.    /******** routines have to be bound in (e.g., the              ********/
434.    /******** "getTriggers" routine is different for               ********/
435.    /******** each FSM).                                           ********/
436.    /*********************************************************************/
437.
438.    /******************************************************************/
439.    /*                    enterHistory                           */
440.    /*                                                           */
441.    /* return to the history of the state <st>. If               */
442.    /* the state has never been entered before,                  */
443.    /* then execute its initial transition if it                 */
444.    /* has one.                                                  */
445.    /******************************************************************/
446.
447.    void enterHistory (state st)
448.
449.        {
450.        if (historyOf (st) == noHistory)
451.            doInitTransFor (st);
452.        else
453.            doHistoryFor (st);
454.        };
455.
456.    /******************************************************************/
457.    /*                    executeExits                           */
458.    /*                                                           */
459.    /* execute exit actions of any nested states up              */
460.    /* to and including the state <st> that is                   */
461.    /* responding to the current event. This is the              */
462.    /* routine where history is recorded.                        */
463.    /******************************************************************/
464.
465.    void executeExits (state st)
466.
467.        {
468.        state nxtSt = currentState ();            // start with the current state
469.        while (nxtSt >= st)
470.            {
471.            doExitFrom (nxtSt);                  // execute exit action of nested state
472.            state prev = nxtSt;
473.            nxtSt = parentOf (prev);
474.            if (nxtSt != noParent)
475.                setHistory (nxtSt, prev);        // remember history of this state
476.            };
477.        };
478.
479.    /******************************************************************/
```

```
480.   /*                    resetFSM                        */
481.   /*                                                    */
482.   /* reset the FSM specified by the input parame-       */
483.   /* ter. This routine initializes all the local        */
484.   /* variables of the FSM and also resets the           */
485.   /* history variables back to default values           */
486.   /*****************************************************/
487.
488.   void resetFSM (fsmCB* fsmPtr)
489.
490.       {
491.       initVars (fsmPtr);
492.       for (int i = 0; i < (fsmPtr->numSt); ++i)
493.           (fsmPtr->states[i])->history = noHistory;
494.       fsmPtr->curState = top;
495.       };
496.
497.   /*****************************************************/
498.   /*                    processMsg                      */
499.   /*                                                    */
500.   /* this is the main message handling loop that        */
501.   /* is invoked whenever an FSM receives a mes-         */
502.   /* sage. Starting with the current state, this        */
503.   /* procedure searches for a state that reacts         */
504.   /* to the current message. If it finds one, it        */
505.   /* executes all the exit actions of all states        */
506.   /* that are nested within that state and then         */
507.   /* invokes the appropriate transition chain           */
508.   /* routine to handle the actual transition. If        */
509.   /* no state reacts to this event the default          */
510.   /* unexpected message handler is invoked.             */
511.   /*****************************************************/
512.
513.   void processMsg
514.       (
515.       fsmCB* fsmPtr,              // pointer to the CB of the receiving fsm
516.       msgHeader* aMsgPtr         // ptr. to msg. just received
517.       )
518.
519.       {
520.       // set up common pointers expected by utility routines:
521.
522.       fsm = fsmPtr;
523.       msg = aMsgPtr;
524.       state st = currentState ();        // start from current state
525.       int trigger = noTrigger;           // tells us if msg was accepted by a state
526.
```

```
527.        // now search for a state that responds to the current message:
528.
529.        while (st >= top)
530.            {
531.            trigger = getTriggers (st); // check if state <st> responds
532.            if (trigger > noTrigger)
533.                {
534.                executeExits (st); // execute all exit actions required
535.                transitionChains (trigger);
536.                return; // event handled successfully -------->
537.                }
538.            else
539.                st = parentOf (st); // try the parent state
540.            }; // end of loop
541.
542.        // if we reach here, no state responded to the message:
543.
544.        unhandledMsg ();
545.
546.        }; // end of processMsg
547.
548.    /******************************************************************/
549.    /*                    startFSM                                    */
550.    /*                                                                */
551.    /* initialize the FSM specified by the input                      */
552.    /* parameter by forcing a reset of the FSM and                    */
553.    /* executing the initial transition of its top                    */
554.    /* state.                                                         */
555.    /******************************************************************/
556.
557.    void startFSM
558.        (
559.        fsmCB* fsmPtr,
560.        msgHeader* initMsg
561.        )
562.
563.        {
564.        resetFSM (fsmPtr); // reset local vars and history
565.        // ensure proper settings for initial message
566.        initMsg->signal = init;
567.        initMsg->port = sysPort;
568.        processMsg (fsmPtr, initMsg);
569.        };
570.
571.    /******************************************************************/
572.    /*                    terminateFSM                                */
573.    /*                                                                */
```

```
574.    /* destroy the specified FSM and release its            */
575.    /* resources back to the system                         */
576.    /*****************************************************************/
577.
578.    void terminateFSM (fsmCB* fsmPtr)
579.
580.        {
581.        releaseVars (fsmPtr);
582.        for (int i = 0; i < fsmPtr->numSt; ++i)
583.            free (fsmPtr->states[i]);
584.        free (fsmPtr);
585.        fsmPtr = NULL;
586.        };
```

B.1.7   Main Program

The following sample "main" program is included for illustrative purposes only and
would not be found, in this form, in any real implementation. It shows how the four main
FSM interface procedures (**createFSM**, **startFSM**, **processMsg**, and **terminateFSM**) are used. This program allocates a message block, and then re-uses it for the
following four different messages:

- An initialization message (with no initial data). This message normally is provided
  by the run-time system and emanates from the "system" port **sysPort** that is
  automatically associated with every actor.

- A message with a signal value of **sig1** on **port1**.

- A message with a signal value of **sig2** on **port1**.

- A message with a signal value not recognized by the FSM (unexpected message).

```
587.    /********************************************/
588.    /**** main program                      ****/
589.    /**** used for testing only             ****/
590.    /********************************************/
591.
592.    main ()
593.    {
594.
595.    // create the FSM:
596.
597.    struct fsmCB* fsmPtr = createFSM();
598.
599.    // allocate a message block and start up the FSM:
600.
601.    struct msgHeader* aMsgPtr = malloc (sizeof(msgHeader));
602.    aMsgPtr->signal = init;
603.    aMsgPtr->port = sysPort;
```

```
604.    startFSM (fsmPtr, aMsgPtr);
605.
606.    // create a <sig1, port1> message and process it:
607.
608.    aMsgPtr->signal = sig1;
609.    aMsgPtr->port = port1;
610.    processMsg (fsmPtr, aMsgPtr);
611.
612.    // create a <sig2, port1> message and process it:
613.
614.    aMsgPtr->signal = sig2;
615.    processMsg (fsmPtr, aMsgPtr);
616.
617.    // create an invalid message and process it:
618.
619.    aMsgPtr->signal = 3; // invalid signal
620.    processMsg (fsmPtr, aMsgPtr);
621.
622.    // now terminate the FSM:
623.
624.    terminateFSM (fsmPtr);
625.    }
```

APPENDIX C

Rationale
for ROOMcharts

In order to explain the rationale behind the answer chosen in ROOM, as well as to encourage exploration of other suitable formalisms, this appendix provides a general review of the various approaches to describing behavior and lists the criteria that may be used for selecting between them. For those interested in detailed theoretical issues, this appendix concludes with a discussion of the differences between ROOMcharts and statecharts.

C.1   Methods of Describing Behavior

The ROOM structural framework places the following constraints on behavior:

- All behavior is located within the behavior components of actors.

- All communication between actors is achieved by the exchange of messages through end ports, SAPs, and SPPs. Note that message-based communications does not necessarily imply that the communication model must be asynchronous.

The behavior of an actor must conform to the combined set of protocol specifications of its behavior interface (end ports, SAPs, and SPPs). It almost seems as if this process could be automated. Unfortunately, no such methods for automatic synthesis exist yet, so we must depend on the creative abilities of human designers to synthesize the desired behavior. This imposes the following pragmatic criteria on the type of formalism that can be used:

- *Expressiveness.* The chosen formalism must be capable of describing the characteristic phenomena of large distributed real-time systems in a succinct, yet understandable, way.

- *Familiarity.* The formalism must be sufficiently accepted in practice so that it does not require major retraining of current domain experts. Simply speaking, it is unrealistic to propose concepts that would require a dramatic paradigm shift of current experts.

- *Efficiency.* It must be possible to derive efficient and economical real-time implementations from the behavior specifications, using current computing technology. This is in accord with the fundamental objective of ROOM (eliminating discontinuities in the development process). To understand the significance of this, we only need to remind the reader that many real-time applications still are being realized with assembly language, more than 30 years after high-level programming languages have been introduced.

In general, the two approaches to specifying behavior are *assertional* and *operational*. In assertional modeling, the behavior of a system is defined implicitly by asserting that a system must meet a set of properties. Examples of such techniques include various types of formal logic (for example, temporal logic [Manna92], interval logic [Schwartz83], and trace-based methods [Hoffman85]). Operational methods describe behavior by explicitly specifying a mechanism that exhibits the desired behavior. Techniques in this category include algebraic methods ([Milner85] [Hoare85]), various algorithmic forms, and state machines. The essential difference between the two approaches is that assertional techniques specify the "what," whereas operational techniques specify the "how."

C.1.1   Assertional Methods

Assertional methods are appealing, since they are more explicit and less technology dependent than operational methods. In this case, a system is specified in terms of its desired effect, rather than in terms of its implementation. As technologies evolve, it is possible to take advantage of them without having to reformulate the specification. An example of the assertional approach can be found in the Prolog programming language.

The basic assumption behind assertional methods is that some automatic synthesis system will generate the desired behavior from the assertional specification. However, we have already noted that general automated synthesis methods do not exist yet. Even in those special cases where automated synthesis exists (for example, as in Prolog), the generated behavior usually is not efficient enough to meet the performance objectives of many real-time systems. Thus, assertional methods generally fail the efficiency criterion.

There is another significant problem with assertional methods. We illustrate this by using a classical example from number theory: an assertional specification of the desired "behavior" of natural numbers (that is, the non-negative integers 0, 1, 2, 3, ...). This consists of a set of the following five axioms [Daintith89]:

1. 0 is a *natural number.*

2. Every natural number n has another natural number *succ(n)* as its *successor.*

3. 0 is not the successor of any natural number.

4. If *succ(n)* = *succ(m)* then $n = m$.

5. If P is a *property* and 0 has P, then whenever a number x has P, then *succ(x)* also has P, then it follows that all natural numbers have P. (This axiom captures the principle of mathematical induction.)

These assertions are known as Peano's postulates after the Italian mathematician Giuseppe Peano, who formulated them in 1889. Mathematicians agree that Peano's postulates truly capture the essence of natural numbers. In computing terminology, we can claim that Peano's postulates represent a portion of the *abstract data type* definition of the class of natural numbers.

We can draw several conclusions from this example. First, to someone untrained in mathematics and logic, the postulates are not self-explanatory and require some reflection before their true meaning is understood. Second, as with all requirements, it can be extremely difficult to specify precisely what is desired. Even experts often have difficulty in proposing a complete and consistent set of assertions that formally capture everything that is desired. Peano's postulates, for example, were the culmination of a large body of previous work on number theory, and yet they deal with the simplest of mathematical objects.

In contrast, consider an operational specification of complex numbers defined by the formula

$$x + iy$$

in which variables x and y belong to the set of real numbers.[1] This specification is clearly simpler and more intuitive than an equivalent assertional one. The properties of this class are determined by the combination of the semantics of the "+" operation and the semantics of the class of real numbers. Unfortunately, while we may have a good intuition about the semantics resulting from this combination, generally we cannot claim with certainty that it is devoid of undesirable behavior. This is the price paid for the simplicity of operational specifications.

In summary, assertional techniques have problems with all three of the basic criteria for behavior. They are inefficient for many real-time needs, their expressive power is sometimes curtailed by our incapacity to specify precisely what the desired behavior should be, and their mathematical foundations mean that they are unfamiliar to a large segment of software practitioners. Nevertheless, we do not discount the usefulness of assertional methods. They are best used in conjunction with operational techniques. That is, assertions can be made and related to an operational specification. In some cases, it is possible to validate whether an operational specification contradicts an assertion either by formal analytical means or by testing.

C.1.2 Operational Methods

With operational methods, there are two styles of describing the behavior of concurrent objects. In the first case, we try to follow, as much as possible, a *sequential* style consisting of a series of elementary action steps (P_0) similar to the conventional form of imperative programming languages:

---

[1] This example is interesting because it shows that operational specifications are used even in that most formal of domains—mathematics.

P_0: $action_1$;
         $action_2$;
         receive (e_1);
         $action_3$;
         $action_4$;
         receive (e_2);

         .

         .

         etc.

Note that some of the actions involve synchronization with the environment (for example, other concurrent objects) during which the object receives external events.

The advantage of this model is obvious: Sequential composition is simple and easy to understand. We can directly follow a sequence from beginning to end, concentrating on one step at a time. A key assumption of the sequential model is that the external events occur in the precise order specified by the action sequence (e_1 followed by e_2 and so on). Since most concurrent environments are not that well-behaved, it is necessary to provide the object with control over which events it is willing to receive at a particular time. This "selective receive" is a form of synchronization. It allows the object to reorder the occurrence of external events to conform to its expectations. This is illustrated in Figure C.1.

Figure C.1   Sequential Model

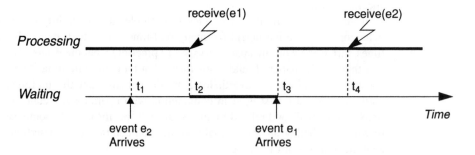

When event e_2 occurs at time t_1, the object is not prepared to receive any events. At time t_2, it executes the "receive" action for event e_1. Since e_1 has not yet occurred, the execution thread is suspended. It is reactivated when the anticipated event, e_1, finally arrives at time t_3. Finally, when the object executes the receive action for event e_2 at time t_4, the execution thread is not suspended, since that event has already occurred. Thus, as far as the object is concerned, event e_1 occurred before event e_2. Some form of event queueing is required to ensure that an event stays around if it is not immediately consumed.

The alternative style of describing operational behavior of concurrent objects is called *event-driven* and it characterized by the following generic form:

```
do forever
    listen for next event;
    process event;
enddo;
```

In other words, the object alternates between a "listening" mode, during which it is ready to receive *any* new events, and a "processing" mode, during which the consequences of the most recent event are computed (see Figure C.2). In the event-driven model, events are handled in the order in which they arrive.

Figure C.2   Event-Driven Model

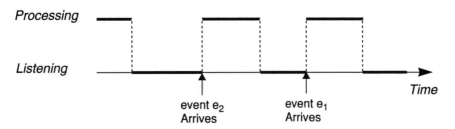

An implicit assumption of the sequential model is that the behavior being described is, in essence, some form of progression. In reactive systems, this is not always true. For example, a cruise control system for an automobile continually monitors for deviations from the desired settings and makes the necessary adjustments. This is much closer to the event-driven model, since there really is no long-term progression.

Even in those cases where the behavior of a reactive system can be modeled as a progression, it frequently happens that the progression is highly susceptible to disruptions. For example, component failures requiring recovery actions or high-priority asynchronous service requests may interrupt the current progression. Recall that real-time reactive systems have the following properties:

- The relative order and time of occurrence of events cannot always be predicted.

- A timely response must be provided for the majority of inputs.

The first property means that, at any given moment, many different events are possible, while the second property implies that an event must be handled with minimum delay. In the sequential model in Figure C.1, event e_2 is ignored for the entire interval between t_1 and t_4. During that time, processing actually is suspended while awaiting event e_1 (interval t_3-t_2), even though event e_2 is pending. This further delays the handling of e_2.

From this perspective, the event-driven approach is clearly more appropriate for real-time reactive systems because it minimizes delays in processing events and also because it deals better with asynchronous (nonprogressive) behavior.

C.2   A Comparison of Statecharts and ROOMcharts

As noted previously, ROOMcharts were inspired by the statecharts formalism [Harel87]. The basic graphical concepts (such as hierarchical states, group transitions, and history) are derived from their statechart analogs. However, in their original form, statecharts include certain simplifying idealizations that are problematic for modeling practical real-time software. This pertains, in particular, to the following assumptions:

- The communication model of statecharts assumes a fully reliable and instantaneous broadcast.

- The statechart execution model assumes that transitions from one state to the next are instantaneous (the so-called "zero" time assumption).

The latter is derived from the view that a system always must be in some state. Hence, the period between states must be infinitesimally small. In ROOMcharts, the time spent between states is finite but, because of the run-to-completion model, an actor cannot be interrupted by some other event while executing a transition. This means that the time interval between states (during which the behavior is not in any definite state) is not critical, since an actor cannot be observed by other actors during this time.

These two idealizations are key to some of the most powerful modeling concepts in statecharts, including, for instance, the decomposition of a state into orthogonal substates called "and" states. As a result, in many practical scenarios, specifications that are modeled using these concepts may not be feasible to implement, at least not with current technology. We have noted on several occasions that distributed systems are particularly sensitive to imperfections in communications so that assumptions about reliable instantaneous communications can lead to fundamental design flaws.

The modifications and extensions to statecharts in ROOM were motivated by the following objectives:

- It must be possible to *automatically* generate *efficient* software implementations from high-level behavioral specifications.

- The behavioral specification formalism must be *formally related* to other ROOM concepts, such as ports and actors.

- The behavior formalism must take advantage of the essential features of the object model, such as encapsulation and inheritance.

The first point is crucial to meeting the higher objective of a seamless development process and, in particular, to the elimination of the error-prone discontinuity between design and implementation. This directly led to the elimination of certain idealizations and the concepts that were based on them. The second objective also contributes to the achievement of a seamless process and also ensures the ability to produce operational models early in the development process. The third objective opens up the possibility of securing the main benefits of the object paradigm in the very specific domain of reactive systems.

Meeting these objectives requires trading off some of the expressive power of statecharts. The major loss is probably because of the elimination of "and" states. Fortunately, this facility can be emulated to a degree by combining some of the other ROOMchart features.

We illustrate this method using a much-simplified example of a digital alarm clock. This system provides the following functionality:

- A basic timekeeping function
- An alarm that is triggered when a particular time of day is reached
- A display function that displays the current time in either 24-hour or 12-hour mode

In the basic statechart formalism, the state of this system may be modeled by a composite state consisting of the state of the display, the state of the alarm, and the state of the timekeeping function, as shown in Figure C.3. Each of these three high-level states also contains a sub-machine that describes the behavior of the particular function.

Figure C.3 A Statechart for an Alarm Clock

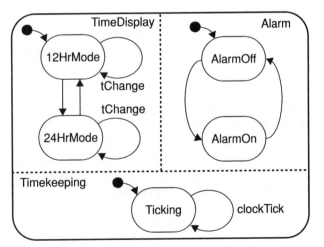

The basic function here is the timekeeping function that measures the progress of time by a series of clock ticks (generated by some hardware device). When a clock tick occurs, it increments the current time maintained in a special numeric variable. We assume that the resolution of the hardware clock exceeds the resolution of the time display, so that the display is updated only after a certain number of ticks has expired (indicated by a tChange event) and not on every clock tick. When the specified alarm time value is reached, an event is generated that triggers a transition of the alarm function from the "alarm off" state to the "alarm on" state.

In the object model, each of the orthogonal states of the alarm clock (Timekeeping, Alarm, and TimeDisplay) can be modeled as a distinct object. This is possible because the mechanisms required to implement the time display function are distinct from the mechanisms required to realize the alarm function, even though they may share some common functionality (for example, the timekeeping function). This approach suggests that each orthogonal state can be represented by an actor. (Since the orthogonal states are concurrent, they must be modeled by concurrent objects.) Shared functionality, such as the timekeeping function, may be modeled by a layer or a peer actor. The result is a layered system such as the one shown in Figure C.4. The state machines within the individual actors would be similar to the corresponding ones in Figure C.3.

Figure C.4   A ROOM Model of the Alarm Clock

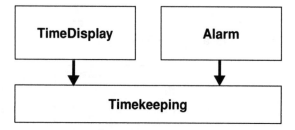

The layer connections are used to inform the clients of the "timekeeping" service when the events of interest have occurred.

Perhaps the principal difference between ROOMchart and statechart models is in the communication forms used. In the ROOMchart model, all communication is explicit. The clients of the timekeeping service explicitly request services and receive in return explicit notification messages when appropriate. This requires more effort from the modeler, since the communication protocols and message formats must be formally defined. On the other hand, by making the interaction between concurrent entities explicit, unintentional couplings between orthogonal states are avoided. Such a coupling can occur when an action associated with one transition unexpectedly generates an event that triggers a transition in another orthogonal state. (In the worst-case scenario, this can lead to an infinite cycle of mutual triggering.) The likelihood of an unintentional coupling is increased by the fact that, in statecharts, an event is not necessarily generated as an explicit communication, but could be the side effect of some other operation (for example, incrementing a counter).

APPENDIX D

ROOM Graphical Notation Summary

For convenience, in this appendix we summarize the elements of the ROOM graphical notation used at the Schematic Level. Note that all the graphical elements are supplemented by additional textual specifications.

D.1   Structure Notation

All high-level structure is captured by actor class diagrams. The notational symbols in this set include the following:

```
┌─────────────────────────┐
│                         │
│      ActorClass         │
│                         │
│                         │
│                         │
└─────────────────────────┘
```

Actor Class: A rectangular box with a thick black border is used to specify an *actor class*. The inside space is used to define the decomposition frame and may contain component actors, behavior end ports, bindings, and layer connections. The border also may contain class relay ports and class end ports of various kinds.

```
┌─────────────────────────┐
│                         │
│     actorReference      │
│                         │
└─────────────────────────┘
```

Actor Reference: A rectangular box with a thinner black border is used to specify an *actor reference*. An actor reference can only appear in the context of a decomposition frame of some actor class specification. It may have reference ports on its outside border. The class of the actor reference is specified by an associated textual annotation.

Actor reference symbols can be modified in several ways to indicate different properties. Note that, in most cases, these modifiers can be combined to specify the desired composite set of actor reference properties.

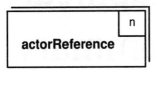

Replicated Actor Reference: This type of actor reference symbol is used to specify a *replicated actor reference*. The replication factor is specified in the box in the upper right-hand corner.

Optional Actor Reference: This type of actor reference symbol is used to specify an *optional actor reference*. It cannot be combined with the imported actor reference modifier.

Imported Actor Reference: This type of actor reference symbol is used to specify an *imported actor reference*. It cannot be combined with the optional actor reference modifier.

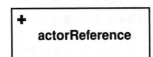

Substitutable Actor Reference: A "+" symbol within an actor reference symbol is used to specify a *substitutable actor reference*.

Class ports are ports that are used to define the internal and external ports of an actor class. Note that these may serve as anchor points for a binding. In all cases, the protocol class associated with the port is specified by a textual annotation.

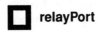

Class Relay Port: This symbol can only appear on the border of an actor class symbol.

Conjugated Class Relay Port: This symbol can only appear on the border of an actor class symbol.

Class End Port: This symbol can only appear on the border of an actor class symbol.

⬤	**endPort**	**Conjugated Class End Port:** This symbol can only appear on the border of an actor class symbol.
◻	**relayPort**	**Replicated Class Relay Port:** This symbol can only appear on the border of an actor class symbol. The replication factor is not included in the graphical representation.
◼	**relayPort**	**Conjugated Replicated Class Relay Port:** This symbol can only appear on the border of an actor class symbol. The replication factor is not included in the graphical representation.
◯	**endPort**	**Replicated Class End Port:** This symbol can only appear on the border of an actor class symbol. The replication factor is not included in the graphical representation.
⬤	**endPort**	**Conjugated Replicated Class End Port:** This symbol can only appear on the border of an actor class symbol. The replication factor is not included in the graphical representation.

In addition to class ports, ports can appear on the outer border of an actor reference. These can be used as anchor points for bindings. The class of the associated protocol can be determined from the corresponding actor class specification. The following symbols are used here:

■	**referencePort**	**Reference Port:** This symbol can only appear on the border of an actor reference symbol.
☐	**referencePort**	**Conjugated Reference Port:** This symbol can only appear on the border of an actor reference symbol.

referencePort

Replicated Reference Port: This symbol can only appear on the border of an actor reference symbol. The value of the replication factor is provided by an associated textual annotation.

referencePort

Conjugated Replicated Reference Port: This symbol can only appear on the border of an actor reference symbol. The protocol class and the value of the replication factor are not included in the graphical representation.

Communication relationships are indicated by arcs.

binding

Binding: This symbol indicates a binding between two ports. The same symbol is used for both simple and replicated bindings.

layerConnection

Layer Connections and Export Connections: This symbol indicates a layer connection between one or more SAPs and SPPs. The same symbol is used to indicate an export connection in which an SPP is being exported through a containing actor.

D.2 Behavior Notation

The behavioral notation that is used for capturing the high-level behavior of actors is called ROOMcharts and contains the following elements:

State Context: A rectangular box with rounded edges and a thick black border is used to specify a *state context*. The inside space is used to define a state machine. Except for the top state, a state context can have incoming and outgoing transition points on the border.

State: A rectangular box with rounded edges and a thin black border is used to specify a *state* (or substate) within a state context.

Transition Segment: A directed arc indicates a *transition segment*. The code of the transition and the triggering conditions are specified through a textual annotation.

Textual Definitions: This is used to list the textual declarations of extended state variables, functions, and so on, associated with a state context.

Non-Extending Transition Point: This point is located on the border of a state context and is used as a transition end point for transitions that do not extend outside the context (for example, internal self-transitions).

Initial Transition Point: This point is located within a state context and is used as the origination point for the initial transition in that context.

Incoming Transition Point: This point is located on the state context border and indicates a transition that is incoming into the context.

Outgoing Transition Point: This point is located on the state context border and indicates a transition that is outgoing from the context.

Choicepoint: This point is located within a state context at the end of a transition segment. The number of branches is variable. One of the branches must be the default branch.

Transition to History: An incoming transition segment that ends on an outer state context without a continuing transition segment within the context represents a *transition into the history* of a state.

Group Transition: An outgoing transition segment that begins on the state context and that has no chained incoming transition is a *group transition*.

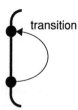

Internal Self-Transition: A transition segment that begins and ends on the same state context, and that has neither a chained incoming transition nor a chained outgoing transition, is an *internal self-transition*. This transition is a combination of the group and history transitions described previously. It will not trigger the exit or entry actions of its containing context. However, the entry and exit actions of any contained current states will be executed.

APPENDIX E

ROOM Linear Form Representation—Concrete Syntax

While graphical representations are much more appropriate for human understanding of complex specifications, textual representations are much better suited for processing by computer programs. For example, we may want to subject our ROOM model specification to some type of analysis, or we may wish to transform it into a particular programming language. This appendix provides a standard *ROOM linear form* that can be used to represent ROOM specifications in textual format. This form is a concrete version of the formal specifications (abstract syntax) used throughout this book.

There are two limitations in the version of the linear form presented here. It does not specify how attributes are inherited. That is, all attributes of a class are included in the linear form specification whether they are inherited from a superclass or defined locally in the class. Also, since ROOM incorporates a standard programming language for expressing Detail Level attributes, it is impractical to include specifications of these items, as they are different for each programming language.

E.1   Notational Conventions

We use a BNF (Backus-Naur Form) representation to specify the syntax of the linear form. The following notational conventions are adopted:

[ ]	Items contained within square brackets are optional.
*	An asterisk *after* an item indicates a sequence of *zero* or more occurrences of that item.
+	A plus sign *after* an item indicates a sequence of *one* or more occurrences of that item.
|	A vertical bar indicates two or more alternative production rules.
( )	Items in brackets are grouped, allowing a modifier such as an asterisk or plus sign to be applied equally to all grouped terms.
<non-terminal>	Nonterminal productions are shown in angle brackets.

    <non-terminal>   Nonterminal productions in italics indicate items that are not defined
                       further (usually because they are language-specific).

    terminal   A bold item indicates a reserved word or symbol.

E.2   BNF for ROOM Linear Form

E.2.1   General

<class-specification>	::=	<actor-class-spec> |
		<protocol-class-spec> |
		<data-class-spec>
<comment>	::=	/* [<comment-text>] */
<class-name>	::=	*<ROOM-identifier>*
<root-id>	::=	**root**
<replication-factor>	::=	**[** *<integer-literal>* **]**

E.2.2   Actor Classes

<actor-class-spec>	::=	[*<comment>*]
		actor class *<actor-class-name>*
		derived from *<actor-superclass-id>*
		{ *<actor-interface-spec>*
		<actor-implem-spec> **} ;**
<actor-class-name>	::=	*<class-name>*
<actor-superclass-id>	::=	<root-id> |
		<actor-class-name>
<actor-interface-spec>	::=	**interface: {** [<interf-ref-list>] **}**
<interf-ref-list>	::=	(<interf-ref-item> **;**)+
<interf-ref-item>	::=	<port-ref-item> |
		<spp-ref-item>
<spp-ref-item>	::=	[<comment>] **spp** <spp-ref-name>
		[<replication-factor>] **isa**
		<protocol-class-name>
<spp-ref-name>	::=	*<ROOM-identifier>***:**
<port-ref-item>	::=	[<comment>] **port** <port-ref-name>
		[<replication-factor>] **isa** [**conjugated**]
		<protocol-class-name>
<port-ref-name>	::=	*<ROOM-identifier>***:**
<actor-implem-spec>	::=	**implementation: {**
		<structure-spec>
		<behavior-spec> **}**

E.2.2.1 **Actor Classes—Structure**

<structure-spec>	::=	**structure: {**
		[<end-ports-spec>]
		[<saps-spec>]
		[<spps-spec>]
		[<components-spec>]
		[<contracts-spec>]
		[<equivs-spec>] **}**
<saps-spec>	::=	**saps: {** <saps-list> **}**
<saps-list>	::=	(<sap-ref-item> **;**)+
<sap-ref-item>	::=	[<comment>]
		sap <sap-ref-name> **isa** <sap-class-name>
<sap-ref-name>	::=	*<ROOM-identifier>*
<sap-class-name>	::=	**Frame** |
		Timing |
		Exception |
		<protocol-class-name>
<spps-spec>	::=	**spps: {** <spps-list> **}**
<spps-list>	::=	(<spp-ref-item> **;**)+
<spp-ref-item>	::=	[<comment>]
		spp <spp-ref-name>
		[<replication-factor>] **isa** <protocol-class-name>
<sap-ref-name>	::=	*<ROOM-identifier>*
<end-ports-spec>	::=	**end ports: {** [<port-ref-list>] **}**
<components-spec>	::=	**components: {** <components-list> **}**
<components-list>	::=	(<actor-ref-item> **;**)+
<actor-ref-item>	::=	[<comment>] **actor** <actor-ref-name>
		[<replication-factor>] **isa** <dynamics-type>
		[**substitutable**] <actor-class-name>
<actor-ref-name>	::=	*<ROOM-identifier>*
<dynamics-type>	::=	**optional** |
		fixed |
		imported
<contracts-spec>	::=	**contracts: {** [<bindings-spec>]
		[<layer-conns-spec>] **}**
<layer-conns-spec>	::=	**layer connections: {** <layer-conns-list> **}**
<layer-conns-list>	::=	(<conn-item> **;**)+
<conn-item>	::=	**connection** <conn-name>
		isa <protocol-class-name>
		[**: {** [<srce-pt-spec>] [**to** <dest-pt-spec>] **}**]
<srce-pt-spec>	::=	<actor-class-name> |
		<sap-ref-name> **/** <actor-ref-name>

<dest-pt-spec>	::=	<spp-ref-name> / <actor-ref-name>
<bindings-spec>	::=	**bindings:** { <bindings-list> }
<bindings-list>	::=	(<binding-item> ;)+
<binding-item>	::=	**binding** <binding-name> : {
		<end-pt-spec> (**to** <end-pt-spec>)+ }
<end-pt-spec>	::=	<port-ref-name> /
		(<actor-ref-name> | <actor-class-name>)
<equivs-spec>	::=	**equivalences:** { <equivs-list> }
<equivs-list>	::=	(<equiv-item> ;)+
<equiv-item>	::=	[<comment>] **set** <equiv-name> :
		{ <paths-list> }
<equiv-name>	::=	<ROOM-identifier>
<paths-list>	::=	<actor-path-id> (**and** <actor-path-id>)+
<actor-path-id>	::=	<actor-ref-name> (/ <actor-ref-name>)*

E.2.2.2   Actor Classes—Behavior

<behavior-spec>	::=	**behavior:** {
		[<comment>]
		<language-spec>
		[<inclusions-spec>]
		[<functions-spec>]
		<fsm-spec> }
<language-spec>	::=	**language:** *<language-identifier>*
<inclusions-spec>	::=	**inclusions:** { <inclusions-list> }
<inclusions-list>	::=	(<inclusion-spec>;)+
<inclusion-spec>	::=	**include** <inclusion-name>
<functions-spec>	::=	**functions:** { <functions-list> }
<functions-list>	::=	(<function-spec>;)+
<function-spec>	::=	**function** <function-name>:
		[*<functions-attributes>*]
		{ *<function-code>* }
<function-name>	::=	*<ROOM-identifier>* (:*<ROOM-identifier>*:)*
<fsm-spec>	::=	[<comment>] **top fsm:** { <state-spec> }
<state-spec>	::=	[<vars-spec>]
		[<entry-action-spec>]
		[<exit-action-spec>]
		[<substates-spec>]
		[<choicepoints-spec>]
		[<transitions-spec>]
<vars-spec>	::=	**vars:** { <vars-list> }
<vars-list>	::=	(<var-item> ;)+
<var-item>	::=	[<comment>]

		var *<var-name-desc>* isa *<var-class-desc>*
<entry-action-spec>	::=	entry action: { [*<expression>*] }
<exit-action-spec>	::=	exit action: { [*<expression>*] }
<substates-spec>	::=	substates: { <states-list> }
<states-list>	::=	(<state-item> ;)+
<state-item>	::=	[<comment>] state <state-name> : { [<state-spec>] }
<state-name>	::=	*<ROOM-identifier>*
<choicepoints-spec>	::=	choicepoints: { <choicepoint-list> }
<choicepoint-list>	::=	(<choicepoint-item> ;)+
<choicepoint-item>	::=	[<comment>] choicepoint <choicept-name> : { (<choicepoint-case>)+ }
<choicepoint-case>	::=	<case-name> : { *<boolean-expression>* }
<case-name>	::=	*<ROOM-identifier>* | default
<choicept-name>	::=	*<ROOM-identifier>*
<transitions-spec>	::=	transitions: { <transition-list> }
<transition-list>	::=	(<transition-item> ;)+
<transition-item>	::=	[<comment>] transition <transition-name> : { <trans-source-pt> <trans-dest-pt> [<trans-triggers>] [<trans-code>] }
<transition-name>	::=	*<ROOM-identifier>* [/ <source-name>]
<source-name>	::=	<state-name> | <choicept-end> | top
<choicept-end>	::=	choicepoint <choicept-name> [case-name case]
<trans-source-pt>	::=	source: <tr-point-spec>
<tr-point-spec>	::=	state <state-name> | <choicept-end> | initial point | state border [<cont-trans>]
<cont-trans>	::=	to transition <transition-name> | [from transition <transition-name>]*
<trans-dest-pt>	::=	destination: <tr-point-spec>
<trans-triggers>	::=	triggered by: { [<events-list>] }
<events-list>	::=	<event-item> | <event-item> or <events-list>
<event-item>	::=	event: { signals: { <signals-list>} on: { <interfaces-list> } [guard: { [*<boolean-expression>*] }] } }

<signals-list>	::=	<signal-literal> | <signal-literal> **or** <signals-list>
<interfaces-list>	::=	<interface-name> | <interface-name> **or** <interfaces-list>
<interface-name>	::=	<port-ref-name> | <sap-ref-name> | <spp-ref-name>
<trans-code>	::=	**code:** { [*<expression>*] }

E.2.3   Protocol Classes

<protocol-class-spec>	::=	[*<comment>*] **protocol class***<protocol-class-name>* **derived from** *<protocol-superclass-id>* <protocol-spec> ;
<protocol-class-name>	::=	<class-name>
<protocol-superclass-id>	::=	<root-id> | *<protocol-class-name>*
<protocol-spec>	::=	{ <service-spec> <messages-spec> }
<service-spec>	::=	**service:** *<service-name>*
<messages-spec>	::=	**message types:** { <in-messages-spec> <out-messages-spec> }
<in-messages-spec>	::=	**in:** { <message-types-list> }
<out-messages-spec>	::=	**out:** { <message-types-list> }
<message-types-list>	::=	(<message-type-spec> ;)+
<message-type-spec>	::=	{ **signal:** <signal-literal> **data class:** <data-class-name> }
<signal-literal>	::=	%<signal-name>
<signal-name>	::=	*<ROOM-identifier>*

References
and Bibliography

[Ada90] Ada 9X Project Office, *Ada 9X Requirements*. Ada 9X Project Report. Washington, DC: Office of the Under Secretary of Defense for Acquisition, 1990.

[Agha86] Agha, Gul. *Actors: A Model of Concurrent Computation in Distributed Systems*. Cambridge, MA: The MIT Press, 1986.

[Anderson81] Anderson, T., and P. Lee. *Fault Tolerance: Principles and Practice*. Englewood Cliffs, NJ: Prentice-Hall International, 1981.

[Andrews83] Andrews, Gregory R., and Schneider, Fred B. "Concepts and Notations for Concurrent Programming." *ACM Computing Surveys* 15, no. 1 (March 1983): 3–43.

[ANSI76] American National Standards Institute. *American National Standards Programming Language PL/I*. ANSI X3.53-1976. New York: American National Standards Institute, 1976.

[ANSI83] American National Standards Institute and Ada Joint Program Office. *Military Standard: Ada Programming Language*. ANSI/MIL-STD-1815A-1983. New York: American National Standards Institute; Washington, DC: US Government Department of Defense, Ada Joint Program Office, 1983.

[Allworth87] Allworth, S.T., and R.N. Zobel. *Introduction to Real-time Software Design*. 2nd ed., New York: Springer-Verlag New York Inc., 1987.

[America87] America, Pierre H. "POOL-T: A Parallel Object-Oriented Language." in *Object-Oriented Concurrent Programming*, ed. by A. Yonezawa and M. Tokoro. Cambridge, MA: The MIT Press, 1987.

[Arnold91] Arnold, Patrick et. al. *An Evaluation of Five Object-Oriented Development Methods*. HP Laboratories Technical Report HPL-91-52, Bristol: Hewlett-Packard Company, June 1991.

[Bedard77] Bedard, C., F. Mellor, and W. Older. "A Message-Switched Operating System for a Multiprocessor." in *Proceedings IEEE Computer Software and Applications Conference (COMPSAC 77)*, 1977: 772–777.

[Birtwistle73] Birtwistle, Graham, Ole-Johan Dahl, Bjorn Myrhaug, and Kristen Nygaard. *Simula Begin*. New York: Auerbach Publishers, 1973.

[Boehm81] Boehm, Barry W. *Software Engineering Economics*. Englewood Cliffs, NJ: Prentice Hall, 1981.

[Boehm88] ———. "A Spiral Model of Software Development and Enhancement." *IEEE Computer* 21, no. 5 (May 1988): 61–72.

[Booch91] Booch, Grady. *Object-Oriented Design with Applications*. Menlo Park, CA: Benjamin/Cummings, 1991.

[Booch93] ———. Correspondence with author, 15 January 1993.

[Brooks75] Brooks, Frederick P. *The Mythical Man-Month*. Reading, MA: Addison-Wesley, 1975.

[BSE92] Berard Software Engineering, Inc. *A Comparison of Object-Oriented Development Methodologies*. Gaitherburg, MD: Berard Software Engineering, Inc. 1992.

[Buhr92] Buhr, Ray, and Ron Casselman. "Architectures with Pictures." in *Proceedings of the Seventh Conference on Object-Oriented Programming Systems, Languages, and Applications (OOPSLA'92)*, 466–483, Vancouver: ACM Press, October 1992.

[Cardelli85] Cardelli, Luca, and Peter Wegner. "On Understanding Types, Data Abstraction, and Polymorphism." *ACM Computing Surveys* 17, no. 4 (December 1985): 471–522.

[Chen76] Chen, P.P. "The Entity-Relationship Model—Towards a Unified View of Data." *ACM Transactions on Database Systems* 1, no. 1 (March 1976): 9–36.

[Coad91a] Coad, Peter, and Ed Yourdon. *Object-Oriented Analysis. 2nd ed*. Englewood Cliffs, NJ: Prentice-Hall, 1991.

[Coad91b] ———. *Object-Oriented Design*. Englewood Cliffs, NJ: Prentice-Hall, 1991.

[Codd70] Codd, E.F. "A Relational Model of Data for Large Shared Data Banks." *Communications of the ACM* 14, no. 6 (June 1970): 377–387.

[Colbert91] Colbert, Edward. *Introduction to the Object-Oriented Software Development Method—Comparison of Object-Oriented Software Methods*. Seminar Notes. Los Angeles: Absolute Software Co., Inc., 1991.

[Constantine93] Constantine, Larry L. "Work Organization: Paradigms for Project Management and Organization." *Communications of the ACM* 36, no. 10 (October 1993): 34–43.

[Cook89] Cook, W.R. "A Proposal for Making Eiffel Type-safe." *The Computer Journal* 32, no. 4, (1989): 305–311.

[Cook92] Cook, W.R. "Interfaces and Specifications for the Smalltalk-80 Collection Classes." in *Proceedings of the Seventh Conference on Object-Oriented Programming Systems, Languages, and Applications (OOPSLA'92)*, 1–15, Vancouver: ACM Press, October 1992.

[Coplein92] Coplein, James. *Advanced C++ Programming Styles and Idioms*. Reading, MA: Addison-Wesley, 1992.

[Coplein93] ———. "Objects, Multiple Paradigm Integration and Organization Structure. " in *Proceedings of the Dependable Software Technology Exchange*, C. Weinstock, ed. Pittsburgh, PA: Software Engineering Institute, Carnegie Mellon University, March 1993.

[Dahl66] Dahl, Ole-Johan, and Kristen Nygaard. "SIMULA—An Algol-based Simulation Language." *Communications of the ACM* 9, no. 9 (September 1966): 671–678.

[Dainthith89] Daintith, John, and R.D. Nelson, ed. *The Penguin Dictionary of Mathematics*. London: Penguin Books, 1989.

[Danforth88] Danforth, Scott, and Chris Tomlinson. "Type Theories and Object-Oriented Programming." *ACM Computing Surveys* 20, no. 1 (March, 1988): 29–72.

[Davies88] Davies, P., and J. Brown. *Superstrings: A Theory of Everything?* Cambridge: Cambridge University Press, 1988.

[deChampeaux91] de Champeaux, Dennis. *A Comparative Study of Object-Oriented Analysis Methods*. HP Laboratories Technical Report HPL-91-41. Penelope Faure, Nutech: Hewlett-Packard Company, April 1991.

[DeMarco78] DeMarco, Tom. *Structured Analysis and System Specification*. New York: Yourdon Press, 1978.

[Dijkstra68] Dijkstra, Edsger. "Cooperating Sequential Processes." in F. Genuys ed., *Programming Languages*. New York: Academic Press, 1968.

[Dijkstra72] ———. "Structured Programming ." in O.-J. Dahl, E. Dijkstra, and C. Hoare, *Structured Programming*, New York: Academic Press, 1972.

[Ellis90] Ellis, Margaret, and Bjarne Stroustrup. *The Annotated C++ Reference Manual*. Reading, MA: Addison-Wesley, 1990.

[ESA89a] European Space Agency. *HOOD Reference Manual*. WME/89-173/JB, Issue 3.0. Noordwijk: European Space Research and Technology Centre, September 1989.

[ESA89b] ———. *HOOD User Manual*. WME/89-353/JB, Issue 3.0. Noordwijk: European Space Research and Technology Centre, December 1989.

[Flew79] Flew, Antony, ed. *A Dictionary of Philosophy*. London: Pan Books Ltd in association with MacMillan Press, 1979.

[Goldberg83] Goldberg, Adele, and David Robson. *Smalltalk-80: The Language and its Implementation*. Reading, MA: Addison-Wesley, 1983.

[Gray78] Gray, J.N. "Notes on Database Operating Systems." in *Operating Systems an Advanced Course*, Lecture Notes in Computer Science 60, New York: Springer-Verlag, 1978.

[Gupta70] Gupta, Someshwar C., and Lawrence Hasdorff. *Fundamentals of Automatic Control*. New York: John Wiley and Sons, 1970.

[Guillemont82] Guillemont, Marc. "The Chorus Distributed Operating System: Design and Implementation." in *Proceedings of the International Symposium on Local Computer Networks*, 207–221. Florence, Italy: IFIP 1982.

[Halpern84] Halpern, Joseph, and Yoram Moses. "Knowledge and Common Knowledge in a Distributed Environment." in *Proceedings of the Third ACM Symposium on Principles of Distributed Systems*, 50–61. Vancouver: ACM Press, 1984.

[Harel87a] Harel, David. "Statecharts: A Visual Formalism for Complex Systems." *Science of Computer Programming* 8 (July 1987): 231–274.

[Harel87b] Harel, D., A. Pnueli, J.P. Schmidt, and R. Sherman. "On the formal semantics of statecharts." in *Proceedings of the Second IEEE Symposium on Logic in Computer Science*, 54–64. New York: IEEE Press, 1987.

[Hatley87] Hatley, Derek J., and Imtiaz A. Pirbhai. *Strategies for Real-Time System Specification*. New York: Dorset House Publishing, 1987.

[Harrison65] Harrison, Michael A. *Introduction to Switching and Automata Theory*. New York: McGraw-Hill, 1965.

[Heppenheimer85] Heppenheimer, T. A. "Man Makes Man." in M. Minsky ed., *Robotics*, New York: Anchor Press/Dobuleday, 1985.

[Hoare85] Hoare, C.A. *Communicating Sequential Processes*. Englewood Cliffs, NJ: Prentice Hall, 1985.

[Hoffman85] Hoffman, D. "Trace Specification of Communication Protocols." *IEEE Transactions on Computers* C-34, no. 12 (December 1985): 1102–1113.

[Hogg91] Hogg, John, and and Rodney Iversen. "Representing Concurrent Communication Systems," in *Proceedings of the ECOOP/OOPSLA Workshop in Object-Oriented Concurrent Programming*, 37–39, ACM OOPS Messenger 2, no. 2 (April 1991).

[Jacobson92] Jacobson, Ivar, et al. *Object-Oriented Software Engineering*. Reading, MA: Addison-Wesley, 1992.

[Johnson88] Johnson, Ralph, and Brian Foote. "Designing Reusable Classes." *Journal of Object-Oriented Programming* 1, no. 2 (June/July 1988): 22–30, 35.

[Kay93] Kay, Alan. "The Early History of Smalltalk." *ACM SIGPLAN Notices* 28, no. 3 (March 1993): 69–96.

[Kitchenham90] Kitchenham, Barbara, and Roland Carn. "Research and Practice: Software Design Methods and Tools," Chapter 4.2 of *Psychology of Programming*, ed. J.-M. Hoc et al. New York: Academic Press, 1990.

[Kleinrock76] Kleinrock, Leonard. *Queueing Systems; Volume 2: Computer Applications*. New York: John Wiley and Sons, 1976.

[Krueger92] Krueger, Charles W. "Software Reuse." *ACM Computing Surveys* 24, no. 2 (June 1992): 131–184.

[Lamport78] Lamport, Leslie. "Time, Clocks, and the Ordering of Events in a Distributed System." *Communications of the ACM* 21, no. 7 (July 1978): 558–565.

[Lemay87] Lemay, John, and James McGee. "A Distributed Network Architecture for the Competitive Network Environment," in *Proceedings International Switching Symposium*, vol. 3, 524–531. 1987.

[Liskov74] Liskov, Barbara H., and Stephen N. Zilles. "Programming with Abstract Data Types." ACM SIGPLAN Notices 9, no. 4 (April 1974): 50–59.

[Liskov76] Liskov, Barbara H. "Introduction to CLU," in *New Directions in Algorithmic Languages* 1975, S. A. Schuman, ed., INRIA, 1976.

[Liskov79] Liskov, Barbara, and Allan Snyder. "Exception Handling in CLU." *IEEE Transactions on Software Engineering* SE-5, no. 6 (November 1979): 546–558.

[Leduc87] Leduc, et al. "Architectural and Behavioural Modelling in Computer Communication," in *Distributed Processing*, ed. M. Barton et al., 53–70, Amsterdam: North-Holland, 1988.

[Lynch88] Lynch, Nancy, and Mark Tuttle. *An Introduction to Input/Output Automata*. Report MIT/LCS/TM-373 (TM-351 Revised), Cambridge, MA: Laboratory for Computer Science, MIT, 1988.

[Manna92] Manna, Zohar, and Amir Pnueli. *The Temporal Logic of Reactive and Concurrent Systems: Specification*. New York: Springer-Verlag, 1992.

[McDermid93] McDermid, John. "Dependability Requirements: Orthodoxy and a Goal-structured Approach," in *Proceedings of the Dependable Software Technology Exchange*, C. Weinstock, ed. Pittsburgh, PA: Software Engineering Institute, Carnegie Mellon University, March 1993.

[Meyer88] Meyer, Bertrand. *Object-Oriented Software Construction*. Englewood Cliffs, NJ: Prentice Hall, 1988.

[Meyers90] Meyers, M.N. "The AT&T Telephone Network Outage of January 15, 1990." Invited presentation given at the 20th International Symposium on Fault-Tolerant Computing, Newcastle-upon-Tyne, U.K., June 1990.

[Milner85] Milner, Robin. *Communication and Concurrency*. Englewood Cliffs, NJ: Prentice-Hall, 1985.

[Monarchi92] Monarchi, David E., and Gretchen I. Puhr. "A Research Typology for Object-Oriented Analysis and Design." Communications of the ACM 35, no. 9 (September 1992): 35–47.

[Moore56] Moore, E. "Gedanken-Experiments on Sequential Machines." in *Automata Studies*, Princeton: Princeton University Press, 1956.

[Nierstrasz90] Nierstrasz, Oscar, and Michael Papathomas, "Towards a Type Theory for Active Objects." in *Object Management*, D. Tsichritzis ed., 295–304, Geneva: University of Geneva, July 1990.

[Nierstrasz91] Nierstrasz, Oscar. "The Next 700 Concurrent Object-Oriented Languages," in *Object Composition*, D. Tsichritzis ed., 165–188. Geneva: University of Geneva, June 1991.

[ObjecTime92a] ObjecTime Limited. *Programming Guide for Run-Time System Services—RPL*, Technical manual, Release 4.0, Version 3.0, Ottawa: ObjecTime Limited, 1992.

[OMG92] Object Management Group. *Object Management Architecture Guide*, R. M. Soley ed., 2nd ed. The Object Management Group, November 1992.

[OSF90] Open Software Foundation, *Distributed Computing Environment Specification*. Document OSF-DCE-PD-1090-2, Cambridge, MA: Open Software Foundation, November 1990.

[Parnas71] Parnas, David L. "Information Distribution Aspects of Design Methodology." in *Proceedings of the 1971 IFIP Congress*. Amsterdam: North-Holland, 1971.

[Parnas72] ———. "On the Criteria To Be Used in Decomposing Systems into Modules." *Communications of the ACM* 15, no. 12 (December 1972): 1053–1058.

[Parnas86] Parnas, David L., and Paul C. Clements. "A Rational Design Process: How and Why to Fake It. " *IEEE Transactions of Software Engineering* SE-12, no. 2 (February 1986): 251–257.

[Pernici90] Pernici, Barbara. "Class Design and Meta-Design," in *Object Management*, D. Tsichritzis ed., 117–132. Geneva: University of Geneva, July 1990.

[Perry90] Perry, Dewayne E., and Gail E. Kaiser. "Adequate Testing and Object-Oriented Programming." *Journal of Object-Oriented Programming* 2 (January/February 1990): 13–19.

[Peters87] Peters, L. *Advanced Structured Analysis and Design*. Englewood Cliffs, NJ: Prentice Hall, 1987.

[Peterson81a] Peterson, G.L. "Myths About the Mutual Exclusion Problem." *Information Processing Letters* 12, no. 3 (June 1981): 115–116.

[Peterson81b] Peterson, James L. *Petri Net Theory and Modeling of Systems*. Englewood Cliffs, NJ: Prentice Hall, 1981.

[Pfleeger91] Pfleeger, Shari L. *Software Engineering. 2nd ed.* New York: Macmillan, 1991.

[Royce70] Royce, W.W. "Managing the Development of Large Software Systems: Concepts and Techniques." in *Proceedings of WESCON*, August 1970.

[Rumbaugh91] Rumbaugh, James, at al., *Object-Oriented Modeling and Design*. Englewood Cliffs, NJ: Prentice Hall, 1991.

[Rumbaugh92] Rumbaugh, James. "Let there be objects: a short guide to reification." *Journal of Object-Oriented Programming* 5, no. 7 (November/December 1992): 9–14.

[Saltzer81] Saltzer, James, et al. "End-to-End Arguments in System Design," *ACM Transactions on Computing Systems* 2, no. 4 (November 1984): 277–288.

[Schwartz83] Schwartz, Richard, et al. "An Interval-based Temporal Logic," in *Proceedings of the Workshop on Logics of Programs*, E. Clarke and D. Kozen eds., Lecture Notes in Computer Science 164, New York: Springer-Verlag, 1983.

[SEI91] Software Engineering Institute. *Capability Maturity Model for Software*. Report CMU/SEI-91-TR-24. ESD-TR-91-24. Pittsburgh: Software Engineering Institute, Carnegie Mellon University, February 1993.

[Selic92] Selic, Bran. "Experiences with Smalltalk on a Large Development Project." *The Smalltalk Report* 2, no. 1 (September 1992): 1–7.

[Selic92a] Selic, Bran, et al. "ROOM: An Object-Oriented Methodology for Developing Real-Time Systems." in *Proceedings Fifth International Workshop on Computer-Aided Software Engineering (CASE '92)*. July 1992.

[Shlaer92] Shlaer, Sally, and Stephen Mellor. *Object Lifecycles: Modeling the World in States*. Englewood Cliffs: Prentice Hall, 1992.

[Simon69] Simon, Herbert A. *The Sciences of the Artificial*. Cambridge, MA: MIT Press, 1969.

[Stefik86] Stefik Mark, and Daniel Bobrow. "Object-Oriented Programming: Themes and Variations." The AI Magazine 6, no. 4 (Winter 1986): 182–199.

[Stroustrup93] Stroustrop, Bjarne. "A History of C++: 1979-1991." *ACM SIGPLAN Notices* 28, no. 3 (March 1993): 271–298.

[Tanenbaum88] Tanenbaum, Andrew. *Computer Networks. 2nd ed.* Englewood Cliffs, NJ: Prentice Hall, 1988.

[Turing36] Turing, Alan. "On Computable Numbers with Applications to the Entscheidungsproblem. " in *Proceedings of the London Mathematical Society, Ser.* 2, vol. 42, 230–265. London: London Methematical Society, 1936.

[Walston77] Walston, C.E., and C.P. Felix. "A Method of Programming Measurement and Estimation." *IBM Systems Journal* 16, no. 1 (1977): 54–73.

[Ward85] Ward, Paul T., and Stephen J. Mellor. *Structured Development for Real-Time Systems: Introduction and Tools.* Englewood Cliffs, NJ: Prentice Hall, 1985.

[Wegner87] Wegner, Peter. "Dimensions of Object-Based Language Design." in *Proceedings of the Second Conference on Object-Oriented Programming Systems, Languages, and Applications (OOPSLA'87),* 168–182. ACM Press, October 1987.

[Wegner90] ———. "Concepts and Paradigms of Object-Oriented Programming." *ACM OOPS Messenger* 1, no. 1 (August 1990): 7–87.

[Wirfs-Brock90] Wirfs-Brock, Rebecca, Brian Wilkerson, and Lauren Wiener. *Designing Object-Oriented Software.* Englewood Cliffs, NJ: Prentice Hall, 1990.

[Yourdon79] Yourdon, Ed, and Larry Constantine. *Structured Design.* Englewood Cliffs, NJ: Prentice Hall, 1979.

[Zave82] Zave, Pamela. "An Operational Approach to Requirements Specification for Embedded Systems." *IEEE Transactions on Software Engineering* SE-8, no. 3 (May 1982): 250–269.

[Zave84] ———. "The Operational Versus the Conventional Approach to Software Development." *Communications of the ACM* 27, no. 2 (February 1984): 104–118.

[Zimmerman80] Zimmerman, H. "OSI Reference Model - The ISO Model of Architecture for Open System Interconnection." *IEEE Transactions on Communications* COM-28, no. 4 (April 1980): 425–432.

Index